1841 Lakeshore
Lane

"Composed in the style of the great medieval *catenae*, this new anthology of patristic commentary on Holy Scripture, conveniently arranged by chapter and verse, will be a valuable resource for prayer, study and proclamation. By calling attention to the rich Christian heritage preceding the separations between East and West and between Protestant and Catholic, this series will perform a major service to the cause of ecumenism."

AVERY DULLES, S.J.
Laurence J. McGinley Professor of Religion and Society
Fordham University

"The initial cry of the Reformation was *ad fontes*—back to the sources! The Ancient Christian Commentary on Scripture is a marvelous tool for the recovery of biblical wisdom in today's church. Not just another scholarly project, the ACCS is a major resource for the renewal of preaching, theology and Christian devotion."

TIMOTHY GEORGE
Dean, Beeson Divinity School, Samford University

"Modern church members often do not realize that they are participants in the vast company of the communion of saints that reaches far back into the past and that will continue into the future, until the kingdom comes. This Commentary should help them begin to see themselves as participants in that redeemed community."

ELIZABETH ACHTEMEIER
Union Professor Emerita of Bible and Homiletics
Union Theological Seminary in Virginia

"Contemporary pastors do not stand alone. We are not the first generation of preachers to wrestle with the challenges of communicating the gospel. The Ancient Christian Commentary on Scripture puts us in conversation with our colleagues from the past, that great cloud of witnesses who preceded us in this vocation. This Commentary enables us to receive their deep spiritual insights, their encouragement and guidance for present-day interpretation and preaching of the Word. What a wonderful addition to any pastor's library!"

WILLIAM H. WILLIMON
Dean of the Chapel and Professor of Christian Ministry
Duke University

"Here is a nonpareil series which reclaims the Bible as the book of the church by making accessible to earnest readers of the twenty-first century the classrooms of Clement of Alexandria and Didymus the Blind, the study and lecture hall of Origen, the cathedrae of Chrysostom and Augustine, the scriptorium of Jerome in his Bethlehem monastery."

GEORGE LAWLESS
Patristic Institute and Augustianum, Rome

"We are pleased to witness publication of the
Ancient Christian Commentary on Scripture. It is most beneficial for us to learn
how the ancient Christians, especially the saints of the church
who proved through their lives their devotion to God and his Word, interpreted
Scripture. Let us heed the witness of those who have gone before us in the faith."

METROPOLITAN THEODOSIUS
Primate, Orthodox Church in America

"As we approach the advent of a new millennium there has emerged across Christendom a
widespread interest in early Christianity, both at the popular and scholarly level. . . .
Christians of all traditions stand to benefit from this project, especially clergy
and those who study the Bible. Moreover, it will allow us to see how our traditions are
both rooted in the scriptural interpretations of the church fathers while at
the same time seeing how we have developed new perspectives."

ALBERTO FERREIRO
Professor of History, Seattle Pacific University

"The Ancient Christian Commentary on Scripture fills a long overdue need for scholars and
students of the church fathers. . . . Such information will be of immeasurable
worth to those of us who have felt inundated by contemporary interpreters and novel theories
of the biblical text. We welcome some 'new' insight from the
ancient authors in the early centuries of the church."

H. WAYNE HOUSE
Professor of Theology and Law
Trinity University School of Law

Chronological snobbery—the assumption that our ancestors working without benefit of
computers have nothing to teach us—is exposed as nonsense by this magnificent
new series. Surfeited with knowledge but starved of wisdom, many of us are
more than ready to sit at table with our ancestors and listen to their holy
conversations on Scripture. I know I am.

EUGENE H. PETERSON
James Houston Professor of Spiritual Theology
Regent College

"Few publishing projects have encouraged me as much as the recently announced Ancient Christian Commentary on Scripture with Dr. Thomas Oden serving as general editor. . . . How is it that so many of us who are dedicated to serve the Lord received seminary educations which omitted familiarity with such incredible students of the Scriptures as St. John Chrysostom, St. Athanasius the Great and St. John of Damascus? I am greatly anticipating the publication of this Commentary."

FR. PETER E. GILLQUIST
Director, Department of Missions and Evangelism
Antiochian Orthodox Christian Archdiocese of North America

"The Scriptures have been read with love and attention for nearly two thousand years, and listening to the voice of believers from previous centuries opens us to unexpected insight and deepened faith. Those who studied Scripture in the centuries closest to its writing, the centuries during and following persecution and martyrdom, speak with particular authority. The Ancient Christian Commentary on Scripture will bring to life the truth that we are invisibly surrounded by a 'great cloud of witnesses.' "

FREDERICA MATHEWES-GREEN
Commentator, National Public Radio

"For those who think that church history began around 1941 when their pastor was born, this Commentary will be a great surprise. Christians throughout the centuries have read the biblical text, nursed their spirits with it and then applied it to their lives. These commentaries reflect that the witness of the Holy Spirit was present in his church throughout the centuries. As a result, we can profit by allowing the ancient Christians to speak to us today."

HADDON ROBINSON
Harold John Ockenga Distinguished Professor of Preaching
Gordon-Conwell Theological Seminary

"All who are interested in the interpretation of the Bible will welcome the forthcoming multivolume series Ancient Christian Commentary on Scripture. Here the insights of scores of early church fathers will be assembled and made readily available for significant passages throughout the Bible and the Apocrypha. It is hard to think of a more worthy ecumenical project to be undertaken by the publisher."

BRUCE M. METZGER
Professor of New Testament, Emeritus
Princeton Theological Seminary

ANCIENT CHRISTIAN
COMMENTARY ON SCRIPTURE

NEW TESTAMENT
VIII

GALATIANS,
EPHESIANS,
PHILIPPIANS

EDITED BY
MARK J. EDWARDS

GENERAL EDITOR
THOMAS C. ODEN

InterVarsity Press
Downers Grove, Illinois

InterVarsity Press
P.O. Box 1400, Downers Grove, IL 60515
World Wide Web: www.ivpress.com
E-mail: mail@ivpress.com

InterVarsity Press® is the book-publishing division of InterVarsity Christian Fellowship/USA®, a student movement active on campus at hundreds of universities, colleges and schools of nursing in the United States of America, and a member movement of the International Fellowship of Evangelical Students. For information about local and regional activities, write Public Relations Dept., InterVarsity Christian Fellowship/USA, 6400 Schroeder Rd., P.O. Box 7895, Madison, WI 53707-7895.

Cover photograph: Scala / Art Resource, New York. View of the apse. S. Vitale, Ravenna, Italy.

Spine photograph: Byzantine Collection, Dumbarton Oaks, Washington D.C. Pendant cross (gold and enamel). Constantinople, late sixth century.

ISBN 0-8308-1493-0

Printed in the United States of America ∞

Library of Congress Cataloging-in-Publication Data

Galatians, Ephesians, Philippians/edited by Mark J. Edwards.
      p.   cm.— (Ancient Christian commentary on Scripture. New
Testament; 8)
  Includes bibliographical references and index.
  ISBN 0-8308-1493-0 (alk. paper)
  1. Bible. N.T. Galatians—Commentaries.   2. Bible. N.T.
Ephesians—Commentaries.   3. Bible. N.T. Philippians—
Commentaries.   4. Fathers of the church.   5. Bible. N.T.
Galatians—Criticism, interpretation, etc.—History—Early church,
ca. 30-600—Sources.   6. Bible. N.T. Ephesians—Criticism,
interpretation, etc.—History—Early church, ca. 30-600—Sources.
7. Bible. N.T. Philippians—Criticism, interpretation, etc.—
History—Early Church, ca. 30:600—Sources.   I. Edwards, Mark J.,
1962-   .   II. Series.
BS2685.3.G355 1998
227'.077—dc21

98-48175
CIP

| 26 | 25 | 24 | 23 | 22 | 21 | 20 | 19 | 18 | 17 | 16 | 15 | 14 | 13 | 12 | 11 | 10 | 9 | 8 | 7 | 6 | 5 | 4 | 3 |
| 22 | 21 | 20 | 19 | 18 | 17 | 16 | 15 | 14 | 13 | 12 | 11 | 10 | 09 | 08 | 07 | 06 | 05 | 04 | 03 | 02 | 01 | 00 | 99 |

ANCIENT CHRISTIAN COMMENTARY
PROJECT RESEARCH TEAM

GENERAL EDITOR
Thomas C. Oden

ASSOCIATE EDITOR
Christopher A. Hall

TRANSLATIONS PROJECTS DIRECTOR
Joel Scandrett

RESEARCH DIRECTOR
Michael Glerup

EDITORIAL SERVICES DIRECTOR
Susan Kipper

TRANSLATION EDITOR
Dennis McManus

GRADUATE RESEARCH ASSISTANTS

Vincent Bacote	*Jeffrey Finch*
Brian Brewer	*Peter Gilbert*
Thomas Buchan	*Patricia Ireland*
Jill Burnett	*Alexei Khamine*
Hunn Choi	*Sergey Kozin*
Meesaeng L. Choi	*Thomas Mauro*
Joel Elowsky	*Wesley Tink*

Bernie Van De Walle

COMPUTER & TECHNICAL SUPPORT
Michael Kipper

ADMINISTRATIVE ASSISTANTS
Roberta Willison Kisker
Colleen Van De Walle

Contents

General Introduction

The Ancient Christian Commentary on Scripture has as its goal the revitalization of Christian teaching based on classical Christian exegesis, the intensified study of Scripture by lay persons who wish to think with the early church about the canonical text, and the stimulation of Christian historical, biblical, theological and pastoral scholars toward further inquiry into scriptural interpretation by ancient Christian writers.

The time frame of these documents spans seven centuries of exegesis, from Clement of Rome to John of Damascus, from the end of the New Testament era to A.D. 750, including the Venerable Bede.

Lay readers are asking how they might study sacred texts under the instruction of the great minds of the ancient church. This commentary has been intentionally prepared for a general lay audience of nonprofessionals who study the Bible regularly and who earnestly wish to have classic Christian observation on the text readily available to them. The series is targeted to anyone who wants to reflect and meditate with the early church about the plain sense, theological wisdom and moral meaning of particular Scripture texts.

A commentary dedicated to allowing ancient Christian exegetes to speak for themselves will refrain from the temptation to fixate endlessly upon contemporary criticism. Rather, it will stand ready to provide textual resources from a distinguished history of exegesis that has remained massively inaccessible and shockingly disregarded during the last century. We seek to make available to our present-day audiences the multicultural, multilingual, transgenerational resources of the early ecumenical Christian tradition.

Preaching at the end of the first millennium focused primarily on the text of Scripture as understood by the earlier esteemed tradition of comment, largely converging on those writers that best reflected classic Christian consensual thinking. Preaching at the end of the second millennium has reversed that pattern. It has so forgotten most of these classic comments that they are vexing to find anywhere, and even when located they are often available only in archaic editions and inadequate translations. The preached word in our time has remained largely bereft of previously influential patristic inspiration. Recent scholarship has so focused attention upon post-Enlightenment historical and literary methods that it has left this longing largely unattended and unserviced.

This series provides the pastor, exegete, student and lay reader with convenient means to see what Athanasius or John Chrysostom or the desert fathers and mothers had to say about a particular text for preaching, for study and for meditation. There is an emerging awareness among Catholic, Protestant and Orthodox laity that vital biblical preaching and spiritual formation need deeper grounding beyond the scope of the historical-critical orientations that have governed biblical studies in our day.

Hence this work is directed toward a much broader audience than the highly technical and specialized scholarly field of patristic studies. The audience is not limited to the university scholar concentrating on the study of the history of the transmission of the text or to those with highly focused philological interests in textual morphology or historical-critical issues. Though these are crucial concerns for specialists, they are not the paramount interest of this series.

This work is a Christian Talmud. The Talmud is a Jewish collection of rabbinic arguments and comments on the Mishnah, which epitomized the laws of the Torah. The Talmud originated in approximately the same period that the patristic writers were commenting on texts of the Christian tradition. Christians from the late patristic age through the medieval period had documents analogous to the Jewish Talmud and Midrash (Jewish commentaries) available to them in the *glossa ordinaria* and catena traditions, two forms of compiling extracts of patristic exegesis. In Talmudic fashion the sacred text of Christian Scripture was thus clarified and interpreted by the classic commentators.

The Ancient Christian Commentary on Scripture has venerable antecedents in medieval exegesis of both eastern and western traditions, as well as in the Reformation tradition. It offers for the first time in this century the earliest Christian comments and reflections on the Old and New Testaments to a modern audience. Intrinsically an ecumenical project, this series is designed to serve Protestant, Catholic and Orthodox lay, pastoral and scholarly audiences.

In cases where Greek, Latin, Syriac and Coptic texts have remained untranslated into English, we provide new translations. Wherever current English translations are already well rendered, they will be utilized, but if necessary their language will be brought up to date. We seek to present fresh dynamic equivalency translations of long-neglected texts which historically have been regarded as authoritative models of biblical interpretation.

These foundational sources are finding their way into many public libraries and into the core book collections of many pastors and lay persons. It is our intent and the publisher's commitment to keep the whole series in print for many years to come.

Thomas C. Oden
General Editor

A Guide to Using This Commentary

Several features have been incorporated into the design of this commentary. The following comments are intended to assist readers in making full use of this volume.

Pericopes of Scripture

The scriptural text has been divided into pericopes, or passages, usually several verses in length. Each of these pericopes is given a heading, which appears at the beginning of the pericope. For example, the first pericope in the commentary on Galatians is "1:1-5, Greeting and Blessing." This heading is followed by the Scripture passage quoted in the Revised Standard Version (RSV) across the full width of the page. The Scripture passage is provided for the convenience of readers, but it is also in keeping with medieval patristic commentaries, in which the citations of the Fathers were arranged around the text of Scripture.

Overviews

Following each pericope of text from Galatians, Ephesians and Philippians is an overview of the patristic comments on that pericope. The format of this overview varies within the volumes of this series, depending on the requirements of the specific book of Scripture. The function of the overview is to provide a brief summary of all the comments to follow. It tracks a reasonably cohesive thread of argument among patristic comments, even though they are derived from diverse sources and generations. Thus the summaries do not proceed chronologically or by verse sequence. Rather they seek to rehearse the overall course of the patristic comment on that pericope.

We do not assume that the commentators themselves anticipated or expressed a formally received cohesive argument but rather that the various arguments tend to flow in a plausible, recognizable pattern. Modern readers can thus glimpse aspects of continuity in the flow of diverse exegetical traditions representing various generations and geographical locations.

Topical Headings

An abundance of varied patristic comment is available for each pericope of these letters. For this reason we have broken the pericopes into two levels. First is the verse with its topical heading. The patristic comments are then focused on aspects of each verse, with topical headings summarizing the essence of the patristic comment by evoking a key phrase, metaphor or idea. This feature provides a bridge by which modern readers can enter into the heart of the patristic comment.

Identifying the Patristic Texts

Following the topical heading of each section of comment, the name of the patristic commentator is given. An English translation of the patristic comment is then provided. This is immediately followed by the title of the patristic work and the textual reference—either by book, section and subsection or by book-and-verse references.

The Footnotes

Readers who wish to pursue a deeper investigation of the patristic works cited in this commentary will find the footnotes especially valuable. A footnote number directs the reader to the notes at the bottom of the right-hand column, where in addition to other notations (clarifications or biblical crossreferences) one will find information on English translations (where available) and standard original-language editions of the work cited. An abbreviated citation (normally citing the book, volume and page number) of the work in a modern edition is provided. A key to the abbreviations is provided on page xv. Where there is any serious ambiguity or textual problem in the selection, we have tried to reflect the best available textual tradition.

For the convenience of computer database users the digital database references are provided to either the Thesaurus Lingua Graecae (Greek texts) or to the Cetedoc (Latin texts) in the appendix found on pages 291-95.

ABBREVIATIONS

BT	Marius Victorinus. *Bibliotheca Scriptorum Graecorum et Romanorum Teubneriana*. Edited by A. Locher. Leipzig: Teubner, 1824-.
CAO	Clement of Alexandria. *Opera*. Edited by W. Dindorf. Oxford: Clarendon, 1869.
CCL	Corpus Christianorum Series Latina. Turnhout, Belgium: Brepols, 1953-.
CGPEP	Theodore of Mopsuestia. *Catena Graecorum Patrum in Epistulas Pauli*. Edited by J. A. Cramer. Oxford: Clarendon, 1842-1854.
COJG	*The Commentary of Origen on Saint John's Gospel*. Edited by A. E. Brooke. Cambridge: Cambridge University Press, 1896.
CPE	Theodoret. *Commentarius in omnes B. Pauli Epistolas*. Edited by C. Marriott. Oxford: J. H. Parker, 1852-.
CSEL	Corpus Scriptorum Ecclesiasticorum Latinorum. Vienna: Tempsky, 1866-.
Eran	Theodoret. *Eranistes*. Edited by G. H. Ettlinger. Oxford: Clarendon, 1975.
GCS	Die Griechischen Christlichen Schriftsteller der ersten Jahrhunderte. Leipzig and Berlin: Hinrichs, 1897-.
GNO	*Gregorii Nysseni Opera*. Edited by W. Jaeger. Leiden: E.J. Brill, 1952-.
IOEP	John Chrysostom. *Interpretatio Omnium Epistularum Paulinarum*. Edited by F. Field. Oxford: Clarendon, 1849-1862.
JThS	*The Journal of Theological Studies* 3.
LCL	St. Basil, *The Letters*, 4 vols. Edited by R. Deferrari. Loeb Classical Library. Cambridge, Mass.: Harvard University Press, 1926-1934.
NPNF	P. Schaff et al., eds. A Select Library of the Nicene and Post-Nicene Fathers of the Christian Church. 2 series (14 vols. each). Buffalo, N.Y.: Christian Literature, 1887-1894. Reprint, Grand Rapids, Mich.: Eerdmans, 1952-1956. Reprint, Peabody, Mass.: Hendrickson, 1994.
OECT	Cyril of Alexandria. *Select Letters*. Translated and edited by L. R. Wickham. Oxford Early Christian Texts. Edited by H. Chadwick. Oxford: Oxford University Press, 1983.
OSA	*The Orations of St. Athanasius: Against the Arians According to the Benedictine Text*. Translated and edited by W. Bright. Oxford: Clarendon, 1873.
PG	J.-P. Migne, ed. Patrologia Graeca. 166 vols. Paris: Petit-Montrouge: apud. J.-P. Migne, 1857-1886.
PL	J.-P. Migne, ed. Patrologia Latina. 221 vols. Paris: Migne, 1844-1864. (Reference by volume, column and bracketed subsection.)
PO	*The Philocalia of Origen*. Edited by J. A. Robinson. Cambridge: Cambridge University Press, 1893.
PTS	Patristische Texte und Studien. Berlin: de Gruyter, 1964-.
SC	H. de Lubac, J. Daniélou et al., eds. Sources Chrétiennes. Paris: Editions du Cerf, 1941-.
TEM	Theodoret of Mopsuestia. *Epistolas B. Pauli Commentarii*. Edited by H. B. Swete. Cambridge: Cambridge University Press, 1880-1882.
TF	Leo the Great. "Tomus ad Flavianum." In *De Fide et Symbolo*. Translated and edited by C. Heurtley. Oxford: Parker, 1911.

Introduction to
Galatians, Ephesians, Philippians

The Pauline letters—at least the minor letters, which are the subject of this volume—are far more often quoted than discussed in the early church. The most exacting arguments, the most intricate definitions, are fortified by a simple appeal in most cases to texts that are assumed to be self-interpreting or at best to a catena of citations without further exposition or argument.

Much patristic literature consists of popular homilies or sermons, where stringent exegesis would be a tax upon the patience of the listener. Still less can we expect from many of the private letters and artificial speeches from the later Roman Empire, where the words of Paul are often used for ornament and are all the more highly prized the more remote the situation of the writer is from him. It is therefore not surprising that the majority of the excerpts that make up this book should have been derived from authors who assumed the task of expounding one or more of Paul's epistles verse by verse. I shall speak of them not in chronological order but according to their influence on subsequent interpreters of Paul.

The Commentators

Exposition is only part of the object of John Chrysostom, who as bishop of Antioch and Constantinople achieved a dangerous popularity through his attacks on the profligacy of a reigning empress. His homilies cover the whole of the Pauline corpus, giving due weight to every word and every difficulty, but the commentary is interspersed with polished declamations that eschew the rough idiom of the New Testament to bring its lessons home to the more cultivated audience of the fourth century. Yet, classical though Paul's style may be, Chrysostom sees the apostle also as a master of persuasion, and his free use of rhetorical nomenclature lends some support to those who like to analyze Paul's writings in the language of the Greek and Roman schools. It should be observed, however, that he always treats Paul's eloquence as a spontaneous expression of his character, never as the application of an acquired and imitable technique.

Jerome is reckoned one of the four great doctors of the Western church, not so much for his merits as an original theologian as for his rendering of the Old Testament from Hebrew into Latin. Of all our commentators he is the one who says the most on points of grammar, etymology and textual variation. He could not learn not to love the pagan classics and disparages the construction of Paul's sentences with a candor that is seldom imitated. Every modern scholar will, however, admit the value of those comments that compare the apostle's use of Hebrew Scripture with the opinions and traditions of the rabbis. A volume of this nature can accommodate only specimens of such learning, but it can give a better notion of the skill with which he handled other tools of exegesis. We can also get the measure of his temper from such passages as his admonition to bishops at Galatians 6:4. Where Chrysostom was the champion of the lowly, Jerome was the censor of the great.

Chief among Jerome's hermeneutical instruments was allegory, the art of finding mysteries or lessons for the soul beneath the superficial meaning of a text. His master in this discipline, and the source of many of his discoveries in the epistle to the Ephesians, was Origen, a Greek theologian of the previous century, whose influence was matched only by his ill repute among the orthodox. Fragments of his commentary on Ephesians survive in Greek, and the substance of the rest can be inferred from many passages in the commentary by Jerome that either coincide with the known opinions of Origen or recur in other writers, such as Gregory of Nyssa, who are known to have been greatly in Origen's debt. Other texts from Origen cited in this volume have survived either in Greek or in the Latin of Jerome's contemporary Rufinus. Jerome himself, in later life, was one of those vituperative polemicists who ensured that the greater part of Origen's writings would be lost.

Marius Victorinus was a teacher of grammar and rhetoric who did not share Jerome's aversion to the use of speculation in theology. He was perhaps the earliest Christian to attempt a philosophical exposition of the Trinity. The refutation of heresies was for him an important task of exegesis. Its principal aim, however, was to perfect the faith of those whose understanding was still wedded to the senses and the mere letter of the Scriptures. For him it was the spirit, not the body, that was the theme of revelation, and one could never use too many words in the attempt to divine the meaning proper to it. Some no doubt would think him too original in this respect. His comment on Philippians 3:21, for example, defends the resurrection of the body in such a way as almost to deny it. And his statement that the Son will be subjected to the Father was later to be rejected as a heresy at the Council of Constantinople, held in 381. It is to his credit, however, that, using fewer technical words than Chrysostom, he does more to define Paul's terms and to follow his elliptical processes of thought. Eloquence, it would seem, mattered nothing to him. It is hard to guess how anyone learned either grammar or rhetoric from this obscure and slipshod writer. The lacunae in my translation act as a curb on his prolixity but also spare me the duty of translating certain passages that I cannot even parse.

Also verbose at times but more intelligible at all times is Augustine, the foremost theologian of antiquity, to whom we owe the doctrine of original sin and the classic formulation of the view that catholicity is the hallmark of the church. He was not, in the strictest sense, a commentator, but everything that he wrote in later life was tied to Scripture, and the excerpts in this volume have been culled from an unusual variety of writings. To the homilies and sermons that are no small part of his prodigious *oeuvre* he added a continuous exposition of Galatians, in which his originality and insight more than outweigh the defects entailed by his lack of Greek and his indifference to the works of other authors. In his extensive comment on Galatians 5:17 we find a most succinct and cogent summary of his teaching on the function of the law in the reprobation of human sin, as well as its cooperation with the Holy Spirit to imbue Christian neophytes with a righteousness that is real but not their own.

Martin Luther could not have found his own account of Paul precisely stated in any of the Fathers, though he might have felt that Marius Victorinus and Augustine had a sound view of the primacy of grace in our election and our consequent good works. Others, even if they never deny that it is God who ordains salvation, tend to take the position that his choice depends on our foreseen response to his invitation. This is true, for example, of the author whom we call Ambrosiaster, though no one speaks more frequently of the "righteousness of faith" that is imparted through the cross. For the rest, Ambrosiaster is a more pedestrian commentator, seldom profound though always careful and perceptive, who owes his name to the fact that his works were once included erroneously among those of Augustine's teacher Ambrose. Ambrosiaster's statements often resemble those of Chrysostom and Jerome, and like them he sometimes comments on Paul's rhetorical procedure but not with the pertinacity of Chrysostom or with Jerome's pungency. Nevertheless he may have grasped the essence of Paul's gospel better than others when he took the "peace" that is promised at Philippians 4:9 to mean peace with God.

His counterpart among the Greeks is Theodoret, a scholarly and irenic theologian who achieved originality by accident when he coined the phrase "one person in two natures" as a formula for the union of God and humanity in Christ. Scripture and consensus were his usual guides, and his comments on Paul's letters are often mere paraphrases or epitomes of Chrysostom. Only as a historian is he generally his own person. It was he who put a sentence at the end of every letter stating its origin and destination. He is the one who tells us how the prediction of Paul's return at Philippians 1:25 was verified. And he wrote an ingenious paragraph to corroborate the prevalent opinion that the James who is called the Lord's brother in Galatians 2 could not have been the fruit of Mary's womb. He makes occasional observations on Paul's method. Where the followers of Origen would have argued that the text is designed to lead us anagogically from carnal thoughts to higher meditations, Theodoret generally prefers to say that the aim is psychagogic—that is, working upon the feelings of an audience in a temporary state of doubt and need.

This compilation might have been expected to give more room to Theodore, bishop of Mopsuestia, the founder of the Antiochene school of literal and historical exegesis to which both Chrysostom and Theodoret belonged. Most of Theodore's writings perished after his condemnation in 553, when he was said to have denied that the divinity and humanity of Christ were united in a single person. Until the late nineteenth century, the only recognized fragments of his commentaries on Paul were a few quotations in a Byzantine anthology or catena, from which I have made some excerpts for this volume. In 1880 H. B. Swete observed that a Latin commentary on the minor Pauline letters, hitherto attributed to Ambrose of Milan, was largely a translation of Theodore. Two large volumes were therefore published under his name, but on the whole I have made very little use of them, as the Latin is sometimes difficult to render and seems unlikely to be an accurate equivalent of the Greek. In any case, a great part of it is either bald periphrasis or grammatical annotation. The best of the interpretative and homiletic comments have parallels in Theodoret and Chrysostom. I have thought it better to use their words and have gone to the Latin only for a comment on Galatians 4:24, which may stand as a manifesto of Antiochene exegesis against the tendencies of the allegorizing school.

Scripture in the Service of Orthodoxy

The verses that attract most frequent notice in the works of other Christians are those that might be thought to endorse a heresy and those that governed the church's understanding of the nature of God or Christ. Ephesians 2:3, for example, might be thought to countenance the Gnostic tenet that humans are created good or evil and are thus deprived of choice in their salvation. Philippians 2:13 is another text that might seem to deny the freedom of the will. And Galatians 5:17 could be adduced by the Manichaeans to insinuate that the flesh is the creation of some being other than God. All the patristic exegetes agree that nothing bad comes from the hand of the Creator and that flesh is an inalienable part of the human person. The Eastern and Western positions on the freedom of the will are often thought to be in conflict; one will often find in this collection that where Marius Victorinus or Augustine insist that God is the source of everything, the Greeks will be reluctant to admit any curtailment of our freedom. In our compilation on Philippians 2:13, however, we find that even Augustine will affirm that human beings are responsible for their actions, while even Chrysostom maintains that our capacity for willing comes from God.

One theory, which essayed to reconcile predestination with demerit, taught that souls had once existed in a state of perfect innocence and had then undergone the Fall, with a consequent loss of freedom, as a punishment for sin. Origen is the most famous though neither the first nor the most consistent holder of this opinion, and he was followed in part by Marius Victorinus. Both, speaking of Ephesians 1:4, maintained that God could not elect a soul before it came into being. Origen deduced the fall of souls from the word *katabolē*, which Paul had used in this verse to denote the foundation— or, as one might say, the deposition—of this world. I have included only a little of this controversy, but enough to show that even those who agreed that predestination ought to depend on merit insisted that the merits were foreseen from the beginning and dependent on the eternal will of God expressed in Christ.

On one point all were agreed: good works after baptism were both possible and obligatory. Even if perfection would be possible only in heaven, one who failed to pursue it in the present life was forgetting that the God who gave up his Son for us was the God who wrote the law. The difference between the Christian and the Jew is thus that one obeys in love and one in fear. The latter of course is bound to fail, and readers of Philippians 3:5 could hold that even if Paul was outwardly a perfect Jew he could be guilty of inward sins, for which he blames himself elsewhere. Thus one could maintain against Pelagius that all human beings sin and also hold, against Marcion and the Gnostics, that the law is a rule of life. This conviction did not always save our commentators from the anti-Semitism that was prevalent among some Christians of this epoch. Marius Victorinus does himself and truth more credit on Ephesians 3:9 than others (not included here) who interpreted it to mean that "all" are included in God's purpose except the Jews.

Exegesis and Christology

The sense of sin was strong and carried with it a belief that we require a special act to reconcile us with the giver of the law. Personal sin was not the only barrier, for the realm of flesh was ruled by fallen angels, who had acquired the right to punish us for the sins that they themselves had instigated. On the basis of Ephesians 1:10, some maintained that these beings also had been reconciled when Christ the Word took flesh and thus summed up or "recapitulated" all things in himself by his obedience to God. Others cited Ephesians 4:8 to show that Christ had rather vanquished than redeemed the hostile powers, spoiling them of the captives whom they held by a merely arbitrary right. Still another view held that God could not cheat Satan of his due and therefore had to pay our ransom in the precious blood of Christ. This is supported in the present volume by interpreters of Ephesians 1:7. In patristic writings on Galatians we find theories of deception (Gal 1:4), substitutionary offering (Gal 3:13) and the incorporation of all humanity in the flesh of Christ (Gal 6:15). It could not be denied by any, however, that Christ's humiliation was his glory. It was only because his love surpassed all knowledge that he became a curse for us, as Galatians 3:13 declares. If he seemed to "empty himself" of glory in the present world, it was only so that we might share his glory in eternity.

Everyone felt bound to have an opinion on the phrase that says "he emptied himself." The hymn to Christ in Philippians 2 was both a pattern of orthodoxy and a catalyst for many sorts of error. It speaks of Christ as having been in "the form of God" (Phil 2:6) and therefore might be taken to suggest that he was God in form but not in his proper nature. It says that he "did not think it a robbery to be equal with God," a verse that for many remains obscure to the present day. When it goes on to declare that he assumed the form of a slave (Phil 2:7) and the fashion of a man (Phil 2:8), it seemed to some to lend some color to the theory called Docetism, which claims that Christ was never truly human and that his body was a phantom. These assumptions had to be answered. Finally, we are told that on account of Christ's obedience God has given him a name that is above all names (Phil 2:9), from which some could infer that he acquired his divinity only by adoption, while others argued even that he must still be a lesser being than the Creator, who cannot be named in any human tongue.

To the reader of the voluminous annotations to this passage it will be obvious that the multitude of voices is not matched by the diversity of opinions. All affirm that Christ is God by origin and nature; all affirm that he took a human body without disguise and that the name bestowed upon him before the world was a declaration of the Godhead that he had secretly possessed from the beginning. The value of this collation is to reveal the unanimity of doctrine that prevailed among the Fathers and that left no room for the modern theories sometimes traced to them. No one held that the Word had undergone a real *kenōsis*, or self-emptying, in order to effect the incarnation. Even the archheretic Nestorius, condemned by two church councils, never argued that the union of the natures was dependent on the voluntary obedience of the manhood to the Word.

Therefore we look in vain here for any developed theory of *kenōsis* or even for any refined theory of the incarnation. The glosses on Philippians 2:7 are more defensive than constructive, more concerned to limit than to define the new experience that befell the second Person of the Trinity as a result of his conjunction with the flesh. This is equally true, for example, in Galatians 3:13, where Paul declares that Christ became a curse for us. The ancient exegetes insist that it was impossible to part him from his holiness but do not fully explain how he made atonement through the cross. The exegete fulfilled his primary duty by forestalling error and in his own capacity assuming that he should only uphold, not try to make, the doctrine of the universal church.

Some verses that preoccupy modern scholars did not exercise these readers. Everyone had read, of course, at Galatians 3:28 that in Christ there is neither male nor female, bond nor free; but no one deduced that Christians were bound to seek the abolition of slavery or that women could be priests. The function of the Bible, as it was then perceived, was not to change society but to reveal the mind of God. Where God himself was the subject, curiosity was insatiable. The God who is "above all and through all and in all" (Eph 4:4) is a string of syllables to many modern readers, but the ancients detected an adumbration of the Trinity in the prepositions *above*, *in* and *through*.

Some Peculiarities of Ancient Exegesis

In the same way ancient exegetes see Christ where he is invisible to modern commentators. Thus, when we are told at Galatians 3:19 that the law was given by the hand of a mediator, it is obvious to us that this is Moses, in conjunction with the angels. But the Fathers read the New Testament as a single book and believed the term must here denote the same person as in Hebrews and 1 Timothy, where it clearly refers to Christ. Even Paul's vocation could be cited to prove an orthodox Christology, for if he was an apostle not by humans but by Jesus Christ, as he says in the first verse of Galatians, it seemed to follow logically that the Christ who had been revealed to him was truly God. The humanity was not to be forgotten, and a pillar of orthodoxy was Philippians 3:21, which, by making the flesh participate in the glorious resurrection of the Savior, shows us what is to be expected in our own. Paul becomes almost speechless at Ephesians 3:18 when he contemplates the "breadth and length and height and depth" of the blessings that are laid up for the saints. But his early interpreters found no difficulty in equating each of these with both a portion of the world and a dimension of the cross.

The modern reader calls this *allegory* and dislikes it. Some Greek fathers also regard this method with suspicion, as we see from Chrysostom's comments on Galatians 4:24, where Paul himself employs a cognate term. Chrysostom and Theodoret make little use of allegory under any name, as they represent the Antiochene tradition, which identified the meaning of the text with the historical intentions of its author. But other Greeks, among them Origen and Gregory of Nyssa, are as ready as some Latin commentators to believe that the Holy Spirit has permeated the sacred text with a wealth of figurative suggestions. Ephesians 5:31, with its allusions to a great mystery, appears to confirm this principle. Were it otherwise, we could never find the promise of the New Testament in the Old, as every Christian did at that time. And as Gregory of Nyssa makes clear in his remarks on the Philippian hymn, no human speech can ever be fully transparent or unambiguous when it undertakes to make us comprehend the ineffable mysteries of God.

The moral injunctions of the Pauline letters were expanded and applied to new circumstances in the preaching of the clergy and in detailed handbooks of early monastic discipline. This was, then as now, at once the most common and the most fruitful use of Scripture. But since such precepts fall outside the normal definition of a commentary, they have rarely been included in this volume. The early commentators are most instructive on the texts where the author's meaning is ambiguous, as when we are told at Ephesians 4:26 not to let the sun set on our anger. The passages of most interest to the historian are those that show, like Chrysostom's reflections on the lot of slaves (Eph 6:5), how far the ethic of the gospel was in conflict with the custom of the age. It would seem that certain readers of Philippians 1:23 had been too eager to "depart and be with Christ." While some of our witnesses are silent here, others are content with drawing lessons in Christology, and others argue that Paul had never meditated suicide but merely wished to indicate how much he bore for our sake by coming into the world.

The skill with which Paul works upon his audience was frequently commended, above all by John Chrysostom, who earned his surname "Golden Mouth" by his copious eloquence. Rhetorical theory taught that the surest way to arouse a feeling is to make a parade of feeling. That Paul did this was evident, but, since he was an apostle, it was never to be supposed that he was being disingenuous when he expressed his fear, compassion, anger or fatherly concern. What he said was always true for his time and can be true again for us on a comparable occasion. Jerome agreed, and when he found Paul styling himself "the least of all the saints" at Ephesians 3:8, he argues that this must be true in some way, since no pretense would have been a proper implement for a man of God. Yet Jerome himself, though free of false humility, was not wholly unacquainted with deception, and he did believe that Paul also was capable of it when he entered into a staged debate at Antioch. Theodoret too maintains that the dispute between Paul and Peter, as described in Galatians 2, was a pedagogic simulation. But Jerome came to hear of an expostulatory letter by Augustine, for whom mendacity in any form was the root of sin. The resulting correspondence, too long and too unedifying to be included here, taxed Augustine's powers of flattery and Jerome's stores of wit.

Some Editorial Problems in This Volume

A few of the Fathers' eccentricities could not now be imitated because they either used a different text or, if they wrote in Latin, relied on a translation that would not commend itself to the critical scholarship of our day. Since they may not always be wrong and since the value and interest of their observations need not be impaired by slight inaccuracies of this kind, I have included many such comments, translating them in such a way as to make sense of the author. Even where there is no discrepancy in substance, I have sometimes found it best to admit a trivial deviation from the language of the Revised Standard Version or to incorporate a variant in square brackets when I quote it. The reader will no doubt be aware that no one English version can supply a complete or definitive equivalent to the Greek.

Some comments refer to heresies that are now defunct or at least no longer recognized. Rather than repeat the same information in different footnotes, I have given brief accounts of these in a glossary, where I also provide biographical information on all the authors who have been excerpted in the present volume. References to ancient texts are given according to the conventional divisions or according to page numbers in the latest editions known to me. Where these are not part of Migne's *Patrologia* they are named in the bibliography, together with all the texts on which translations have been based in the present volume.

For those who wish to examine a given patristic text in its context, the easiest mode of reference to the edition consulted here is to look up the number of the scriptural verse in the version indicated or to track down the reference in the footnotes. Digital references may be found in the Thesaurus Linguae Graecae or the Cetedoc digital edition of the Latin fathers (see appendix). Where there is more than one comment by the same author on a single verse, it may be assumed, unless I indicate otherwise, that I am following the order of the Greek or Latin text.

A project of this kind would be inconceivable without a team of graduate-student researchers to pan the vast beds of knowledge now available on computers and ensure that not an ounce of gold is lost. In sifting their results, I have confined my attention to the first five centuries, the age of the doctrine makers; but even within this period, a thorough search could be performed only by several hands. I am therefore glad to acknowledge the punctuality and diligence of Joel Elowsky, Joel Scandrett,

Jeff Finch and several others. I hope that the volume born of our collective toil will demonstrate to all readers that the piety, the eloquence and the intellectual acumen of the Fathers are not antiquated treasures but belong to the disposable resources of the church.

M. J. Edwards
Christ Church, Oxford

THE EPISTLE TO THE GALATIANS

1:1-5 GREETING AND BLESSING

[1]*Paul an apostle—not from men nor through man, but through Jesus Christ and God the Father, who raised him from the dead—* [2]*and all the brethren who are with me,*

To the churches of Galatia:

[3]*Grace to you and peace from God the Father and our Lord Jesus Christ,* [4]*who gave himself for our sins to deliver us from the present evil age, according to the will of our God and Father;* [5]*to whom be the glory for ever and ever. Amen.*

OVERVIEW: Speaking vehemently for their sake (CHRYSOSTOM), Paul tells the Galatians that true apostles are made by God (CASSIODORUS, JEROME) and used by him (AUGUSTINE). He indicates that Christ was more than man (ORIGEN) and equal to God the Father (THEODORET). He mentions "all the brethren" to shame the Galatians (MARIUS VICTORINUS) and defend himself (CHRYSOSTOM) in the face of a general secession from the gospel (THEODORET). He wishes them both grace and peace (AUGUSTINE), reminding them of their duty to the Father (CHRYSOSTOM), who is united with the Son in mission (AMBROSIASTER). Christ outwitted the devil on our behalf, thus giving us grace instead of the law (AMBROSIASTER) and freeing us from the propensity to sin (THEODORET). He did this voluntarily (JEROME). We should both recognize the Father's will in him (CHRYSOSTOM) and imitate his submission (AUGUSTINE) as we contemplate God's marvelous work (CHRYSOSTOM).

1:1a *Paul an Apostle*

HIS AUTHORITY IS NOT OF HUMAN ORIGIN. CASSIODORUS: When he calls himself an apostle not of human making but through Christ Jesus, he does away with those who had only human authority for styling themselves apostles. The churches at that time were being thrown into turmoil by false preachers. He greets these churches with all the brethren who are with him. In that greeting he also blesses them, so that their fitness to receive the word of the Lord may be established. SUMMARY OF GALATIANS 1.1.1.[1]

1:1b *Not from Humans or Through Humans*

---

[1]Migne PL 70:1343C.

1

PAUL SPEAKS WITH PASSION. CHRYSOSTOM: [The first verse] is full of great passion and strong sentiment; and not the prologue only but, as it were, the whole letter. For always to speak mildly to those who are being taught, even when they need vehemence, is not the part of a teacher but of a corrupter and an enemy. HOMILY ON GALATIANS 1.1-3.[2]

PAUL, NOT ONE OF THE TWELVE, DEFINES HIS APOSTOLATE. JEROME: Not in pride, as some suppose, but by necessity, he said that he was not an apostle from men or through man . . . so that by this he might confound those who were alleging that Paul was not one of the twelve apostles or ordained by his elders. This might also be taken as aimed obliquely at Peter and the others, because the gospel was committed to him not by the apostles but by the same Jesus Christ who had chosen those apostles. EPISTLE TO THE GALATIANS 1.1.1.[3]

TRUTH DOES NOT COME FROM HUMAN SOURCES PRONE TO LIE. AUGUSTINE: The one sent *from men* is a liar; the one sent *through man* tells the truth, as God too, who is truthful, may send truth through men. The one, therefore, who is sent not from men or through man but *through God* derives his truthfulness from the One who makes truthful even those sent through men. EPISTLE TO THE GALATIANS 2.[4]

1:1c *Through Jesus Christ and God the Father*

DIVINELY APPOINTED. ORIGEN: We are clearly given to understand that Jesus Christ was not a [mere] man but was of divine nature. . . . Because he knew him to be of a more sublime nature, he therefore said that he was not appointed by a man. APOLOGY FOR ORIGEN.[5]

THE SON IS NOT LESS THAN THE FATHER. THEODORET: So that no one might suppose the Son to be a mere ancillary to the Father, finding the word *through* in this passage, he immediately adds *but through God the Father, who raised him from the dead*. For he has applied the word *through* to both persons, teaching that this usage does not imply any difference of nature. And the phrase "the one who raised him from the dead" does not hint at any defect in the Son's divinity, for the suffering did not happen to the Godhead but illustrates the concord of the gospel, because it was not the Son alone who bestowed the mystery of the divine incarnation, but the Father himself is a sharer in this dispensation. EPISTLE TO THE GALATIANS 1.1.[6]

CHRIST-TAUGHT. MARIUS VICTORINUS: His reason for saying *through Christ and God the Father, who raised him from the dead* is that what God does he does through Christ. And so that people would not say, "How did you learn from Christ?" since Paul had not previously been a follower of Christ and Christ was dead, he said that God raised Christ from the dead. By this he implies that it is Christ himself, who taught him, who has been raised from the dead—raised, that is, by the power of God the Father. EPISTLE TO THE GALATIANS 1.1.1.[7]

---

[2]IOEP 4:1. [3]Migne PL 26:311A-B [373]. [4]Migne PL 35:2107, italics added. [5]Migne PG 17:584-85. [6]CPE 1:327-28. [7]BT 1972:3 [1148B].

RAISED FROM THE DEAD. CHRYSOSTOM: To say *who raised him from the dead* is to encapsulate the essence of God's beneficence toward us, which coincides in no small part with his present purpose. For the majority are much less apt to listen to words that establish the majesty of God than to those which demonstrate his good will to humanity. HOMILY ON GALATIANS 1.1-3.[8]

1:2a All the Brethren with Me

ALL THE BROTHERS WITH ME. MARIUS VICTORINUS: Whereas he was accustomed to call himself simply Paul the apostle to the Romans and Corinthians,[9] in order to startle the Galatians and reprove them for a grave error he has joined with himself all the brothers who were with him, saying that they themselves were writing to the Galatians, making them feel the shame of thinking contrary to everyone, so as to give more weight to his own injunctions and the gospel that he preaches. EPISTLE TO THE GALATIANS 1.1.1.[10]

PAUL SPEAKS WITH THE CONSENT OF OTHERS. CHRYSOSTOM: Why does he nowhere else add this in his letters? For he puts his own name alone, or names two or three;[11] but here he speaks of the whole community and therefore mentions no one's name. Why then does he do this? Because their slander against him was that he was the only person proclaiming this and was introducing novelty to doctrine. So as to destroy their calumny, therefore, and to show that his opinions are shared by many, he adds on *the brothers*, showing that what he writes he writes with their consent. HOMILY ON GALATIANS 1.1-3.[12]

1:2b To the Churches of Galatia

ADDRESSED TO THE WHOLE CHURCH OF GALATIA. CHRYSOSTOM: This fire had overtaken not one city, or two or three, but the whole Galatian people. And let me point out here his extreme irritation. He does not write "to the beloved" or "to the sanctified" but *to the churches of Galatia*. This is the act of one who is intensely displeased and showing his pain, that he addresses them not with love nor with the names of honor but only by that of the congregation. He does not even say "to the churches of God" but "to the churches of Galatia."[13] HOMILY ON GALATIANS 1.1-3.[14]

WRITTEN FROM ROME. THEODORET: The epistle to the Galatians was written from Rome. The divine apostle had already seen and taught them. EPISTLE TO THE GALATIANS 6.18.[15]

1:3 Grace and Peace from God the Father and Our Lord Jesus Christ

DISTINGUISHING GRACE AND PEACE. AUGUSTINE: The grace of God, by which our sins are forgiven, is the condition of our being reconciled to him, whereas peace is that wherein we are reconciled. EPISTLE TO THE GALATIANS 3 [1B.1.3-5].[16]

WHY WE CALL GOD "FATHER." CHRYSOSTOM: He calls God "Father" here not to flat-

---

[8]IOEP 4:6. [9]See Rom 1:1; 1 Cor 1:1; 2 Cor 1:1. [10]BT 1972:2 [1147B-C]. [11]E.g., 2 Cor 1:1; Phil 1:1; 1 Thess 1:1. [12]IOEP 4:7. [13]Cf. 1 Thess 2:14; 2 Thess 1:4. [14]IOEP 4:7-8; cf. Theodoret *Epistle to the Galatians* 1.2 [CPE 1:328]. [15]CPE 1:365. [16]Migne PL 35:2108.

ter them but vehemently reproving them and reminding them how it was that they became sons. For it was not through the law but through the bath of regeneration that they were deemed worthy of this honor.... "You slaves and enemies and aliens," [he says], "why are you so quick to call God your Father? Surely it was not the law that gave you this kinship? So why do you desert the one who was leading you to this sense of affiliation and return to your previous mentor?" HOMILY ON GALATIANS 1.1-3.[17]

SUSTAINED BY THE FATHER AS MUCH AS BY THE SON. AMBROSIASTER: He shows that the human race is sustained by the goodness of both, as much Father as Son. Nor does he indicate that the Son is less than the Father when he calls him our Lord, nor that the Father is greater when he calls him our God. He will not be a true Father unless he is also Lord, nor will the Son be a true Lord unless he is also God. EPISTLE TO THE GALATIANS 1.3.[18]

1:4a Christ Gave Himself for Our Sins

WHY CHRIST GAVE HIMSELF UP. AMBROSIASTER: For when the human race was held in the dominion of the devil, the Savior offered himself to the willing devil, so that deceiving him by the power of his virtue—for the devil wanted to take possession of one whom he was unable to hold—he could carry off those whom the devil was detaining by a false right. EPISTLE TO THE GALATIANS 1.4.1.[19]

FOR OUR SINS. AMBROSIASTER: Now Christ by atoning for our transgressions not only gave us life but also made us his own, so that we might be called children of God, made so

through faith. What a great error it is, therefore, to go under the law again after receiving grace. EPISTLE TO THE GALATIANS 1.4.2.[20]

1:4b Delivering Us from This Evil Age

IS THE WORLD THEREFORE EVIL? THEODORET: By *the evil age* he does not mean the elements, as the Manichaeans[21] portentously assert, but the present life, that is, this secular human way of living, in which sin has made a home. For, being enveloped in a mortal nature, some of us venture on the greater sins, some on the lesser. But when we make the transition to that immortal life, and are free from our present corruption and have put on incorruption, we shall be made able to conquer sin.... Yet the present age as such is not vile, but vileness is the enterprise of some who live in it. EPISTLE TO THE GALATIANS 1.3-4.[22]

1:4c The Will of Our God and Father

IS CHRIST THEREFORE SUBORDINATE TO GOD? JEROME: Neither did the Son give himself without the Father's will, nor did the Father give up the Son without the Son's will. ... The Son gave himself, that he himself, as righteousness, might do away with the unrighteousness in us. Wisdom gave itself that it might oust foolishness. EPISTLE TO THE GALATIANS 1.1.3.[23]

CHRIST MADE HIS FATHER OUR FATHER. CHRYSOSTOM: Since they thought that they

---

[17]IOEP 4:8. [18]CSEL 81.3:6. [19]CSEL 81.3:7. [20]CSEL 81.3:7. [21]To the followers of Manes, who conflated Judeo-Christian with Indo-Iranian doctrines, the earth and its elements are evil. [22]CPE 1:328-29. [23]Migne PL 26:314A [376].

were disobeying God, as the giver of the law, and were afraid to forsake the old and pass to the new, he corrects this reasoning of theirs, saying that this also pleased the Father. And he said not simply "of the Father" but *of your Father*. He adds this immediately, exhorting them by showing that Christ made his Father our Father. HOMILY ON GALATIANS 1.4.[24]

1:5a Glory for Ever and Ever

CHRIST DID NOT SEEK HIS OWN GLORY. AUGUSTINE: How much more, therefore, ought men not to claim the credit for themselves if they perform any good work, when the very Son of God in the Gospel said that he sought not his own glory. Nor had he come to do his own will but the will of him who sent him! This will and glory of the Father the apostle now commemorates, that he also, by the example of the Lord who sent him, may indicate that he seeks not his own glory or the performance of his own will in the preaching of the gospel, just as he says a little later, "if I were to please men, I should

not be a servant of Christ."[25] EPISTLE TO THE GALATIANS 3 [1B.1.3-5].[26]

1:5b Amen

WHY SAY "AMEN" SO EARLY? CHRYSOSTOM: We nowhere find the word *amen* placed at the beginning or in the prologue of his letters but after many words. But here, showing that what he has said is a sufficient accusation of the Galatians and that the argument is closed, he made this the prologue. For it does not take long to establish charges that are patently true. . . . But not only for this reason does he do it but because he is exceedingly astonished by the magnitude of the gift, the excess of grace and what God did at once in a tiny space of time for those in such a state. Unable to express this in words, Paul breaks into a doxology. He holds up for the whole world a blessing, not indeed worthy of the subject but such as was possible to him. HOMILY ON GALATIANS 1.5.[27]

---

[24]IOEP 4:12. [25]Gal 1:10. [26]Migne PL 35:2108; cf. NPNF 1 13:6*. [27]IOEP 4:12.

1:6-9 THE INTEGRITY OF THE GOSPEL

[6]*I am astonished that you are so quickly deserting him who called you in the grace of Christ and turning to a different gospel—* [7]*not that there is another gospel, but there are some who trouble you and want to pervert the gospel of Christ.* [8]*But even if we, or an angel from heaven, should preach to you a gospel contrary to that which we preached to you, let him be accursed.* [9]*As we have said before, so now I say again, If any one is preaching to you a gospel contrary to that which you received, let him be accursed.*

OVERVIEW: Showing that the Galatians have been carried away by Satan (JEROME), Paul both blames and flatters them by professing astonishment, asserting that they have sinned against the Father (CHRYSOSTOM), who is the author of the gospel (THEODORET). Any other gospel is no gospel (AUGUSTINE)—indeed, an illusion (JEROME). The slightest innovation is an apostasy (THEODORE OF MOPSUESTIA), though the gospel can never be overthrown (JEROME). Not sparing himself (THEODORET) or even angels (JEROME), Paul expresses his indignation (AMBROSIASTER) yet shows by repetition that he has neither spoken in haste (CHRYSOSTOM) nor cursed without warning (JEROME).

1:6a *Their Quick Desertion*

WHO HAS PROMPTED THE DESERTION?
JEROME: The word for "being carried away"[1] is first found in Genesis where God carries Enoch away and he is not found.[2] . . . The one whom God carries away is not found by his enemies . . . but he whom the devil carries away is carried into that which appears to be but is not. EPISTLE TO THE GALATIANS 1.1.6.[3]

THE ABRUPTNESS OF THEIR LAPSE.
CHRYSOSTOM: The one who is carried away after a long time is worthy of blame, but the one who falls at the first attack and in the initial skirmish has furnished an example of the greatest weakness. And with this he charges them also, saying "What is this, that those who deceive you do not even need time, but the first assault suffices to rout and capture you?" . . . At the same time he shows in what great and high estimation he holds them. For if he had thought them

mere nobodies and easily deceived, he would not have been surprised by what occurred. HOMILY ON GALATIANS 1.6.[4]

1:6b *Called in the Grace of Christ*

THE DECEITFULNESS OF THE LAPSE. CHRYSOSTOM: And he did not say "from the gospel" but *from God*, for he used terms that were more horrifying and more likely to astound them. For those who wished to deceive them did not do so all at once but gently estranged them from the faith in fact, leaving the names unchanged. For such are the wiles of the devil, not to make apparent the instruments of his hunt. For if they had said, "Depart from Christ," the Galatians would have shunned them as deceivers and corrupters. As it was, the deceivers allowed them still to remain in the faith while they were undermining the whole edifice with impunity. The language these tunnelers used was covered with these familiar names as with awnings. HOMILY ON GALATIANS 1.6.[5]

DEPARTING FROM THE ONE WHO CALLS US TO GRACE. THEODORET: He is saying, "You have not departed from this teaching to that but from the one who called you. . . . The very Father who gave the law is the one who called you to this gospel. . . . And if you desert this gospel, you will not find another. For the Lord does not preach some things through us and others through the other apostles." EPISTLE TO THE GALATIANS 1.6-7.[6]

---

[1]The literal translation of the word rendered *desertion* by Paul. [2]See Gen 5:24, "because God translated him" (LXX). [3]Migne PL 26:317C-318A [380-81]. [4]IOEP 4:13. [5]IOEP 4:13. [6]CPE 1:329-30.

1:6c-7a *Turning to a Different Gospel*

Why Is It Not a Gospel? AUGUSTINE: If it were another gospel other than the one that the Lord has given through himself or through some other, it would not be a gospel. EPISTLE TO THE GALATIANS 4 [1B.1.6-9].[7]

There Is No Other Gospel. JEROME: Not another gospel, because all that is false is insubstantial, and that which is contrary to truth finally has no existence. EPISTLE TO THE GALATIANS 1.1.6.[8]

1:7b *Perverting the Gospel of Christ*

They Can Do No More Than "Want to" Pervert the Gospel. JEROME: They wish, he says, to disturb the gospel of Christ but cannot prevail, because it is of such a nature that it cannot be other than the truth. EPISTLE TO THE GALATIANS 1.1.6.[9]

Debasing the Currency. THEODORE OF MOPSUESTIA: Just as with royal currency—anyone who cuts off a little from the impress has debased the whole currency—so one who makes even the smallest change in sound faith adulterates the whole. EPISTLE TO THE GALATIANS.[10]

1:8a *An Angel and a Contrary Gospel*

Could Angels Ever Deceive? JEROME: This could be understood as a hyperbolic statement, not meaning that an apostle or an angel could preach otherwise than they had spoken. . . . [Yet] angels are also mutable if they have not held fast to their ground. . . . Lucifer, who rose in the morning, also fell. He who dispensed deceit to all nations is to

be trampled on the earth. EPISTLE TO THE GALATIANS 1.1.8.[11]

Might a Holy Angel Deny the Gospel? THEODORET: He mentioned the angels, not speculating that any of the holy angels would say something contrary to the divine gospel, for he knew this to be impossible. But through this he reprehended every novelty of humanity. EPISTLE TO THE GALATIANS 1.8.[12]

1:8b *Let False Teachers Be Accursed*

Indignant for Their Salvation. AMBROSIASTER: Let no one be surprised that the apostle, when quieting ferocious characters, was so annoyed. He is indignant, for the sake of the Galatians' salvation, with the enemies of the Christian way of life. For this indignation shows that it is no light sin to transfer allegiance to the law after receiving faith. EPISTLE TO THE GALATIANS 1.9.1.[13]

1:9a *The Apostle's Reiteration*

Why He Repeats. CHRYSOSTOM: Lest you should think that the words came from passion or were spoken hyperbolically or through a loss of self-control, he says the same things over again. HOMILY ON GALATIANS 1.9.[14]

1:9b *An Anathema*

Has Paul Cursed Without Warning?

---

[7]Migne PL 35:2108. [8]Migne PL 26:318C [381]. Since there is no other gospel, to speak as if there were a different gospel is to speak of that which is unreal. [9]Migne PL 26:319A [382]. [10]CGPEP 6:16. [11]Migne PL 26:319C-320A [382-83]. [12]CPE 1:330. [13]CSEL 81.3:9-10. [14]IOEP 4:19. Cf. Theodoret *Epistle to the Galatians* 1.9 [CPE 1:330].

JEROME: He indicates that he initially, fearing this very thing, denounced an anathema on those who would preach in this way. Now, after it has been preached, he decrees the anathema that he formerly predicted. EPISTLE TO THE GALATIANS 1.1.8.[15]

---

[15]Migne PL 26:320C [384].

1:10-17 PAUL'S CONVERSION

[10]*Am I now seeking the favor of men, or of God? Or am I trying to please men? If I were still pleasing men, I should not be a servant[a] of Christ.*

[11]*For I would have you know, brethren, that the gospel which was preached by me is not man's[b] gospel. [12]For I did not receive it from man, nor was I taught it, but it came through a revelation of Jesus Christ. [13]For you have heard of my former life in Judaism, how I persecuted the church of God violently and tried to destroy it; [14]and I advanced in Judaism beyond many of my own age among my people, so extremely zealous was I for the traditions of my fathers. [15]But when he who had set me apart before I was born, and had called me through his grace, [16]was pleased to reveal his Son to[c] me, in order that I might preach him among the Gentiles, I did not confer with flesh and blood, [17]nor did I go up to Jerusalem to those who were apostles before me, but I went away into Arabia; and again I returned to Damascus.*

a Or slave b Greek according to man c Greek in

OVERVIEW: Though there may be times for pleasing people, Paul is not doing so here (AUGUSTINE, JEROME). He relates his conversion to refute the false apostles (CHRYSOSTOM), arguing that human thoughts cannot understand the gospel (MARIUS VICTORINUS, AUGUSTINE). The fact that he is taught by Christ, not people, enhances his authority (ORIGEN, CHRYSOSTOM) and qualifies him as the teacher for the Galatians (THEODORET). He reinforces his point (MARIUS VICTORINUS) by showing that it was harder for him than for them to reject Judaism (CHRYSOSTOM), which is now condemned (AUGUSTINE), though the law is not (JEROME). Chosen in foreknowledge of his merits (AMBROSIASTER) yet by grace (MARIUS VICTORINUS), Paul has received a new revelation (JEROME, FILASTRIUS). Whether or not he means the apostles by "flesh and blood" (CHRYSOSTOM, JEROME), he does not disparage them in his account of his conversion (CHRYSOSTOM). He went to Arabia to sow the gospel in new places (AMBROSIASTER). From his brief words we learn humility (CHRYSOSTOM).

1:10a *Seeking Divine or Human Favor?*

ON NOT DESPISING HUMAN OPINIONS.
JEROME: Let us not suppose that the apostle is teaching us by his example to despise the judgments of others . . . but if it can happen that we can please God and others equally, let us also please others. . . . The word *now* is inserted specially here, to show that people are to be pleased or displeased according to the circumstances, so that he who is now displeasing for the sake of gospel truth was at one time pleasing for the sake of people's salvation. EPISTLE TO THE GALATIANS 1.1.10.[1]

HOW WE ARE BEST PLEASED THROUGH THE TRUTH. AUGUSTINE: No one persuades God, for all things are manifest to him. But a person does well in wishing to persuade others when it is not himself that he wishes them to like but the truth that he persuades them of. . . . When one pleases others on account of truth, it is not the proclaimer himself but the truth that pleases. . . . Thus the sense is, "Do I then persuade men or God? And since it is men that I persuade, do I seek to please them? If I still sought to please men I should not be Christ's servant. For he bids his servants to learn from him to be meek and lowly of heart, which is utterly impossible for one who seeks to please men on his own account, for his own private and special glory." . . . Both then can be rightly said: "I please" and "I do not please." EPISTLE TO THE GALATIANS 5 [1B.1.10].[2]

1:10b *A Servant of Christ*

PERSONAL EVIDENCE. CHRYSOSTOM: He has

said this because he is about to rehearse his previous life and his sudden conversion and to show through manifest proofs that there was truth in his conversion, lest [his opponents] should imagine that he was saying this to defend himself against them and be elated. . . . For he knew the proper season for the correction of his pupils and how to say something sublime and grand. Now, there was a time to demonstrate the truth of his preaching in another way: from signs, from wonders, from dangers, from imprisonments, from daily deaths, from hunger and thirst and nakedness, and from other things of the kind. But since his argument now was not with pseudoapostles but with apostles, and since they had been partakers of these dangers, he employs a different method of argument. HOMILY ON GALATIANS 1.10.[3]

1:11 *The Gospel Paul Preached*[4]

WHY DOES HE SAY "NOT ACCORDING TO MAN"? MARIUS VICTORINUS: Possibly because the Savior himself is not a man [merely], as some think. Nor because he is sent in the form of a man is he therefore a man but God in a mystery taking flesh to overcome the flesh. . . . If "from a man" means one thing, "after the manner of man" will mean another. And again if *I did not receive from a man* is one thing, *not after the manner of man* will be another. Therefore "after the manner of man" can be understood to mean "so that you may understand in a corporeal manner," seeing that the argument received is that "which I did not re-

---

[1]Migne PL 26:321A-B [384-85]. [2]Migne PL 35:2109.
[3]IOEP 4:21. [4]Not "man's gospel" or "according to man."

ceive from man." EPISTLE TO THE GALA-
TIANS I.I.II.[5]

THE MAN FROM GOD. AUGUSTINE: The gos-
pel that is *according to men* is a lie, for every
person is a liar,[6] seeing that whatever truth
is found in a man is not from the man but
through the man from God. EPISTLE TO THE
GALATIANS 6 [IB.I.II-I2].[7]

1:12a A Gospel from God

THE GOSPEL RECEIVED FROM GOD. ORIGEN:
Therefore he shows plainly that Jesus was
not a [mere] man; and if he is not a man
then without doubt he is God. APOLOGY FOR
ORIGEN.[8]

NO HUMAN TEACHER. CHRYSOSTOM:
Those who are taught by men, when they
have been vehement and hot in the opposite cause, require time and much ingenu-
ity for their conversion. But he who was so
suddenly converted and was rendered
clean and sober at the very peak of his mad-
ness had obviously received a divine vision
and teaching. HOMILY ON GALATIANS I.I2.[9]

1:12b A Revelation of Jesus Christ

THE RISEN LORD APPEARED TO HIM. THEO-
DORET: It was very shrewd of him to mention revelation, for the Lord Jesus had been
taken up and was no longer seen equally of
all.[10] But to Paul he had appeared on the
road and made him worthy of the ministry
of proclamation.[11] And this again he sets
against their slanders, showing that in this
too he did not fall short of the apostles. For
just as the Galatians received the gospel
from him, so likewise he had Christ himself

as a teacher. EPISTLE TO THE GALATIANS
I.I2.[12]

1:13 One Who Persecuted the Church

WHY HE REMINDS THEM OF HIS OWN
STORY. MARIUS VICTORINUS: The point of
telling this about himself is to show that
he did not learn from a man or through
man but from God and Jesus Christ. The
aim of this is to prevent the Galatians
from entertaining another opinion or sup-
posing that anything needs to be added to
the gospel. EPISTLE TO THE GALATIANS
I.I.I3-I4.[13]

WHETHER THE LAW ITSELF IS TO BLAME FOR
LEGALISTIC SERVITUDE. AUGUSTINE: If
therefore he showed prowess in Judaism by
persecuting and wasting God's church, it is
obvious that Judaism is contrary to the
church of God, not through that spiritual
law which the Jews had received but
through their carnal habit of servitude. And
if Paul as a zealot—that is, an imitator of
late Judaic traditions—persecuted the
church of God, his paternal traditions are
contrary to God's church, but the blame
does not belong to the law itself. For the law
is spiritual and does not allow itself to be in-

---

[5]BT 1972:8 [1151B]. The Savior is God in human form in a
mystery of taking flesh to overcome the flesh. He is not
man alone, nor is he God sent imaginarily in the form of a
man, as if to appear that he is a man. Paul distinguished between "from a man" and "after the manner of a man." He
did not receive the gospel from humans. He is not living
out of it "after the manner of man," that is, in a fleshly manner, as his own experience shows. [6]Cf. Rom 3:4. [7]Migne
PL 35:2109. [8]Migne PL 17:585; imitated by Jerome *Epistle
to the Galatians* 1.1.11-12 [PL 26:322A (385)]. [9]IOEP
4:22. [10]Cf. Lk 24:44-53. [11]See Acts 9:1-19. [12]CPE 1:331.
[13]BT 1972:9 [1152B].

terpreted carnally.[14] That is the fault of those who understand carnally the things that they have received and who also have handed down many things of their own, undermining, as the Lord said, the command of God through their traditions. EPISTLE TO THE GALATIANS 7 [1B.1.13-14].[15]

1:14 *Advanced in Judaism*

ZEAL FOR GOD. CHRYSOSTOM: What he is saying is, "If what I then did against the church was done not on man's account but through zeal for God—mistaken but zeal nonetheless—how can I now be acting for vainglory when I operate on behalf of the church and know the truth?" HOMILY ON GALATIANS 1.14.[16]

SUBMISSION TO JEWISH TRADITION. JEROME: He prudently inserts the statement that he served not so much God's law as the paternal traditions—that is, those of the Pharisees, who teach doctrines and precepts of men[17] and reject the law of God to set up their own traditions. EPISTLE TO THE GALATIANS 1.1.13.[18]

1:15a *Set Apart Before Birth*

SET APART. AMBROSIASTER: Just as he said to Jeremiah, "Before I formed you in the womb I knew you,"[19] so, knowing what Paul would be, God called him because he was able to serve. EPISTLE TO THE GALATIANS 1.16.2.[20]

1:15b *Called Through Grace*

CALLED THROUGH GRACE FROM THE WOMB. MARIUS VICTORINUS: The God who caused me to be born, who separated me from my mother's womb, also called me through his grace. For no one knows God except one who has been called. EPISTLE TO THE GALATIANS 1.1.15-16.[21]

1:16a *The Son Revealed to Paul*[22]

WHY REVEALED "IN" HIM? JEROME: If something is revealed to someone, that may be revealed to him which was not in him before; but if it is revealed in him, that is revealed which was previously in him and had been subsequently revealed . . . from which it clearly appears that there is natural knowledge of God in all. EPISTLE TO THE GALATIANS 1.1.15.[23]

WHAT WAS REVEALED. FILASTRIUS: This means that he showed him the meaning of the Law and the Prophets. BOOK OF HERESIES 155.5.[24]

1:16b *Preaching Christ Among the Gentiles*

PAUL'S FITNESS TO PREACH. AMBROSIASTER: When he had faith in the law, not knowing that it was not the time for observance of the law, and was intensely striving to resist the gospel of Christ, he thought that he acted by God's will. God, seeing that his zeal was

---

[14]In a fleshly sense, or according to its idolatrous orientation toward the flesh. [15]Migne PL 35:2109-10. [16]IOEP 4:22. [17]Cf. Mt 15:1-20; Mk 7:1-23. [18]Migne PL 26:324B [388]. [19]Jer 1:5. [20]CSEL 81.3:14; cf. Jerome *Epistle to the Galatians* 1.1.15 [Migne PL 26:325A-326B (389-91)]. [21]BT 1972:13 [1154C]. [22]"Pleased to reveal his Son to me"; literally, "in me." [23]Migne PL 26:326A-B [391]. What was revealed was not alien to humanity's created nature. [24]CCL 9:319.

good, though he lacked knowledge, chose to summon him into his grace. He knew that this man was suitable to preach his gospel to the Gentiles. For if he was so swift and faithful in so poor a cause through boldness of conscience, not through adulation of anyone, how much more constant would he be in preaching the gift of God through the hope of the promised reward? EPISTLE TO THE GALATIANS 1.15.1.[25]

1:16c Not Conferring with Flesh and Blood

TO WHOM IS HE REFERRING? CHRYSOSTOM: *I did not confer with flesh and blood.* Here he is hinting at the apostles, describing them by their human nature. Yet if he means to refer here to all the apostles we shall not contradict him. HOMILY ON GALATIANS 1.15-16.[26]

COULD THERE BE ANOTHER MEANING? JEROME: I know that many think that this was said of the apostles . . . but far be it from me to reckon Peter, John and James as "flesh and blood," which cannot possess the kingdom of God.[27] . . . It is obvious that Paul did not confer with flesh and blood after the revelation of Christ because he would not throw pearls before swine or that which is holy to the dogs.[28] EPISTLE TO THE GALATIANS 1.1.16.[29]

1:17a Paul and the Apostles in Jerusalem

PAUL'S MOTIVE NOT ARROGANCE. CHRYSOSTOM: If one interprets these words by themselves they seem suggestive of some great conceit or a sentiment not worthy of an apostle. To rely on one's own choice and have no

one else to share one's estimate seems a mark of folly. . . . But we should not interpret bare words, or many absurdities follow. . . . Let us now interpret the mind of Paul when he wrote these words. Let us consider his aim and his whole attitude to the apostles, and then we shall know his intention in saying this. . . . For since those who plunder the church were saying that one should follow the apostles, who did not forbid these things, he is forced to withstand them stoutly, not wishing to disparage the apostles but to restrain the folly of those who were falsely puffed up. HOMILY ON GALATIANS 1.17.[30]

1:17b Into Arabia and Damascus

WHY ARABIA? AMBROSIASTER: He set out from Damascus to Arabia, therefore, to preach where none of the apostles had been and where Judaizing had not been promoted through the intrigues of pseudoapostles. And from there he returned again to Damascus so that he could attend to those who were still immature when he preached to them the gospel of God's grace. EPISTLE TO THE GALATIANS 1.17.2.[31]

HIS MODESTY. CHRYSOSTOM: And let me point out to you his humility. For, having said *I went up to Arabia,* he has added *and I returned to Damascus.* He does not recount his conversions or what people and how many he instructed, even though he showed such zeal after his baptism that the Jews were enraged against him, and their animos-

---

[25]CSEL 81.3:13-14. [26]IOEP 4:23. [27]Cf. 1 Cor 15:50. [28]Cf. Mt 7:6. [29]Migne PL 26:326C-327A [391]. [30]IOEP 4:25. [31]CSEL 81.3:15.

ity became so intense that they laid an ambush for him and wanted to kill him, along with the Greeks.[32] . . . But he says nothing of these things here, nor would he have spoken of them in that place had he not seen that the occasion demanded that he recount his own history. HOMILY ON GALATIANS 1.17.[33]

COULD THERE BE A DEEPER MEANING? JEROME: How are we to explain this narrative, if we read later that Paul went immediately to Arabia after the revelation of Christ?[34] . . . He teaches that the Old Testa-

ment, that is, the son of the bondwoman, was established in Arabia. And so, as soon as Paul believed, he turned to the Law, the Prophets and the symbols of the Old Testament that were then lying in obscurity and sought in them the Christ whom he was commanded to preach to the Gentiles. EPISTLE TO THE GALATIANS 1.1.17.[35]

---

[32] Here Chrysostom cites 2 Corinthians 11:32. [33]IOEP 4:28. [34]Here follows a citation of Galatians 4:24-26 on the allegory of the two covenants, Sinai and Jerusalem. [35]Migne PL 26:328C-329A [394]. Paul sought in the Old Testament the texts that explain Christ in the New.

1:18-24 THE JOURNEY TO JERUSALEM

[18]*Then after three years I went up to Jerusalem to visit Cephas, and remained with him fifteen days. [19]But I saw none of the other apostles except James the Lord's brother. [20](In what I am writing to you, before God, I do not lie!) [21]Then I went into the regions of Syria and Cilicia. [22]And I was still not known by sight to the churches of Christ in Judea; [23]they only heard it said, "He who once persecuted us is now preaching the faith he once tried to destroy." [24]And they glorified God because of me.*

OVERVIEW: Paul visited Peter simply from goodwill (AUGUSTINE) and because of his high standing (MARIUS VICTORINUS), thus demonstrating his own humility (CHRYSOSTOM). He remained long enough for a friend (CHRYSOSTOM), not long enough for a disciple (JEROME). He recognizes James as an apostle (JEROME) and as the "brother of the Lord" (CHRYSOSTOM), though this is not meant literally (THEODORET). With an oath

that does not transgress Christ's precept (AUGUSTINE, JEROME) Paul shows that his gospel had taken effect even in his absence (MARIUS VICTORINUS) and that he had neither preached circumcision (CHRYSOSTOM) nor learned Christianity in Judea (JEROME), where Jews and Gentiles remained separate (AUGUSTINE). He candidly recalls his former sins (CHRYSOSTOM) and, though aware that his conversion was remarkable (MARIUS VIC-

TORINUS), claims no merit (CHRYSOSTOM).

1:18a *Visiting Peter in Jerusalem*

WHETHER HIS KNOWLEDGE CAME FROM PETER, TO WHOM CHRIST COMMITTED SO MUCH AUTHORITY. MARIUS VICTORINUS: For if the foundation of the church was laid in Peter, to whom all was revealed, as the gospel says, Paul knew that he ought to see Peter. When he speaks of seeing Peter, it is as one to whom Christ had committed so much authority, not as one from whom he was to learn anything. . . . "How," [he implies], "could I learn this great knowledge of God from Peter in such a short time?" EPISTLE TO THE GALATIANS 1.1.18.[1]

WHY VISIT PETER? CHRYSOSTOM: What greater humility of soul could there be? For after so many conversions, having no need of Peter or of speech with him but being equal with him in honor—for I say no more at present—he nonetheless goes up to him as to one who is greater and senior . . . and he says not "to see Peter" but *to visit Peter*, as people say when acquainting themselves with great and splendid cities. HOMILY ON GALATIANS 1.18.[2]

FRATERNAL LOVE MAGNIFIED. AUGUSTINE: If, when Paul had evangelized Arabia, he subsequently saw Peter, it was not so that he might learn the gospel from Peter himself (for then he would have seen him before) but so that he might enhance familial love by being with the apostles. EPISTLE TO THE GALATIANS 8 [1B.1.15-19].[3]

1:18b *Remaining for Fifteen Days*

WHY SO LONG? CHRYSOSTOM: Now to remain with him was an act of honor, but to remain with him so many days was one of friendship and extreme love. HOMILY ON GALATIANS 1.18.[4]

WHY NOT LONGER? JEROME: He who had prepared himself for so long a time did not need any long instruction. And, though it seems excessive to some to investigate numbers in Scripture, yet I think it not beside the point to say that the fifteen days that Paul spent with Peter signifies [in late Judaic piety] the fullness of wisdom and the perfection of doctrine, seeing that there are fifteen psalms in a psalter and fifteen steps by which people go up to sing to God. EPISTLE TO THE GALATIANS 1.1.18.[5]

1:19 *Seeing James the Lord's Brother*

SOME NOT AMONG THE TWELVE WERE CALLED APOSTLES. JEROME: That some were called apostles apart from the twelve is a consequence of the fact that all who had seen the Lord and subsequently preached him were called apostles.[6] EPISTLE TO THE GALATIANS 1.1.19.[7]

THE SOLEMN TITLE. CHRYSOSTOM: *And I saw no other but James the brother of the Lord.* See how much greater is his friend-

---

[1]BT 1972:14 [1555A-B]. [2]IOEP 4:19. Cf. Theodoret *Epistle to the Galatians* 1.18 [CPE 1:332-33]. Paul learned the gospel not from Peter but from Christ. [3]Migne PL 35:2110. [4]IOEP 4:30. [5]Migne PL 26:329C [395]; citing 1 Cor 15:5-7. Jerome sees an analogy between the fifteen days Paul spent with Peter and the fifteen Psalms of Ascent (Ps 120—134), which reenacted the fifteen steps up to the temple in Jerusalem. [6]Here Jerome cites 1 Corinthians 15:5-11. [7]Migne PL 26:330B-C [396].

ship for Peter, for he stayed on his account. . . . [He says of James] *I saw*, not "I was taught." But see with what honor he named this man also. For he says not simply James but adds the solemn title. So free of jealousy was he. For had he wished only to indicate whom he meant he could have identified him by another name and called him the son of Clopas, as the Evangelist does.[8] HOMILY ON GALATIANS 1.19.[9]

WAS JAMES THE LITERAL, NATURAL BROTHER OF THE LORD? THEODORET: He was called "the brother of the Lord" but was not so by nature. For he was not, as some suppose,[10] the son of Joseph by a previous marriage but the son of Clopas and cousin of the Lord. For his mother was the sister of the Lord's mother.[11] . . . He was thought by others to be the Lord's brother, both because their mothers had the same names and because the families shared one house. And he was so called even by believers, both because of the extreme virtue that he possessed (for he was called "the Just") and because of the kinship. For the sacred story of the Gospels tells us that the Blessed Virgin had no other son. For seeing her by the cross, the Lord gave her to the most divine John,[12] but he would not have committed her to another if the blessed James, a man possessed of extreme virtue, had been her son. EPISTLE TO THE GALATIANS 1.19.[13]

1:20 I Do Not Lie!

WHETHER A SACRED OATH DEFIES THE COMMANDMENT TO NOT SWEAR. AUGUSTINE: He certainly swears, and what oath could be more sacred? But an oath is not against the commandment when the "evil cause"[14] is not in the swearer but in the incredulity of him to whom he is forced to swear. For we understand from this that what the Lord meant in prohibiting oaths was that everyone, so far as in him it lies, should not swear the oaths that many do, having the oath on their lips as though it were something lofty and elegant. EPISTLE TO THE GALATIANS 9 [1B.1.20-24].[15]

THE DEEPER SENSE. JEROME: Or perhaps this could be taken in a deeper sense, that "what I say to you is before God, that is, worthy of God's countenance.[16] And why worthy of God's countenance? Because I do not lie." EPISTLE TO THE GALATIANS 1.1.20.[17]

1:21 Into Syria and Cilicia

WHAT THIS PROVES. MARIUS VICTORINUS: What does he prove by all this? That his gospel had persuaded everyone, even in his absence. EPISTLE TO THE GALATIANS 1.1.21-22.[18]

1:22 Not Known by Sight to the Judean Churches

WHAT SLANDER IS PAUL REBUTTING? CHRYSOSTOM: What is his aim in saying *I was unknown by face to the churches of Judea?* That you may understand he was so far from preaching circumcision to them that they did not even know him by sight. HOMILY ON GALATIANS 1.22-23.[19]

---

[8]Cf. Mk 15:40; Jn 19:25. [9]IOEP 4:30. [10]Ambrosiaster *Epistle to the Galatians* 1.19 [CSEL 81.3:15-16]. [11]Here Theodoret quotes Mark 15:40 and the Syriac version of Luke 24:10. [12]Jn 19:26-27. [13]CPE 1:333. [14]Cf. Mt 5:37. [15]Migne PL 35:2110-11. [16]Ready to come into God's presence. [17]Migne PL 26:331B [397]. [18]BT 1972:16 [1157A]. [19]IOEP 4:31.

THE BEARING OF HIS SHORT TIME IN JUDEA ON HIS APOSTLESHIP. JEROME: He discreetly returns to the main point, establishing that he had spent so short a time in Judea that he was unknown even by face to the believers. Hence he shows that he had no teachers—not Peter, not James, not John—but Christ, who had revealed his gospel to him. EPISTLE TO THE GALATIANS 1.1.[20]

THE VITALITY OF JEWISH CHURCHES APART FROM JERUSALEM. AUGUSTINE: It should be observed that Jews had believed in Christ not only in Jerusalem, nor were they so few that they had been absorbed into the Gentile churches, but they were so numerous that churches came into being from them. EPISTLE TO THE GALATIANS 9 [IB.1.20- 24].[21]

1:23 The Persecutor Preaches the True Faith

HYPERBOLE AND MODESTY. CHRYSOSTOM: What soul could be more modest than this? For when he is discussing the things that bring opprobrium on him, such as his persecution and plundering of the church, he narrates it with great hyperbole, putting his previous life on show; but the things which would enhance his reputation he passes by. HOMILY ON GALATIANS 1.23.[22]

1:24 Glorifying God Because of Paul

RECEIVING ONE PREVIOUSLY ASSAILED. MARIUS VICTORINUS: By *glorified God in me* he means they called him great. For what is so magnificent as to have your own opinion turned around and receive the one whom you previously assailed? This being so, you also should follow nothing else than the gospel preached to you by the one who is a miracle among the Gentiles, because he preaches the faith of Christ. EPISTLE TO THE GALATIANS 1.1.24.[23]

DOES PAUL CLAIM ANYTHING FOR HIMSELF? CHRYSOSTOM: See here too how exactly he follows the principle of humility. For he says not "they were amazed at me," "they praised me" or "they were astonished," but he has shown that all was of grace by saying *they glorified God in me.* HOMILY ON GALATIANS 1.24.[24]

---

[20]Migne PL 26:332A [398]. [21]Migne PL 35:2111. [22]IOEP 4:31. [23]BT 1972:16 [1157B-C]. [24]IOEP 4:31.

2:1-10 THE FIRST VISIT TO JERUSALEM

[1]*Then after fourteen years I went up again to Jerusalem with Barnabas, taking Titus along with me.* [2]*I went up by revelation; and I laid before them (but privately before those who were of repute) the gospel which I preach among the Gentiles, lest somehow I should be running or had run in vain.* [3]*But even Titus, who was with me, was not compelled to be circumcised, though he was a Greek.* [4]*But because of false*

brethren secretly brought in, who slipped in to spy out our freedom which we have in Christ Jesus, that they might bring us into bondage—⁵to them we did not yield submission even for a moment, that the truth of the gospel might be preserved for you. ⁶And from those who were reputed to be something (what they were makes no difference to me; God shows no partiality)—those, I say, who were of repute added nothing to me; ⁷but on the contrary, when they saw that I had been entrusted with the gospel to the uncircumcised, just as Peter had been entrusted with the gospel to the circumcised ⁸(for he who worked through Peter for the mission to the circumcised worked through me also for the Gentiles), ⁹and when they perceived the grace that was given to me, James and Cephas and John, who were reputed to be pillars, gave to me and Barnabas the right hand of fellowship, that we should go to the Gentiles and they to the circumcised; ¹⁰only they would have us remember the poor, which very thing I was eager to do.

OVERVIEW: Paul went up to Jerusalem at last to refute his detractors (AMBROSIASTER). He took Titus and Barnabas as witnesses (MARIUS VICTORINUS), just as Acts indicates (THEODORET). His journey was occasioned by divine revelation (CHRYSOSTOM). He had learned nothing from the Jerusalem apostles that he had not already known by revelation, though he solicited their judgment (MARIUS VICTORINUS, CHRYSOSTOM). His visit to the apostles was an act of humility (JOHN CASSIAN), undertaken privately to avoid causing scandal to others (JEROME). Thus others could not suspect him of having run in vain (AUGUSTINE), nor did he thus accuse himself (MARIUS VICTORINUS). He was more submissive to the apostles than to the false brethren (CHRYSOSTOM, MARIUS VICTORINUS), but he could be wary even of the apostles (CHRYSOSTOM). He knew that God is the only true judge of human worth (AUGUSTINE). Paul stood in accord with the apostles, teaching them more than he learned from them (JEROME, AUGUSTINE). Barnabas accompanied Paul as a fellow trustee of the gospel (MARIUS VICTORINUS). Paul acknowledged Peter's singular role (AMBROSIASTER). He noted that he and Peter had distinguishable but complementary callings (JEROME), as made evident by their works (THEODORET). Because the other apostles support the church they are called *pillars* (MARIUS VICTORINUS), fully deserving their reputation (JEROME). So we too should be pillars reared on truth (GREGORY OF NYSSA).

In refusing to circumcise Titus, Paul confronted the legalistic brothers, setting an example to the Galatians (AMBROSIASTER, AUGUSTINE), who had gone overboard by making compulsory what the apostles merely allowed (CHRYSOSTOM). The care of those who had been impoverished by persecution (CHRYSOSTOM) was committed to Paul as a gospel duty (MARIUS VICTORINUS), and he performed it with zeal (JEROME). Paul steadfastly maintained the centrality of his vocation to the Gentiles (AMBROSIASTER, THEODORET).

2:1a Going Again to Jerusalem

THE OCCASION FOR THE JOURNEY TO JERUSALEM. AMBROSIASTER: His renown had been growing for a long time among all the Jews, though he had not been seen face to face . . . but on account of the law he had acquired a bad reputation among the Jews, as though his preaching was out of harmony with the preaching of the other apostles. Many were having doubts on account of this, which were sufficient to make the Gentiles anxious, in case they had been trained in something other than that which was preached by the apostles who had been with the Lord. For on this precise occasion the Galatians were undermined by Jews who were saying that Paul taught something other than Peter taught. This is the reason for his going up to Jerusalem, at the bidding of the Lord's revelation, disclosing to them the implications of his preaching, with Barnabas and Titus as witnesses of his preaching, one from the Jews and one from the Gentiles, so that if any took offense at him it might be assuaged by their testimony. EPISTLE TO THE GALATIANS 2.2.1.[1]

2:1b With Barnabas and Titus

THE CONFIRMING COMPANIONSHIP OF BARNABAS AND TITUS. MARIUS VICTORINUS: These men he had as witnesses, through whom he proved that his gospel was given to him through revelation, seeing that he said Barnabas went up with me, and he also took Titus, whose faith and gospel were approved by everyone.

EPISTLE TO THE GALATIANS 1.2.1.[2]

WHERE DOES THIS FIT INTO THE NARRATIVE OF ACTS? THEODORET: Both [Barnabas and Titus] spent an extended time in Antioch, making a large body of converts and binding them to live according to the law of grace. But some supporters of the law who arrived from Judea tried to persuade the Gentiles to adopt the way of life according to the law.[3] But those great heralds of the truth, Paul and Barnabas, repudiated the teaching they promoted. They wished to persuade the congregation of the faithful that this was also the view of the great apostles. So they immediately went straightway to Judea, to apprise the apostles of what was going on. EPISTLE TO THE GALATIANS 2.1-2.[4]

2:2a I Went Up by Revelation

WHY "BY REVELATION"? CHRYSOSTOM: The purpose for his saying through revelation was that even before the solution to the question [why he spoke of running in vain] no one should accuse him of any ignorance, knowing that what occurred was not of human origin but of a certain divine dispensation which had in view many things, both present and to come. What then is the reason for this journey? When he first went up from Antioch to Jerusalem it was not for his own sake, for he himself knew that he ought to follow strictly the teachings of Christ. Rather he wanted to win over those who opposed him. He

---

[1]CSEL 81.3:17-18. [2]BT 1972:16-17 [1157C-D]. [3]See Acts 15:1. [4]CPE 1:334-35.

himself had no need at this point to ascertain whether he ran in vain, but [he went up] to satisfy his detractors. HOMILY ON GALATIANS 2.2.[5]

2:2b The Gospel Preached Among the Gentiles

THOSE WHO WERE OF REPUTE. MARIUS VICTORINUS: That is, those through whom the commandments and gospel of God were being handed down, such as apostles and the rest. "To these men," he says, "I privately explained my gospel, which I preach among the Gentiles, so that if there was anything that they were handing on otherwise, they could correct it or could emend anything that I myself was handing on otherwise. This therefore was the cause of my going up to Jerusalem, and for this reason it was revealed to me that I should go up, so that it might be more readily known that my gospel to the Gentiles and their gospel to the Jews were the same." Now the purpose of his expounding it privately was that shame might be taken from among them, and they might communicate to one another the mysteries that they knew. Since they all shared one opinion and one gospel, what was it that he labored to persuade them of? That they should not add anything new or join anything to it. That is the cause of the present sin of the Galatians in following Judaism and the practice of circumcision, the sabbath and other things. EPISTLE TO THE GALATIANS 1.2.2.[6]

WHY HE MET THEM PRIVATELY. JEROME: What he says [about meeting privately] could be understood as meaning that the grace of evangelical liberty and the obsoles-cence of the law that was now abolished was discussed in confidence with the apostles on account of the many Jewish believers who were not yet able to hear that Christ was the fulfillment and end of the law. And these men, when Paul was absent, had boasted in Jerusalem that he was running and had run in vain when he supposed that the old law was not to be followed. EPISTLE TO THE GALATIANS 1.2.1-2.[7]

PAUL'S MOTIVE. CHRYSOSTOM: It is indeed true that one who is eager to set right a common doctrine undertakes this not privately but in public. But it was not so with Paul, for he did not wish to learn or correct anything but rather to overthrow the pretext of those who were intent on deception. For since everyone in Jerusalem was scandalized if someone transgressed the law . . . he did not attempt to come forward openly and reveal his own preaching. HOMILY ON GALATIANS 2.2.[8]

THE CALL TO CONFER WITHIN THE APOSTOLATE. JOHN CASSIAN: Who could be so presumptuous and blind as to dare to trust his own judgment and discretion, when the vessel of election bears witness that he needs the partnership of his coapostles? CONFERENCES 2.15.[9]

2:2c Not Running in Vain

SO AS NOT TO RUN VAINLY. MARIUS VIC-

---

[5]IOEP 4:32. [6]BT 1972:17 [1158A-B]. [7]Migne PL 26:333 B-C [399-400]; cf. Jerome Letter 112.8.3 [CSEL 55:374]. [8]IOEP 4:33. Cf. Theodoret Epistle to the Galatians 2.2 [CPE 1:334-35]. [9]CSEL 13:59; citing Abba Moses (a translation of a comment in Greek).

TORINUS: *So that I should not run or have run in vain.* That is [he says], "lest I should fail to preach a full gospel. For if I have preached anything less, I have run in vain or I now run in vain." EPISTLE TO THE GALATIANS 1.2.2.[10]

TO WHOM ADDRESSED. AUGUSTINE: *So that I should not run or have run in vain* we should understand to be addressed as if in a question, not to those with whom he compared his gospel in private but to those to whom he was writing, so that it might appear that he was not running and had not run in vain from the fact that by the testimony of the others he was certified not to dissent from the truth of the gospel. EPISTLE TO THE GALATIANS 10 [IB.2.1-2].[11]

2:3 *The Circumcision of Titus*

THE CASE OF TITUS. AMBROSIASTER: The implication is "Why should you be circumcised, when Titus was not compelled to undergo circumcision by the apostles? Titus, who had an important role, was accepted without circumcision." EPISTLE TO THE GALATIANS 2.3.[12]

THE GRAVITY OF THE CASE. AUGUSTINE: It was because of the intrigues of false brethren that Titus was not compelled to be circumcised. It was not possible to require circumcision of him. Those who had crept in to spy on their liberty had a vehement expectation and desire for the circumcision of Titus. They wanted, with Paul's testimony and consent, to preach circumcision as necessary to salvation. EPISTLE TO THE GALATIANS 11 [IB.2.3-5].[13]

2:4a *False Brethren*

IT IS FALSE TO CONSIDER CIRCUMCISION A NECESSITY. CHRYSOSTOM: No small thing is at stake here. The question is, if the apostles at this point consented to circumcision, why did Paul apply the term "false brothers" to those who also imposed circumcision in accordance with the sentiment of the apostles? First of all, it is one thing actively to impose an act and another passively to consent to it once done. For the one who zealously imposes it makes it necessary and paramount. But the one who, without imposing it, does not prevent the one who wants it, does not consent to it as a necessity but rather through passive consent seeks to accomplish other purposes.[14] . . . Second, the apostles did this only in Judea, but the false apostles had gone about everywhere. They had all the Galatians in their grip. HOMILY ON GALATIANS 2.4.[15]

2:4b *Spying Out Our Freedom*

THEIR DECEPTIVE METHODS. AMBROSIASTER: By *secretly* he means that they had entered by deception, passing themselves off as brothers when they were enemies. By *slipped in* he means that they came in a humble manner, feigning friendship. . . . To *spy out* is to enter in such a way as to invent one thing and discover another, whereby they may challenge our liberty. . . . *Liberty in Jesus Christ* means not being subject to the law. *That they might bring us into bondage* means . . . to subject us to the law of circum-

---

[10]BT 1972:17 [1158B]. [11]Migne PL 35:2111. [12]CSEL 81.3:19. [13]Migne PL 35:2111-12. [14]Here Chrysostom cites 1 Corinthians 7:5-7. [15]IOEP 4:33-34.

cision. EPISTLE TO THE GALATIANS 2.5.3-4.[16]

2:5 We Did Not Submit to Them

RESISTING A NEW SLAVERY. CHRYSOSTOM: See how noble and emphatic his words are. . . . For [the false brethren] did not do this in order to teach anything profitable but that they might subject and enslave them. "For this reason," [he says,] "we yielded to the apostles but not to [the false brethren]." HOMILY ON GALATIANS 2.5.[17]

CHALLENGING ARROGANT OPINIONS. THEODORET: "Not even for a short while," [he says,] "would we endure their arrogant opinions, but we preferred the truth of the gospel before all things." He says this about those who obeyed the law by custom. For since it was likely that the Galatians would say that even the first of the apostles also kept the law, and the divine apostle knew that they were forced to do this in deference to believers from among the Jews who were still weak, he was caught in the middle. It would have been highly perverse to condemn them, yet he did not wish to reveal their aim, in case he might do harm to the new dispensation.[18] So he steers a middle course. And while he does indeed profess to be angry at what occurred, he is nonetheless not disposed to say anything more about them. So he commits everything to the verdict of God. EPISTLE TO THE GALATIANS 2.5.[19]

2:6a Those Reputed to Be Something

THOSE REPUTED TO BE SOMETHING ARE NOTHING. MARIUS VICTORINUS: [He means] those who have sprung from those same pseudoapostles but nonetheless "are something," that is, have undergone change and now follow the gospel. Even if they have sprung from these phonies they are now whole, for that is what it is truly to be something. "It is nothing to me," he says, "what kind of people they were before, at some past time." And he adds the reason: God shows no partiality but looks at one's mental attitude and faith. Whether one be Greek or Jew, whether one *was* anything, is not what God accepts, but what one *is* and whether one has received faith and the gospel. EPISTLE TO THE GALATIANS 1.2.6.[20]

THE TEMPTATION TO APPEASEMENT. CHRYSOSTOM: Here he not only offers no defense of the apostles but is hard on the saints so that he may assist the weaker among them. What he is saying is something like this: "If these men enjoin circumcision, they will give an account to God. For God will not accept their persons because they are great and in authority." Yet he has not said this openly, but sparingly. . . . And he does not say "what they are" but what they were, indicating that they also later gave up the preaching of circumcision, once the gospel was manifest everywhere. . . . It is as though he were saying, "I do not condemn or disparage those saints; for they knew what they were doing, and they will give an account to God." HOMILY ON GALATIANS 2.5-6.[21]

2:6b God Shows No Partiality

BEING SOMETHING, BEING NOTHING. AUGUSTINE: If people were reputed to be anything,

---

[16]CSEL 81.3:20. [17]IOEP 4:35. [18]The time of Christ's coming. [19]CPE 1:335-36. [20]BT 1972:20 [1160A]. [21]IOEP 4:35-36.

that was a human reputation, for they themselves are not anything to boast of. For even if they are good ministers of God, it is Christ in them, not they through themselves, who are something. For if they were something through themselves they would always be something. "What they were" at one time means that it is nothing to him that they themselves were sinners. God accepts no one because of the office one holds. He calls all to salvation, not imputing their transgressions to them.... No one should suppose that Paul said [this] to disparage his predecessors, for they too, as spiritual people, wished to stand against the carnal people who thought themselves to "be something" on their own rather than out of Christ in them. They were extremely glad when persuaded that they themselves, Paul's predecessors, like Paul had been justified by the Lord from a state of sin. But carnal people, if anything is said about their previous life, grow angry and take it as disparagement. So they assume that the apostles are of their own mind. Now Peter, James and John were more honored among the apostles because the Lord showed himself on the Mount to these same three as a sign of his kingdom.[22] EPISTLE TO THE GALATIANS 12-13 [IB.2.6-9].[23]

2:7a The Gospel to the Uncircumcised

TWO POSSIBLE READINGS. JEROME: This intricate passage, full of intervening matter, might be briefly construed as follows: "Those who were conspicuous added nothing to me, but *on the contrary* gave the right hand of fellowship to me and Barnabas." An alternative sense is hidden to avoid boasting of himself: "Those who were conspicuous added nothing to me, but on the contrary I

have added to them, and they have become more steadfast in the grace of the gospel." EPISTLE TO THE GALATIANS 1.2.7-8.[24]

THE FULLNESS OF THE GOSPEL TO THE UNCIRCUMCISED. AUGUSTINE: The apostles were not therefore found to disagree in anything. Otherwise, when Paul claimed to have received the gospel perfectly, they might have denied this and wished to add to his teaching, as though he were incomplete. On the contrary, instead of reproving Paul's imperfection, they approved his perfection.... His saying *on the contrary* might also be understood in such a way as to yield the following meaning: "Upon me those who had a reputation imposed nothing further. On the contrary, they consented with me and Barnabas, joining the right hand of fellowship, that we, for our part, should go among the Gentiles, who are contrary to the circumcision, while they for their part should go to those of the circumcision." EPISTLE TO THE GALATIANS 12 [IB.2.6-9].[25]

2:7b The Gospel to the Circumcised

THE UNIQUE AUTHORITY OF PETER. AMBROSIASTER: He names Peter alone because he has received the primacy in the founding of the church;[26] and he himself had likewise been chosen to have the primacy in the founding of Gentile churches, but with the proviso that Peter should preach to the Gentiles, should cause arise, and Paul to the Jews. EPISTLE TO THE GALATIANS 2.7.8.[27]

---

[22]Here Augustine cites Matthew 16:28; compare Matthew 17:1-8. [23]Migne PL 35:2112-13. [24]Migne PL 26:336A [403]. Cf. Chrysostom *Homily on Galatians* 2.7 [IOEP 4:35]. [25]Migne PL 35:2112. [26]Mt 16:18. [27]CSEL 81.3:23-24.

2:8 The Mission to the Gentiles

MISSION TO THE GENTILES UNCOM-PROMISED. JEROME: Paul allows that Peter, following Jewish custom, was without blame in his temporary observation of what was amiss so as not to lose those entrusted to him. But it was Paul's own duty for the sake of the gospel truth to do what was entrusted to him among the uncircumcised, so that the Gentiles would not depart from their faith and belief in Christ through fear of the burdens and rigor of the law. EPISTLE TO THE GALATIANS 1.2.7-8.[28]

2:9a The Grace Given to Paul

COLLABORATION WITH GRACE. THEODORET: They knew this from the facts; for [he says] "just as divine grace worked with Peter for the preaching to the Jews, so it collaborated with me for the salvation of the Gentiles." EPISTLE TO THE GALATIANS 2.8.[29]

2:9b The Pillars

ONE GOSPEL. MARIUS VICTORINUS: That is, those who supported the church were like pillars supporting roofs and other things. "These men, then," he says, "being of such quality and so great, gave me their right hands, that is, joined in friendship, peace and steadfastness and declared that they had only one gospel. In view of this accord, Galatians, you are sinning and follow neither my gospel nor that of Peter, James and John, who are the pillars of the church, when you add things that are not approved by any of them." EPISTLE TO THE GALATIANS 1.2.7-9.[30]

ALL BELIEVERS WHO OVERCOME THE ENEMY

ARE PILLARS. JEROME: Three times above we read that the apostles were *reputed*.[31] . . . And so I was wondering what this word meant. Now he has delivered me from all doubt when he describes them as those "who appeared to be pillars." Therefore it means the apostles, and above all Peter, James and John, two of whom were deemed fit to go up the Mount with Jesus. One of these introduces the Savior in the Apocalypse saying *He who has overcome I shall make him a pillar in the temple of my God*.[32] This teaches us that all believers who have overcome the enemy can become pillars of the church. EPISTLE TO THE GALATIANS 1.2.7-8.[33]

THE FOUNDATION OF TRUTH. GREGORY OF NYSSA: Since we must also ascertain how it is possible to become a *pillar*, so that we too may become worthy of this calling, we ought to hear this again from the dictum of the apostle Paul, who says that the pillar is *the foundation of truth*.[34] ORATION 14 ON SONG OF SONGS 5.15.[35]

2:9c Fellowship Given to Paul and Barnabas

NOT TO ME ALONE. MARIUS VICTORINUS: "Not to me alone," [he says], "did they give the right hand of fellowship, but also to Barnabas who was my companion." He

---

[28]Migne PL 26:336C-D [404]. Both Peter and Paul had a duty to those entrusted to them. In Peter's case it was temporarily to allow circumcision, and in Paul's case it was to disallow circumcision. [29]CPE 1:336. [30]BT 1972:21 [1160C-D]. [31]"To be something" or "of repute." [32]Rev 3:12. [33]Migne PL 26:337A-B [404-5]. But on 2:7 compare Augustine *Epistle to the Galatians* 12 [1b.2.6-9; Migne PL 35:2112]. [34]1 Tim 3:15. [35]GNO 6:416.

made the addition so that it should not appear that he alone had received the trust. EPISTLE TO THE GALATIANS 1.2.7-9.[36]

WHETHER BARNABAS RECEIVED EQUAL PRIMACY. AMBROSIASTER: Just as he allots to Peter companions who were the outstanding men among the apostles, so he joins to himself Barnabas, who was associated with him by God's appointment. Yet he claims that the grace of his primacy was entrusted to him alone by God, just as the primacy among the apostles was entrusted solely to Peter. EPISTLE TO THE GALATIANS 2.10.1-2.[37]

2:10a Remembering the Poor

BEING MINDFUL OF THE POOR. MARIUS VICTORINUS: When Paul and Barnabas were having these discussions with John and Peter and James, the gospel was accepted and established in the way that Paul describes. The only thing that they did not hear willingly in this dispute was that works were not part of salvation. Their sole injunction, however, was that they should be mindful of the poor. Thus they agree on this point also, that the hope of salvation does not reside in the activity of doing works for the poor, but they simply enjoin—what?—that we be mindful of the poor. Not that we should spend all our efforts on it but that we should share with those who have not what we are able to have. We are instructed simply that we should be mindful of the poor, not that we should place our care and thought upon our own capacity to hold on to our salvation by this means. Thus he is almost corrected and admonished in this matter, but this is not all Paul says. *That we should be mindful*, he says, not "that we should do this" but

"that we should keep them in mind," which is less than putting our work into this and fulfilling this alone. He adds that he took thought even for this matter outside the gospel that he preached, which consisted in being mindful of the poor and bestowing whatever he could upon them. In truth, indeed, no one is poor if, simply keeping faith and trusting in God, he awaits the riches of his salvation. EPISTLE TO THE GALATIANS 1.2.10.[38]

WHO ARE THESE POOR? CHRYSOSTOM: Many believers of Jewish origin in Palestine had been robbed of all their goods and were being persecuted on all sides. . . . Those who had been converted from Greek backgrounds did not suffer such antagonism from those who had remained Greek as much as the believers of Jewish origin had suffered from their own people. Therefore he takes great pains that they should receive all assistance, as also when writing to the Romans and Corinthians.[39] HOMILY ON GALATIANS 2.10.[40]

2:10b Care for the Poor

THE HOLY POOR. JEROME: The holy poor, care of whom was specially committed to Paul and Barnabas by the apostles, are those believers in Judea who brought the price of their possessions to the feet of the apostles[41] to be given to the needy, or because they were incurring hatred and punishment from their kin, family and parents as deserters of the law and believers in a crucified man.

---

[36]BT 1972:21 [1161A]. [37]CSEL 81.3:24. [38]BT 1972:21-22 [1161B-C]. [39]Rom 15:25-29; 1 Cor 16:1-4. [40]IOEP 4:40; but cf. Jerome on 2:10b. [41]Acts 4:32-37.

How much labor the holy apostle expended in ministering to these his letters bear witness, as he wrote to Corinth, the Thessalonians and all the churches of the Gentiles that they should prepare this offering to be taken to Jerusalem through himself or others. For

this reason he now says confidently *which very thing I have been careful to do.* EPISTLE TO THE GALATIANS 1.2.10.[42]

---

[42]Migne PL 26:337C-338A [405].

2:11-14 THE CONFRONTATION AT ANTIOCH

[11]*But when Cephas came to Antioch I opposed him to his face, because he stood condemned.* [12]*For before certain men came from James, he ate with the Gentiles; but when they came he drew back and separated himself, fearing the circumcision party.* [13]*And with him the rest of the Jews acted insincerely, so that even Barnabas was carried away by their insincerity.* [14]*But when I saw that they were not straightforward about the truth of the gospel, I said to Cephas before them all, "If you, though a Jew, live like a Gentile and not like a Jew, how can you compel the Gentiles to live like Jews?"*

OVERVIEW: Peter, now called Cephas (JEROME) found himself in a debate with Paul (CHRYSOSTOM) because Peter himself was being wrongly condemned (JEROME) after the people "came from James" (THEODORET). Paul's rebuke is repeated here to edify the Galatians (MARIUS VICTORINUS). Peter's fear has wholesome grounds. Insincerity is wrong (AUGUSTINE), at least if it is practiced for the wrong reason (MARIUS VICTORINUS). It is doubtful that an apostle should ever make use of it (AUGUSTINE). Grace is available where the law is unavailing (CASSIODORUS). The reprimand, publicly delivered to be more effective (AUGUSTINE), is

made on behalf of Gentiles (CHRYSOSTOM), whose duty is to keep the law in spirit (AUGUSTINE).

2:11a *Opposing Peter at Antioch*

WHY PETER IS NOW CALLED CEPHAS.
JEROME: It is not that Peter and Cephas signify different things, but what we would call in Latin and Greek *petra* ("stone") the Hebrews and Syrians both, because of the affinity of their languages, call *cephas.* . . . Nor is it surprising that Luke was silent on this matter, when there are many other things that Paul claims to have suffered which Luke

omits with the freedom of a historian. EPIS-
TLE TO THE GALATIANS 1.2.11.[1]

2:11b *Standing Condemned*

WHETHER THEY REALLY DISAGREED.
CHRYSOSTOM: Many of those who read this
passage of the letter superficially believe that
Paul rebuked the hypocrisy of Peter. But it
is not so—it is not so, far from it! For we
shall find that there was here a deep though
hidden understanding between Paul and Peter for the good of those who listen.[2] . . .
How could one who risked his life before such
a multitude have ever played the hypocrite?
. . . Paul does not now say this to condemn
Peter, but in the same spirit as when he said
those who are "reputed to be something," he
now says this too. . . . The apostles, as I said
before, consented to circumcision in Jerusalem, because it was not possible to tear them
away from the law all at once. But when they
came to Antioch they did not henceforth observe anything of the kind but lived indifferently with believers of Gentile origin. Peter
also did this. But when people came from
Judea and saw him preaching there in this
way, he gave up this practice, fearing to disturb them, and changed his ways. He had a
twofold purpose, to avoid scandalizing the
Jews and to give Paul a plausible reason to
confront him. For if Peter himself, having included circumcision in his preaching in Jerusalem, had changed in Antioch, those of
Jewish origin would have surmised that he
did this from fear of Paul, and his disciples
would have condemned his excessive compla-
cence. . . . And so Paul rebukes and Peter voluntarily gives way. It is like the master who
when upbraided keeps silent, so that his disciples might more easily change their ways.

HOMILY ON GALATIANS 2.11-12.[3]

2:12a *Eating with the Gentiles*

**WHY THIS PUZZLING STORY HAD TO BE
TOLD.** MARIUS VICTORINUS: Perhaps indeed
he would at this point have kept silent about
the sin that he says he reproved in Peter, for
it was enough that Peter had been corrected
by popular reproof and Paul's open accusation. But it is profitable and extremely requi-
site for this letter. He has two reasons for
relating the incident. First, his own gospel
was not reproved, and he himself, when he
reproved Peter, heard no reproof from Peter. Next, this too, as I said, was extremely
pertinent: it is because the Galatians
thought that they needed to add to the principles of the gospel to obtain life . . . that this
letter is being written to them. Hence it is
very good to tell the story, because it is this
very fault that was reproved by Paul in Peter
and by the people also.[4] In this way it follows that the Galatians too are sinning. EPIS-
TLE TO THE GALATIANS 1.2.12-13.[5]

**THE IMPLICATION OF EATING WITH THE
GENTILES.** THEODORET: While active in
Judea the holy apostles were forced to live according to the law on account of the weakness of the believers from Jewish backgrounds, for they held fast to the regulations
of the law. But when they shifted to the cit-

---

[1]Migne PL 26:341B-C [409-10]. [2]He cites many proofs of
Peter's zeal (e.g., Mt 16:16, 22; 17:4; Jn 21:7), including
preaching to the Jews in Acts 2. [3]IOEP 4:40-41. Compare
similar passages in Theodoret *Epistle to the Galatians* 2.11
[CPE 1:337-38] and Jerome *Epistle to the Galatians* 1.2.11
[Migne PL 26:338C]. [4]"He stood condemned." [5]BT
1972:23 [1162B-C]. This comment assumes Peter's fault to
be genuine.

ies of the Gentiles they had no need of such an accommodation but lived according to the freedom of the gospel. This is what the godly Peter did when he arrived in Antioch. He ate freely with the Gentiles. But when some of the Jews came he separated from the Gentiles, so that he might not give those who came from the Jews any pretext for doing harm. This is the meaning of "fearing those of the circumcision." For he who did not fear the whole host of the Jews did not succumb to fear of men, but he did not wish to furnish them with a pretext for scandal. EPISTLE TO THE GALATIANS 2.12-13.[6]

2:12b Fearing the Circumcision Party

PETER'S FEAR. MARIUS VICTORINUS: But in what way was Peter sinning? He had not adopted this ruse to bring in the Jews, meeting them on their own terms (which Paul himself had done and glories in having done,[7] meeting the Jews on their own terms but for their profit). Rather the sin of Peter lay in the fact that he withdrew, through fear of those who were of the circumcision. EPISTLE TO THE GALATIANS 1.2.12-13.[8]

APPROPRIATE FEAR OF APOSTASY. CHRYSOSTOM: He was not afraid of his own endangerment; for one who had no fear at the beginning would have all the less at that time. Rather, he feared their apostasy. Just as Paul himself says to the Galatians, *I am afraid I have labored over you in vain.*[9] HOMILY ON GALATIANS 2.11-12.[10]

2:13a Acting Insincerely

PETER'S AMBIVALENCE. AUGUSTINE: Paul never fell into any pretense, for he every-

where observed a principle which seemed fitting both to Gentile and to Jewish churches, that he should nowhere take away a custom whose observation did not prevent the receiving of God's kingdom. . . . Peter, however, when he came to Antioch, was rebuked by Paul not because he observed the Jewish custom in which he was born and reared, although he did not observe it among the Gentiles, but because he wanted to impose it on the Gentiles. This happened after seeing certain persons come from James—that is, from Judea, since James was the head of the church in Jerusalem. It was therefore in fear of those who still thought that salvation resided in these observances that Peter separated himself from the Gentiles and pretended to consent in imposing those burdens of servitude on the Gentiles. EPISTLE TO THE GALATIANS 15 [1B.2.11-16].[11]

2:13b Barnabas Carried Away by Their Insincerity

EVEN BARNABAS. MARIUS VICTORINUS: What then should we understand by *their insincerity*? Even Peter and Barnabas and the other Jews had not truly gone to the length of living their lives according to Jewish practice. They even pretended to do so as an ad hoc measure, because of the fears of those around them. And therefore, he says, even Barnabas acquiesced in their insincerity. EPISTLE TO THE GALATIANS 1.2.12-13.[12]

2:14a The Truth of the Gospel

---

[6]CPE 1:338. [7]1 Cor 9:20. [8]BT 1972:24-25 [1163B-C]. [9]Gal 4:11. [10]IOEP 4:43. [11]Migne PL 35:2113-14. [12]BT 1972:24-25 [1163B-C].

THE IMPLICATION OF THE CHARGE. AUGUS-
TINE: Those who wish to defend Peter from
error and from the depravity of life into
which he had fallen[13] overturn the very way
of religion in which lies the salvation of all.
This shatters and diminishes the authority
of the Scriptures. They do not see that in
this defense they are implicitly charging the
apostle Paul not only with the crime of lying
but even with perjury in the very teaching of
piety, that is, in the letter in which Paul pro-
claims the gospel. It is for this reason he
says, before narrating these things [in 1:20],
*What I write to you, understand before God
that I do not lie.* ON LYING 43.[14]

2:14b *Rebuking Peter Openly*

BEFORE THEM ALL. AUGUSTINE: That he rebuked him *before all* was necessary, in order
that everyone might be bettered by his rebuke. For it was not expedient to correct in
secret an error that was doing public harm.
It should be added that in his steadfastness
and charity Peter, to whom the Lord had
said three times, *Do you love me? Feed my
sheep,*[15] was very ready to bear this rebuke
from a junior shepherd for the salvation of
the flock. For the one who was being rebuked was himself more remarkable and
more difficult to imitate than the one rebuking. For it is easier to see what one should
correct in others than to see what ought to
be corrected in oneself. It is easier to correct
others by admonishing and rebuking than to
be corrected readily even by yourself, let
alone by another, still less if you add another
and *before all.* EPISTLE TO THE GALATIANS
15 [1B.2.11-16].[16]

2:14c *Born a Jew, Living Like a Gentile*

THE SUBSTANCE OF THE REPROACH. PSEUDO-
AUGUSTINE: The apostle Peter would not
have been rebuked if he had separated himself from the Gentiles for fear of giving scandal to the Jews. But what was rebuked in the
apostle Peter was that, when he previously
had been living in Gentile fashion with believers, he started to teach that the Gentiles
ought to follow Jewish practice because he
was overcome by fear upon the arrival of
Jews from James. Therefore it was said to
him, *If you, being a Jew, live in Gentile fashion, why do you force the Gentiles to follow
Jewish practice?* For he had introduced
doubt about discipleship in the gospel,
which is a crime, since he was destroying
what he had built. Thus it is that the apostle
Paul calls this *insincerity.* QUESTIONS ON
THE NEW TESTAMENT, APPENDIX 60.2.[17]

**GRACE IS AVAILABLE WHERE THE LAW IS
UNAVAILING.** CASSIODORUS: He says this so
that Hebrews no less than Gentiles may be
compelled to accept the grace of faith, not
the impositions of the law, which no one
could fulfill. SUMMARY OF GALATIANS 3.2.6.[18]

2:14d *Compelling Gentiles to Live
Like Jews*

**THE PALATABLE WAY THE REBUKE WAS
PHRASED.** CHRYSOSTOM: What is Paul's design? To preempt suspicion in his reproach.
For if Paul had said, "You do wrong in observing the law," those from Judea would
have reproached him, as one who insulted

---

[13]By colluding temporarily with the circumcision party.
[14]Migne PL 40:517-18, openly contradicting Jerome,
Chrysostom and Theodoret. [15]Jn 21:15-17. [16]Migne PL
35:2114. [17]CSEL 50:454. [18]Migne PL 70:1344C.

the teacher. But now, rebuking Peter on account of his own disciples—those of Gentile origin I mean—Paul makes his argument palatable. And not in this way only, but by declining to reproach everyone and making the whole reproof fall on the apostle [Peter] alone. HOMILY ON GALATIANS 2.14.[19]

GRACE ENABLES THE FULFILLMENT OF THE LAW. AUGUSTINE: So that one might fulfill the works of the law, his infirmity being assisted not by his own merit but by the grace of God,[20] they were not to demand from the Gentiles a fleshly observation of the law but were to understand that through the same grace of God they were able to fulfill the spiritual works of the law. EPISTLE TO THE GALATIANS 15 [IB.2.II-16].[21]

---

[19]IOEP 4:44. [20]But only the free reception of grace by which the spiritual law is fulfilled. [21]Migne PL 35:2114.

2:15-21 FROM LAW TO GRACE

[15]*We ourselves, who are Jews by birth and not Gentile sinners,* [16]*yet who know that a man is not justified*[d] *by works of the law but through faith in Jesus Christ, even we have believed in Christ Jesus, in order to be justified by faith in Christ, and not by works of the law, because by works of the law shall no one be justified.* [17]*But if, in our endeavor to be justified in Christ, we ourselves were found to be sinners, is Christ then an agent of sin? Certainly not!* [18]*But if I build up again those things which I tore down, then I prove myself a transgressor.* [19]*For I through the law died to the law, that I might live to God.* [20]*I have been crucified with Christ; it is no longer I who live, but Christ who lives in me; and the life I now live in the flesh I live by faith in the Son of God, who loved me and gave himself for me.* [21]*I do not nullify the grace of God; for if justification*[e] *were through the law, then Christ died to no purpose.*

d Or reckoned righteous; *and so elsewhere* e Or righteousness

OVERVIEW: The ceremonies of the law have served their purpose (THEODORET). Even the patriarchs were saved by faith, and no one is saved by works without Christ (JEROME). The accusers of Paul make Christ a sinner (THEODORET), as do Gentiles who slavishly adopt the law (MARIUS VICTORINUS, CHRYSOSTOM). Paul shows that even Jews have forsaken the law (JEROME, AUGUSTINE). We are called to die to the letter (MARIUS VICTORINUS), as we die to the world in union with the crucified Lord (AM-

BROSIASTER), so as to share in the living bread of heaven (AMBROSE) in the company of saints and angels. Christ dwells in us as our sins are forgiven (AMBROSIASTER), though we are never completely freed from sin in the flesh (AUGUSTINE). Paul expresses his gratitude with passion (CHRYSOSTOM), knowing the cost to Christ (JEROME). To avoid nullifying grace we must remember Christ's death for our sins (AMBROSIASTER). To make him die in vain is the worst of heresies (CHRYSOSTOM).

2:15 Jews by Birth, Not Gentiles

WE JEWS BY BIRTH. JEROME: A Jew by nature is one of Abraham's stock, who has been circumcised by his parents on the eighth day.[1] One who is a Jew "not by nature" is one of Gentile origin who has been subsequently made so. That I may embrace the whole argument in a brief discourse, the sense of the text is as follows: "We are Jews by nature, doing those things that were precepts of the law. We are not sinners who come from the Gentiles—either in the sense of those who are sinners generically because they worship idols or those whom Jews now regard as unclean. Yet we know that we cannot be saved by the works of the law but rather by faith in Christ. We have believed in Christ that what the law had not given us our faith would guarantee to us. Seceding from the law in which we could not be saved, we have gone over to faith, in which not the circumcision of the flesh but the devotion of a pure heart is demanded. But what if we now belatedly declare by seceding from the Gentiles that whoever is uncircumcised is unclean? In that case faith in Christ —by which we previously thought we were

saved—would rather become a minister of sin than of righteousness. For faith would under that assumption take away the circumcision without which one is unclean." EPISTLE TO THE GALATIANS 1.2.15.[2]

PRIDE IN PERCEIVING GENTILES AS SINNERS. AUGUSTINE: The Jews had given the name of sinners to the Gentiles through a certain pride, already inveterate. It is as though they themselves were just, seeing the mote in another's eye and not the beam in their own.[3] EPISTLE TO THE GALATIANS 16 [IB.2.15-18].[4]

2:16 Not Justified by Works of the Law

PATRIARCHS, PROPHETS AND SAINTS PRIOR TO CHRIST WERE JUSTIFIED BY FAITH, NOT WORKS. JEROME: Some say that if Paul is right in asserting that no one is justified by the works of the law but from faith in Christ, the patriarchs and prophets and saints who lived before Christ were imperfect. We should tell such people that those who are said not to have obtained righteousness are those who believe that they can be justified by works alone. The saints who lived long ago, however, were justified from faith in Christ, seeing[5] that Abraham saw in advance Christ's day. EPISTLE TO THE GALATIANS 1.2.16.[6]

NO ONE CAN FULFILL THE LAW IN EVERY RESPECT BY MORAL EFFORT ALONE. JEROME: In this place we must consider how many are the precepts of the law which no one can ful-

---

[1]Gen 17:9-12. [2]Migne PL 26:343A-B [411-12]. [3]See Mt 7:3-5; Lk 6:41-42. [4]Migne PL 35:2115. [5]Jn 8:56. [6]Migne PL 26:343C-D [412].

fill. And it must also be said that some works of the law are done even by those who do not know it. But those who perform it are not justified, because this happens without faith in Christ. EPISTLE TO THE GALATIANS 1.2.16.[7]

MUCH OF THE LAW IS KNOWN BY NATURAL CONSCIENCE. THEODORET: The necessary commandments of the law were taught even by nature. That is, "You shall not commit adultery, you shall not murder, you shall not steal, you shall not bear false witness against thy neighbor, honor your father and mother, and the rest of this kind." But the commandments about the sabbath and circumcision and lepers and menstruation and sacrifice were peculiar to the [Jewish] law, since nature taught nothing about these matters. These are what he now calls *works of the law*. The transgression of these is sin, yet the mere keeping of them is not the way of maintaining perfect righteousness. For these were symbols of other things. Nonetheless they were appropriate to the Jews in their due time. EPISTLE TO THE GALATIANS 2.15-16.[8]

2:17 Can Christ Be an Agent of Sin?

WHETHER CHRIST BECOMES AN AGENT OF SIN TO THOSE WHO RETURN TO THE LAW. MARIUS VICTORINUS: Suppose that we, after receiving faith in Christ, do in Christ what the Jews do. Suppose we have received faith in Christ and wish to be justified in it. Suppose we have understood that a man is not justified by the works of the law. Would we not then, by observing the works of the law, be made sinners? Then it would be the case that Christ, whom we received in order not to sin, would himself become a minister of

sin. Now, when after receiving him we return to sin—that is, to the old covenant—is Christ made a minister of sin? Let this possibility, Paul says, be far from us. One ought not to think in this way and act so as to make Christ a minister of sin, when he suffered in order that sin might perish. EPISTLE TO THE GALATIANS 1.2.17.[9]

WHETHER CHRIST COULD EVEN BE CONCEIVED AS AN AGENT OF SIN. THEODORET: Paul says in effect: "We have forsaken the law and come over to Christ, expecting to enjoy righteousness through faith in him. But suppose that this itself is counted as a transgression. The fault would then pertain to Christ the Lord himself. For it was he who gave us the New Testament. Far be it from us to tolerate such blasphemy!" EPISTLE TO THE GALATIANS 2.17.[10]

2:18 Rebuilding the Law Makes One a Trangressor

ONE WHO REESTABLISHES THE LAW IS A TRANSGRESSOR AGAINST NOT FAITH BUT THE LAW ITSELF. CHRYSOSTOM: Note the shrewdness of Paul. For they wanted to show that the one who does not keep the law is a transgressor; but he turns the argument upside down, showing that the one who observes the law is a transgressor not against faith but against the law itself. What he says is as follows: "The law has ceased, as we ourselves agree, in so far as we have left it and taken refuge in the salvation of faith. If we now strive to establish it, we become

---

[7]Migne PL 26:344A-B [413]. [8]CPE 1:340. [9]BT 1972:26-27 [1165A-B]. [10]CPE 1:341; here Theodoret follows Chrysostom *Homily on Galatians* 2.17 [IOEP 4:45].

transgressors by this very fact, as we strive to observe the precepts dissolved by God." HOMILY ON GALATIANS 2.18.[11]

2:19 Dying to the Law, Living to God

VARIED WAYS OF UNDERSTANDING THE LAW. MARIUS VICTORINUS: Now it is possible to see Paul as speaking of two laws— one of Moses, the other of Christ—so that he is saying he is dead to that law, which was given to the Jews, through the law that was given through Christ . . . that is, "I am dead through the law of Christ to the law formerly given to the Jews." But Paul may also be seen as doing what both he and the Savior himself often do, so that he speaks of two laws because it is itself, as it were, twofold: one thing when it is understood carnally,[12] another when understood spiritually. . . . Thus the sense will be *For I through the law*, which is now spiritually understood, *am dead to the law*— that law obviously which is understood carnally. And since this is so, *I am dead to the carnal law* because I understand the law spiritually, *so that I live to God*. For what it means for someone to live to God is that he understands those precepts contained in the law not carnally but spiritually, that is, what it is to be truly circumcised and what the true sabbath is. EPISTLE TO THE GALATIANS 1.2.19.[13]

2:20a Crucified with Christ

NO LONGER I WHO LIVE. AMBROSE: This means, "Not I, who once ate from the earth [like Adam]. Not I who was once grass, as all flesh is grass,[14] but Christ who lives in me. That is, there lives that living bread

which comes from heaven, there lives wisdom, there lives righteousness, there lives the resurrection." ON PARADISE 76.[15]

WHERE I AM NOT I, I AM MORE HAPPILY I. AUGUSTINE: The human spirit, cleaving to the Spirit of God, struggles against the flesh,[16] that is, against itself and on its own behalf. Those impulses natural to humanity, whether in the flesh or in the soul, which remain because of our acquired debility, are restrained by discipline for the sake of obtaining salvation. So the human being who does not live according to human nature can already say, *I live, yet not I, but Christ lives in me*. For where I am not I, I am more happily I. Thus when any reprobate impulse arises according to my old human nature, to which I who serve the law of God with my mind do not consent, I may now say this: *now I am not the one doing that*.[17] ON CONTINENCE 29.[18]

2:20b Christ Lives in Me

IS PAUL UNIQUE? ORIGEN: Since Christ was in Paul, who will doubt that he was also likewise in Peter and John and in every individual among the saints, and not only in those who are on earth but also in those in heaven? For it is absurd to say that Christ was in Peter and Paul but not in the archangel Michael or Gabriel. ON FIRST PRINCIPLES 4.4.29.[19]

---

[11]IOEP 4:47; cf. Theodoret *Epistle to the Galatians* 2.18 [CPE 1:341]. [12]According to or pertaining to the flesh. [13]BT 1972:27-28 [1165C-D]. [14]Is 40:6. [15]CSEL 32.1:335. [16]Gal 5:17. [17]Rom 7:17. [18]Migne PL 40:369; cf. Augustine *Against Julian of Eclanum* 6.70 [Migne PL 44:865-66]. [19]GCS 22:351; from Rufinus's Latin translation.

DEAD TO THE WORLD. AMBROSIASTER: One who is fixed to the cross of Christ is one who, in imitation of his footsteps, is not ensnared by any worldly desire. Living to God, he appears dead to the world. EPISTLE TO THE GALATIANS 2.19.[20]

2:20c *Living by Faith in the Son of God*

SNATCHED FROM DEATH. AMBROSIASTER: There is no doubt that Christ lives in the one who is delivered from death by faith. When Christ forgives the sins of one who is worthy of death, he himself lives in that person, since by his protection the person is snatched from death. EPISTLE TO THE GALATIANS 2.20.[21]

2:20d *Christ Gave Himself for Me*

MAKING THE UNIVERSAL GOD MY OWN. CHRYSOSTOM: What are you doing, Paul, making common things your own, and claiming for yourself what was done on behalf of the whole world? For he says not "who loved us" but "who loved me." . . . But Paul speaks in this highly personal voice, aware of the culpability of human nature and the ineffable compassion of Christ, aware of what he redeems us from and what grace he confers upon us. Burning with desire toward him, he utters this. In just this way did the prophets often make the universal God their own, crying, *My God, my God, I invoke you.*[22] He shows that each of us ought to render as much thanks to Christ as though Christ had come for him alone. For God would not have withheld this gift even from one person. He has the same love for every individual as for the whole world. HOMILY ON GALATIANS 2.20.[23]

HE HANDED HIMSELF OVER. JEROME: Judas and the priests, with the princes, handed him over, and Pilate, to whom he was finally handed over, handed him over again. But the Father handed him over that he might save the abandoned world. Jesus gave himself, that he might do the Father's will. But Judas and the priests and elders of the people and Pilate unwittingly handed over their lives to death. EPISTLE TO THE GALATIANS 1.2.20.[24]

2:21a *Not Nullifying the Grace of God*

ON NOT NULLIFYING GRACE. AMBROSIASTER: Since a future life is promised to Christians, the one who now lives with God's assistance lives in the faith of the promised life. For this one contemplates his image, having the pledge of the future life, which was procured for us by Christ's love in accordance with God's will. The one who is grateful to Christ is therefore the one who endures in faith toward him. He knows that he has no benefit from anyone but Christ and treats Christ with dishonor if he compares any other to him. EPISTLE TO THE GALATIANS 2.21.[25]

2:21b *Justification Not Through the Law*

THE REASON FOR CHRIST'S DEATH. AMBROSIASTER: The law could not give remission of sins, nor triumph over the second death nor free from captivity those who were bound because of sin. The reason for Christ's death was to provide those things

---

[20]CSEL 81.3:28. [21]CSEL 81.3:29. [22]Ps 62:1 (LXX). [23]IOEP 4:50. [24]Migne PL 26:346B [415]. [25]CSEL 81.3:28.

that the law could not. He did not die in vain, for his death is the justification of sinners. EPISTLE TO THE GALATIANS 2.21.[26]

THE ABSURDITY OF THE CONTRARY ARGUMENT. CHRYSOSTOM: How could an act so great, so awesome and surpassing human reason be to no purpose? How could a mystery so ineffable, for which the prophets yearned in travail, the patriarchs foresaw and the angels were astonished to behold, acknowledged by all as the crown of God's loving care—how could one say that this was vain and futile? Considering therefore how exceedingly absurd it would be for them to say a deed of such significance and magnitude had been superfluous . . . Paul adopts an indignant tone toward them saying O foolish Galatians. HOMILY ON GALATIANS 2.21.[27]

---

[26]CSEL 81.3:28. [27]IOEP 4:51.

3:1-5 THE FOLLY OF THE GALATIANS

¹*O foolish Galatians! Who has bewitched you, before whose eyes Jesus Christ was publicly portrayed as crucified?* ²*Let me ask you only this: Did you receive the Spirit by works of the law, or by hearing with faith?* ³*Are you so foolish? Having begun with the Spirit, are you now ending with the flesh?* ⁴*Did you experience so many things in vain?—if it really is in vain.* ⁵*Does he who supplies the Spirit to you and works miracles among you do so by works of the law, or by hearing with faith?*

OVERVIEW: Paul scolds the Galatians for their own good (CHRYSOSTOM) yet implicitly compliments them on their progress (THEODORET). No literal belief in witchcraft is here implied (JEROME). By faith the Galatians saw the crucifixion (CHRYSOSTOM), as do we (JEROME). Rejecting eloquence (CHRYSOSTOM), Paul shows that faith cannot coexist with an external legalism (AUGUSTINE). Reminding them of the persecution they have suffered courageously (AMBROSIASTER), the miracles they have experienced (AMBROSIASTER) and the advances they have already made (CHRYSOSTOM), he cajoles even as he reprimands (MARIUS VICTORINUS). Reserving logical argument for later points (CHRYSOSTOM), he shows that faith, not law, has been the cause of their progress so far (MARIUS VICTORINUS).

3:1a A Rebuke for Folly

HIS BRUSQUE MANNER. CHRYSOSTOM: Having established himself as a trustworthy teacher, he speaks from now on with greater personal authority, drawing a comparison between the law and faith. Earlier he had said: *I am amazed that you have so quickly departed.*[1] Now he says: *O foolish Galatians.* Then he was pregnant with indignation. Now, having made his defense of what pertained to him, he lets it burst into the open and brings it forth afterward for demonstration. And if he calls them fools, do not be surprised. In doing this, he does not transgress Christ's law, which forbids one to call his brother a fool,[2] but rather is protecting them. For who could have more justly deserved this term, when after so many great things they held to the former ways as though nothing had happened? HOMILY ON GALATIANS 3.1.[3]

THE HIDDEN COMMENDATION. THEODORET: This indicates their previous zeal for piety and manifests the fatherly affection of the apostle. He grieves over them for their loss of wealth accumulated. EPISTLE TO THE GALATIANS 3.1.[4]

A COLLOQUIAL EXPRESSION. JEROME: We must expound what follows—*Who has bewitched you?*—in a way worthy of Paul, who even if rough in his speech is not so in his understanding. It must not be interpreted in such a way as to make Paul legitimize the witchcraft that is popularly supposed to do harm. Rather he has used a colloquial expression, and as elsewhere so here he has adopted a word from everyday speech. . . . In the same way as tender infants are said to be harmed by witchcraft, so too the Galatians, recently born in the faith of Christ and nourished with milk, not solid food,[5] have been injured as though someone has cast a spell on them. EPISTLE TO THE GALATIANS 1.3.1.[6]

3:1b *Christ's Crucifixion Publicly Portrayed*

THE EYES OF FAITH SEE THE PORTRAYAL CLEARLY FROM AFAR. CHRYSOSTOM: Since Christ was crucified not in the Galatians' territory but in Jerusalem, what does he mean by this phrase *before whose eyes?* He is illustrating the power of faith, which is able to see even things far off. And he said not "crucified" but *portrayed as crucified,* showing that with the eyes of faith they saw more accurately than those who were there and witnessed the events. . . . And he says this both to reprimand and to commend them. He commends them for having received the facts with such enthusiasm. He blames them because, having seen Christ stripped, crucified, nailed, spat on, mocked, drinking vinegar, insulted by thieves, pierced with a spear . . . they have forsaken this man and run back to the law, showing no awareness of Christ's sufferings. HOMILY ON GALATIANS 3.1.[7]

WE ARE ALSO WITNESSES. JEROME: Christ is rightly said to be portrayed before us, since the whole chorus of Old Testament prophets spoke of his gallows and passion, his blows and whippings. . . . Nor was it a small number of Galatians who believed in the crucifixion as it has previously been portrayed for them. It was of course by this means that, reading the prophets continually and knowing all the ordinances of the law,

---

[1]Gal 1:6. [2]Mt 5:22. [3]IOEP 4:52-53. [4]CPE 1:342. Similar points are made by Chrysostom *Homily on Galatians* 3.1 [IOEP 4:52-53], and Marius Victorinus *Epistle to the Galatians* 1.3.1 [BT 1972:29-30 (1166D-1167B)]. [5]Cf. 1 Cor 3:2. [6]Migne PL 26:347B-348A [417-18]. [7]IOEP 4:53.

they were led in due course to belief. EPIS-
TLE TO THE GALATIANS 1.3.1.[8]

3:2a Asking a Single Question

SWIFT PROOF. CHRYSOSTOM: Paul says, in effect, "For since you do not pay heed to high-
flown words and will not consider the
greatness of God's gift, I want to persuade
you through a concise argument with a very
swift proof, since you seem to be utterly unaware." HOMILY ON GALATIANS 3.2.[9]

3:2b Law or Faith?

TONGUES AND THEIR INTERPRETATION AS
EVIDENCES OF THE GIFTS OF THE SPIRIT.
AMBROSIASTER: He sets forth a tenet that
could not at that time be denied: the Holy
Spirit dwells in believers. This gift was manifested by God to recollect the rudiments of
the faith, as it was at the beginning when it
was practiced among the apostles and the
other disciples.[10] . . . On these the Holy
Spirit descended and gave the capacity to
speak in many tongues,[11] with the gift of interpretation, so that no one dared deny the
presence of the Spirit of God in them. EPIS-
TLE TO THE GALATIANS 3.3.3.[12]

CEREMONIAL AND MORAL OBSERVANCE DIS-
TINGUISHED FROM FAITH. AUGUSTINE: Here
he begins to demonstrate in what sense the
grace of faith is sufficient for justification
without the works of the law. . . . But so
that this question may be carefully treated
and no one may be deceived by ambiguities,
we must first understand that the works of
the law are twofold; for they reside partly in
ceremonial ordinances and partly in morals.
To the ordinances belong the circumcision

of the flesh, the weekly sabbath, new
moons,[13] sacrifices and all the innumerable
observances of this kind. But to morality belong "You shall not kill, you shall not commit adultery, you shall not bear false
witness" and so on.[14] Could the apostle possibly not care whether a Christian were a mur-
derer and adulterer or chaste and innocent,
in the way that he does not care whether he
is circumcised or uncircumcised in the flesh?
He therefore is specially concerned with the
works that consist in ceremonial ordinances,
although he indicates that the others are
sometimes bound up with them. But near
the end of the letter he deals separately with
those works that consist in morals, and he
does this briefly, but he speaks at greater
length regarding the [ceremonial] works. . . .
For nothing so terrifies the mind as a ceremonial ordinance that is not understood. But
when it is understood it produces spiritual joy
and is celebrated gladly and in due season. It is
read and treated only with a spiritual sweetness. Now every sacrament,[15] once understood
in this way, is applied either to the contemplation of truth or to good morals. The contemplation of truth is founded in the love of God
alone, good morals in the love of God and the
neighbor,[16] and on these two precepts depend
the whole Law and the Prophets. EPISTLE TO
THE GALATIANS 19 [1B.3.1].[17]

---

[8]Migne PL 26:348B [418]. [9]IOEP 4:54. [10]Here Ambrosiaster cites Acts 19:2. [11]"Facility in many tongues" could refer
to many known languages (as in Acts 2:8-10) or ecstatic utterance (as in the Corinthian controversy; cf. 1 Cor 12:10).
[12]CSEL 81.3:31. For a similar comment see Theodoret Epistle to the Galatians 3.2 [CPE 1:343]. [13]E.g., Col 2:16-17.
[14]Ex 20; Deut 5. [15]Or proto-Christian levitical ordinance,
which Christianly understood is an anticipatory type of Christian liturgical practice. [16]Mt 22:37-40. [17]Migne PL 35:2117.

3:3 Beginning with the Spirit, Ending with the Flesh

CARRIED BACK TOWARD LESS. CHRYSOSTOM: What he means is, "Whereas the advance of time should bring increase, you not only have not improved but have actually been pushed backward. For those who have begun from small things gradually proceed to greater ones. But you, on the contrary, beginning from great things, have been carried back to less . . . from performing spiritual signs back to practicing fleshly circumcision." HOMILY ON GALATIANS 3.3.[18]

3:4 Did You Experience Many Things in Vain?

REPRIMAND AND ADMONITION. MARIUS VICTORINUS: Such a subtle comment requires patience to understand. It both negatively reprimands and positively admonishes. He reprimands them by saying *You have suffered so much in vain.* At the same time he admonishes them by saying *you have suffered so much,* aware that they withstood many things with fortitude when they received faith. EPISTLE TO THE GALATIANS 1.3.4.[19]

THE PRIZE OF PERSEVERANCE. MARIUS VICTORINUS: Lest he should seem to despair needlessly, he has corrected his own reprimand by saying *if indeed it is in vain.* For they could be corrected. If so, what they have suffered will not be without meaning. The meaning they will have will be perseverance in faith, the prize and the confirmation of promises derived from faith in Christ. EPISTLE TO THE GALATIANS 1.3.4.[20]

THEIR FORMER SUFFERING MADE USELESS BY THEIR RETURN TO LEGALISTIC BONDAGE. AMBROSIASTER: At that time believers were subject to reproach from others, whether at home or abroad, being pointed out as guilty of treason.[21] Hence the Galatians, who had likewise suffered a great deal, were more perverse than those who had been spared, because they had lost the merit of their suffering by their resubmission to the law. EPISTLE TO THE GALATIANS 3.4.[22]

3:5 Works of the Law or Hearing with Faith

THE SPIRIT REQUIRES NO ADDED LAW. CHRYSOSTOM: His opponents had turned this about and upside down by saying that faith is of no avail if the law is not added. He shows, on the contrary, that if the law's precepts are added, faith will no longer be of any use. HOMILY ON GALATIANS 3.5.[23]

MIRACLES UNDESERVED. MARIUS VICTORINUS: After confirming that they have suffered and consequently that the Spirit has been given to them, he rightly goes on to ask whether God worked virtues in them from the works of the law or from the hearing of faith. "Obviously not from works," [he says], "for it was not from yourselves that any works proceeded, but you heard in faith and were attentive to faith. And for this reason God worked virtues in you; and if he worked, he gave you the Spirit." EPISTLE TO THE GALATIANS 1.3.5.[24]

---

[18]IOEP 4:54. [19]BT 1972:31 [1167D-1168A]. [20]BT 1972:31 [1168A]. [21]Against interpretation of law. [22]CSEL 81.3:32. [23]IOEP 4:55. [24]BT 1972:31-32 [1168B-C].

3:6-14 FAITH AGAINST LAW

[6]*Thus Abraham "believed God, and it was reckoned to him as righteousness."* [7]*So you see that it is men of faith who are the sons of Abraham.* [8]*And the scripture, foreseeing that God would justify the Gentiles by faith, preached the gospel beforehand to Abraham, saying, "In you shall all the nations be blessed."* [9]*So then, those who are men of faith are blessed with Abraham who had faith.*

[10]*For all who rely on works of the law are under a curse; for it is written, "Cursed be every one who does not abide by all things written in the book of the law, and do them."* [11]*Now it is evident that no man is justified before God by the law; for "He who through faith is righteous shall live";[f]* [12]*but the law does not rest on faith, for "He who does them shall live by them."* [13]*Christ redeemed us from the curse of the law, having become a curse for us—for it is written, "Cursed be every one who hangs on a tree"—* [14]*that in Christ Jesus the blessing of Abraham might come upon the Gentiles, that we might receive the promise of the Spirit through faith.*

f Or the righteous shall live by faith

OVERVIEW: Paul urges us all to become Abraham's children through faith (MARIUS VICTORINUS). Asserting that Abraham anticipates our condition (CHRYSOSTOM), Paul takes circumcision as a sign for us (JEROME) and the promise as a foretaste of the gospel (AUGUSTINE). From praising faith Paul goes on to disparage legalism (THEODORET), showing that the law has no power to curse the one under the gospel (CHRYSOSTOM) as it curses the natural man (EPIPHANIUS), though he does not deny that good works are called for (MARIUS VICTORINUS). The law brings only knowledge of sin (AUGUSTINE) and gives present but not future life (PSEUDO-AUGUSTINE). Christ became a victim for us (AMBROSIASTER), taking our sins upon himself (GREGORY OF NAZIANZUS). Even as our sacrifice (CHRY-

sosTOM) he vindicated the law (EPIPHANIUS). As a result the blessing of Abraham descends to us and prepares us for the Spirit (CHRYSOSTOM).

3:6 Abraham's Belief Counted as Righteousness

DISSOLVING FEAR IN KINSHIP WITH ABRAHAM. CHRYSOSTOM: Since the argument was about the law, Paul develops another highly controversial argument, bringing Abraham to the fore, and most effectively. . . . "For the power of faith," he says, "is shown by the miracles that occurred among you; but if you wish I shall also try to convince you from the ancient records. . . . There was no law then," he says, "and now too there is no law. . . . Just as in Abraham's time the law was not yet given, so now, having been given, it has ceased." And since they thought it a great thing to be descended from Abraham and were afraid that if they abandoned the law they would be deprived of their kinship, Paul turns this argument on its head and dissolves fear by showing that it is faith above all that produces affinity with Abraham. HOMILY ON GALATIANS 3.6.[1]

3:7 People of Faith Are Abraham's Descendants

SOLA FIDE. MARIUS VICTORINUS: Every mystery which is enacted by our Lord Jesus Christ asks only for faith. The mystery was enacted at that time for our sake and aimed at our resurrection and liberation, should we have faith in the mystery of Christ and in Christ. For the patriarchs prefigured and foretold that man would be justified from faith. Therefore, just as it was reckoned as righteousness to Abraham that he had faith, so we too, if we have faith in Christ and every mystery of his, will be sons of Abraham. Our whole life will be accounted as righteous. EPISTLE TO THE GALATIANS 1.3.7.[2]

3:8a Scripture Foresaw the Gentiles' Justification by Faith

THE ONE WHO GAVE THE LAW DECREED BEFORE THE LAW THAT THE GENTILES BE JUSTIFIED BY FAITH ALONE. CHRYSOSTOM: For since they were perturbed by the greater antiquity of the law and the fact that faith came after the law, he destroys this surmise of theirs, showing that faith is older than the law. That is obvious from Abraham, since he was justified before the appearance of the law. . . . "The one who gave the law," he

says, in effect "was the one who decreed before the law was given that the Gentiles should be justified." And Paul does not say "revealed" but "preached the gospel" [beforehand to Abraham], so that you may understand that even the patriarch rejoiced in this kind of righteousness and greatly desired its advent. HOMILY ON GALATIANS 3.8.[3]

How Joshua's Circumcised People Anticipate the Spiritual Circumcision of Jesus' People. JEROME: God, providing that the descendants of Abraham should not be mixed with the other nations . . . marked off the Israelite people by a particular rite: circumcision. . . . After that for forty years no one was circumcised in the wilderness. They were living without any intermixing with other nations. . . . As soon as the people crossed the river Jordan and the host poured out onto the territory of Judea in Palestine, he made provision by a necessary circumcision against the future error from miscegenation with the Gentiles. But the fact that the people are said to have been circumcised a second time by their leader Joshua[4] signifies that circumcision had ceased in the wilderness, though practiced in Egypt for a good reason. Believers now are cleansed by our Lord Jesus Christ through a spiritual circumcision. EPISTLE TO THE GALATIANS 3.7.[5]

3:8b The Gospel Preached to Abraham

THE GOSPEL BEFOREHAND TO ABRAHAM. AUGUSTINE: The greatest cause for triumph

---

[1]IOEP 4:56. [2]BT 1972:32 [1169A]. [3]IOEP 4:57. [4]Joshua is a prototype of Jesus. He "circumcised the people of Israel" a second time (Josh 5:2). [5]Migne PL 26:352C-353A [423-24].

in Abraham was that, before his circumcision, faith was reckoned to him for righteousness.[6] This is most correctly referred to the promise that *All nations shall be blessed in you,*[7] meaning of course by the following of his faith, by which he was justified even before the ordinance of circumcision, which he received as a token of faith, and long before the servitude of the law,[8] which was given much later. EPISTLE TO THE GALATIANS 20 [IB.3.2-9].[9]

3:9 People of Faith Blessed with Abraham, Who Had Faith

BLESSED WITH ABRAHAM. THEODORET: Paul has thus eulogized faith and shown what fruits it has from the gracious gifts of the Spirit. He also has shown that it is older than the law from the witness of the law itself—for the Old Testament describes the events concerning Abraham. Finally, he sets the law alongside faith, showing how it differs. EPISTLE TO THE GALATIANS 3.7-9.[10]

3:10a The Results of Reliance on the Law

A CHRISTIAN'S GOOD WORKS DISTINGUISHED FROM WORKS OF THE LAW. MARIUS VICTORINUS: From his saying *works of the law* we are to understand that there are also good works in the Christian life, especially those that the apostle frequently commends, such as that we should be mindful of the poor and the other precepts for living that are contained in this very letter. The fulfillment of all these works is the calling of every Christian. The cursed works of the law referred to here are therefore other things: obviously observations [of

days,] sacrifices of lambs and other such works that they perform concerning circumcision and the choice of foods. But now the paschal feast has been consummated through Christ. EPISTLE TO THE GALATIANS 3.10.[11]

THE CURSE NOW TURNED TO BLESSING. EPIPHANIUS: The words *they are under a curse* mean that in the law there was a curse against Adam's transgression, until the advent of the one who came from above and who, clothing himself with a body from the mass of Adamic humanity, turned the curse into blessing. PANARION 42.12.3, FIRST REFUTATION OF MARCION.[12]

ONLY ONE WHO ADHERES TO FAITH ALONE IS BLESSED. CHRYSOSTOM: This dissolves the fear, cleverly and shrewdly turning it on its head. . . . For they said that the one who does not keep the law is cursed, while he shows that the one who strives to keep it is cursed and the one who does not strive to keep it is blessed. They said also that the one who adheres to faith alone is accursed, while he shows, on the contrary, that the one who adheres to faith alone is blessed. HOMILY ON GALATIANS 3.9-10.[13]

3:10b The Text of the Law

WHICH VERSION OF THE HEBREW TEXT OF DEUTERONOMY 27:26 WAS PAUL FOLLOWING? JEROME: We perceive that the apostle, as elsewhere, has written down the sense of

---

[6]Gen 15:6. [7]Gen 22:18. [8]The late Judaic bondage to interpretations of Mosaic law. [9]Migne PL 35:2118. [10]CPE 1:344. [11]BT 1972:33-34 [1169D-1170A]. [12]GCS 31:156. [13]IOEP 4:7-8.

the passage rather than the words. We consider it uncertain whether the seventy interpreters [of the Septuagint] have added *everyone* and *in all* or whether it was in the old Hebrew and deleted by the Jews. What makes me suspect this is that the apostle, a man skilled in Hebrew learning, would never have added these words *everyone* and *all* as if they were necessary to his meaning in the proof that all who perform the works of the law are accursed, unless they were in the Hebrew copies. Therefore, reading over the Hebrew copies of the Samaritans, I found the word *kol* written, which means *all* or *in all* and concurs with the Seventy. EPISTLE TO THE GALATIANS 2.3.[14]

3:11a No One Is Justified by the Law

THE PURPOSE OF THE LAW. AUGUSTINE: The law leads to knowledge of sin and at length to the transgression of the law itself. It is thus with the knowledge and increase of sin that grace may be sought through faith. AGAINST TWO LETTERS OF PELAGIUS 1.14.[15]

3:11b Righteousness Through Faith

NOT PAUL'S ARGUMENT ALONE BUT ALSO THE PROPHET'S. CHRYSOSTOM: All have sinned and are under a curse.[16] Yet he does not say this, lest he should seem to be running ahead of his own demonstration. He establishes it by a testimony that succinctly proves both that no one fulfills the law (and therefore they are accursed) and that faith justifies. . . . For the prophet did not say, "The just shall live from law" but from faith.[17] HOMILY ON GALATIANS 3.11.[18]

3:12 The Law Does Not Rest on Faith

RIGHTEOUSNESS IN THE AGE TO COME. PSEUDO-AUGUSTINE: This means the one who follows the law will live and not die for the present. But the righteousness which is from faith makes one righteous in God's sight, so that one may be rewarded eternally in the age to come. QUESTIONS ON THE NEW TESTAMENT, APPENDIX 66.[19]

3:13a Having Become a Curse for Us

REDEEMED FROM THE CURSE OF THE LAW. AMBROSIASTER: Since no one could obey the law, all were convicted by the curse of the law, so that it was right to punish them. But Christ, born as a man and offered for us by his Father, redeemed us from the devil. He was offered for those who were liable to the curse of the law. Jesus was made a curse in the way that under the law a victim offered for sin is said to be sin. . . . Thus he did not say "cursed for us" but *made a curse*. EPISTLE TO THE GALATIANS 3.13.1-2.[20]

WHETHER A REAL CHANGE OCCURRED IN THE LORD'S BECOMING A CURSE FOR US. GREGORY OF NAZIANZUS: It is not that the Lord was changed into these things—for how could that be?—but because he underwent them, *taking up our transgressions and*

---

[14]Migne PL 26:357B-C [431]. Jerome recognized astutely that the Hebrew text said "Cursed be *he* [not *everyone*] who does not confirm the words of *this law* [not *all things*] by doing them." This shows that Jerome had at least three texts of Deuteronomy 27:26 before him: the Hebrew, the Samaritan and the Septuagint. Since Paul would not amend the Hebrew text Jerome concludes that he was stating the sense of the text rather than quoting it verbatim. [15]Migne PL 44:557. [16]Cf. Rom 3:23. [17]Hab 2:4. [18]IOEP 4:58. [19]CSEL 50:460. Cf. Augustine *Epistle to the Galatians* 21 [1B.3.10-12; Migne PL 35:2118-19]. [20]CSEL 81.3:34-35.

bearing our sicknesses.[21] LETTER 101.61.[22]

3:13b *The Curse of the Crucifixion*

HOW THE CURSE WAS LOOSED. EPIPHA-NIUS: The holy apostle, revealing again how the appearance in the flesh and the cross fulfilled the plan for the loosing of the curse and how this was written before-hand in the law and prophesied as coming, then fulfilled in the Savior, has clearly proved that the law is not alien to the Sav-ior. PANARION 42.12.3, SECOND REFUTA-TION OF MARCION.[23]

SUFFERING FROM THE CURSE, HE RELEASED THEM FROM THE CURSE. CHRYSOSTOM: For the people were liable to punishment since they had not fulfilled the whole law. Christ satisfied a different curse: the one that says *Cursed is everyone that hangs on a tree.*[24] Both the one who is hanged and the one who transgresses the law are accursed. Christ, who was going to lift that curse, could not properly be made liable to it yet had to receive a curse. He received the curse instead of being liable to it and through this lifted the curse. Just as, when someone is condemned to death, another innocent per-son who chooses to die for him releases him from that punishment, so Christ also did. . . . Just as by dying he snatched from death those who were going to die, so also when he suffered the curse he released them from the curse. HOMILY ON GALATIANS 3.13.[25]

3:14 *Receiving the Promise of the Spirit*

RECEIVING THE PROMISE OF THE SPIRIT THROUGH FAITH. CHRYSOSTOM: It would not be right that the grace of the Spirit should come to one who was graceless or full of offense. We are blessed first by the taking away of the curse. Then, justified by faith, we receive[26] the grace of the Holy Spirit. So the cross has dissolved the curse, faith has brought righteousness, and by God's own righteousness the grace of the Spirit has been given. HOMILY ON GALATIANS 3.14.[27]

---

[21]Is 53:4. [22]SC 208:62. [23]GCS 31:156. [24]Deut 21:23. [25]IOEP 4:59. [26]Or "draw to ourselves" (cf. NPNF 1 13:27) or "procure." [27]IOEP 4:60.

3:15-20 TESTAMENT AND PROMISE

[15]*To give a human example, brethren: no one annuls even a man's will,*[g] *or adds to it, once it has been ratified.* [16]*Now the promises were made to Abraham and to his offspring. It does not say, "And to offsprings," referring to many; but, referring to one, "And to your offspring," which is Christ.* [17]*This is what I mean: the law, which came four hundred and thirty years afterward, does not annul a covenant previously ratified by God, so as to make the promise void.* [18]*For if the inheritance is by the law,*

it is no longer by promise; but God gave it to Abraham by a promise.

[19]*Why then the law? It was added because of transgressions, till the offspring should come to whom the promise had been made; and it was ordained by angels through an intermediary.* [20]*Now an intermediary implies more than one; but God is one.*

g *Or covenant (as in verse 17)*

OVERVIEW: Using words suited to limited human knowing (JEROME) Paul draws this analogy: Just as no one can change his legal will after his death, that is how unchangeable is God's promise to save by faith (AUGUSTINE). When he says that Christ, not birth, makes people heirs of Abraham (THEODORET), he is true to scriptural usage (JEROME) and includes us in Christ's saving act (THEODORE OF MOPSUESTIA). The law was given to point to the promise (AMBROSIASTER) but cannot overshadow Abraham himself (AUGUSTINE). Showing that the Judaizing position is contradictory (AMBROSIASTER), Paul replies to defenders of the law (THEODORET), asserting that it came either to prevent transgressions or to multiply them (JEROME, AUGUSTINE). It was given by God through angels, like most ancient revelation (AMBROSIASTER, NESTORIUS), and mediated by Moses (THEODORET), looking toward Christ (AUGUSTINE). Christ himself is the mediator of God's unity (PSEUDO-AUGUSTINE). He thus unites the nations (AMBROSIASTER).

3:15a A Human Example

THE GALATIANS NOT YET READY FOR SOLID FOOD. JEROME: The apostle, who was *made all things to all men*[1] . . . is also made a fool for the Galatians, whom he a little while be-fore called fools. For he does not employ the arguments that he used with the Romans but simpler ones and such as the stupid could understand. . . . [He means,] "What I am about to say I say not according to God. I do not speak with regard to the deepest wisdom and those who can eat solid food[2] but with regard to those who feed on milk because of the tenderness of their stomachs." EPISTLE TO THE GALATIANS 2.3.15 SEQ.[3]

3:15b The Analogy of a Will

HOW UNCHANGEABLE IS GOD'S PROMISE TO SAVE BY FAITH. AUGUSTINE: The value that a testator's death has for confirming his testament is final, since he cannot then change his mind. This is the value that the immutability of God's promise has in confirming the inheritance of Abraham, whose faith was reckoned for righteousness. EPISTLE TO THE GALATIANS 23 [IB.3.15-18].[4]

3:16a Promises to Abraham and His Offspring

---

[1]1 Cor 9:22. [2]1 Cor 3:2. [3]Migne PL 26:364B [438-39]. [4]Migne PL 35:2121. Just as no one can change a legal will after his or her death, so unchangeable is God's promise to save by faith.

THE OFFSPRING OF ABRAHAM. THEODORET: The promise made to Abraham is called a testament[5] in the ancient Scripture and so cannot suffer addition, subtraction or dissolution through the imposition of the Mosaic law, which was given a very long time after Abraham. Now the promise was that the God of all would bless the nations through the offspring of Abraham. And this offspring is Christ the Lord, since the promise found its destination in him through whom the nations received a blessing. But all the others, such as Moses, Samuel, Elijah and in a word all who traced their descent from Israel, were called his offspring according to nature, but [this genetic fact] is not what brought the fount of blessings to the nations. . . . The fact that those men too trace their race to Abraham does not mean that they are rightly called his offspring, but this man has that appellation in the proper sense, as being the only One through whom, according to the promise, God has bestowed blessing on the nations. EPISTLE TO THE GALATIANS 3.16-17.[6]

3:16b *One Offspring, Not Many*

SIMPLICITY IN ARGUMENT. JEROME: Passing my eyes and memory over all the Scriptures, I nowhere find *offsprings* written in the plural but everywhere the singular, whether in a good sense or a bad. . . . If anyone carefully collates the Hebrew Scriptures with the [Greek version of the] Seventy, he will find that where *testament* is written, what is meant is not "testament" but "covenant." . . . Whence it is clear that the apostle has done as he promised, not using deeper meanings but everyday ones, and even trivial ones which (if he had not said beforehand I

speak humanly) might have displeased the intelligent. EPISTLE TO THE GALATIANS 2.3.15 SEQ.[7]

3:16c *The One Offspring Is Christ*

WHETHER CHRIST IS THE SOLE RECIPIENT OF THE PROMISE. THEODORE OF MOPSUESTIA: The words *and to his offspring* are found to be strictly fulfilled in Christ in their straightforward sense, since he is Abraham's offspring by nature, as are all those who derive their stock from that source. We, believing in him, are therefore enrolled as children of Abraham and thereby receive fellowship in the blessing. The result is that what appears to be said to one can in fact be understood commonly of many, insofar as all who derive from that source are of Abraham. This promise is completely fulfilled in Christ in the light of the actual events. EPISTLE TO THE GALATIANS.[8]

3:17a *The Law Given After the Promise*

GIVEN SUBSEQUENTLY, THE LAW DOES NOT COMPETE WITH THE PROMISE. AMBROSIASTER: Once the promise had been established, the law was given subsequently, not so that it could undermine the promise but so that it might point to what was to be fulfilled and when it would come. EPISTLE TO THE GALATIANS 3.17.[9]

3:17b *The Law Does Not Annul the Promise*

---

[5]Analogous to a legal will, which cannot be arbitrarily changed. [6]CPE 1:346. [7]Migne PL 26:364C-365A [439]. [8]CGPEP 6:54-55. [9]CSEL 81.3:37.

THE COVENANT NOT ANNULLED WITH ABRA-HAM, FOR WHOM BOTH COMINGS WERE FUTURE EVENTS. AUGUSTINE: If the law justifies, Abraham was not justified, since he lived long before the law. Since they cannot say this, they are forced to admit that a man is justified not by works of the law but by faith. And he compels us to understand that all the ancients who were justified were justified from the same faith. For as we are saved by believing partly in a past event, that is, the first coming of the Lord, and partly in a future one, that is, his second coming, they believed the whole of it, that is, both comings as events. The Holy Spirit reveals this for their salvation. EPISTLE TO THE GALATIANS 23 [1B.3.15-18].[10]

3:18 Inheritance by Faith, Not Law

HEIRS OF THE PROMISE MADE CHILDREN BY FAITH. AMBROSIASTER: The Jews maintain two opposing tenets. For in no way and by no argument can they be persuaded that the promise to Abraham was rendered void by the law, and they are right. But in their short-sighted vanity they maintain another contrary principle, thinking that justification could not come without the practice of the law. They know that Abraham, who is the type [of justification], was justified through faith alone, without the practice of the law. . . . The heirs to the promise of Abraham are therefore those who are his successors in the adoption of the faith by which Abraham was blessed and justified. The testimony of the promise to Abraham is therefore called a covenant [to signify] that after his death there would be heirs in the promise, made sons of Abraham through faith. EPISTLE TO THE GALATIANS 3.18.1-3.[11]

3:19a Why the Law?

THE LAW AS TUTOR. THEODORET: This question should be read as a personification. "What you want to know," he says, "is why the law was imposed. I shall tell you. . . . It was imposed for the tutelage of the race from which that offspring was going to sprout according to the flesh." EPISTLE TO THE GALATIANS 3.19.[12]

3:19b The Law Added Because of Transgressions

AFTER IDOLATRY CAME THE LAW TO FORBID TRANSGRESSIONS. JEROME: It was after the offense of the people in the wilderness, after the adoration of the calf and their murmurings against God, that the law came to forbid transgressions.[13] EPISTLE TO THE GALATIANS 2.3.19-20.[14]

NONE BUT THE HUMBLE ARE READY FOR GRACE. AUGUSTINE: Here arises a rather pertinent question: if faith justifies and even the former saints, who were justified before God, were justified through it, what need was there for the law to be given? . . . The law was given to a proud people, but the grace of love cannot be received by any but the humble. Without this grace the precepts of the law cannot possibly be fulfilled. Israel was rendered humble by transgression, so that it might seek grace and might not arro-

---

[10]Migne PL 35:2121. Abraham, who was promised to be a blessing to the Gentiles, lived before the announcement of the law of Moses. Once ratified, that covenant with Abraham is not annulled. Both the coming of Christ and his future judgment were foreseen and received through faith by Abraham. [11]CSEL 81.3:37. [12]CPE 1:347. [13]See Ex 32. [14]Migne PL 26:366A [440].

gantly suppose itself to be saved by its own merits; and so it would be righteous, not in its own power and might but by the hand of the Mediator who justifies the ungodly. Epistle to the Galatians 24 [ib.3.19-20].[15]

3:19c The Law Given Through an Intermediary

Whether God Gave the Law by Means of the Angels. Nestorius: [It is said that] *God gave the law*[16] and again *by means of angels the Law was given.*[17] They are not lies, nor are they contradictory one to another. It is not that he calls the angels God or that an angel calls himself God. But because he appeared by means of the angels, both are truly said. The Bazaar of Heracleides 56.[18]

Ordained by Angels. Ambrosiaster: By *angels* he means God's messengers—that is, Moses, [Joshua] son of Nun and the other prophets up to John the Baptist.[19] . . . Through these, therefore, the Law and Prophets are ordained and disposed by God in the hand, that is, the power, of the Savior. For he is the Mediator, the reconciler of God and humanity, so that he may save whom he will out of those who have received the law from the angels. Epistle to the Galatians 3.19.1-2.[20]

An Angel Sent to Moses. Theodoret: It was imposed through the ministry of angels, and Moses assisted in this imposition. For Moses is the one that is called an intermediary.[21] . . . For the God of all set Michael over them, as taught by the blessed Daniel.[22] And to the great Moses he promised to send with him an angel to the people.[23] Epistle to the Galatians 3.19.[24]

God the Spirit Worked Through Angels Prior to the Incarnation. Augustine: Now every dispensation of the Old Testament was given through angels, the Holy Spirit working in them and in the very Word of truth, though not yet incarnate, yet never departing from some true ordering of providence. This law was given through angels, sometimes acting in their own person, sometimes in that of God, as was also the way of the prophets. . . . The children [of Abraham] were put in the hand of [Christ] the Mediator so that he himself might liberate them from sin when they were forced by their transgression of the law to admit that they needed grace and mercy from the Lord. Epistle to the Galatians 24 [ib.3.19-20].[25]

3:20 An Intermediary

The Reconciler of Nations. Ambrosiaster: Without doubt, a mediator, that is, arbiter, is not of one but two. For when two peoples[26] were contending against one another, always at odds and enemies because of the disparity in their doctrines, the Savior came as their Mediator, taking from each people the cause of discord so that they might be at peace. So he took from the Gentiles the plurality of gods and cult of the elements, and he took from the Jews the works of the law, that is, new moons, circumcision,

---

[15]Migne PL 35:2121-22. [16]Ex 31:18. [17]Cf. Acts 7:53. [18]BH 53. [19]Here he cites Malachi 3:1. The prophetic tradition from Moses to John the Baptist mediated the requirement of God for Israel through developing historical circumstances. [20]CSEL 81.3:38. [21]Here Theodoret cites Hebrews 2:2. [22]Dan 10:21. [23]Ex 32:34. [24]CPE 1:347. [25]Migne PL 35:2123; cf. Pamphilus *Apology for Origen* [Migne PG 17:589-90]. [26]Jews and Gentiles.

the keeping of the sabbath, the distinction of foods and other things that the Gentiles abhorred. And thus those who were formerly enemies came to be at peace. If then this is the case, how could the Galatians be so dullwitted as to violate this reconciliation by conversion back to Judaism? EPISTLE TO THE GALATIANS 3.20.1-2.[27]

MOSES AS MEDIATOR. THEODORET: For [Moses] mediated between God and the people. But God is the one who both gave the promise to Abraham and imposed the law, and he has shown us the destination of the promise. For it was not one God who dispensed the former and another who dispensed the latter. EPISTLE TO THE GALATIANS 3.20.[28]

CHRIST AS MEDIATOR. PSEUDO-AUGUSTINE: Because this situation had made the Galatians turn to the law, so as to confess one God without the mystery, as if it were inimical to the law for Christ to be called God, he says: "An arbiter (that is, a mediator) is not of one but of course of two. You however, having turned to the law, have rejected the arbiter. God, however, is one." By saying this he bears witness that he is not preaching Christ in such a way as to make him another God or confess two but that there is one God, as the law itself attests. QUESTIONS ON THE NEW TESTAMENT, APPENDIX 80.2.[29]

---

[27]CSEL 81.3:38-39. [28]CPE 1:347. [29]CSEL 50:474.

3:21-29 RESTRAINED BY LAW UNTIL FAITH WAS REVEALED

[21]*Is the law then against the promises of God? Certainly not; for if a law had been given which could make alive, then righteousness would indeed be by the law.* [22]*But the scripture consigned all things to sin, that what was promised to faith in Jesus Christ might be given to those who believe.*

[23]*Now before faith came, we were confined under the law, kept under restraint until faith should be revealed.* [24]*So that the law was our custodian until Christ came, that we might be justified by faith.* [25]*But now that faith has come, we are no longer under a custodian;* [26]*for in Christ Jesus you are all sons of God, through faith.* [27]*For as many of you as were baptized into Christ have put on Christ.* [28]*There is neither Jew nor Greek, there is neither slave nor free, there is neither male nor female; for you are all one in Christ Jesus.* [29]*And if you are Christ's, then you are Abraham's offspring, heirs according to promise.*

OVERVIEW: The law cannot contradict the Lawgiver's promises (MARIUS VICTORINUS). The law prepared us for faith (THEODORET). It provoked sin to make us humble (AUGUSTINE). Only grace can apply the remedy (FULGENTIUS). God supersedes the law. No law gives life (MARIUS VICTORINUS). When the fulfillment of the law appeared in Christ's own person (MARIUS VICTORINUS), the law had no remaining function (CHRYSOSTOM). We are made perfect as children of God (THEODORET) when we assume his form through faith in baptism (CHRYSOSTOM). This excludes unbelievers but unites us in the Spirit (JEROME). Indeed we are all one body (CHRYSOSTOM), though potentially rather than actually at present (AUGUSTINE). Nonetheless we are already Abraham's heirs in spirit, as Christ was in nature (JEROME).

3:21a *The Law and God's Promises*

THE LAW CANNOT STAND AGAINST GOD'S OWN PROMISES. MARIUS VICTORINUS: Since God gave the law, it is not plausible that that same law should be seen as having been given against the promises. It is certainly against the promises if it embroils us in other things, namely, that we should fulfill the works required by the law and not expect from faith what is promised, that we should obtain through faith an inheritance in God. But let us see what is his answer to this. He first denies it unequivocally: *Certainly not!* That is, it is not right that God should make the giving of the law contrary to the promises. . . . And next he adds the reason. EPISTLE TO THE GALATIANS 2.3.21.[1]

3:21b *The Law and Life*

THE LAW CANNOT GIVE LIFE. MARIUS VICTORINUS: We have said that the law given by Moses teaches nothing but sins, admonishing us what sins are and how they are to be avoided. And Scripture draws no other conclusion but lays down all its precepts in the light of and with reference to sin. . . . It is not given so that life may be sought from it but is given so that by its written form it may both include all sins in its teaching and show that they should be avoided. Therefore righteousness is not from the law; that is, justification and salvation come not from the law but from faith, as is promised. EPISTLE TO THE GALATIANS 2.3.21.[2]

3:22a *Scripture Consigned All Things to Sin*

PRIDE BOUND UNDER SIN. AUGUSTINE: For those who are proud it is useful to be more closely bound under sin, so that they would not presume on free will for the performance of righteousness, as though upon their own strength. ON THE GRACE OF CHRIST 9.[3]

BREAKING PRIDE. AUGUSTINE: Transgression of the law was needed to break the pride of those who, glorying in their father Abraham, boasted of having a sort of natural righteousness. They caused more harm to the Gentiles the more arrogantly they flaunted the merits of their circumcision. But the Gentiles could be humiliated very easily even without transgression of this sort of law, for the grace of the gospel found that these men, who knew that they had received

---

[1]BT 1972:36 [1171C-D]. [2]BT 1972:36-37 [1172A]. [3]Migne PL 44:365.

no root of wisdom from their parents, were actually slaves to idols. . . . The law was therefore given not to take away sin but to include all under sin. For the law showed that to be sin which the Jews in their blindness deemed to be righteousness, so that by this humiliation they might know that their salvation was not in their own hands but in the hand of a mediator. . . . This very humility was fitted to the recognition of Christ, who is the paradigm of humility. EPISTLE TO THE GALATIANS 25 [IB.3.21-22].[4]

3:22b The Interplay of Law and Grace

THE DISEASE EXPOSED WITHOUT REMEDY. FULGENTIUS: Law without grace, then, can expose disease but cannot heal. It can reveal the wounds but does not administer the remedy. But so that the law's precepts may be fulfilled, grace provides assistance within. ON THE TRUTH OF PREDESTINATION 1.41.[5]

3:23a Confined Under the Law

THE LAW AS A TUTOR LOOKED FORWARD TOWARD FAITH. MARIUS VICTORINUS: The law was not empty or against the promises. How does he say it was necessary? Because it looked forward to the faith that was to be, and the promise came through faith. "First," he says, "before the law came we were under a tutor; that is, under the law as a sort of custodian and guardian we lived a life that was pure through the avoidance of and repentance for sins, so that when Christ came we, being as it were confined for the purpose of that faith which was to come, should expect his coming; and being prepared through the law, should have faith in him; and, as we avoided sin

and did the works of the law, should easily be able to have what was promised from his advent, namely, faith in Christ." EPISTLE TO THE GALATIANS 2.3.23.[6]

3:23b Restrained Until Faith Is Revealed

THE DOCTOR DESIRED MORE URGENTLY. AUGUSTINE: No person should be unwise enough to say here, "Why then was it no profit to the Jews that they were put in the hand of a Mediator through angels dispensing the law?" It was profitable to them beyond what can be expressed. For what churches of the Gentiles sold their possessions and put the price of them at the apostles' feet, which so many thousands of people so quickly did?[7] . . . And when he praises the church of the Thessalonians before all other churches, he says that they have become like the churches of the Jews, because they had suffered many things from their people on account of their faith, as the others had from the Jews.[8] . . . And the consciousness of a greater sickness, that they were found to be transgressors of the law itself, worked not to the ruin but to the good of those who believed, causing them to desire more fervently a doctor and to love him with more ardor. EPISTLE TO THE GALATIANS 26 [IB.3.23].[9]

3:24a The Law Was Our Custodian

THE PURPOSE OF A CUSTODIAN IS TEMPORARY. JEROME: A custodian is given to infants to rein in an age full of passion and to

---

[4]Migne PL 35:2123-24. [5]CCL 91A:485 [980-83]. [6]BT 1972:37 [1172B-C]. [7]See Acts 4:34-35. [8]1 Thess 2:14-16. [9]Migne PL 35:2124.

restrain hearts prone to vice until tender infancy is refined by growth. . . . Yet the teacher is not a father, nor does the one being instructed look for the custodian's inheritance. The custodian guards another person's son and will depart from him when the lawful time of inheritance arrives. EPISTLE TO THE GALATIANS 2.3.24 SEQ.[10]

3:24b *Justified by Faith*

WHY THE LAW WAS GIVEN. THEODORET: Now it was necessary that the law be given, as it fulfilled our need of a custodian. And it freed us from our previous impiety, taught us knowledge of God and then brought us to Christ the Lord as though to some wise teacher, so that we might be instructed by him in perfect learning and acquire the righteousness that is through faith. EPISTLE TO THE GALATIANS 3.24.[11]

3:25 *Faith Has Come; There Is No Custodian*

HOW FAITH HAS NOW COME. MARIUS VICTORINUS: "That faith has come" means that Christ himself has come—for then faith arose. There began to be a time for faith to fully come and for us to believe in him in whom is all salvation, in contrast to the Jews, who did not believe [in him]. EPISTLE TO THE GALATIANS 2.3.25-26.[12]

THE TIME OF THE CUSTODIAN LIMITED. CHRYSOSTOM: Now if the law was a custodian and we were confined under its direction, it was not opposed to grace but cooperated with it. But if it continues to bind us after grace has come, then it is opposed to grace. . . . Those who maintain

their custody at this point are the ones who bring the child into the greatest disrepute. The custodian makes the child ridiculous when he keeps him close at hand even after the time has come for his departure. HOMILY ON GALATIANS 3.25-26.[13]

3:26 *Chidren of God Through Faith*

HOW THE FAITHFUL INHERIT ETERNAL LIFE. MARIUS VICTORINUS: The metaphor of *inheritance* refers to receiving eternal life. But how does this come about? By faith in Jesus Christ, when we believe in him, that he is the Son of God and that he himself saves us and that he has accomplished every mystery on our behalf. All these things are reported in the gospel. But what should be noticed here is that, while Paul is stating this fact, he addresses it to their persons, offering incentives to persuade them more readily. "You all," he says, "are sons of God." Before, he had said, "We are under a custodian." Now as it were he names them anew, saying "You are sons of God"—but sons from faith in Christ Jesus. EPISTLE TO THE GALATIANS 2.3.25-26.[14]

THE PERFECTION OF BELIEVERS IS BY FAITH ALONE. THEODORET: He has illustrated the perfection of believers. For what is more perfect than to be called sons of God? EPISTLE TO THE GALATIANS 3.26.[15]

3:27 *Baptized into Christ*

HOW ONE IS MADE A SON IN BAPTISM.

---

[10]Migne PL 26:368A-B [443]. [11]CPE 1:348-49. [12]BT 1972:38 [1172D-1173A]. [13]IOEP 4:64. [14]BT 1972:38 [1173A]. [15]CPE 1:349.

CHRYSOSTOM: Since he has said something great and remarkable, he also explains how one is made a son. *For as many of you as were baptized into Christ have put on Christ.* Why didn't he say, "All you who were baptized into Christ have been born of God," since that is the inference from showing that they were sons? Because what he says is more awe-inspiring. For if Christ is the Son of God and you put him on, having the Son inside yourself and being made like him, you have been made one in kind and form. HOMILY ON GALATIANS 3.27.[16]

SPIRITUALLY TRANSFORMED INTO A NEW PERSON. CYPRIAN: One who, having laid bare his sins, has been sanctified by baptism and spiritually transformed into a new man has been made ready to receive the Holy Spirit. The apostle says that all you who have been baptized in Christ have put on Christ. LETTER 74.5.3.[17]

3:28 All Are One in Christ Jesus

THE ANALOGY OF GLOWING WITH THE SPIRIT, WHERE ALL DISTINCTIONS DISAPPEAR. JEROME: When one has once put on Christ and, having been sent into the flame, glows with the ardor of the Holy Spirit, it is not apparent whether he is of gold or silver. As long as the heat takes over the mass in this way there is one fiery color, and all diversity of race, condition and body is taken away by such a garment. EPISTLE TO THE GALATIANS 2.3.27-28.[18]

ONENESS IN CHRIST. CHRYSOSTOM: Do you see how insatiable his soul is? For having said that we have become sons of God

through faith, he does not stop here but seeks out something more to say, which can make still more plain our closer unity with Christ. And having said, "You have put him on," he is not content with this, but interpreting it he speaks of something more intimate than this association and says, "You are all one in Christ"—that is, you have one form, one character, that of Christ. What words could inspire more awe than these? The former Jew or slave is clothed in the form not of an angel or archangel but of the Lord himself and in himself displays Christ. HOMILY ON GALATIANS 3.28.[19]

ONENESS IN CHRIST IS NOT PERFECTLY DISPLAYED WITHIN THE CONDITIONS OF HISTORY. AUGUSTINE: Difference of race or condition or sex is indeed taken away by the unity of faith, but it remains embedded in our mortal interactions, and in the journey of this life the apostles themselves teach that it is to be respected. . . . For we observe in the unity of faith that there are no such distinctions. Yet within the orders of this life they persist. So we walk this path in a way that the name and doctrine of God will not be blasphemed. It is not out of fear or anger that we wish to avoid offense to others but also on account of conscience, so that we may do these things not in mere profession, as if for the eyes of men, but with a pure love toward God. EPISTLE TO THE GALATIANS IB.3.28-29.[20]

3:29 Heirs According to the Promise

---

[16]IOEP 4:65. [17]CCL 3C:570. [18]Migne PL 26:369B [445]. [19]IOEP 4:65-66. [20]Migne PL 35:2125.

DISTINGUISHING THE BODILY AND SPIRITUAL SENSES OF "ABRAHAM'S OFFSPRING." JEROME: Whenever our Lord Jesus Christ is called Abraham's offspring, this must be understood in the bodily sense of his generation from the stock of Abraham. But when it is applied to us who, receiving the Savior's word, believe in him and assume the dignity of Abraham's race, to whom the promise was made, then we should understand the offspring spiritually, as that of faith and preaching. . . . We must also note that, when the Lord is spoken of, Paul mentions *promises* in the plural—the promises are made to Abraham and his offspring—but when he speaks of those who through Jesus Christ are the offspring of Abraham, *the promise* is referred to in the singular, as in the present passage. EPISTLE TO THE GALATIANS 2.3.29.[21]

---

[21] Migne PL 26:369D-370A [445-46].

4:1-7 INHERITANCE THROUGH CHRIST

[1] *I mean that the heir, as long as he is a child, is no better than a slave, though he is the owner of all the estate;* [2] *but he is under guardians and trustees until the date set by the father.* [3] *So with us; when we were children, we were slaves to the elemental spirits of the universe.* [4] *But when the time had fully come, God sent forth his Son, born of woman, born under the law,* [5] *to redeem those who were under the law, so that we might receive adoption as sons.* [6] *And because you are sons, God has sent the Spirit of his Son into our hearts, crying, "Abba! Father!"* [7] *So through God you are no longer a slave but a son, and if a son then an heir.*

OVERVIEW: All humans have become enslaved to death and sin in Adam, under the custody of prophets and princes (JEROME). They all serve the natural elements (MARIUS VICTORINUS, AUGUSTINE), the Jews having their own special days (AMBROSIASTER), while the Gentiles worship the heavenly bodies (JEROME). God was waiting for a time to redeem us (AMBROSIASTER) through his Son, the Lord of times (MARIUS VICTORINUS). He was God's unique Son (AMBROSE), who became incarnate to do his Father's bidding (THEODORET). He was born of a virgin (TERTULLIAN), without the usual human agency (PSEUDO-AUGUSTINE), yet he was true man as he was true God (LEO THE GREAT), becoming human to confer his likeness on us and teaching us to be free of the law (MARIUS VICTORINUS). The Jews, who served without hope, were promised redemption (MARIUS VICTORINUS) but were not the sole beneficiaries (JEROME). Through the Son we receive adoptive sonship (AUGUSTINE), Jew and Gentile alike

(AMBROSIASTER), because of the joint operation of the Trinity (MARIUS VICTORINUS). The cry of "Abba!" unites Jew and Gentile (AUGUSTINE), for the whole human race has obtained the inheritance (JEROME), not by the death but by the eternal life of the Father (AMBROSIASTER).

4:1 The Status of the Heir

THE OWNER OF THE ESTATE AS SLAVE. JEROME: The infant heir . . . signifies the whole human race up to the advent of Christ, and, to speak more largely, right up to the end of the world. For, just as all die in Adam the first man, though they are not yet born, so all those who were born before Christ's advent are now made alive in the second Adam. And so it is that we served the law in the fathers and are saved by grace in the sons. This understanding fits the catholic church, which asserts a single providence in the Old and New Testaments and does not distinguish in time those whom it makes equal in condition. EPISTLE TO THE GALATIANS 2.4.1-2.[1]

4:2 Under Guardians and Trustees

THE AGE OF INFANCY. JEROME: *Guardians and trustees* could be taken as the prophets, by whose words we were made ready, day by day, for the coming of the Savior, just as the law of Moses is described above as a custodian. . . . Or the phrase could be taken to refer to priests and princes, who then held power over the people and are now a reflection of God's purpose. People are correctly said to live under tutors and overseers when, having the spirit of fear, they have not yet deserved to receive the spirit of freedom and

adoption. For the age of infancy feels dread in relation to sin, fears its custodian and does not believe in its own freedom, even if it is sovereign by nature. EPISTLE TO THE GALATIANS 4.1-2.[2]

4:3 Slaves to the Elemental Spirits of the Universe

ALL HUMANITY IN ITS INFANCY SERVED THE NATURAL ELEMENTS. MARIUS VICTORINUS: The elements of the world were thought to have in themselves at the same time their own motions and, as it were, certain necessary consequences of the motion of other beings, such as stars, by whose revolution human life was brought under necessity. And so humans served the elements as the stars ordained and the course of the world required. EPISTLE TO THE GALATIANS 2.4.3-4.[3]

SERVING NEW MOONS BEFORE THE PROMISE FULFILLED. AMBROSIASTER: By the *elements* he means new moons and the sabbath. New moons are the lunar days that the Jews observe, while the sabbath is the day of rest. Therefore, before the promise came (that is, the gift of God's grace) and justified believers by purifying them, we were subject, like those who are infants and imperfect, to our fellow servants as though to custodians. Our pernicious freedom was the matrix of sin. EPISTLE TO THE GALATIANS 4.3.[4]

---

[1]Migne PL 26:370A-B [446]. The analogy is intricate: A single providence embraces all who have already died in Adam though they are not yet born and all born before the Redeemer who are now made alive, including all of the Old and of the New Covenant. [2]Migne PL 26:370C-D [446-47]. [3]BT 1972:41 [1175A-B]. [4]CSEL 81.3:43. Cf. Theodoret *Epistle to the Galatians* 4.3 [CPE 1:350].

POSSIBLE VIEWS OF THESE ELEMENTS.
JEROME: He has used the name *elements of the world* for those whom he called tutors and overseers above.... Some hold that these are angels that preside over the four elements.[5] ... Many think that it is the heaven and earth with their inhabitants that are called the elements of the world, because the wise Greeks, the barbarians and the Romans, the dregs of all superstition, venerate the sun, the moon, ... from which we are liberated by Christ's coming, knowing them to be creatures and not divinities. Others interpret the elements of the world as the law of Moses and the utterances of the prophets, because, commencing and setting out with these letters, we imbibe the fear of God, which is the beginning of wisdom.... The Mosaic law and the prophets can be taken as the elements of writing, because through them syllables and names are put together, and they are learned not so much for their own sake as for their usefulness to others.
... Regarding our interpretation of the law and the prophets as the elements of the world, "world" is customarily taken to signify those who are in the world. EPISTLE TO THE GALATIANS 2.4.3.[6]

PAUL INCLUDES HIMSELF IN THIS SCENARIO OF SUBJECTION. AUGUSTINE: Why does Paul include his own character in this description? He says not "When you were small, you were subject to the elements of this world" but *When we were small we were in servitude under the elements of this world*. This does not have any reference to the Jews, from whom Paul derived his origin. Rather it refers to his identification with the Gentiles in this place at least, since he can properly join himself with the character of

those whom he was sent to evangelize. EPISTLE TO THE GALATIANS 29 [IB.4.1-3].[7]

4:4a *In the Fullness of Time, God Sent His Son*

RIPENESS FOR FAITH IN THE FULLNESS OF TIME. MARIUS VICTORINUS: As there is a fullness in things, so there is in times. For each thing has its fullness in a full and copious perfection that abounds in everything. Christ is the fullness of things. The fullness of times is the consummation of freedom. So that his fullness may be whole and perfect Christ collects his members who are scattered, and in this way his fullness is achieved. So in the same way the fullness of times was achieved when all had become ripe for faith and sins had increased to the utmost, so that a remedy was necessarily sought in the judgment of all things. Hence Christ came when the fullness of time was completed. EPISTLE TO THE GALATIANS 2.4.3-4.[8]

GOD'S WAY OF ADOPTING SINNERS. AMBROSIASTER: *The fullness of time* is the completed time which had been foreordained by God the Father for the sending of his Son, so that, made from a virgin, he might be born like a man, subjecting himself to the law up to the time of his baptism, so that he might provide a way by which sinners, washed and snatched away from the yoke of the law, might be adopted as God's sons by his condescension, as he had promised to those redeemed by the blood of his Son. It

---

[5]Air, earth, fire and water. [6]Migne PL 26:371A-D [447-48]. [7]Migne PL 35:2126. [8]BT 1972:41-42 [1176A-B].

was necessary, indeed, that the Savior should be made subject to the law, as a son of Abraham according to the flesh, so that, having been circumcised, he could be seen as the one promised to Abraham, who had come to justify the Gentiles through faith, since he bore the sign of the one to whom the promise had been made. EPISTLE TO THE GALATIANS 4.5.1.[9]

NOT ONE OF MANY. AMBROSE: He says *his Son*, not one of many, not "a Son" but his own. When he says *his own* he confirms that he has the property of eternal generation.[10] This is the one whom he subsequently declares to have been born from a woman, so as to ascribe the fact of being born not to the Godhead but to the assumed body. He was made from a woman by assuming flesh and made under the law by observing the law. But that heavenly birth of his is prior to the law, while the incarnation happens later. ON THE FAITH 1.14.[11]

4:4b Born of Woman

THE INCARNATE SENDING. THEODORET: It is right to point out that he has linked the sending of the eternal Son with the incarnation. For he does not say "he sent him to come into being as Godhead from a woman," so that we would misunderstand the sending to be the sending of the Godhead. Instead only the Son, not the Godhead, is born of a woman. Now this is peculiar to the incarnation. EPISTLE TO THE GALATIANS 4.4-5.[12]

WHY MARY IS NOT HERE CALLED A VIRGIN. TERTULLIAN: A certain person thought that he had cleverly solved this question: that

Mary was called a woman by the angel and the apostle because she was already betrothed. For a betrothed is in some sense a bride. Yet between "in some sense" and "truly" there is a great distance. . . . He spoke of one who was a virgin and was called *woman* according to a proper usage of this term with respect to the basic quality of a virgin, which is therefore vindicated by the generic term *woman*. ON THE VEILING OF VIRGINS 6.[13]

NOT FROM HUMAN SEED. PSEUDO-AUGUSTINE: Although in this place the *making* might be understood of his nativity, for there is indeed a distinction between making and generation, . . . the apostle spoke in this way since the flesh of the Lord was not produced from a human seed in the virgin's womb and made into a body but by the efficacy and power of the Holy Spirit. For it is one thing for blood to come together with an admixture of seed and cause birth, another to procreate by divine power. QUESTIONS ON THE NEW TESTAMENT, APPENDIX 50.[14]

WHETHER BIRTH IS COMPATIBLE WITH HIS GODHEAD. LEO THE GREAT: He is God in that *all things were made through him and nothing was made without him*.[15] He is human in that he was *made from a woman, made under the law*. The nativity of his flesh shows his human nature. The virgin birth is an indicator of his divine nature. LETTER 28 TO FLAVIAN 4.[16]

---

[9]CSEL 81.3:43. [10]He is eternally the Son of the Father. As eternal Son he is not a created being. [11]CSEL 78:41. [12]CPE 1:351. [13]CCL 1:1215-16. It is not inconsistent to say Jesus was born of a virgin and thus born of a woman. [14]CSEL 50:444-45. [15]Jn 1:3. [16]TF 210.

4:4c Born Under the Law

THE SON'S SUBJECTION TO THE LAW.
MARIUS VICTORINUS: Because he is brought
forth from a woman he can be said to be
made, but made for this temporary purpose:
to be subject to the law. . . . The Galatians
were to understand from this that they had
fallen into error, for the Savior himself, in
whom they believed, was made subject to
the law though he remained the Lord of the
law. EPISTLE TO THE GALATIANS 2.4.3-4.[17]

4:5a To Redeem Those Under the Law

THE REDEMPTION OF ALL WHO BELIEVE.
MARIUS VICTORINUS: Since the law by its
precepts held people bound, as it were, only
to decency of life but not to the hope of deliverance and eternity, God sent his own
Son. He sent him subject to the law, that is,
the law of Israel, that he might redeem those
who were there and lived under the law.
Now this is a great thing, that he says
[Christ came] not merely to show them the
way of life or to stir them up toward eternity
with harsh commands but to redeem them.
This is the mystery of what he performed,
the redemption of all who believed in him,
that they might become sons by adoption.
When, therefore, such a great benefit came
from Christ, nothing was to be added beside
this. The law was no longer a matter of servitude. EPISTLE TO THE GALATIANS 2.4.5.[18]

**THOSE OUTSIDE AND UNDER THE LAW RE-
DEEMED.** JEROME: Someone might raise the
problem: "If then he was made subject to the
law to redeem those who were subject to the
law . . . if he himself was not made also outside the law, he did not redeem those who

had not been subject to the law." Another,
however, will scrutinize the word *redeemed*
more closely and will say that by the *redeemed* are meant those who were once of
God's party and later ceased to be so,
whereas those who were not subject to the
law were not so much redeemed as purchased. EPISTLE TO THE GALATIANS 2.4.4.[19]

4:5b Receiving Adoption

**OUR SONSHIP BY ADOPTION, HIS BY NA-
TURE.** AUGUSTINE: He says *adoption* so that
we may clearly understand that the Son of
God is unique. For we are sons of God
through his generosity and the condescension of his mercy, whereas he is Son by
nature, sharing the same divinity with the
Father. EPISTLE TO THE GALATIANS 30
[IB.4.4-5].[20]

4:6a Sending the Spirit of His Son

THE WORK OF THE TRIUNE GOD. MARIUS
VICTORINUS: Behold the whole array of
those three powers through one power and
one Godhead. For God, he says, who is the
Father, sent his own Son, who is Christ, and
again Christ, who himself being the power
of God is God, . . . sent the spirit of his Son,
who is the Holy Spirit. EPISTLE TO THE
GALATIANS 2.4.6.[21]

**GENTILES BECOME SONS OF GOD BY THE
SPIRIT.** AMBROSIASTER: He says of the Gentiles who believed in Christ, "You are sons,"
having previously been enemies. There can

---

[17]BT 1972:43-44 [1177B-D]. [18]BT 1972:44 [1178A-B].
[19]Migne PL 26:372C-373A [449-50]. [20]Migne PL 35:2126.
[21]BT 1972:44-45 [1178B-C].

be no doubt that believing Jews were also said to be sons of God, since they had long been called by that name. They had received the name of sons at one time as though by anticipation in order that this sonship might subsequently be understood in Christ, being incomplete without the Spirit. EPISTLE TO THE GALATIANS 4.6.1.[22]

4:6b Crying "Abba! Father!"

WHY BOTH ARAMAIC AND GREEK. AUGUSTINE: There are two words that he has set down so that the former may be interpreted by the latter, for *Abba* means the same as *Father*. Now we see that he has elegantly, and not without reason, put together words from two languages signifying the same thing because of the whole people, which has been called from Jews and Gentiles into the unity of faith. EPISTLE TO THE GALATIANS 31 [IB.4.6].[23]

4:7 No Longer a Slave but an Heir

IF SON, THEN HEIR. AMBROSIASTER: There is no doubt that one adopts a son in order to leave him an heir; but inheritance depends on the death of someone. How then can mortals be called the heirs of him who lives forever? The fact is that Scripture speaks in our own manner so that we may understand. In order to show that the Father will give from his goods those things that he is going to give his sons, it calls this *inheritance*. EPISTLE TO THE GALATIANS 4.7.[24]

ONE IN CHRIST. JEROME: What we say in this place we should also observe in others, that the whole human race is being treated under a single term. For all we who believe are one in Christ Jesus and members of his body. EPISTLE TO THE GALATIANS 2.4.7.[25]

---

[22]CSEL 81.3:44. [23]Migne PL 35:2127. [24]CSEL 81.3:45. [25]Migne PL 26:374D-375A [452].

4:8-20 THE BACKSLIDING OF THE GALATIANS

[8]*Formerly, when you did not know God, you were in bondage to beings that by nature are no gods;* [9]*but now that you have come to know God, or rather to be known by God, how can you turn back again to the weak and beggarly elemental spirits, whose slaves you want to be once more?* [10]*You observe days, and months, and seasons, and years!* [11]*I am afraid I have labored over you in vain.*

[12]*Brethren, I beseech you, become as I am, for I also have become as you are. You did me no wrong;* [13]*you know it was because of a bodily ailment that I preached the gospel to you at first;* [14]*and though my condition was a trial to you, you did not scorn or despise me, but received me as an angel of God, as Christ Jesus.* [15]*What has become*

of the satisfaction you felt? For I bear you witness that, if possible, you would have plucked out your eyes and given them to me. ¹⁶Have I then become your enemy by telling you the truth?ʰ ¹⁷They make much of you, but for no good purpose; they want to shut you out, that you may make much of them. ¹⁸For a good purpose it is always good to be made much of, and not only when I am present with you. ¹⁹My little children, with whom I am again in travail until Christ be formed in you! ²⁰I could wish to be present with you now and to change my tone, for I am perplexed about you.

h *Or by dealing truly with you*

OVERVIEW: The Galatians once did not know God through Christ (MARIUS VICTORINUS) and so were ignorant of the Trinity (AUGUSTINE). Addressing them as Gentiles (AUGUSTINE) Paul reminds them that they have come to knowledge of God only by grace (MARIUS VICTORINUS). Yet they are returning to things that are both unstable and inferior to God (AUGUSTINE), namely, the carnal understanding of the law (MARIUS VICTORINUS), which Christ has superseded (JEROME). Hence they are more culpable than they were in the state of ignorance (CHRYSOSTOM) having adopted obsolete practices of the Jews (MARIUS VICTORINUS, JEROME) and connived with Gentile superstitions (AUGUSTINE). Paul's fears express his compassion (CHRYSOSTOM) and show that the matter is no slight one (AUGUSTINE). Paul remembers how he once preached the most basic elements of the gospel to them (JEROME). He mollifies them by recalling their discipleship (CHRYSOSTOM, JEROME), alluding to his sufferings (JEROME). He exposes the absurdity of their change of mind (CHRYSOSTOM) as he recalls how they once received him (MARIUS VICTORINUS) and laments the incompleteness of his own work (JEROME). Their past relationship proves that he is not their enemy (AMBROSIASTER), even

when he confronts them with the truth (JEROME). Paul speaks like a mother in great solicitude (CHRYSOSTOM, JEROME) as he labors a second time (AUGUSTINE). Christ is formed in us by faith and discipline (CYRIL OF ALEXANDRIA), but slowly as growth occurs (JEROME). Paul longs to express the sadness that a letter cannot convey (CHRYSOSTOM), to impress his teaching upon them and to articulate his perplexed feelings (JEROME). The false teachers envy the faith of the Galatians (THEODORET) and wish to stir up divisions (MARIUS VICTORINUS). Falsehood has taken advantage of the teacher's absence (CHRYSOSTOM), as laxity does today (JEROME).

4:8 In Bondage Through Ignorance of God

WHEN THEY DID NOT KNOW GOD. MARIUS VICTORINUS: Not to know God is not to know Christ, for God is known through Christ. But now, since Christ has appeared, who has taught me and has revealed God through himself—both himself as God and the Father through himself—it is no longer permitted not to know God. EPISTLE TO THE GALATIANS 2.4.8.[1]

---

[1]BT 1972:46 [1179C].

IN BONDAGE TO BEINGS THAT ARE NO GODS. AUGUSTINE: *When*, however, he says, *you were in servitude to those who are by nature no gods*, he sufficiently proves that one true God is God by nature, by whose name the triune God is received in the most faithful and catholic bosom of the heart. *Those who are by nature no gods* are described by him as governors and overseers. There is no creature, whether it abides in truth by giving glory to God or fails to abide in truth by seeking its own glory—there is, I say, no creature that does not willy-nilly serve divine providence. . . . But, just as the magistrate under the imperial law does nothing but what is permitted to him, so the governors and overseers of this world do nothing but whatever God allows. EPISTLE TO THE GALATIANS 32 [IB.4.7-8].[2]

4:9a *Knowing God, Being Known by God*

THOSE WHO KNOW GOD ARE THOSE KNOWN BY GOD. MARIUS VICTORINUS: He preserves the essence of his own teaching, that those who come to Christ are the ones whom God sends and God calls, and those who know God are the ones that God knows. . . . For those who are known of God receive the Spirit by which they know God. EPISTLE TO THE GALATIANS 2.4.9.[3]

REVERSION TO BEGGARLY ELEMENTS. AUGUSTINE: What follows, as it were, reintroduces a question that has already been explored. Through the whole letter he has shown that no one has disturbed the faith of the Galatians except those who were of the circumcision, who wished to lead them into carnal[4] observations of the law as though sal-

vation were in them. In this place alone he seems to speak to those who were attempting to return to Gentile superstitions. . . . For in saying *you have reverted*, since he is speaking not to the circumcised but to Gentiles, as appears in the whole letter, he does not say at all that they have reverted to circumcision, in which they had never been, but he says *to the weak and beggarly elements*, which you wish to serve again as before. EPISTLE TO THE GALATIANS 33 [IB.4.9].[5]

4:9b *Turning Back to the Elemental Spirits*

MAKING GODS FROM THE ELEMENTS. MARIUS VICTORINUS: When he introduces the *beggarly elements of this world*, this seems rather to concern the pagans, who make gods for themselves even from the elements of this world. . . . Since, however, the whole of his discourse and the whole of this treatise were undertaken to reprimand the Galatians for their conversion to Judaism, and all these things are to be understood of the Jews, how do we understand *you are turned again to the weak?* When therefore he says *the beggarly elements of this world*, he means those who, understanding the law carnally,[6] have clung to the contingent elements of this world. For the flesh is always hungering. It yearns for the sustenance of food and drink and objects of desire, all of which, however, are weak. EPISTLE TO THE GALATIANS 2.4.9.[7]

---

[2]Migne PL 35:2128. [3]BT 1972:48 [1180C-D]. Note the sequence: to know God is to be known by God. To be known by God is receive the Spirit by which God becomes known. [4]According to an orientation toward the flesh rather than the Spirit. [5]Migne PL 35:2129. [6]In a way that reduces all matters of importance to the natural, the fleshly. [7]BT 1972:47 [1180A-C].

THE LAW AN INFANCY OF WEAKNESS.
JEROME: Now these same elements that he has now styled *weak and beggarly* he called above merely the *elements of the world*.... And so I think that so long as someone is an infant ... he is subject to the elements, namely, the law of Moses. But when after [receiving] the freedom due to an heir he reverts again to the law, desiring to be circumcised and to follow the whole letter of Jewish legal illusions, then those things that were merely the elements of the world to him before are now said to be *weak and beggarly elements*.... The law of Moses, which before was rich, affluent and illustrious, became after Christ's advent and in comparison with him *weak and beggarly*.... The *weak and beggarly elements* are those unworthy traditions of the Jews, which interpret according to the letter. They were poor excuses for interpretations and *commandments that were not good*.[8] EPISTLE TO THE GALATIANS 2.4.8-9.[9]

4:9c Reverting to Slavery

HARSHER DISCIPLINE DUE TO THOSE WHO STILL HUNGER FOR SLAVERY. CHRYSOSTOM: What he is saying is something like this: "When you were in darkness and lived in error you were in an abject condition. But now, when you have known God or rather been known by him, how can you not bring on yourselves a greater and harsher punishment, when you suffer the same disease after so much therapy?" HOMILY ON GALATIANS 4.8.[10]

4:10 Observing Days and Seasons

OBSERVING OBSOLETE SEASONS. MARIUS

VICTORINUS: So that he may be seen to say this to Jews and about Jews—that is, to the Galatians, who combine the Jews' way of life with theirs—he adds, *You observe days and months and seasons and years*.... For it is one thing to observe days, as for example to rest on the sabbath, another to observe months, as for example to observe new moons, ... another to observe years, another again [to observe] seasons such as fasting, the Passover, the feast of unleavened bread and other things of this kind. EPISTLE TO THE GALATIANS 2.4.9-10.[11]

SEASONAL SUPERSTITIONS. AMBROSIASTER: The observers of days are those who say, for example, "Tomorrow there must be no setting out on a journey." ... The observers of months are those who watch the course of the moon, saying, for example, "Contracts must not be sealed in the seventh month." ... Seasons are observed when people say, "Today is the first day of spring, it is a festival and after tomorrow is the feast of Vulcan." ... People pay respect to the year when they say, "The first day of January is the new year," as though a year were not completed every day.... For if God is loved with the whole heart, there ought not to be any dread or suspicion of these phenomena so long as he is near. EPISTLE TO THE GALATIANS 4.10.1-2.[12]

THE YEARS IN JUDAISM. JEROME: By *years* I think he means the seventh year of release, and the fiftieth, which they call the jubilee.[13] EPISTLE TO THE GALATIANS 2.4.10-11.[14]

---

[8]Ezek 20:25. [9]Migne PL 26:375B-C [453]. [10]IOEP 4:67. [11]BT 1972:48 [1181A-B]. [12]CSEL 81.3:46. [13]Lev 25. [14]Migne PL 26:377C [456].

4:11 *Fear of Laboring in Vain*

PAUL'S FEAR FOR THEM. CHRYSOSTOM: Do you see the compassion of the apostle? They were being corrupted. He trembles and fears. Therefore he expresses this in a very solicitous manner, saying "I labored for you," as if to say, "Do not render such strenuous toils ineffectual for me." In saying *I fear* . . . he has both stirred them up for a contest and directed them toward better hopes. HOMILY ON GALATIANS 4.8.[15]

SUPERSTITIOUS OBSERVANCES IMPERIL THE LABOR FOR THE GOSPEL. AUGUSTINE: So, let the reader choose whichever interpretation he wishes,[16] so long as he understands that such superstitious observances of times bring great peril to the soul, so much so that the apostle adds, "I am afraid, *lest perhaps I should have labored in you in vain*." . . . And yet if someone, even a catechumen,[17] is caught observing the sabbath by the Jewish rite, the church is confused. As it is, innumerable members of the church say with great complacency in open view of us, "I do not travel on the day after the first." . . . Alas for human sinfulness, that we only denounce what is unfamiliar, but with familiar things we tolerate them, although they may be great and cause the kingdom of heaven to be shut against them absolutely. It is for them that the Son of God shed his blood. We come to tolerate them through frequent acquaintance with them, and through increased toleration we share in them. EPISTLE TO THE GALATIANS 35 [IB.4.10-11].[18]

4:12a *The Apostle's Plea*

BECOME AS I AM. CHRYSOSTOM: He is saying this to those of a Jewish background, and so he brings himself to the fore, persuading them on this ground also to depart from the ancient ways. "For if you have no one else as a paradigm, it is enough simply to look at me as an instance of this change, and you will easily be encouraged. Consider then: I also was in this state and burned with great zeal for the law, and yet later I was not afraid to discard the law and depart from that way of life." HOMILY ON GALATIANS 4.12.[19]

4:12b *Becoming as You Are*

MADE WEAK FOR YOUR WEAKNESS. JEROME: He is saying something like this: "Just as I was made weak for your weakness and could not speak as to spiritual people . . . so you should also be as I am, that is, understand more spiritually." . . . This he says indeed as an imitator of the Savior, who . . . *was found in fashion as a man*,[20] that we might come to the divine life[21] from being men. EPISTLE TO THE GALATIANS 2.4.12.[22]

4:12c *You Have Done Me No Harm*

A CHANGE OF TONE. CHRYSOSTOM: See how again he addresses them by a name of honor, remembering to be gracious . . . for just as continual flattery ruins people, so a continuously severe mode of speech hardens them. Therefore it is good to maintain a balance everywhere. See now how he defends what he has said, showing that it was not in mere

---

[15]IOEP 4:67. [16]As to whether those addressed are Jews or Gentiles. [17]One preparing for baptism. [18]Migne PL 35:2130. [19]IOEP 4:68. [20]Phil 2:8. [21]Share in the nature of God; participate in God's very nature. [22]Migne PL 26:379A-B [457-58].

indignation but in concern for them that he said what he has said. For since he has given them a deep cut he next injects this appeal like oil. And showing that his words did not come from hatred or enmity, he reminds them of the charity that they displayed toward him and carries on his argument ironically. HOMILY ON GALATIANS 4.8-12.[23]

WHEN HE FIRST PREACHED, THEY DID HIM NO HARM. JEROME: A disciple harms his master if he wastes his precepts and his work by his own neglect. The Galatians had not harmed the apostle, because they had observed his gospel and his commands right up to the present.... Or else [he means]: "When I first preached the gospel to you ... I pretended to be weak that I might be helpful to you in your weakness; did you not receive me as an angel, as Christ Jesus? When, therefore, you did me no harm at that time and thought me in my downcast and lowly state to be like the Son of God, why am I harmed by you when I stir you up to greater things?" EPISTLE TO THE GALATIANS 2.4.13.[24]

4:13 Paul's Reason for Preaching

A BODILY AILMENT. JEROME: This is an obscure passage and demands closer attention. "I preached to you initially," he says, "as if to infants and sucklings on account of your bodily weakness.... This economy and pretense of weakness in preaching was my own policy. You were trying to decide whether things that were rather small in themselves and were presented by me as of little account would be acceptable."... The passage could also be explained another way: "When I came to you ... as a lowly and despised man ... you perceived that my lowliness and the

plainness of my dress were meant to try you." ... Or we might suppose that the apostle was sick when he came to the Galatians. ... And this could also be said, that in his first coming to the Galatians he was subject to abuse and persecution and physical beatings from the adversaries of the gospel. EPISTLE TO THE GALATIANS 2.4.14.[25]

4:14a A Trial to You

PAUL'S CONDITION TESTED THE GALATIANS. CHRYSOSTOM: What is he saying? "I was persecuted, I was flogged, I underwent many near-deaths in preaching to you, and even so you did not despise me." For that is the meaning of *you did not scorn or despise me*. Do you perceive his spiritual understanding? For even in the course of his self-defense he continues to exhort them anew, showing what he has suffered on their account. HOMILY ON GALATIANS 4.14.[26]

4:14b You Did Not Scorn or Despise Me

THEY PASSED THE TEST. AMBROSIASTER: The ailment of the apostle was a temptation to the Galatians. But they were found constant, not doubting as to his faith. For they could have stumbled and said, "What virtue or hope is there in this faith when its minister is so humiliated?" But when he had inspired their minds with future hopes, they did not fear present death for the sake of Christ's name.... This caused them later to blush, because after these laudable acts they became again entrapped so as to deserve re-

---

[23]IOEP 4:6-8. Cf. Ambrosiaster *Epistle to the Galatians* 4.12 [CSEL 81.3:47]. [24]Migne PL 26:380A-B [459]. [25]Migne PL 26:380C-381B [459-61]. [26]IOEP 4:69.

proach. EPISTLE TO THE GALATIANS 4.14.1-2.[27]

4:14c Received as an Angel of God

RECEIVED AS A MESSENGER SENT FROM GOD. MARIUS VICTORINUS: The weakness in my body was no obstacle for you, but you received me as an angel of God, that is, as a messenger, a preacher sent from God (for that is an angel of God); and you received me like Christ Jesus, whom I was preaching to you. And so you truly received Christ Jesus, if you received me as an angel of God,[28] in the same way you received Christ Jesus. EPISTLE TO THE GALATIANS 2.4.14.[29]

THE EARLIER RECEPTION MAKES ABSURD THE LATER NONRECEPTION. CHRYSOSTOM: Do you see the absurdity of receiving him as an angel of God when pursued and persecuted but not receiving him when he commands what is necessary? HOMILY ON GALATIANS 4.14.[30]

4:15 The Satisfaction You Felt

FIRM TO BEGIN, INFIRM TO CONTINUE. MARIUS VICTORINUS: You were satisfied at the time when you received the gospel, because you were zealous at the outset. Yet now, since I do not see the finishing of the edifice, I am forced to say, *where is your satisfaction?* EPISTLE TO THE GALATIANS 2.4.15-16.[31]

4:16 Have I Become Your Enemy?

THE UNEXPECTED REVERSAL. AMBROSIASTER: He says this as to imply: "It is not possible that I should become an enemy to those from whom I received such services. But because no one wants to be exposed when he errs, I seem to be your enemy when I justly reprimand you." EPISTLE TO THE GALATIANS 4.16.[32]

AN ENEMY FOR PREACHING THE TRUTH. JEROME: He has finished his sentence elegantly, asking: *Have I become an enemy for preaching the truth to you?* He says this to show that his initial bodily ailment in preaching was not so much truth as a shadow and image of truth. . . . He has tempered this sentence and made it personal because he has addressed it to the Galatians in person. . . . Today also, so long as we . . . explain the Scripture according to the letter, we are praised and respected and held in admiration. But when we make a small attempt to provoke people personally to pass on to greater things, they stop acclaiming us and become resistant. EPISTLE TO THE GALATIANS 2.4.15-16.[33]

4:17 Making Much of You and Them

GOOD AND BAD EMULATION. MARIUS VICTORINUS: Since *emulate*[34] signifies two things—one when someone emulates what he finds pleasing because it is good and another when people are emulators because they feel envy—these people, he says, emulate you in a bad way, by which he means that they are imitators through envy. . . . When he adds the phrase *so that you may emulate them* [meaning] "that you may fol-

---

[27]CSEL 81.3:47-48. [28]Cf. Mt 25:40. [29]BT 1972:50 [1182C-D]. [30]IOEP 4:69. [31]Migne PL 26:381D-382A [461]. [32]CSEL 81.3:49. [33]Migne PL 26:382C-383A [462-63]. [34]Or "make much of."

low them," he has thus used the double sense of emulation in different places, since emulation is imitation, and especially when it is also directed to what is good. . . . [He continues:] "Emulate therefore better gifts[35] —not those of Jewish law, which are not gifts and are not better; but emulate those things which are good and better gifts. That is, whatever belongs to faith and love, emulate that with regard to Christ and follow it. It is always good to emulate better things. Emulation as such is not good, but the emulation of better things is always good, and not only when I am present." EPISTLE TO THE GALATIANS 2.4.17-18.[36]

THE MALICE BORNE BY FALSE TEACHERS. THEODORET: He says this with reference to those evil teachers. "For seeing your conspicuous faith," he says, "they are grieved and all try by every means to rob you of those goods and subject you to their own authority." For that is what he means by writing *that you may emulate them*. EPISTLE TO THE GALATIANS 4.16.[37]

4:18 *Achieving Stability*

THEIR LOSS OF EQUILIBRIUM IN PAUL'S ABSENCE. CHRYSOSTOM: Here he hints that his absence had caused these troubles and that the truly blessed state is one in which the disciples have the proper opinion not only when the teacher is present but also when he is absent. But since they have not yet advanced to this degree of responsiveness, he does everything to get them there. HOMILY ON GALATIANS 4.18.[38]

THE EPHEMERAL ENDURANCE OF THE FICKLE. JEROME: No wonder indeed that on

the apostle's departure . . . the Galatians were changed, since even now we witness the same occurrence in the church. For never was there a teacher in the church so distinguished in speech and life. . . . We see people busy with haste and fervor about alms, fasting, sexual abstinence, relief of the poor, taking care of graves, etc. But when he departs we see that they waste away and, from loss of their food, grow thin, pale and languid. Then follows the death of all that was thriving before. EPISTLE TO THE GALATIANS 2.4.17-18.[39]

4:19a *Again in Labor*

PARENTING THE FAITH OF THE REGENERATE. MARIUS VICTORINUS: Sons are spoken of in many senses, sometimes as by love, sometimes as by nature, sometimes as by blood, sometimes even as by religion. This is what Paul means now by *my sons*, either because when the new birth occurs through faithful baptism, he who guides the baptized toward maturity or receives them when fully ready is called their father, or because when he calls them back into Christ he makes them his own sons. EPISTLE TO THE GALATIANS 2.4.19.[40]

THE ANALOGY OF THE APOSTLE AS MOTHER. JEROME: He who in another place had spoken like a father[41] now speaks not like a father but like a mother in Christ, so that they may recognize the dutiful anxiety of both parents. EPISTLE TO THE GALATIANS 2.4.19.[42]

---

[35]Cf. 1 Cor 14:1. [36]BT 1972:51-52 [1183C-1184A]. [37]CPE 1:353. [38]IOEP 4:70-71. [39]Migne PL 26:384A-B [464]. They grow thin due to lack of leadership and faith. [40]BT 1972:52 [1184A-B]. [41]Here Jerome cites 1 Corinthians 4:18. [42]Migne PL 26:385A [465].

THE MISCARRIAGES AND ABORTIONS STILL MY CHILDREN. CHRYSOSTOM: Do you see his parental compassion? Do you see the anguish that is fitting for an apostle? Do you see how he has lamented more bitterly than women giving birth? "You have ruined the image of God," he is saying. "You have lost the kinship, you have exchanged the likeness. You need a rebirth and a reformation. Yet nonetheless I still call the miscarriages and the abortions my children." HOMILY ON GALATIANS 4.19.[43]

LIKE A MOTHER HE IS IN TRAVAIL. AUGUSTINE: Humans are conceived in their mother's womb in order to be formed, yet only when fully formed do they go into labor. One might be surprised by his statement: "You with whom I am again in travail until Christ be formed in you." We are to understand this travail to stand for the agonies of concern that they might be born in Christ. Then he labors for them once again because of the dangers of their seduction, by which he sees them being disturbed. EPISTLE TO THE GALATIANS 38 [IB.4.19].[44]

4:19b Until Christ Is Formed in You!

THE LABOR OF THE MOTHER DOES NOT END IN BIRTH. JEROME: This example which he has taken from a pregnant woman deserves our close attention, so that we may understand what is being said. Nature is something to be not ashamed of but revered. For just as the seed is unformed when first sown into the mother . . . then at a determined time issues into the light and is now born with difficulties as great as those with which it is later nourished to keep it from dying— so too, when the seed of Christ's word falls into the soul of the hearer it increases by its proper degrees and . . . remains in jeopardy so long as the one who has conceived it is in labor. Nor does the work end as soon as it emerges. This is but the beginning of a new labor, so that he may lead the infant, by diligent nourishment and study, up to the full maturity of Christ. EPISTLE TO THE GALATIANS 2.4.19.[45]

CHRIST IS FORMED IN YOU BY LIVING FAITH. CYRIL OF ALEXANDRIA: Christ *is formed in you* by nothing else but irreproachable faith and the way of gospel. FESTAL LETTER 10.1.[46]

4:20a Wishing to Be Present

A LETTER CANNOT WEEP. CHRYSOSTOM: Let me show you how impatient, how incensed he is, how he cannot bear these things. For such is love: it is not content with words but seeks also to be personally present. . . . *To change my tone,* he says, that is, to cry out and to make mournful noise and tears and to turn everything into lamentation. For in a letter it was not possible to show his tears and mourning. HOMILY ON GALATIANS 4.20.[47]

THE PRESENT TEACHER IS MORE THAN THE ABSENT WRITER. JEROME: Holy Scripture edifies even when read but is much more profitable if one passes from written characters to the voice. . . . Knowing, then, that speech has more force when addressed to those who are present, the apostle longs to

---

[43]IOEP 4:71. [44]Migne PL 35:2132. [45]Migne PL 26:385B-C [466]. [46]SC 392:194-96. [47]IOEP 4:71.

turn the epistolary voice, the voice confined within written characters, into actual presence. EPISTLE TO THE GALATIANS 2.4.20.[48]

4:20b The Apostle's Perplexity

HIS PRESENT PERPLEXITY INTENSIFIED BY HIS ABSENCE. JEROME: "I used coaxing words to you just now, . . . but for the sake of that love which prevents me from allowing my sons to perish and stray forever I

wish that I were now present—if the bonds of my ministry did not prevent me—and change my coaxing tone to one of castigation. It is not because of fickleness that I am now coaxing, now irate. I am impelled to speak by love, by grief, by diverse emotions." EPISTLE TO THE GALATIANS 2.4.20.[49]

---

[48]Migne PL 26:386B-C [467]. [49]Migne PL 26:387C [468-69].

4:21-31 THE BOND AND THE FREE

[21]*Tell me, you who desire to be under law, do you not hear the law?* [22]*For it is written that Abraham had two sons, one by a slave and one by a free woman.* [23]*But the son of the slave was born according to the flesh, the son of the free woman through promise.* [24]*Now this is an allegory: these women are two covenants. One is from Mount Sinai, bearing children for slavery; she is Hagar.* [25]*Now Hagar is Mount Sinai in Arabia;[i] she corresponds to the present Jerusalem, for she is in slavery with her children.* [26]*But the Jerusalem above is free, and she is our mother.* [27]*For it is written,*

"Rejoice, O barren one who does not bear;
break forth and shout, you who are not in travail;
for the children of the desolate one are many more
than the children of her that is married."

[28]*Now we,[j] brethren, like Isaac, are children of promise.* [29]*But as at that time he who was born according to the flesh persecuted him who was born according to the Spirit, so it is now.* [30]*But what does the scripture say? "Cast out the slave and her son; for the son of the slave shall not inherit with the son of the free woman."* [31]*So, brethren, we are not children of the slave but of the free woman.*

i *Other ancient authorities read* For Sinai is a mountain in Arabia j *Other ancient authorities read* you

Overview: The Law, including the patriarchal narrative (JEROME), is here shown to prefigure the New Testament (AUGUSTINE). Abraham is used by Paul in a new way, to show that birth by spirit is better than birth by flesh (CHRYSOSTOM). Paul describes typology as allegory (CHRYSOSTOM), taking the term from the schools (JEROME), but does not diminish or deny the literal history (THEODORE OF MOPSUESTIA). He relates Hagar to the Sinai testament (AMBROSIASTER) and leaves us to interpret the other wives (AUGUSTINE). We might interpret Hagar by etymology (JEROME). We might suggest four meanings to Jerusalem (JOHN CASSIAN), assuming that the church is the heavenly Jerusalem on earth (AMBROSIASTER). The true Jerusalem, deserted by sinners (AUGUSTINE), has now acquired children in all nations so as to outnumber those of the law's bride, the synagogue (CHRYSOSTOM). Christians obtain by faithful baptism (THEODORET) the promise that Paul holds out to the Galatians (JEROME), even amid Jewish persecutions (CHRYSOSTOM), which will be requited like Ishmael's persecution of Isaac (JEROME). Citing Sarah's banishment of Hagar (THEODORET), Paul exhorts us to claim our freedom (AMBROSIASTER). We share this with the Jewish patriarchs (AUGUSTINE) but not with those who enslave themselves to the law (CHRYSOSTOM).

4:21 Hearing the Law

HEARING THE OLD TESTAMENT NARRATIVE. JEROME: One should note that the whole narrative in Genesis is here called Law, not, according to the popular assumption, simply statements of what is to be done or avoided but everything that is rehearsed concerning Abraham and his wives and sons. EPISTLE TO THE GALATIANS 2.4.21.[1]

HAGAR'S STORY AS PROPHECY. AUGUSTINE: People might suppose that in the case of Hagar Abraham acted [merely from human desire for procreation]. But the apostle makes the reverse clear, viewing this in relation to prophecy. QUESTIONS ON GENESIS 1.70.[2]

THE NEW TESTAMENT PREFIGURED IN THE OLD. AUGUSTINE: Because in the Old Testament the New is prefigured, those men of God who then understood this in the manner appropriate to their times are shown to have been ministers and performers of the old covenant but heirs of the new. AGAINST TWO LETTERS OF PELAGIUS 3.6.[3]

4:22 Two Sons, One by a Slave and One by a Free Woman

WHY RETURN TO ABRAHAM? CHRYSOSTOM: He returns once again to Abraham, not repeating the same thing but because the reputation of Abraham was great among the Jews. He shows that the types have their origin in him and that present things were adumbrated in him. HOMILY ON GALATIANS 4.22.[4]

4:23a A Son According to the Flesh

BIRTH ACCORDING TO THE SPIRIT DOES NOT YIELD LESS KINSHIP THAN BIRTH ACCORDING TO THE FLESH. CHRYSOSTOM: Isaac was not born in the natural manner usual in

---

[1]Migne PL 26:387D [469]. [2]Migne PL 34:566. [3]Migne PL 44:591-92. [4]IOEP 4:72-73.

marriages, or according to the body's natural power, and yet was a lawful son. . . . Natural processes did not produce his conception, nor did the seed conceive him. For Sarah's womb was dead both through age and through sterility. But the Word of God formed him. . . . Nevertheless the one not born according to the flesh was in greater honor than the one who was. Do not, then, be dismayed that you were not born according to the flesh, for your not being born according to the flesh makes you all the more kin to him. For conception that is not according to natural processes is more remarkable and more spiritual. HOMILY ON GALATIANS 4.23.[5]

4:23b *The Son Through the Promise*

MADE HEIR THROUGH A TESTAMENT. JEROME: From God's own Scripture[6] it is evident that the birth of Ishmael also was according to promise. But the answer is that a promise is truly fulfilled in the giving of a covenant. It is one thing to bless, increase and multiply greatly, as is written in Ishmael's case, but another to make an heir through a covenant. EPISTLE TO THE GALATIANS 2.4.22-23.[7]

THE UNIQUENESS OF ISAAC'S BIRTH ACCORDING TO THE PROMISE. AUGUSTINE: Now the fact that Isaac was born of a free wife is not enough to make him signify the people who inherit the New Covenant. What is more important is that he was born according to the promise. For he could have been born according to nature's norms from a slave and in the same way from a free woman, just as Abraham received from Katurah, whom he subsequently married,

sons not according to a promise but according to nature.[8] EPISTLE TO THE GALATIANS 40 [IB.4.21-31].[9]

4:24a *An Allegory: Two Women Are Two Covenants*

ALLEGORY DEFINED. CHRYSOSTOM: *Allegory* is used improperly for typology. His meaning is this: "This story does not say only what is evident but relates other things as well; hence it is called *allegory*." HOMILY ON GALATIANS 4.24.[10]

THE LITERARY TRADITION OF ALLEGORY. JEROME: *Allegory* is properly a term in the art of grammar. How it differs from metaphor and other figures of speech we learn as children. It presents one thing in words and signifies another in sense.[11] . . . Understanding this, Paul (who had a certain knowledge of secular literature also) used the name of the figure of speech and called it *allegory* according to the usage of his own circle. EPISTLE TO THE GALATIANS 2.4.24.[12]

PAUL DOES NOT THEREBY DENY THE PLAIN OR LITERAL SENSE OF SCRIPTURE. THEODORE OF MOPSUESTIA: Those who are at great pains to pervert the meaning of the divine Scriptures . . . abuse this saying of the apostle's, as though they thought that they could derive from it the power to suppress the entire sense of holy Scripture in their aspirations to speak "allegorically," as if in the manner of the apostle. They fail to see how

---

[5]IOEP 4:73. [6]E.g., Gen 17:18-27. [7]Migne PL 26:388C [470]. [8]Gen 25:1-2. [9]Migne PL 35:2133. [10]IOEP 4:73. [11]Cf. Marius Victorinus *Epistle to the Galatians* 4.24.1-2 [CSEL 81.3:50-51]. [12]Migne PL 26:389B-C [471].

great a difference there is between their own position and that of the apostle in this passage. For the apostle does not deny the history or pick apart the events of the distant past, but he has stated them as they happened at the time, while using for his own purpose the interpretation of these events. . . . He would not have said *referred to one who was born* if he had not believed that person had really existed. There cannot be a simile if one takes away the historical reality itself. COMMENTARY.[13]

4:24b Bearing Children for Slavery

WHY THE LAW BEARS CHILDREN FOR SLAVERY. AMBROSIASTER: These women represent the two covenants. Moses, taking the blood of a calf in a vessel, sprinkled the people, saying *this is the blood of the covenant,* etc.[14]. . . The law was given on Mount Sinai. In reciting it to the people Moses called this the book of the testament. He then sprinkled the people with blood, as I have said. This law held sinners as offenders. They soon began to be slaves of sin, as if they had been made sons of Hagar, as if returning to slavery. EPISTLE TO THE GALATIANS 4.24.1-2.[15]

FALSE TEACHERS ARE LIKE SONS OF THE FREE WOMEN WHO BACKSLIDE TO SLAVERY. AUGUSTINE: Under the sure guidance of the apostle we see how clearly he shows that these two are to be taken allegorically. One may also consider the sons of Keturah under some figure of things to come. The fact that such people did these things is recorded not without purpose but under the guidance of the Holy Spirit. We will perhaps find that heresies and schisms are signified in this alle-

gory. For these are sons of the free woman, that is, of the church, and yet they again revert to life according to the flesh, not spiritually according to a promise. EPISTLE TO THE GALATIANS 40 [IB.4.21-31].[16]

4:25 Mount Sinai and the Present Jerusalem

THE ETYMOLOGICAL CLUE IN HAGAR. JEROME: Hagar, who is interpreted as "sojourning," "wandering" or "tarrying," gives birth to Ishmael. . . . No wonder that the Old Covenant, which is on Mount Sinai, which is in Arabia and nearby to Jerusalem, is stated and alleged in writing to be ephemeral and not perpetual. The sojourning of Hagar stands in contrast with perpetual possession. The name of Mount Sinai means "tribulation," while Arabia means "death."[17] EPISTLE TO THE GALATIANS 2.4.25-26.[18]

4:26 The Jerusalem Above

HOW WE ENTER THE HEAVENLY JERUSALEM IN THIS LIFE. AMBROSIASTER: Jerusalem, which he calls our mother, represents the Lord's mystery, through which we are reborn into freedom, just as she is free. And she is called heavenly because heaven is her seat. Those to whom she gives birth will be there with her. EPISTLE TO THE GALATIANS 4.26.[19]

THE FOURFOLD MEANING OF JERUSALEM. JOHN CASSIAN: One and the same Jerusalem can be understood in a fourfold way: histori-

---

[13]TEM 1:73-74. [14]Ex 24:8. [15]CSEL 81.3:51. [16]Migne PL 35:2133. [17]But fancifully. [18]Migne PL 26:390C-D [472-73]. [19]CSEL 81.3:51-52.

cally as the city of the Jews, allegorically as the church of Christ, anagogically[20] as the heavenly city of God, which is the mother of all, and tropologically[21] as the human soul, which is often upbraided or praised under this name by the Lord. CONFERENCES 14.8.4.[22]

4:27a "Rejoice, O Barren One Who Does Not Bear"

SARAH DESERTED BECAUSE OF HER STERILITY. AUGUSTINE: Sarah signifies the heavenly Jerusalem, having been deserted for a long time by her husband's embraces because of her perceived sterility. For men such as Abraham did not use women to satisfy lust but for the procreation of offspring. Now to her sterility age had also been added. . . . The age of Isaac's parents serves to signify that, new though the people of the New Covenant are, their predestination lies nonetheless with God and is that heavenly Jerusalem of old. EPISTLE TO THE GALATIANS 40 [IB.4.21-31].[23]

4:27b The Children of the Desolate One

LIKE SARAH, THE BARREN CHURCH ACQUIRED CHILDREN. CHRYSOSTOM: The church was not only barren like Sarah and did not only become rich in children like her, but it also gave birth in the same way as Sarah. For just as it was not nature but the word of God that made her a mother . . . so too in our own regeneration it is not nature of any kind but the word of God spoken through the presbyter, as the faithful know, in the waters of the font, as in a womb, that fashions and regenerates the one who is being baptized. HOMILY ON GALATIANS 4.27.[24]

4:27c The Children of Her That Is Married

HOW THE ONCE BARREN CHURCH NOW SURPASSES THE SYNAGOGUE IN CHILDBEARING. CHRYSOSTOM: Who is the woman with the husband? Is it not obviously the synagogue [as married to the law]? Yet the barren one has surpassed her in childbearing. For the synagogue contains one nation, whereas the children of the church fill Greece, Africa, land, sea and the whole inhabited world. Do you see how Sarah foreshadowed our future in deeds and the prophet in words? HOMILY ON GALATIANS 4.27.[25]

4:28 Like Isaac We Are Children of Promise

THE GALATIANS CALLED ONCE AGAIN TO BECOME SONS OF THE FREE WOMAN. JEROME: One might ask how he speaks of the Galatians, whom he had called fools. He accused them of starting in the Spirit and finishing in the flesh. When the apostle called them *sons of promise* in the way that Isaac was, he meant that he did not completely despair of their salvation and judged that they would return again to the Spirit, in which they had begun, and become sons of the free woman. EPISTLE TO THE GALATIANS 2.4.28.[26]

CHILDREN OF PROMISE, BORN ACCORDING TO GRACE. THEODORET: We were born not

---

[20]According to a hidden or mysterious meaning, or leading toward an elevated interpretation. [21]According to the figurative turning of a phrase, as a variation of tropes, or figures of speech. [22]CSEL 13:405; quoting Abbot Nestoros. [23]Migne PL 35:2133. [24]IOEP 4:75. [25]IOEP 4:74-75. [26]Migne PL 26:392A [474].

according to nature but according to grace. For, just as in Isaac's case, it was not the law of nature but that of the gospel that fashioned us. Thus the promise given to Abraham engendered us. EPISTLE TO THE GALATIANS 4.28.[27]

4:29 Persecution for Those Born of the Spirit

PERSECUTION ANTICIPATED. CHRYSOSTOM: "And what sort of freedom is this," someone might ask, "when the Jews oppress and beat the faithful, and those who are reckoned free are persecuted?" For that is what happened then, as the faithful were persecuted. "But do not let even this discourage you, for this too he included beforehand in the type." HOMILY ON GALATIANS 4.29.[28]

THE SPIRITUAL PERSECUTED BY THE NATURAL BROTHER. JEROME: Ishmael, the elder brother, persecuted him while still a nursing infant, claiming for himself the prior right of circumcision and the inheritance of the firstborn.... And it is aptly said that he who is born according to nature persecutes the spiritual. The spiritual one never persecutes the natural one but forgives him like an untutored brother, for he knows that he may progress. EPISTLE TO THE GALATIANS 2.4.29-31.[29]

4:30 What Does the Scripture Say?

THE TRUTH AND TYPE OF SCRIPTURE EXPLAINED. THEODORET: By *the words of Scripture* he means those spoken of Sarah[30] explaining the goal of the Scripture, for the sake of which he has written these things

afresh, so that after the truth the type also may be explained. EPISTLE TO THE GALATIANS 4.30.[31]

4:31 Children of the Slave, Now Children of the Free Woman

BEFORE WE WERE CHILDREN OF THE SLAVE. AMBROSIASTER: We were therefore sons of the slave woman when we were liable for our sins. But, having received the remission of sins from Christ, we have been made free. EPISTLE TO THE GALATIANS 4.31.[32]

FOREORDAINED THROUGH AGES. CHRYSOSTOM: He raises and treats all these points in his wish to prove that what has occurred is not an afterthought but was prefigured from above and through many ages. Do you see how it is absurd that those who were foreordained through so many ages and had obtained freedom should happily put themselves again under the yoke of slavery? HOMILY ON GALATIANS 4.31.[33]

NOW CHILDREN OF THE FREE WOMAN. AUGUSTINE: Let us consider whether we should say that the righteous people of old were children of the slave woman or the free. But God forbid that they should be the slave woman's. If therefore they are the free woman's they belong to the new covenant in the Holy Spirit, whose life-giving power the apostle contrasts with *the letter that kills*.[34] AGAINST TWO LETTERS OF PELAGIUS 3.12.[35]

---

[27]CPE 1:355. [28]IOEP 4:75. Cf. Theodoret *Epistle to the Galatians* 4.29 [CPE 1:355]. [29]Migne PL 26:392A [474]. [30]Gen 21:10-12. [31]CPE 1:355. [32]CSEL 81.3:53. [33]IOEP 4:76. [34]2 Cor 3:6. [35]Migne PL 44:596.

5:1-12 EXHORTATIONS TO STEADFASTNESS

[1]*For freedom Christ has set us free; stand fast therefore, and do not submit again to a yoke of slavery.*

[2]*Now I, Paul, say to you that if you receive circumcision, Christ will be of no advantage to you.* [3]*I testify again to every man who receives circumcision that he is bound to keep the whole law.* [4]*You are severed from Christ, you who would be justified by the law; you have fallen away from grace.* [5]*For through the Spirit, by faith, we wait for the hope of righteousness.* [6]*For in Christ Jesus neither circumcision nor uncircumcision is of any avail, but faith working[x] through love.* [7]*You were running well; who hindered you from obeying the truth?* [8]*This persuasion is not from him who calls you.* [9]*A little leaven leavens the whole lump.* [10]*I have confidence in the Lord that you will take no other view than mine; and he who is troubling you will bear his judgment, whoever he is.* [11]*But if I, brethren, still preach circumcision, why am I still persecuted? In that case the stumbling block of the cross has been removed.* [12]*I wish those who unsettle you would mutilate themselves!*

x *Or made effective*

OVERVIEW: Relying on his authority as Christ's instrument (JEROME), Paul warns against seeking salvation through circumcision (AUGUSTINE). He adapts his language to the Gentile church (JEROME). Faith sets us free to believe God's promises (MARIUS VICTORINUS). Taking seriously one precept of the law implies taking seriously all (CHRYSOSTOM). Circumcision is a mere shadow of the true covenant (JEROME). God can make the moral law light for us (EPIPHANIUS), but not if we expect salvation from it (JEROME). Grace comes only from God (MARIUS VICTORINUS). As Christ has the right to abolish both circumcision and uncircumcision (TERTULLIAN), circumcision is now a matter of indifference (CHRYSOSTOM). Meanwhile Gentiles have no advantage (JEROME). Love supplies the content of faith (MARIUS VICTORINUS) and is also the means of sustaining it (CHRYSOSTOM), in contrast to cold belief (AUGUSTINE) and impenitence (FULGENTIUS).

Admonishing the Galatians by means of a rhetorical question (CHRYSOSTOM), Paul reminds them that they have followed human wisdom, not God (AMBROSIASTER, THEODORET). He insists that their offense is not trivial (CHRYSOSTOM), using a simile from breadmaking (MARIUS VICTORINUS). The Galatians are in great danger (AUGUSTINE). Unless corrected the burden will be intolerable (MARIUS VICTORINUS), and they will be to blame (CHRYSOSTOM), for they will have reverted to superstition (JEROME). Yet he has confidence grounded in the Lord (CHRYSOSTOM), for they have been led astray in ignorance (AMBROSIASTER), even if by distinguished persons (JEROME). That will not save them from judgment (MARIUS VICTORINUS). Fighting accusations based on the circumcision of Timothy (CHRYSOSTOM), Paul cannot preach both circumcision and the cross (AUGUSTINE). With a vehemence that shows his love (JEROME) he hints that circumcision is as repugnant as castration (CHRYSOSTOM), understanding that term metaphorically (AMBROSIASTER, AUGUSTINE).

5:1a For Freedom Christ Has Set Us Free

HOW CHRIST SETS FREE. MARIUS VICTORINUS: He obviously means that freedom by which our mother [the church] is free, and she obviously is free by faith. For this is true freedom, to keep faith in God and to believe all God's promises. Therefore by faith Christ has brought us back to freedom and made us free by the freedom of faith. EPISTLE TO THE GALATIANS 2.5.1.[1]

THE FOLLY OF RETURNING TO SLAVERY. CHRYSOSTOM: Do you see how many reasons he employs to lead them away from the error of the Jews? He shows first that it is the utmost foolishness, having become free instead of slaves, to desire slavery again instead of freedom. Second, he reveals them to be unmindful of and ungrateful to their benefactor, despising the one who frees them and preferring that which enslaves them. Third, he shows that this is absurd, since [as Paul says] "the law has no power over you, since another has purchased you once for all from it." HOMILY ON GALATIANS 5.1.[2]

5:1b Stand Fast and Do Not Submit to Slavery

ONE CANNOT STAND WHOSE NECK IS BOWED DOWN. MARIUS VICTORINUS: He had to add an exhortation that they should persevere in the same way that they had first begun to receive from him the gospel and not return to the slavery under the law. He says *stand*, which is not possible for one who is under a heavy yoke. For he bows his neck submissively and therefore cannot stand. EPISTLE TO THE GALATIANS 2.5.1.[3]

THE ABSURDITY OF GOING BACK TO BONDAGE. CHRYSOSTOM: By the name of *yoke* he indicates to them the gravity of the affair. By "again" he shows how profound is their confusion. Paul implies, "If you had no experience of that yoke, you would not deserve such recriminations. But when those who have learned by experience the heaviness of the law submit themselves to it again, what forgiveness do they deserve?" HOMILY ON GALATIANS 5.1.[4]

WHY BE YOKED AGAIN? JEROME: He adds *again*, not because the Galatians had previously kept the law . . . but in their readiness to observe the lunar seasons, to be circumcised in the flesh and to offer sacrifices, they were in a sense returning to the cults that they had previously served in a state of idolatry. EPISTLE TO THE GALATIANS 2.5.1.[5]

---

[1]BT 1972:58 [1188A]. [2]IOEP 4:77. [3]BT 1972:58 [1188A]. [4]IOEP 4:77. [5]Migne PL 26:394A-B [477].

5:2a *Paul's Reminder*

PAUL'S PERSONAL ATTESTATION OF GOD'S WORD. JEROME: His statement,[6] "I, Paul, say to you," implies that the words are to be accepted not as Paul's alone but as God's. EPISTLE TO THE GALATIANS 2.5.2.[7]

5:2b *Receiving Circumcision Makes Christ of No Advantage*

WHAT THE CASE OF TIMOTHY SHOWS. AUGUSTINE: Now Paul says that Christ will profit them nothing if they are circumcised, that is, in the physical way that his opponents wanted, namely, to put their hope of salvation in circumcising their flesh. For Paul himself circumcised Timothy as a young man when he was already a Christian. This he did [to avoid] scandalizing his own people, not at all in dissimulation but from that indifference which made him say *circumcision is nothing, uncircumcision is nothing*.[8] For circumcision is no impediment to the one who does not believe that his salvation lies in it. EPISTLE TO THE GALATIANS 41 [1B.5.1-3].[9]

ROMANS ADDRESSED DIFFERENTLY FROM GALATIANS. JEROME: The letter that he wrote to the Romans was addressed to believers from both Jewish and Gentile backgrounds. . . . But writing to the Galatians he argues differently, since they belonged not to the circumcision party but to the believing Gentiles. EPISTLE TO THE GALATIANS 2.5.2.[10]

5:3 *Circumcision Binds One to Keeping the Whole Law*

THE EXTENSIVE OBLIGATION ATTACHED TO CIRCUMCISION. CHRYSOSTOM: The provisions of the law imply one another. I mean something like this. Attached to circumcision are sacrifice and the observance of days. The sacrifice again entails the observance of a day and place, the place entailing many types of purification. The purifications set up a further string of varied observances. For it is not legitimate for the impure to sacrifice, to intrude upon the holy shrines or to do any such things. Therefore through this one commandment the law drags along many others. Now if you have been circumcised but not on the eighth day; or on the eighth day but without a sacrifice; or with sacrifice but not in the appointed place; or in the appointed place but not under the prescribed forms; or under the prescribed forms but not in a pure state; or in a pure state but purified by inappropriate rites—all these things are wasted. For this reason he says *he is bound to keep the whole*. "Do not keep part but the whole," Paul says, "but if it is not of the Lord, do not keep even part." HOMILY ON GALATIANS 5.3.[11]

THE CIRCUMCISED MUST SUBMIT TO THE WHOLE OF THE LAW. AMBROSIASTER: There are some who serve the law to a certain extent without being circumcised; for many Romans in Judea served the law without circumcision. . . . Yet there is no one who is circumcised without being required to serve the whole law. He is a debtor, since the law was given to the circumcised. His meaning here was that they had

---

[6]Cf. 2 Cor 13:3; Gal 2:20. [7]Migne PL 26:394B-C [477]. [8]1 Cor 7:19. [9]Migne PL 35:2134. [10]Migne PL 26:395A-B [478]. [11]IOEP 4:78.

become so negligent as to deserve to bear all the burdens of the law. EPISTLE TO THE GALATIANS 5.3.[12]

THE LAW AND CHRIST ARE TWO MASTERS. JEROME: Just as no one can serve two masters,[13] so it is difficult to keep both the shadow and the substance of the law. EPISTLE TO THE GALATIANS 2.5.4.[14]

THE LORD CAN MAKE THE BURDEN OF THE LAW LIGHT. EPIPHANIUS: When he says *bound* he is no longer speaking of the law as something unworthy but of a heavy burden which can be made lighter. There is one Lord, who is able to make it either heavy or light according to the choice of those who have not refused to accept salvation through his grace through his appearance in the flesh. PANARION 42.12.3, THIRD REFUTATION OF MARCION.[15]

5:4a *Justification by the Law Severs One from Christ*

JUSTIFICATION BY THE LAW. JEROME: He is refuting those who believed that they were justified in the law, not those who observed its legitimate provisions in honor of him by whom they were commanded, understanding both that they were commanded as a foreshadowing of the truth and that they belonged to a particular time. LETTERS 116.19.3.[16]

5:4b *Fallen Away from Grace*

THE FALL FROM GRACE. MARIUS VICTORINUS: All the virtue of the one who believes in Christ is by the grace of God. Grace is not from merits but from readiness to believe God. Therefore [Paul writes] "You

have already fallen from grace if you place your justification in the law, because (for example) you serve works, because you observe the sabbath or on account of your circumcision. If you believe that you are justified by this, *you have fallen from grace and been made void of Christ*. You no longer have your faith from Christ nor hope for grace for yourselves from his passion and resurrection, if you believe that justification comes from the law." EPISTLE TO THE GALATIANS 2.5.4.[17]

THOSE FREED FROM THE DEBT PREFER INDEBTEDNESS. AUGUSTINE: Because it is they, not Christ, who are injured, he adds: *you have fallen from grace*. For when the effect of Christ's grace is that those who were debtors to the works of the law were freed from this debt, these people, ungrateful to such great grace, prefer to be debtors to the whole law. Now this had not yet happened, but, because the will had begun to be moved, he therefore speaks frequently as though it had already happened. EPISTLE TO THE GALATIANS 42 [1B.5.4-12].[18]

5:5 *We Wait for the Hope of Righteousness*

THE TONE CHANGES. CHRYSOSTOM: Having now multiplied their fear and shaken their minds and shown them the shipwreck that they are about to suffer, he reveals to them the haven of grace close by. This he does everywhere, showing thereby how extremely benign and safe salvation is. . . . "We need none

[12]CSEL 81.3:54-55. [13]Mt 6:24. [14]Migne PL 26:397B [481]. [15]GCS 31:156. [16]CSEL 55:410. [17]BT 1972:60 [1189B-C]. [18]Migne PL 35:2135.

of those legal provisions," Paul says, "for grace sufficiently gives the Spirit to us, through whom we are offered righteousness and a multitude of great goods." HOMILY ON GALATIANS 5.5.[19]

5:6a In Christ Jesus Neither Circumcision nor Uncircumcision Avails Us

NEITHER CIRCUMCISION NOR UNCIRCUMCISION CAN COUNT IN CHRIST'S KINGDOM. TERTULLIAN: Since circumcision and uncircumcision belonged to the one God, both therefore were annulled in Christ because of the priority given to faith, this being the faith of which it was written *the Gentiles shall believe in his name.*[20] AGAINST MARCION 5.4.11.[21]

THE ANALOGY OF CHOOSING ATHLETES ON THE BASIS OF THE COLOR OF THEIR SKIN OR LENGTH OF THEIR NOSES. CHRYSOSTOM: [Circumcision] is indifferent for those who have it already before believing but not for those who are circumcised after believing. Note how he has rejected it, putting it after uncircumcision. What makes the difference is faith. For just as when one is choosing athletes, it matters nothing in this trial whether they be hook-nosed or snub-nosed, dark or fair, but all that need be looked for is that they be strong and skillful. So when a person is to be enrolled in the new covenant, the lack of these bodily trappings does no harm, just as they do no good if they be present. HOMILY ON GALATIANS 5.6.[22]

NOR DOES UNCIRCUMCISION COUNT FOR RIGHTEOUSNESS. JEROME: [Lest Gentiles

should say] that uncircumcision, in which *Abraham pleased God and had his faith counted for righteousness,*[23] is better than circumcision, which was given as a sign and was of no profit to Israel though it possessed it, we shall see that this arrogant boast has also been excluded with the greatest foresight. EPISTLE TO THE GALATIANS 2.5.6.[24]

5:6b Faith Working Through Love

FAITH WORKS THROUGH LOVE. MARIUS VICTORINUS: Everywhere he says that faith in the gospel of Christ accords no value to rank or sex or works done with regard to the body or from the body or for the sake of the body, such as circumcision, works and other things of this kind. None of these, he says, has saving value in Christ. Circumcision is therefore vain, nor by uncircumcision do we gain value in Christ. Because we have conceived faith in him and because we have believed his promises and because through his resurrection we too rise and have suffered all things with him and rise to life with him but also through him, our faith is sure. Through this faith comes works fitting to salvation. This comes about through the love that we have for Christ and God and thus toward every human being. For it is these two relationships above all that set life straight and fulfill the whole sense of the law. They contain all the commands in the Decalogue—if it follows necessarily that he who keeps faith will also keep love,

---

[19]IOEP 4:79. [20]Is 42:4; Mal 1:11; Mt 12:21. [21]CCL 1:674. [22]IOEP 4:79. [23]Gen 15:6. [24]Migne PL 26:400A-B [484].

since these two fulfill all the precepts of the law of Christ. EPISTLE TO THE GALATIANS 2.5.6.[25]

NO DRIFT TOWARD BONDAGE. CHRYSOSTOM: He strikes them here with a great blow by showing that it is their failure to be rooted in love for Christ that has given entrance to this error. For what is looked for is not only faith but also faith abiding in love. It is as though he said, "Had you loved Christ as you ought, you would not have gone voluntarily into slavery, you would not have insulted your deliverer." And here he also alludes obliquely to those who have plotted against them, showing that if they had love for them they would not have dared to do this. He also wishes to amend their lives through this saying. HOMILY ON GALATIANS 5.7.[26]

THE FAITH THAT WORKS THROUGH LOVE DISTINGUISHED FROM THE FAITH OF DEMONS. AUGUSTINE: This is the faith that separates the righteous from the unclean demons, for they too, as the apostle James says, *believe and tremble,*[27] but their actions are not good. Therefore they do not have that faith by which *the righteous live.*[28] ON GRACE AND FREE WILL 18.[29]

LOVING FAITH IS EFFICACIOUS AND GUILTLESS. FULGENTIUS: If anyone, holding the faith that works through love, repents of his former sin in such as a way that he from then on turns his back on it, he will be guiltless of the blasphemy that is spoken against the Holy Spirit [namely, impenitence], which is not forgiven to the speaker either in this age or in the one to come. ON THE REMISSION OF SINS 1.24.1.[30]

5:7 Who Hindered Obeying the Truth?

THE QUESTION ITSELF IS A TESTIMONY OF LOSS. CHRYSOSTOM: These are not the words of one who asks a question but of one who is at a loss and grieving. [Paul means] "How was so great a race cut short? Who had strength to do such a thing? You who were superior to all and were in the position of teachers have not even remained in the position of disciples." HOMILY ON GALATIANS 5.7.[31]

5:8 Persuasion Not from God

THE CALL TO GRACE. AMBROSIASTER: The truth is that the Jews imposed the yoke of the law on them by a human decision, not by the judgment of God, who was calling them to grace through his apostle. EPISTLE TO THE GALATIANS 5.8.[32]

THIS PERSUASION NOT FROM THE GOD WHO CALLS YOU. THEODORET: It is for God to call and hearers to obey. EPISTLE TO THE GALATIANS 5.8.[33]

5:9 A Little Leaven

KEEP THE BREAD UNLEAVENED. MARIUS VICTORINUS: All leaven corrupts the bread, and the corrupted bread is flour. When the mass of flour is left it sours, and then comes the leavening. Now when a small amount of the leaven is put into the mass, the mass is corrupted. "You," he says, "must be unleavened bread. There-

---

[25]BT 1972:60-61 [1189D-1190A]. [26]IOEP 4:80. [27]Jas 2:19. [28]Gal 3:11. [29]Migne PL 44:892. [30]CCL 91A:673. [31]IOEP 4:80. [32]CSEL 81.3:56. [33]CPE 1:357.

fore that little addition of yours, which you thought a small amount, namely, your observing of circumcision and the rest, because it is corrupt, corrupts the mass of our gospel. If so, you do not have full hope in Christ, and neither does Christ regard you as his own or people whose hope depends on him. For it is faith that sets free, and, as I have said, he has no faith who hopes for any sort of help apart from Christ, even along with Christ." EPISTLE TO THE GALATIANS 2.5.9.[34]

THIS PERSUASION COULD LEAD TO RAMPANT JUDAIZING. CHRYSOSTOM: Some may say, "Why do you blow up the matter so portentously by your words? We have kept a single command of the law, and are you clamoring because of that?" But Paul is concerned not only for their present but for their future. . . . "For," he says, "this little evil, if uncorrected, has the strength to lead you into complete Judaizing, just as leaven acts on the lump." HOMILY ON GALATIANS 5.9.[35]

5:10a Confidence in the Lord and in Them

THE ERROR CORRECTABLE. AMBROSIASTER: He says that he has this ground for trusting in them, that they had entered on the path of error not of their own accord, but they had been taken unawares. Thus he trusts that when they are shown the true road they will easily be able to return. EPISTLE TO THE GALATIANS 5.10.[36]

PAUL'S CONFIDENCE IN THE FAITHFUL IN THE LORD. CHRYSOSTOM: He did not say "I know" but *I have confidence.* "I trust God,"

Paul says. "I am confident when I call on the Lord to assist in your amendment." And he has not said, "I have confidence in the Lord" but "I have confidence *in you* in the Lord." Everywhere he interweaves his admonitions with praises. It is as though he said, "I know my disciples, I know your uprightness. My confidence is based first on the Lord who does not allow the least thing to be lost, and then on you, who can quickly recover control of yourselves." At the same time, he asks them to bring their own zeal, since we cannot receive from God without bringing something of our own. HOMILY ON GALATIANS 5.10.[37]

5:10b The Troubler Will Bear His Judgment

THE TROUBLER WAS SOMEONE OTHER THAN PETER. JEROME: Some say that Paul is tacitly attacking Peter, whom he says he *opposed to his face*[38] . . . but Paul would not speak with such offensive aggression of the head of the church, nor did Peter deserve to be held to blame for disturbing the church. Therefore it must be supposed that he is speaking of someone else who had either been with the apostles, or was from Judea, or was one of the believing Pharisees, or at any rate was reckoned important among the Galatians. EPISTLE TO THE GALATIANS 3.5.10.[39]

5:11a Why Am I Persecuted?

HIS ANSWER TO THE CHARGE OF HYPOC-

---

[34]BT 1972:61-62 [1190C]. [35]IOEP 4:80. [36]CSEL 81.3:56. [37]IOEP 4:80-81. [38]Gal 2:11. [39]Migne PL 26:403C-D [490].

RISY IN THE CIRCUMCISION OF TIMOTHY. CHRYSOSTOM: Since they were slandering him as one who constantly Judaized and was a hypocrite in his preaching, see how blamelessly he meets the challenge, calling them to admit the truth. "For you know that this is the pretext for persecuting me, that I ask you to avoid the law. But if I preach circumcision, why am I persecuted? For the Jews have nothing to charge me with but this one thing." . . . What then? Did he not preach circumcision? Did he not circumcise Timothy? He did indeed circumcise him. How then can he say "I do not preach"? Now learn here his precise meaning. He did not say "I do not perform circumcision" but *I do not preach it,* that is, "I do not tell you to believe in this way." HOMILY ON GALATIANS 5.11.[40]

5:11b *The Stumbling Block of the Cross Removed*

THE CROSS AS STUMBLING BLOCK. AUGUSTINE: Since he speaks of a stumbling block here he is reminding them that the principal reason for the Jews' taking offense at Christ was that they often saw him ignoring and disdaining those ceremonial observances which they believed themselves to have for their very salvation. What he says here, then, is as much as to say: "It was therefore in vain that the Jews in their indignation crucified Christ when he disdained these commandments. Now they still try to enjoin such things on those for whom he was crucified." EPISTLE TO THE GALATIANS 42 [1B.5.4-12].[41]

5:12 *A Question About Cutting Off or Mutilation*

A LAPSE INTO UNCHARITABLE EXAGGERATION? JEROME: It is asked how Paul, a disciple of him who said, *Bless those who curse you,*[42] . . . now curses those who were disturbing the churches of Galatia. . . . The words that he speaks are prompted not so much by anger against his opponents as by affection for the churches of God. . . . Nor is it any wonder that the apostle, as a man still enclosed in a frail vessel and seeing the law in his own body taking him captive and leading him into the law of sin, should have spoken like this once, when we observe such lapses to be frequent in holy people.[43] EPISTLE TO THE GALATIANS 3.5.12.[44]

NOT TO BE TAKEN IN ITS LITERAL SENSE ALONE. CHRYSOSTOM: If they will, let them be not only circumcised but emasculated. But where are those who dare to emasculate themselves, drawing upon themselves the curse, slandering the divine creation and acting like the Manichaeans?[45] For the latter say that the body itself is a deceiver and the work of evil matter. By their deeds they have given an impetus to these evil doctrines. For they cut off the member as an enemy and an intriguer. . . . Yet no physical member is responsible but free will. If you do not accept this, why not cut out the tongue on account of blasphemy, the hands on account of theft, the feet on account of their swiftness in pursuing evil, and, as it were, the whole body? . . . But this is absolutely illicit and a satanic aberration. It is necessary only to correct the disorderly impulse of the soul, the evil de-

---

[40]IOEP 4:81. [41]Migne PL 35:2136. [42]Lk 6:28. [43]Cf. Rom 7:23. [44]Migne PL 26:405B-D [492-93]. [45]Who considered the flesh evil.

mon, who rejoices unceasingly in murder, who has persuaded you to cut off the instrument as though the Creator had erred. HOMILY ON GALATIANS 5.6.[46]

A METAPHORICAL INTERPRETATION. AMBROSIASTER: [The point is] that those who had deprived the Galatians of the grace of God should themselves be cut off from the grace of God. EPISTLE TO THE GALATIANS 5.12.[47]

---

[46]IOEP 4:83. [47]CSEL 81.3:57-58.

5:13-18 FREEDOM IN THE SPIRIT

[13]*For you were called to freedom, brethren; only do not use your freedom as an opportunity for the flesh, but through love be servants of one another.* [14]*For the whole law is fulfilled in one word, "You shall love your neighbor as yourself."* [15]*But if you bite and devour one another take heed that you are not consumed by one another.*

[16]*But I say, walk by the Spirit, and do not gratify the desires of the flesh.* [17]*For the desires of the flesh are against the Spirit, and the desires of the Spirit are against the flesh; for these are opposed to each other, to prevent you from doing what you would.* [18]*But if you are led by the Spirit you are not under the law.*

OVERVIEW: Love constrains the abuse of freedom (CHRYSOSTOM). Paul equates freedom and true virtue (THEODORET). The goodness of the law is shown in its commendation of love (EPIPHANIUS), which renders circumcision irrelevant (CHRYSOSTOM) but also excludes all wrongdoing (MARIUS VICTORINUS). The Galatians have been set at odds by this dispute (THEODORET), which legalistic attitudes have exacerbated (JEROME).

The Spirit intends to free us from law (MARIUS VICTORINUS) and reveal to us the way of love (CHRYSOSTOM). We retain the choice between Spirit and the sinful nature, which is not the created nature as such but the mind that is fixated on the flesh (CHRYSOSTOM). It is the proper function of the human spirit to rule the flesh (AUGUSTINE). The Spirit makes slow headway against the sinful nature in this life (AUGUSTINE), sometimes remarkably so (JOHN CASSIAN). All Christians struggle with the old nature, but the aim is to make virtue a second nature (AUGUSTINE). Scripture is to be read spiritually (JEROME). We obey the law spiritually when we act out of love, not fear (AUGUSTINE), remembering that the law is good (CHRYSOSTOM) and the patriarchs were saved under it (JEROME). Only the resurrection can complete sanctification (AUGUSTINE).

5:13a Called to Freedom

LOVE CONSTRAINS CHRISTIAN FREEDOM. THEODORET: He now shifts to ethical exhortation and commends the practice of virtue. "For it was not in order to sin without fear," he says, "that we have been freed from the law." From this it is clear that in rejecting the superfluous parts of the ceremonial law he is commending the observance of the moral law and, above all, love. EPISTLE TO THE GALATIANS 5.13.[1]

5:13b Misusing Freedom

USING FREEDOM AS AN OPPORTUNITY FOR THE SIN NATURE. CLEMENT OF ALEXANDRIA: One who is free and follows the spirit and the truth in the higher sense may look beyond the mere letter of Scripture with its types and precursors. But he should not therefore despise the less mature nor give some cause to lose hope to those who cannot grasp the deeper sense. For even if they are weak and fleshly in comparison with those who are spiritual, they remain the body of Christ. STROMATA 10.[2]

CALLED TO FREEDOM BUT NOT AS AN OCCASION FOR SIN. AUGUSTINE: From this point Paul begins to discuss those works of the law which . . . no one denies also pertain to the new covenant, but with another aim, appropriate to those who perform good works *in freedom*. These acts aim for the rewards of a love that hopes for eternal things and looks forward in faith. This is quite unlike the Jews, who were forced to fulfill these commandments from fear, and not that righteous fear which endures to eternity but one that made them fear for the present life. The result: they fulfill certain works of the law which consist in ceremonies but are completely unable to fulfill those that consist in good conduct. For nothing fulfills these except love. . . . And so the apostle now says, "You are called into freedom, brethren, but on condition that you do not let your freedom be an opportunity for the sin nature. Do not suppose, upon hearing the word *freedom*, that you can sin with impunity." EPISTLE TO THE GALATIANS 43 [IB.5.13].[3]

5:13c Be Slaves to One Another

BE OBEDIENT TO LOVE IN THE MOST RADICAL SENSE. CHRYSOSTOM: He then also shows the way by which this rectification[4] may be easily accomplished. *Be slaves to one another in love*, Paul says. Here again he hints that love of strife, faction, ladder climbing and folly were the causes of their error. The mother of heresies is desire for power. From this foolishness and conceit he is calling them to *be slaves to one another*. Therefore Paul applies this corresponding remedy: "Since you have been torn apart by your desire to rule one another, be slaves to one another. In this way you will be brought together again." He does not openly state their fault, but he states the remedy openly, so that through the remedy they may also

---

[1]CPE 1:358, following Chrysostom *Homily on Galatians* 5.13 [IOEP 4:84]. [2]Migne PG 11:105A-B; cited by Jerome *Epistle to the Galatians* 3.5.13 [Migne PL 26:406C (494)]. [3]Migne PL 35:2136-37. [4]The removal of the yoke of the law.

better grasp the fault. . . . He did not say "love one another" but *be slaves to one another,* to express the most intense possible love. HOMILY ON GALATIANS 5.13.[5]

5:14a *The Whole Law Fulfilled in One Word*

BOTH COVENANTS FROM THE ONE LORD. EPIPHANIUS: What need is there for the holy apostle to make use of the law, if the new covenant is foreign to the old legislation? He wants to show both covenants are from the one Lord. They are best perceived as sharing the same intent. The fulfillment of the law is through the love of one's neighbor, because love is that which effects the perfect good. He therefore says that love is the fulfilling of the law. PANARION 42.12.3, FIFTH REFUTATION OF MARCION.[6]

5:14b *Loving One's Neighbor as Oneself*

THE WHOLE LAW FULFILLED BY LOVE. MARIUS VICTORINUS: The whole work of the law is fulfilled by this one command: love. For one who loves another neither murders nor commits adultery nor steals. . . . Now Paul himself adds a text[7]: *You shall love your neighbor as yourself.* But we ought to understand by *neighbor* every human being and then constantly view Christ as our neighbor. "And you too must love one another but in the spirit." Here he now seems, as if neglecting the previous question and discussion, to urge them to avoid discord. And this can happen if you love one another in the Spirit, not in the flesh nor for the works of the flesh nor in natural observances. For he who loves another feels no envy, nor steals from an-

other, nor despises or abuses him. EPISTLE TO THE GALATIANS 2.5.14.[8]

THE LAW IS OBSERVED NOT IN CIRCUMCISION BUT IN LOVE. CHRYSOSTOM: "Since I have turned the law upside down, if you wish to fulfill it, do not be circumcised; for it is fulfilled not in circumcision but in love." Notice that he does not forget his grief. He keeps on touching upon what troubled him even as he turns to ethical issues. HOMILY ON GALATIANS 5.14.[9]

5:15 *Take Heed That You Are Not Consumed*

THE LAW ALONE WILL EAT YOU UP. JEROME: Paul is not here erupting suddenly into ad hoc legal precepts against the tenor and sequence of the whole letter. He is still discussing circumcision and the observance of the law. . . . If you read the whole Old Testament and understand it according to the text *an eye for an eye, a tooth for a tooth*[10] . . . what appears as justice will eat you away, not avenging anything but consuming everything. EPISTLE TO THE GALATIANS 3.5.15.[11]

BITING AND DEVOURING. CHRYSOSTOM: He does not accuse explicitly, but he speaks hypothetically, so as not to irk them. He has said not "Since you bite one another" but "If you bite." Again, he has not said explicitly here, "You will be destroyed by one another," but instead he says "Take care lest you be destroyed by one another." He is ex-

---

[5]IOEP 4:85; cf. NPNF 1 13:40. [6]GCS 31:157. [7]Lev 19:18. [8]BT 1972:63-64 [1191D-1192A]. [9]IOEP 4:85. [10]Deut 19:21. [11]Migne PL 26:410B-C [499].

pressing his concern and admonition rather than his condemnation. . . . He does not refer only to biting, as the act of a person out of control, but also to devouring, which implies malice. For the one who bites satisfies the immediate passion of anger, but the one who devours proves he is acting like an animal. By *bitings and devourings* he does not mean a literal biting and devouring. He refers to something more pernicious. The harm done by one who tastes human flesh is not so great as that done by the one who sinks his teeth into the soul. In proportion as the living soul is more precious than the corruptible body, so much the worse is the harm done to it. HOMILY ON GALATIANS 5.15.[12]

LOVE OVERCOMES ALL DIFFERENCES. THEODORET: Here Paul hints that, while some had been circumcised under duress, others had relied on their faith and stood firm. Nevertheless, they were at odds, some praising the legalistic way of life, others showing due admiration for the gifts of grace. For this reason Paul focuses his attention on the exhortation to love. EPISTLE TO THE GALATIANS 5.15.[13]

5:16 Walk by the Spirit

WALK IN THE SPIRIT. MARIUS VICTORINUS: The whole essence of the gospel is to think according to the Spirit, to live according to the Spirit, to believe according to the Spirit, to have nothing of the flesh in one's mind and acts and life. That means also having no hope in the flesh. *Walk, then,* he says, *in the Spirit*—that is, "Be alive. If you do so you will not consummate the desire of the flesh. You will admit into consciousness no sin,

which is born of the flesh." EPISTLE TO THE GALATIANS 2.5.16.[14]

THE SPIRIT ABIDES AS THE STRENGTH OF LOVE. CHRYSOSTOM: See how he also shows a better way. It makes virtue uncomplicated and rightly accomplishes what he has previously said—a way that brings forth love and is sustained by love. For nothing, *nothing* makes people so lovable as to be formed by the Spirit. And nothing so causes the Spirit to abide in us as the strength of love. . . . After having stated the cause of the illness he also shows the remedy that bestows health. HOMILY ON GALATIANS 5.16.[15]

5:17a The Desires of the Flesh Are Against the Spirit

NOT A CONDEMNATION OF THE BODY. CHRYSOSTOM: The body as such does not cause motion but is moved. It is not an agent but is acted upon. For desire is not of the body but of the soul. . . . How then does Paul say *the flesh struggles against the spirit*? By *flesh* he means not the physical body but the evil choice. . . . What then? Ought one to suppress the flesh? Was not the one who said this himself clothed with flesh? . . . By *flesh* here he means earthly thoughts that are apathetic and heedless. This is not a condemnation of the body but a reproach of the apathetic soul. For the flesh is an instrument, and no one repudiates and hates the instrument as such, but only the one who handles the instrument badly. . . . Yet, one may argue, even this is a con-

---

[12]IOEP 4:86. [13]CPE 1:358. [14]BT 1972:64 [1192B-C]. [15]IOEP 4:86.

demnation of the body, to call the faults of the soul by the name of the *flesh*. Now I agree that the body is less precious than the soul, yet it is itself good as created. For what is less than truly good may remain proximately good. Evil is not less than the good but opposed to it. . . . The eucharistic mysteries too, and the whole church, are customarily called by the name of *flesh* in Scripture, which is called *the body of Christ*[16] . . . But if he says *the flesh struggles against the Spirit*, he is speaking of two opposing ways of thinking. The things that oppose each other are virtue and wickedness, not the soul and the body. For if the latter are opposed, each is the destruction of the other . . . but if the soul cares for the body . . . and the body serves the soul . . . how can they be contraries and at war with one another? HOMILY ON GALATIANS 5.17.[17]

THE SPIRITUAL SENSE OF SCRIPTURE STRUGGLES AGAINST BEING REDUCED TO ITS HISTORICAL SENSE. JEROME: The *flesh struggles against the Spirit*: that is, the literal and flat understanding of Scripture fights against allegory and spiritual doctrine. . . . And the carnal[18] sense of Scripture, which cannot be fulfilled (since we cannot do all that is written), shows that we do not have it in our power to fulfill the law when even if we wish to follow the letter we are prevented by its impossibility. EPISTLE TO THE GALATIANS 3.5.17.[19]

BOTH FLESH AND SPIRIT ARE GOOD AS CREATED. AUGUSTINE: The fact is that both are good: the spirit is good and the flesh too is good. And the whole person who consists of both, one ruling and one obeying, is indeed good but a changeable good. Yet these chang-

ing goods could not arise were it not for the immutable good, which is the source of every created good, whether small or great. But however small might be one particular good, it is nonetheless made by the one incomparably good. Yet however great, it is in no way comparable to the greatness of its Maker. But in this human nature, good as it is in origin and constitution, there is now war, because there is not yet salvation. ON CONTINENCE 18.[20]

5:17b *The Desires of the Spirit Are Against the Flesh*

WHETHER THE SPIRIT SUCCEEDS. AUGUSTINE: The *flesh struggles against the spirit* yet does not subdue it, since the spirit *also struggles against the flesh*. Although that same law of sin holds something of the flesh as its prisoner and thereby resists the law of the mind,[21] it does not, however, reign in our body, mortal though it is, if our body does not voluntarily obey its desires. ON MARRIAGE AND CONCUPISCENCE 1.35.[22]

AGAINST THE FLESH. JOHN CASSIAN: An inward war is being waged every day within us. The desires of the flesh and of the spirit are within one and the same person. The lust of the flesh rushes headlong into vice, delights in the worldly enjoyments that seem to satisfy. By contrast the opposed desire of

---

[16]E.g., Rom 7:14; 1 Cor 10:16; 12:27; Eph 4:12. [17]IOEP 4:87. Cf. Origen *On First Principles* 3.4.1-5 [GCS 22:263-70]. [18]The Scripture understood as God's command, apart from the fulfillment of God's promise. [19]Migne PL 26:413A-B [502-3]. [20]Migne PL 40:360. [21]Cf. Rom 7:25. [22]Migne PL 44:433.

the spirit is so eager to cleave entirely to spiritual pursuits that it in an exaggerated way chooses even to exclude the necessary uses of the flesh. By wishing to be so inseparably attached to spiritual things it refuses to take care of its own bodily fragility. CONFERENCES 4.11.2.[23]

5:17c Flesh and Spirit Are Opposed

NO IMPLANTED SINLESSNESS. AUGUSTINE: Now this, I think, he writes to the Galatians, to whom he says, *Who gave you the Spirit. . . . ?*[24] From this it is apparent that he is speaking to Christians, people to whom God had given the Spirit, and therefore to the baptized. See, the sinful nature is an adversary even within the baptized, and there is not in them that possibility [of sinlessness] which [Pelagius[25]] says is so implanted in our nature that it cannot be annulled. ON NATURE AND GRACE 61.[26]

UNDER NATURE, LAW AND GRACE. AUGUSTINE: People think that the apostle here denies that we possess free will. They do not perceive what he is saying to them: If they refuse to hold fast to the grace they have received, through which alone they are able to walk in the Spirit and avoid fulfilling the desires of the flesh, they will not be able to do as they wish. . . . It is love that *fulfills the law.*[27] But *the wisdom of the flesh* by following temporal goods opposes spiritual love. How can it be made subject to the law of God (that is, freely and obediently fulfill righteousness and not be opposed to it) when even as it tries it must be vanquished? The flesh imagines that it can procure a greater temporal good by iniquity than by maintaining righteousness. The first stage,

the *natural life* of a human being, precedes the law, when no wrongdoing or malice is prohibited. The natural being makes no resistance at all to base desires, since there is no one to prohibit them. The second stage is *under law* before grace, when he is indeed prohibited and tries to abstain from sin but is overcome because he does not yet love righteousness for God's sake and its own but wishes to observe it in the hope of earthly acquisitions. And therefore, when he sees righteousness on one side and temporal good on another, he is dragged by the weight of his temporal desire and thus forsakes righteousness, which he was trying to maintain only in order to have that which he now sees that he is going to lose by maintaining it. The third stage of life is the one *under grace,* when no temporal good is preferred to righteousness. This cannot happen except by spiritual love, which the Lord has taught by his example and bestowed by grace. For in this life, even if there remain desires of the flesh from the mortality of the body, yet they do not subdue the mind to consent to sin. EPISTLE TO THE GALATIANS 46 [IB.5.17].[28]

5:18 Led by the Spirit, Not Under the Law

TWO WAYS OF LIFE. AUGUSTINE: A person is *under the law* when he is conscious of abstaining from works of sin through fear of the torments threatened by the law rather than by love of righteousness. He is not yet

---

[23]CSEL 13:105; citing Abbot Daniel. [24]Gal 3:5. [25]Pelagius defended the possibility of continuing sinlessness. [26]Migne PL 44:276-77. [27]Cf. Rom 13:8, 10; Gal 5:14. [28]Migne PL 35:2138-39.

free, not yet a stranger to the will to sin. For he does wrong by his very willing, since he would prefer if it were possible that there should be nothing for the will to fear, so that he might do freely what he secretly desires. . . . By the law which he has used to instill fear [God] has not imparted love. Godly love is suffused in our hearts not through the letter of the law but through the Holy Spirit, which is given to us. ON NATURE AND GRACE 67.[29]

THE LAW NOT DISPARAGED. CHRYSOSTOM: Yet it seems to me that here he has pronounced a great and remarkable eulogy on the law. For the power of the law was such as to put it in the place of the office of the Spirit before the Spirit came to us. That is not to say that one should therefore cleave to this custodian. For then we were properly under the law, so that by fear we might restrain our desires, the Spirit not yet having appeared. But what need is there now of the law when the Spirit has been given? This grace does not merely bid us to abstain from the commands of the old covenant but also quenches them and leads us on to a higher rule of life. HOMILY ON GALATIANS 5.18.[30]

WHETHER THE PROPHETS WERE UNDER THE LAW. JEROME: The holy prophets and Moses, walking in the Spirit and living in the Spirit, were not under the law. But they lived as if under the law, so that they appeared indeed to be under the law, but only in order to benefit those who were under the law and spur them on from the lowliness of the letter toward the heights of the Spirit. EPISTLE TO THE GALATIANS 3.5.18.[31]

PERSEVERANCE UNDER GRACE. AUGUSTINE: He did not say "Walk in the Spirit so that you will not have desires of the flesh" but *so that you will not gratify them*. Not to have them at all, indeed, is not the struggle but the prize of struggle, if we shall have obtained the victory by perseverance under grace. For it is only the transformation of the body into an immortal state that will no longer have desires of the flesh. EPISTLE TO THE GALATIANS 47 [IB.5.18].[32]

---

[29]Migne PL 44:280. [30]IOEP 4:89. [31]Migne PL 26:413D-414A [503]. [32]Migne PL 35:2139.

5:19-26 FRUITS AND WORKS

[19]*Now the works of the flesh are plain: fornication, impurity, licentiousness,* [20]*idolatry, sorcery, enmity, strife, jealousy, anger, selfishness, dissension, party spirit,* [21]*envy,*[k] *drunkenness, carousing, and the like. I warn you, as I warned you before, that those who do such things shall not inherit the kingdom of God.* [22]*But the fruit*

of the Spirit is love, joy, peace, patience, kindness, goodness, faithfulness, [23]*gentleness, self-control; against such there is no law.* [24]*And those who belong to Christ Jesus have crucified the flesh with its passions and desires.*

[25]*If we live by the Spirit, let us also walk by the Spirit.* [26]*Let us have no self-conceit, no provoking of one another, no envy of one another.*

k *Other ancient authorities add* murder

OVERVIEW: The works of the sin nature are easily detected (JEROME). They are the offspring of the world (AMBROSIASTER). They come from the mind, not the body as such (THEODORET). Love is the first of Christian virtues (JEROME). The others are correlated with Scripture's list of evil works (AUGUSTINE). There is no complete list of fruits (AUGUSTINE). This list has the same number as the Decalogue (AMBROSIASTER). It is not exhaustive (JEROME), nor does it exclude repentance (FULGENTIUS). The Spirit produces fruit whereas flesh as such is fruitless (JEROME). Neither flesh nor spirit can be alive without the soul (CHRYSOSTOM). We must mortify our sinful passions (CHRYSOSTOM), taking our baptism as an act of crucifixion (BASIL OF CAESAREA), not refusing to suffer in the flesh (EPIPHANIUS). Zeal for truth may breed strife among saints (JEROME). Spiritual Christians must persevere in rejecting the law (CHRYSOSTOM) but not let this perseverance lead to quarrels (THEODORET). Love and peace are the sources of all spiritual goods (AMBROSIASTER). Paul condemns witchcraft (JEROME). Envy and jealousy are real though different faults (AUGUSTINE).

5:19 Works of the Flesh: Fornication, Impurity, Licentiousness

WORKS OF THE FLESH. AMBROSIASTER: These and others like them are the members of sin, which the apostle calls *the works of the flesh,* because these errors come from the world, from which also the flesh comes. For all these sins arise from the side of the flesh, not from that of the Spirit. EPISTLE TO THE GALATIANS 5.21.[1]

THE WORKS OF THE FLESH ARE PLAIN. JEROME: By saying that *the works of the flesh are plain* he means that they are known to all because they are so self-evidently bad and abhorrent, so much so that even those who do them desire to hide their deeds. Or else it may mean that they are plain only to believers in Christ. EPISTLE TO THE GALATIANS 3.5.19-21.[2]

5:20 Works Not of Flesh Alone

THESE WORKS NOT ASCRIBED TO THE FLESH ALONE. THEODORET: Now it is clear that idolatry and sorcery and things of that kind belong not to the flesh but to the soul. In fact it is not the flesh that he is condemning but the wayward mind. EPISTLE TO THE GALATIANS 5.19-21.[3]

SORCERY FORBIDDEN. JEROME: So that poi-

---

[1]CSEL 81.3:60. [2]Migne PL 26:414D-415A [505]. [3]CPE 1:359. Cf. Chrysostom *Homily on Galatians* [IOEP 4:89-90].

soning and sorcery might not appear to be condoned in the New Testament, they are included among the works of the flesh. This happens when people love and are loved through magical arts. Epistle to the Galatians 3.5.19-21.[4]

Enmity, Strife and False Doctrine. Jerome: It often happens that dissensions arise in the interpretation of Scripture, from which heresies, here numbered among the works of the flesh, boil over. For if *the wisdom of the flesh is at enmity with God*[5] (and all false doctrines, being repugnant to God, are at enmity), heresies also, being at enmity with God, are consequently included among the works of the flesh. Epistle to the Galatians 3.5.19-21.[6]

5:21a Envy, Drunkenness, Carousing

Envy Distinguished from Jealousy. Augustine: Let no one suppose that *envy* is the same thing as *jealousy*. For they are indeed neighbors and because of that very neighborhood either of them is often freely substituted for the other.... But because each is distinguished here they require us to make a distinction. *Jealousy* is the mind's anguish when someone achieves something that two or more were seeking but which can be had only by one. Jealousy is cured by *peace*, in which all may obtain that which is sought and thus become one. *Envy* on the other hand is the grief one feels in one's mind when an unworthy person appears to have obtained something, even if it is not being sought by others. Envy is overcome by *meekness*, when all who yearn appeal to the judgment of God and do not resist his will, trusting rather in the justice of what he does

than in one's own estimate of what people deserve. Epistle to the Galatians 52.[7]

The Catalog of Vices. Jerome: It would have been a long task to enumerate all the works of the flesh and make a catalog of vices, so Paul has wrapped this all up in one phrase: "and the like." I wish that we could avoid these vices as easily as we can see them! Epistle to the Galatians 3.5.19-21.[8]

5:21b A Warning About Inheriting God's Kingdom

Must Inheritors of the Kingdom Be Perfect? Fulgentius: Since God is righteous, such people do not obtain the kingdom of heaven so long as they do such things. But since God is merciful, the wicked, if they cease doing revolting things by which they try God's patience and turn to God in humble amendment, they do without doubt obtain the kingdom of God. On the Remission of Sins 1.15.3.[9]

5:22 The Fruit of the Spirit: Love, Joy, Peace, Patience, Kindness, Goodness, Faith

Good Works Require Grace, While Evil Works Come From Distorted Freedom. Chrysostom: He didn't say "the works of the Spirit" but *the fruits*. Therefore [it may seem that] the soul is superfluous. For if the statement mentions the flesh and the Spirit, where is the soul? Is Paul then speaking of soulless beings? For if the evil belongs to the

---

[4]Migne PL 26:415D [506]. [5]Cf. Rom 8:1-16. [6]Migne PL 26:417A [507]. [7]Migne PL 35:2142. [8]Migne PL 26:418A-B [509]. [9]CCL 91A:663.

flesh and the good to the Spirit, then the soul would be superfluous. Not at all; for the ordering of the passions is the work of the soul and concerns the soul. The soul is situated in the middle of the struggle between virtue and vice. If the soul uses the body as it should, it makes itself more spiritual. But if it departs from the Spirit and yields itself to evil desires, it renders it more earthy. Do you see how everywhere he is not speaking of the essence of the flesh but of moral choice that is inclined toward virtue or vice? So why does he refer to *the fruits of the Spirit*? Because evil works come from us alone, and hence he calls them works, while the good works require not only the resolution of our will but the kindness of God. HOMILY ON GALATIANS 5.22.[10]

FRUIT, NOT WORKS. JEROME: He has spoken elegantly by allotting works to the flesh and fruits to the Spirit. Vices come to nothing and perish in themselves. Virtues multiply and abound in fruit. EPISTLE TO THE GALATIANS 3.5.22.[11]

BEGINNING WITH LOVE. JEROME: What deserves to hold the first place among the fruits of the Spirit if not love? Without love other virtues are not reckoned to be virtues. From love is born all that is good. EPISTLE TO THE GALATIANS 3.5.22.[12]

JOY, PEACE AND THE SPIRIT'S FRUITS. JEROME: By *joy* people mean an elation of mind over things that are worthy of exultation, whereas *gaiety* is an undisciplined elation of mind which knows no moderation. . . . We should not suppose that *peace* is limited to not quarreling with others. Rather the peace of Christ—that is, our inheri-

tance—is with us when the mind is at peace and undisturbed by conflicting emotions. Among the *fruits of the Spirit* faith holds the seventh and sacred place, being elsewhere one of three—*faith, hope and love*.[13] Nor is it remarkable that hope is not included in this catalog, since the object of hope is already included as a part of faith. EPISTLE TO THE GALATIANS 3.5.22.[14]

FORNICATION AND LOVE. AUGUSTINE: He put fornication at the head of carnal vices and love at the head of spiritual virtues. Anyone who takes pains in the study of divine Scripture will be prompted to inquire attentively into the rest. Fornication is love divorced from legitimate wedlock. It roves everywhere in search of an opportunity to fulfill its lust. Yet nothing is so rightly suited for spiritual procreation as the union of the soul with God. The more firmly it adheres, the more blameless it is. Love is what enables it to cleave. Rightly then the opposite of fornication is love. It is the sole means by which chastity is preserved. Now impure acts come from all those disturbances produced from the lust to fornicate, to which the joy of tranquillity is opposed. And bondage to idolatry is the ultimate fornication of the soul. A most furious war is waged against the gospel and against those who have been reconciled to God. The remnants of fornication, though long lukewarm, can nonetheless still be rekindled. The contrary of this war is the peace by which we are reconciled to God. When the same peace of God is maintained toward humans, the vices

---

[10]IOEP 4:90. [11]Migne PL 26:419A [510]. [12]Migne PL 26:418C [510]. [13]1 Cor 13:13. [14]Migne PL 26:419B-420B [510-12].

of poisonings, enmity, strife, deceit, animosity and dissension are healed among us, so others among us may be treated with due moderation. Forbearance fights to endure these vices, kindness to assuage them and goodness to forgive them. Furthermore faith struggles against heresy, meekness against envy, continence against drunkenness and gluttony. EPISTLE TO THE GALATIANS 51 [IB.5.22-23].[15]

5:23 Gentleness and Self-Control: Against These There Is No Law

THE ANALOGY OF TEN. AMBROSIASTER: Paul did not mention more than ten excellent behaviors because he is referring to the fruits of the Spirit. These fruits embrace everything in the tablets of God's covenant, in which no more than ten words of command are succinctly handed down. EPISTLE TO THE GALATIANS 5.24.2.[16]

AGAINST SUCH THINGS. AUGUSTINE: He did not say "against these," so that they would not be thought the only ones—though in fact even if he had said this we ought to understand all the goods of this kind that can be imagined. No, he says *against such things*, namely, both these and whatever is like them. ON CONTINENCE 9.[17]

AGAINST SUCH THERE IS NO LAW. AUGUSTINE: He has added *against such there is no law* so that we understand that those on whom the law must be imposed are those in whom these excellent behaviors do not already reign. For those in whom they reign are the ones who apply the law legitimately, since the law is not imposed on them with coercive intent, seeing that righteousness is

already their overwhelming preference. . . . These spiritual fruits reign in one in whom sins do not reign. These good things reign if they are so delightful that they themselves uphold the mind in its trials from falling into consent to sin. For whatever gives us more delight, this we necessarily perform. EPISTLE TO THE GALATIANS 49 [IB.5.22-23].[18]

5:24 Crucifying the Flesh

WHAT SORT OF PERSON IS ONE WHO HAS CRUCIFIED THE FLESH? CHRYSOSTOM: So that no one may ask, "And who is like this?" he points to people who perform such good things by their works. Once again he makes flesh stand for evil deeds. He does not mean that they had destroyed their flesh; otherwise how were they going to live? For the crucified person is dead and inactive. But what he means is strict discipleship. Even if desires press hard they rage in vain. Since the power of the Spirit is such, let us live according to it, and let us be content with it. HOMILY ON GALATIANS 5.24.[19]

BEGINNING WITH BAPTISM. BASIL OF CAESAREA: We *crucify* the flesh, of course, by being baptized in the water of baptism, which is a likeness of the cross and his death, his entombment and his resurrection, as it is written. ON BAPTISM 1.15.[20]

MUST THE FLESH SUFFER? EPIPHANIUS: If those who are Christ's have crucified the flesh, it is therefore clear that the slaves of

---

[15]Migne PL 35:2141-42. [16]CSEL 81.3:61; commenting on Gal 5:24. [17]Migne PL 40:354-55. [18]Migne PL 35:2140-41. [19]IOEP 4:90-91. [20]SC 357:150 [1552]; alluding also to Rom 6.

Christ have presented their flesh in purity along with its desires and passions. They are participating in Christ, thus acknowledging that he crucified the flesh. That is why the faithful, thinking the same thoughts as their Lord, have crucified the flesh. And if believers have crucified the flesh it is unthinkable that those who suffered on Christ's behalf should not be reigning with him. PANARION 42.12.3, SEVENTH REFUTATION OF MARCION.[21]

5:25 Live by the Spirit, Walk by the Spirit

LIVING AND WALKING BY THE SPIRIT. CHRYSOSTOM: What he means by *walk by the Spirit* is "let us be content in the power of the Spirit, and let us not seek to augment it with the law." Then, having shown that those who introduce circumcision are doing this through ambitious motives, he says, "Let us not become proud, which is the cause of evils, calling one another out to factiousness and strife, in jealousy of one another. For jealousy comes from vainglory, and from vainglory all those other evils." HOMILY ON GALATIANS 5.25.[22]

5:26 No Self-Conceit, Provoking, Envy

NO ENVY. AMBROSIASTER: What he is saying is that if we live well and honestly we should also express this in good conduct. This is what it is to live in the Spirit: to have an unblemished life. We walk in the Spirit if we study peace. For this is what engenders love. It is, on the other hand, empty glory to seek a victory where there is no prize, so that someone would end up having only a zeal for strife and spiritual competition. These things tend toward discord and wrangling. EPISTLE TO THE GALATIANS 5.26.[23]

NO PROVOKING. THEODORET: Some who were grounded in faith were showing a constant disdain of their oppressors. They were thereby provoking them to strife. Paul exhorts them to offer their hands to those who have inclined toward the law. EPISTLE TO THE GALATIANS 5.26.[24]

---

[21]GCS 31:158-59. [22]IOEP 4:91. [23]CSEL 81.3:61-62; citing 2 Tim 2:24. [24]CPE 1:360.

6:1-5 SPIRITUAL ADMONITION

[1]*Brethren, if a man is overtaken in any trespass, you who are spiritual should restore him in a spirit of gentleness. Look to yourself, lest you too be tempted.* [2]*Bear one another's burdens, and so fulfil the law of Christ.* [3]*For if any one thinks he is something, when he is nothing, he deceives himself.* [4]*But let each one test his own work, and then his reason to boast will be in himself alone and not in his neighbor.* [5]*For each man will have to bear his own load.*

OVERVIEW: It is the duty of the Spirit-led to be gentle (CHRYSOSTOM, AUGUSTINE). Gentleness will convert the sinner (AMBROSIASTER), especially when some trouble is taken (JEROME). All of us are subject to temptation (JEROME). Bear with the common weakness of the body (ORIGEN), forgiving sins as Christ did (JEROME), remembering that we too are imperfect (THEODORET). Love is the essence of the law (AUGUSTINE). All pride is sinful (JEROME) and arises from our great distance from God (AMBROSIASTER). We must scrutinize our lives and only then boast—if we must (CHRYSOSTOM). We need not be afraid to associate with sinners in need (AMBROSIASTER), for the coming judgment will leave each of us with our own burden of conscience (JEROME).

6:1a Overtaken in Any Trespass

CAUGHT UNAWARES. CHRYSOSTOM: The Galatians were gratifying their private feelings under pretext of rebuke. They appeared to be doing this to correct the sins of others. Paul wanted to put a stop to their love of being first. He says, *Brothers, if someone is overtaken in any trespass*. Note that he does not say "if he trespasses" but *if he is overtaken*, that is, if he is caught off guard. HOMILY ON GALATIANS 6.1.[1]

THE MEANING OF OVERTAKEN. AUGUSTINE: One is overtaken on those occasions either when one sins without seeing at the time that it is a sin or when one sees this and is still overcome. One sins either in ignorance of truth or under the limitations of infirmity. ON LYING 22.[2]

6:1b Restoration in a Spirit of Gentleness

SPURRED WITH KINDNESS. AMBROSIASTER: Now Paul speaks to those who were spiritually stronger, lest by becoming proud in their own good life they should think it right to despise and reject one who had perhaps been overtaken by sin. And so they must be told that people struggling with sin are to be spurred toward reform with kindness. If they were to be more harshly punished with coercive authority they would not accept reproof. They would begin to defend themselves against seeming to be base and worse. If you protect a person from strife and arrogance he will become meek in relation to you, since humility tends to make even the proud humble. EPISTLE TO THE GALATIANS 6.2.1-2.[3]

RESTORATION. CHRYSOSTOM: Paul does not say "punish" or "pass judgment" but *restore*. Nor did he even stop there, but showing that he strongly desired them to be patient with those who stumbled he adds *in a spirit of gentleness*. He does not say "in gentleness" but *in a spirit of gentleness*, showing that this also is the will of the Spirit and that the capacity to correct another's faults is a spiritual gift. HOMILY ON GALATIANS 6.1.[4]

THE SPIRIT OF GENTLENESS. JEROME: The Spirit-led person should correct a sinner gently and meekly. He must not be inflexible, angry or aggrieved in his desire to correct him. He should stir him up with the promise of salvation, promising remission and bringing forth the testimony of Christ. EPIS-

---

[1]IOEP 4:91-92. [2]Migne PL 40:532. [3]CSEL 81.3:62. [4]IOEP 4:91.

TLE TO THE GALATIANS 3.6.1.[5]

THE TEST OF THE SPIRIT-LED PERSON.
AUGUSTINE: There is no surer test of the spiritual person than his treatment of another's sin. Note how he takes care to deliver the sinner rather than triumph over him, to help him rather than punish him and, so far as lies in his capacity, to support him. EPISTLE TO THE GALATIANS 56 [IB.6.I].[6]

6:1c Beware Lest You Be Tempted

IN AMENDING ANOTHER'S WRONGDOING, THINK OF WHAT MIGHT BEFALL YOU.
JEROME: Maybe Paul is saying that you should identify with the sinner in order to do him good. This is not to imply, of course, that one should seemingly commit the same wrong and pretend that one is also subject to it. No, in another's wrongdoing one should think of what might befall oneself. Help the other with the same compassion that one would hope to receive from another. LETTER 116.29.2.[7]

ALL ARE TEMPTED. JEROME: It is reasonable to ask why one should instruct the sinner in a spirit of gentleness. It is good to reflect that one might oneself be tempted. Would the righteous person, who is certain of his own resolve and confident that he cannot fall, therefore have no duty to instruct the sinner in the spirit of gentleness? To this we reply that even if the righteous one has prevailed, knowing with what difficulty he prevailed over his own temptations he should rather be ready to extend pardon to the sinner. . . . Overcoming or not overcoming is sometimes in our

own power. But being tempted is in the power of the tempter. The Savior himself was tempted.[8] So who of us can be sure that he might cross this sea of life without any temptation? EPISTLE TO THE GALATIANS 3.6.1.[9]

6:2 Bearing Burdens, Fulfilling the Law of Christ

BEARING THE BURDENS OF THE POOR.
ORIGEN: By *burdens* he means the needs of the body. So to the extent that anyone is richer in resources, he is called to bear the poor person's burden and relieve poverty by his abundance. COMMENTARY ON ROMANS 10.6.[10]

THE BURDEN THE SAVIOR BORE FOR US.
JEROME: Sin is a burden, as the psalmist affirms.[11] . . . This burden the Savior bore for us, teaching by his life what we ought to do. He himself bears our iniquities and grieves for us and invites those who are cast down by the burden of sin and the law to take up the light yoke of virtue.[12] Therefore the one who does not demean his brother's salvation extends his hand as needed. So far as it lies within him he weeps with him as he weeps; he shares the neighbor's weakness. He counts another's sins as his own. Such is the one who fulfills the law of Christ through love. EPISTLE TO THE GALATIANS 3.6.2.[13]

---

[5]Migne PL 26:425B-C [518]. [6]Migne PL 35:2143. [7]CSEL 55:417. [8]E.g., Mt 4:1-11; Mk 1:12-13; Lk 4:1-13. [9]Migne PL 26:425B-426C [518-20]. [10]Migne PG 14:1257 [671]; from Rufinus's Latin translation. Followed by Jerome *Epistle to the Galatians* 3.6.2 [Migne PL 26:427B-428A]. [11]E.g., Ps 38. [12]Mt 11:30. [13]Migne PL 26:427B-C [520-21].

LOVE SUMS UP THE LAW. AUGUSTINE: *The law of Christ* means the law of love. The one who loves his neighbor fulfills the law. The love of neighbor is strongly commended even in the Old Testament.[14] The apostle elsewhere says that it is by love that all the commands of the law are summed up.[15] If so, then it is evident that even that Scripture which was given to the covenant people was the law of Christ, which, since it was not being fulfilled by fear, he came to fulfill by love. The same Scripture, therefore, and the same law is called the old covenant when it weighs down in slavery those who are grasping after earthly goods. It is called the new testament when it raises to freedom those who are ardently seeking the eternal good. EPISTLE TO THE GALATIANS 58 [IB.6.2].[16]

LOVE FULFILLED WHEN YOU BEAR EACH OTHER'S BURDEN. THEODORET: This means: "You have one deficiency but not another. The neighbor's case is the opposite. He has another deficit but not the one you have. You must bear his and he yours. For thus is the law of love fulfilled." By *the law of Christ* he means love, for he himself said, "I give you a new commandment, to love one another."[17] EPISTLE TO THE GALATIANS 6.2.[18]

6:3 Humility Curbs Self-Deception

HUMILITY ENABLES GROWTH. AMBROSIASTER: It is true, and no one is unaware of it, that if we consider honestly our acts and thoughts we find ourselves superior to no one and cannot easily pass judgment on another. For the person who is puffed up as if he were something special is misled, since he does not know that humility becomes a means of growth. For he does not have before his eyes the words and deeds of the Savior, who, though he be Lord of all, humbled himself so as to give us a pattern that we might follow should we wish to grow. If we were to exalt ourselves, we would stumble as a result of the ignorance of a heart elated by the hope of presuming to be more worthy of praise. EPISTLE TO THE GALATIANS 6.4.1.[19]

TWO WAYS TO READ: SELF-DECEPTION OR BECOMING NOTHING THROUGH ONE'S ARROGANCE. JEROME: This [verse] can be read in two distinct ways. . . . The sense of the first is "If someone thinks he is something when he is nothing, he deceives himself." The second is deeper and more meaningful to me: "If someone thinks he is something, by the very fact of thinking himself something and judging himself, not from his love toward his neighbors but from his own work and labors, contented with his own virtue, he himself becomes nothing through this very arrogance and is his own deceiver.". . . The meaning of this passage is also linked to circumcision and the law in the following way: One who is spiritual yet has no compassion for his neighbor, despising the lowly because of his own self-elevation, is his own deceiver, not knowing that the spirit of the law adds up finally to loving one another. EPISTLE TO THE GALATIANS 3.6.3.[20]

6:4a Testing One's Own Work

STRINGENT SELF-EXAMINATION. CHRYSOS-

---

[14]Lev 19:18. [15]Rom 13:10. [16]Migne PL 35:2145. [17]Jn 13:34. [18]CPE 1:361. [19]CSEL 81.3:63. [20]Migne PL 26:428C [522].

TOM: Here Paul shows that we must scrutinize our lives. We must test what we have done not cheaply but stringently. For example, suppose you have done something good. Consider whether it might have been through vanity or through necessity, or with animosity, or in hypocrisy, or through some other self-centered motive. HOMILY ON GALATIANS 6.4.[21]

6:4b Reason to Boast

IS PAUL ENCOURAGING BOASTFULNESS? CHRYSOSTOM: He says this not by way of command but by way of concession. It is as though he had said, "It is absurd to boast, but if you must, do not boast against your neighbor, like the Pharisee."[22] The person who learns this lesson will also soon give up boasting altogether. Thus Paul's reason for conceding this was to drive out the larger malady by small steps. For the one who is accustomed to boast with regard to himself alone, and not against others, will soon reform this fault also. If he does not think himself better than others—for that is the meaning of not looking to the other—but is chastened by examining himself by himself, he will later stop this boasting too. HOMILY ON GALATIANS 6.4.[23]

6:5 Each Person Bears His or Her Own Load

NO ONE INCRIMINATED FOR ANOTHER'S SIN. AMBROSIASTER: Finally he wants it to be clear to those who are proud that nobody is incriminated for another's sin. So no one should be afraid to associate with a sinner or to aid him if he comes to him so that he may be of benefit to him. EPISTLE TO THE GALATIANS 6.5.[24]

WHETHER THIS VERSE IS COMPATIBLE WITH 6:2. JEROME: This seems to contradict the words above.[25] . . . But one must see that he was there telling us, as sinners in the present life, to support one another and be a help to one another in the present age. Here he is speaking of the Lord's judgment of us, which is not based on the sin of another or by comparison with others but according to one's own work. EPISTLE TO THE GALATIANS 3.6.5.[26]

---

[21]IOEP 4:93. [22]Lk 18:11. [23]IOEP 4:93-94. [24]CSEL 81.3:63. [25]Gal 6:2: "Bear one another's burdens." [26]Migne PL 26:429A-B [523].

6:6-10 PRECEPTS FOR DISCIPLESHIP

[6]*Let him who is taught the word share all good things with him who teaches.* [7]*Do not be deceived; God is not mocked, for whatever a man sows, that he will also reap.* [8]*For he who sows to his own flesh will from the flesh reap corruption; but*

he who sows to the Spirit will from the Spirit reap eternal life. [9]And let us not grow weary in well-doing, for in due season we shall reap, if we do not lose heart. [10]So then, as we have opportunity, let us do good to all men, and especially to those who are of the household of faith.

OVERVIEW: Paul turns from spiritual to temporal goods (JEROME). He proposes an absolute community of goods between disciple and master (CHRYSOSTOM), assuming that the master is worthy (AMBROSIASTER). He reminds those who fail in this (JEROME) and those who observe the law (MARIUS VICTORINUS) that God is never deceived. Both those who cling to the law (MARIUS VICTORINUS) and those who indulge the carnal vices (CHRYSOSTOM) will get what they deserve. To avoid sowing in a fleshly way we must sow in God's Spirit (JEROME), suppressing the body's lusts by righteous conduct (AUGUSTINE), not hoping for immediate rewards (MARIUS VICTORINUS). Alternately cajoling and threatening (CHRYSOSTOM) Paul reminds his hearers that both life and the world must end (MARIUS VICTORINUS). The law is replaced by universal love (CHRYSOSTOM). This is shown most profitably in those who practice it (MARIUS VICTORINUS) and perhaps especially in teachers (JEROME).

6:6 Sharing Between Disciple and Teacher

SHARE ALL GOOD THINGS WITH THE TEACHER. CHRYSOSTOM: He means "let him display complete freedom in giving to him." For this is what he was hinting at by saying "in all good things." "Nothing," he says, "is to be the disciple's own, but everything is to

be common; for he receives more than he gives, as much more as things heavenly exceed things earthly." HOMILY ON GALATIANS 6.6.[1]

THE TEACHER'S RESPONSIBILITY. AMBROSIASTER: He says this so that hearers may share all their goods with their teachers. But if teachers practice otherwise than they teach, hearers should protest rather than share these goods. It may be clear thereby that the law is your guide rather than the person. For it will be his problem, not yours. EPISTLE TO THE GALATIANS 6.6.[2]

REAPING AND SHARING TEMPORAL GIFTS. JEROME: The meaning is this: Since previously he has been speaking to those who are spiritual about ethics . . . he now on the contrary speaks to those who are still rather weak, who are disciples yet live according to the flesh. Just as they reap spiritual gifts from their teacher, so they are called to give material gifts in return. EPISTLE TO THE GALATIANS 3.6.6.[3]

6:7a God Is Not Mocked

AVOID FURTHER ERRORS. MARIUS VICTORINUS: He adds another principle which is generally stated but is relevant to what he

---

[1]IOEP 4:95. [2]CSEL 81.3:63-64. [3]Migne PL 26:429C [524].

said above to prevent their following anything beside the gospel (that is, adding also a legalistic way of life and works). Do not err, he says, for all those things which are grounded apart from the gospel are error-prone. And he has added the force of necessity to his precept: *God*, he says, *is not mocked*. He does not say, "God knows all," lest they should hope for some sort of cheap pardon for their error or for something that might be hidden. Rather *God is not mocked*, and Paul clarifies what will happen to those who err and those who hold fast to worldly life. EPISTLE TO THE GALATIANS 2.6.[4]

ANTICIPATING EVASIONS. JEROME: Foreseeing in the Spirit that those who ought to furnish sustenance for the necessities of life to their teacher might plead poverty . . . he adds, *Make no mistake; God is not mocked*. EPISTLE TO THE GALATIANS 3.6.7.[5]

6:7b-8a *Whatever One Sows, One Reaps*

SOWING AND REAPING IN THE SPIRIT. MARIUS VICTORINUS: Some Galatians, who thought that they ought to adopt the Jewish way of life, so as to observe the sabbath and undergo circumcision and do other things of this sort in their carnal understanding, could have hope in the flesh and from the flesh. Anyone, therefore, who has hope in the flesh and sows his own hope in the flesh will have a harvest from the flesh, that is, fruit from the flesh. But what fruit? Corruption, he says; for indeed the flesh is corrupted, and this is its end, that it grows corrupt and putrid. It perishes and dies. All things, then, that are of the flesh grow putrid and suffer corruption. . . . Therefore it is better to have hope in the Spirit, so that we may have hope

[in what comes] from the Spirit: the hope and the fruit of the Spirit. This is what it means to sow in the Spirit—eternal life. For this present life indeed is life but not life eternal. But the one who lives here in the Spirit and acts according to the Spirit and does nothing corrupt sows for himself eternal life. And this will be his harvest, that on departing he will receive eternal life. EPISTLE TO THE GALATIANS 2.6.8.[6]

A WARNING AGAINST "SOWING TO ONE'S OWN FLESH." CHRYSOSTOM: The one who sows with his body luxury, drunkenness and insane desires will reap what comes from these. And what is that? Punishment, vengeance, shame, ridicule and destruction. . . . For as these things themselves perish they corrupt the body with them. The fruits of the Spirit are not so but quite contrary. Consider now: If you sow merciful acts, heavenly habitations and eternal glory await you.[7] If you sow love a crown of honor waits for you—the blessings of angels and the athlete's victory. HOMILY ON GALATIANS 6.7-8.[8]

6:8b *Sowing to the Spirit Reaps Eternal Life*

TWO FIELDS. JEROME: All that we say, do or think is sown in two fields, the fallen nature and the Spirit. If what comes from our hand, mouth and heart is good, it is sown in the Spirit and will produce fruits of eternal life. If it is bad, when harvested from the field of the sin nature it will produce an unsavory crop of corruption for us. . . . It should be ob-

---

[4]BT 1972:67 [1194B-C]. [5]Migne PL 26:430C [525]. [6]BT 1972:67-68 [1194C-1195A]. [7]Lk 16:9. [8]IOEP 4:96. Cf. Theodoret *Epistle to the Galatians* 6.8 [CPE 1:361-62].

served that to the one who sows in the flesh is given an additional term, *in his flesh*. But the one who sows in the Spirit is said not to sow in his spirit but simply *in the Spirit*. For the one who sows good things sows not in his own spirit but in God's, from whom he will also reap eternal life. EPISTLE TO THE GALATIANS 3.6.8.[9]

REAPING ETERNAL LIFE. AUGUSTINE: To sow in the spirit is to serve righteousness from faith and with love and not to heed the desires of sin, even though they arise from mortal flesh. . . . When we are under grace[10] we sow in tears, when desires arise from our animal body, which we resist by not consenting, so that we may reap in joy. We reap when, by the reformation of our body, no vexation or peril of temptation comes to trouble us from any physical source. EPISTLE TO THE GALATIANS 61 [IB.6.7-10].[11]

6:9 *Not Losing Heart*

ON NOT GROWING WEARY IN DOING GOOD. MARIUS VICTORINUS: It is not enough that we do good; for our goodness will not be recognized straight away by God if we do good, but only if we *do not grow weary in doing good*. Many begin, many in a way persevere, yet later they give up, either tired or led astray. He justly warns them that they should not grow weary in any way, lest by their weariness they leave off what they began when they began to do well. EPISTLE TO THE GALATIANS 2.6.9.[12]

6:10a *As Opportunity Allows, Do Good to All People*

TIME IS LIMITED. MARIUS VICTORINUS: He

gives the strongest possible imperative to well-doing: time is short. Life is quickly reaching its term. The end of the world is at hand. *As we have opportunity* means either while we have our own life or while there is life in this world. EPISTLE TO THE GALATIANS 2.6.10.[13]

WHILE WE HAVE TIME, DO GOOD. CHRYSOSTOM: On one side he exhorts them and draws them on, while on the other he drives and pushes them, saying *therefore, while we have time, let us do good*. For just as it is not always within our power to sow, neither is it to show mercy. For when the opportunity is taken away, however vehemently we may desire it back we shall not have it. HOMILY ON GALATIANS 6.9.[14]

THE TABLE OF MERCY. CHRYSOSTOM: By this especially he sets them free from the narrowness inherent in the Jewish code. For the whole of Jewish philanthropy was toward those of their own race. But the way of life that comes from grace takes the whole land and sea as the table of mercy, even while it also shows the greater care that is due toward one's household. HOMILY ON GALATIANS 6.9-10.[15]

6:10b *The Household of Faith*

DOING GOOD TO THE HOUSEHOLD OF FAITH. MARIUS VICTORINUS: Hence we are to work, and we are to work good and to work it to all so that there is no partiality toward persons. We are to do nothing except do

---

[9]Migne PL 26:430D-432A [525-27]. [10]Cf. Gal 5:17. [11]Migne PL 35:2146. [12]BT 1972:68 [1195A-B]. [13]BT 1972:68 [1195B-C]. [14]IOEP 4:96. [15]IOEP 4:97.

good and good to all. For indeed if love edifies[16] and every person is beloved, then every good that we work we ought to work on behalf of all. . . . However, he makes the distinction that the good that we work on behalf of all is to be worked most of all on behalf of the household of faith, that is, those who have come to believing trust in Christ and God. He comes to the climax of his argument in urging this. It was particularly germane to the Galatians. For they, by making certain additions to faith from Judaism, were not acting out of faith. They believed that they would gain fruit from works and mere ritual observance. Therefore he adds, "Let us above all do good to the household of faith, because they have adopted faith in the gospel only, that is, in Christ and God." EPISTLE TO THE GALATIANS 2.6.10.[17]

A REFERENCE TO TEACHERS? JEROME: It seems to me possible that this passage relates to an earlier statement,[18] so that he is using the name "household of faith" to refer to teachers, who ought, as he says, to be supplied with all that is reckoned good by those who hear them. EPISTLE TO THE GALATIANS 3.6.10.[19]

---

[16]1 Cor 8:2. [17]BT 1972:68-69 [1195C-D]. [18]Cf. Gal 6:6-7. [19]Migne PL 26:433A-B [528].

6:11-18 FINAL INJUNCTIONS

[11]*See with what large letters I am writing to you with my own hand.* [12]*It is those who want to make a good showing in the flesh that would compel you to be circumcised, and only in order that they may not be persecuted for the cross of Christ.* [13]*For even those who receive circumcision do not themselves keep the law, but they desire to have you circumcised that they may glory in your flesh.* [14]*But far be it from me to glory except in the cross of our Lord Jesus Christ, by which[1] the world has been crucified to me, and I to the world.* [15]*For neither circumcision counts for anything, nor uncircumcision, but a new creation.* [16]*Peace and mercy be upon all who walk by this rule, upon the Israel of God.*

[17]*Henceforth let no man trouble me; for I bear on my body the marks of Jesus.*

[18]*The grace of our Lord Jesus Christ be with your spirit, brethren. Amen.*

1 Or through whom

OVERVIEW: Paul writes in his own hand (JEROME), revealing his deep personal concern for the Galatians (CHRYSOSTOM). The Judaizers please people, not God (AMBROSI-

ASTER), fearing to be oppressed by either the Romans (JEROME) or the Jews (AUGUSTINE). The circumcised, who glory in proselytes (AUGUSTINE), cannot keep the law, because they forget its promises (EPIPHANIUS). They are too weak to observe its moral precepts (JEROME) and cannot even rightly perform its ceremonies (THEODORET). Paul glories in the cross, which incorporates the faithful in Christ's passion (MARIUS VICTORINUS) and unbinds fixation on worldly affairs (CHRYSOSTOM). The cross has taught Paul to transcend his Jewish heritage (CHRYSOSTOM). Christians are the new Israel (CHRYSOSTOM). A foretaste of the new creation is seen in the resurrection (THEODORET). Though some may continue to provoke Paul (AMBROSIASTER), he is not troubled inwardly (CHRYSOSTOM). He shares Christ's lacerations (JEROME), for the perfection of his virtue (GREGORY OF NYSSA) and as an example to the rest (MARIUS VICTORINUS). He invokes a blessing upon the faithful (CHRYSOSTOM), tacitly recapitulating his case against the law (JEROME).

6:11 Letters Written in Paul's Hand

WITH MY OWN RECOGNIZABLE HAND I WRITE. JEROME: Those who wanted the Galatians to be circumcised had put it about that Paul preached one way and acted another, destroying his words by his own deeds, since he who proclaimed the abolition of the law was found to be obeying the law. Because Paul could not refute their opinions in person in the sight of all (being prevented by the chains that he bore as a testimony to Christ), he acts as his own lawyer through his letter. So that no suspicion that the letter was false might arise, he himself has written it from this point right to the end, showing that the preceding part was copied by another's hand.[1] . . . It is not that the letters were larger (though indeed the word would bear this sense in Greek) but because the marks of his own handwriting were known to them. So when they recognized the angles and contours of his own letters, they would feel that they had encountered him. . . . Paul wrote his letter in great characters because the meaning of the characters was great and had been traced out by the Spirit of God, not merely by pen and ink. EPISTLE TO THE GALATIANS 3.6.11.[2]

To STOP THE SLANDER. CHRYSOSTOM: Observe what great grief occupies that blessed soul [Paul]. . . . Having said a little about morals, he now returns to the things that were causing the greatest disturbance to his soul, saying see in what large letters I have written to you. Here he hints at nothing except that he himself wrote the whole letter, which is a sign of the greatest authenticity. For in the other epistles he may have composed, but another wrote. . . . By so large he seems to me to be indicating not the size but the poor form of the characters, all but saying, "Although I do not write well, I have nonetheless been compelled to write for myself, so as to silence those who slander me." HOMILY ON GALATIANS 6.11.[3]

6:12a Those Who Would Compel You

To MAKE A GOOD SHOW IN THE FLESH. AMBROSIASTER: To please "in the flesh" means

---

[1]Cf. 2 Thess 3:17-18; Col 4:18. [2]Migne PL 26:433D-434D [529-30]. [3]IOEP 4:97.

to please human beings. For those he calls false apostles, in order that they gain the approval of the Jews or at least not elicit their hostility, were preaching Christ in such a way that they also taught the necessity of observing the law. Paul was never intimidated by his opponents. He consistently refused to keep silent about the truth. He constantly was attentive to what he was teaching and how he was living. EPISTLE TO THE GALATIANS 6.12.[4]

6:12b *Avoiding Persecution for the Cross of Christ*

THE PLOY OF EVADING ROMAN PERSECUTION BY BECOMING CIRCUMCISED. JEROME: Caius [Julius] Caesar and Octavianus Augustus, and Tiberius the successor of Augustus, had published laws that permitted the Jews scattered throughout the whole sphere of the Roman Empire to live by their own code and observe their ancestral ceremonies. Whoever was circumcised, therefore, even if he was a Christian, was reckoned as a Jew by the Roman authorities. But anyone who was not circumcised and by his uncircumcision proclaimed himself no Jew became liable to persecution, both from Jews and from Gentiles! So those who were leading the Galatians into evil, wishing to evade the persecution, were persuading the disciples to circumcise themselves for protection. This the apostle calls "making a good show" in the flesh. EPISTLE TO THE GALATIANS 3.6.12.[5]

PERSECUTION ALSO FROM THE JEWS. AUGUSTINE: The Jews were inflicting great persecution on those who seemed to be deserting their traditional observances such as circumcision. Paul's lack of fear has been demon-

strated through his composing such a letter in his own handwriting. In this way he shows that those who force the Gentiles into circumcision are operating under fear's control, as though they were subject to the law. EPISTLE TO THE GALATIANS 62 [1B.6.11-14].[6]

6:13a *Receiving Circumcision, Not Keeping the Law*

CHRIST'S MORE PERFECT LAW AND MORE PERFECT CIRCUMCISION. EPIPHANIUS: The former circumcision was not inappropriate in its own time. But the law announced that Christ would come to dispense the law of freedom. Then the circumcision in the flesh would no longer be of service in the time of Christ. For through Christ came the true One[7] of which the law was a shadow. From now on those who have been sealed with circumcision, even if they keep the whole law, would no longer gain any credit from their keeping this part of the law.[8] . . . Nevertheless, the law is good and in its time so is circumcision, since through both we know Christ, who is the more perfect law and the more perfect circumcision. PANARION 42.12.3, EIGHTH REFUTATION OF MARCION.[9]

FAILURE TO KEEP THE LAW. JEROME: Because of the weakness of the sin nature, Paul says, the law cannot be fulfilled. Hence the Jews keep the commands and traditions of the elders rather than God's commands, performing neither the whole body of the law (which is impossible) nor the spirit of the

---

[4]CSEL 81.3:66. [5]Migne PL 26:435A-B [531]. [6]Migne PL 35:2146. [7]The Messiah. [8]Here Epiphanius cites Deuteronomy 18:15 and Romans 2:25. [9]GCS 31:159.

law, which they did not understand. EPISTLE
TO THE GALATIANS 3.6.12.[10]

**THE LAW CANNOT BE KEPT A LONG DIS-
TANCE FROM JERUSALEM.** THEODORET: For
how can they totally keep the law while they
are traveling far from Jerusalem? How can
they perform the feasts; how can they offer
the sacrifices; how can they be cleansed after
touching impure things? No, it is obvious
that they have conspired to have you circumcised in their desire to boast of having made
you change. EPISTLE TO THE GALATIANS
6.13.[11]

6:13b *Glorying in Your Flesh*

**THE UNWORTHY MOTIVES OF THE JUDAIZ-
ERS.** AUGUSTINE: Not only did [the Judaiz-
ers] wish to avoid persecution from the
Jews, who were absolutely unwilling to let
the law be given to the uncircumcised, but
they desired to boast to the Jews about the
number of proselytes they made. EPISTLE TO
THE GALATIANS 62 [1B.6.11-14].[12]

6:14a *Glorying in the Cross of Our Lord
Jesus Christ*

**FAR BE IT FROM ME TO GLORY EXCEPT IN
THE CROSS.** CHRYSOSTOM: Now indeed [the
cross] appears to be a reprehensible thing,
but only to the world and to unbelievers. In
heaven and for believers it is the highest
glory. For poverty too is reprehensible, yet it
is a cause of boasting to us. Many mock simplicity, but we are disciplined by it. In this
way the cross ironically is also a cause of
boasting for us. Paul did not say "I do not
boast" or "I do not wish to boast" but *God
forbid*, as though he were deprecating some-

thing absurd and calling on the aid of God to
set this right. But what is this boasting in
the cross? That on my behalf Christ took the
form of a slave and suffered what he suffered
on account of me the slave, the enemy, the
ingrate. HOMILY ON GALATIANS 6.14.[13]

6:14b *The World Crucified to Me and
I to the World*

**THE WORLD DEAD TO ME AND I TO THE
WORLD.** CHRYSOSTOM: By *world* he means
not heaven nor earth but the affairs of life,
human praise, distinguished positions, reputation, wealth and all things that have a show
of splendor. All such things are dead to me.
Such should be the case for all Christians. Nor
is he satisfied only with the former ordinary
mode of dying, but he also introduces another
kind of death: dying to the world itself. HOM-
ILY ON GALATIANS 6.14.[14]

**THE WORLD CRUCIFIED THROUGH CHRIST
SINCE HE SUFFERED FOR ALL.** MARIUS VIC-
TORINUS: When Paul writes that the cross is
glory, he means obviously "the cross of our
Lord Jesus Christ." When in that mystery
his body hung from the cross and in it
crushed the power of this world, the whole
world was crucified through him. In the
cross he identified with every person in the
world. In doing so he made everything that
he suffered universal, that is, he caused all
flesh to be crucified in his death. Therefore I
too am fixed to the cross and to the world. *I*
means the one who was living carnally,
whose thoughts were of the flesh. Such a

---

[10]Migne PL 26:435C [531]. [11]CPE 1:363. [12]Migne PL
35:2147. [13]IOEP 4:99. [14]IOEP 4:100.

one is now "nailed to the world," that is, the worldly things in him are subjected to death. EPISTLE TO THE GALATIANS 2.6.14.[15]

6:15 Neither Circumcision nor Uncircumcision but a New Creation

THE SOUL RENEWED BY BAPTISM. CHRYSOSTOM: Do you see the power of the cross, to what a height it has raised the apostle? For not only has it made all the things of the world dead to him, but it has set him far above the older way of life. What equals the strength of the cross? Paul at one time was willing to be slain and to slay others for the cause of circumcision. Now he has been persuaded by the cross to let circumcision fall to the level of uncircumcision. Now he seeks new and strange things which are above the heavens. By the *new creation* he means our own new way of life, both on account of what is past and what is to come. We are renewed by what is past, because our soul, having grown old in sin, has been immediately renewed by baptism. It is as if recreated again that we seek a new and heavenly way of life. We are being renewed by what is to come, because the heaven and the earth and all creation will be changed into incorruption along with our own bodies. HOMILY ON GALATIANS 6.15.[16]

A NEW CREATION. THEODORET: Paul also mentions a new creation in his letter to the Corinthians.[17] . . . The strict meaning of *new creation* is the transformation of all things which will occur after the resurrection from the dead. For then the creation will be freed from sin's burden and redeemed. Paul demonstrates that saving baptism is an image of things to come. In it we put off the old na-

ture and put on the new. And we, ridding ourselves of sin's burden, receive the grace of the Spirit. Yet neither the most holy baptism nor the life to come recognizes any difference between circumcision and uncircumcision. By *world* he means the affairs of life—honor, glory and wealth. To these he declares himself dead. EPISTLE TO THE GALATIANS 6.15.[18]

6:16 Peace and Mercy upon the Israel of God

WHO ARE THE ISRAEL OF GOD? CHRYSOSTOM: Those who pursue this new creation will enjoy peace and goodness, and truly deserve to be called by the name of the true Israel. But those who oppose it, even if they have been born of Israel and carried Israel's name with them, have fallen away from Israel and from that name and family. For those who can truly be Israelites are those who keep this rule,[19] abstain from the old ways and pursue what belongs to grace. HOMILY ON GALATIANS 6.16.[20]

THOSE WHO WALK BY THIS RULE. AUGUSTINE: Paul means those who are truly prepared for the vision of God. These are distinguished from those who are called by this name [Israel] and in their carnal blindness refuse to see the Lord, spurning his grace, still desiring to be enslaved by temporal things. EPISTLE TO THE GALATIANS 63 [IB.6.15-16].[21]

---

[15]BT 1972:70 [1196C-D]. [16]IOEP 4:100. [17]Here Theodoret cites 2 Corinthians 5:17. [18]CPE 1:363-64. [19]The new rule of faith in the coming reign of God. [20]IOEP 4:101. [21]Migne PL 35:2148.

6:17a *Let No One Trouble Me*

CASE CLOSED. AMBROSIASTER: He does not wish to be annoyed any longer by people advocating circumcision—people who would force him to write another letter. He wants the Galatians to respond quickly to his letter and get rid of their mistakes. This hard work will result in genuine rest. If, however, they show themselves to be reluctant and stubborn, refusing to change, Paul wants to be left alone. Let the Galatians spend their time and effort trying to please the Judaizers in an empty search for temporary reward. EPISTLE TO THE GALATIANS 6.17.[22]

HENCEFORTH. CHRYSOSTOM: Paul does not write these things because he is tired or demoralized. How could one chosen by God to bear and do all things for his disciples give up now? . . . Why does he says this now? To give direction to lazy Christians by helping them see how serious their situation is, to reinforce the teachings he has given and to refuse to let them abandon it. HOMILY ON GALATIANS 6.17.[23]

6:17b *I Bear on My Body the Marks of Jesus*

READINESS TO SUFFER FOR THE TRUTH. MARIUS VICTORINUS: Paul's point is this: "All that Christ experienced on the cross—the imprint of the nails, the spear thrust in his side, the other marks of the crucifixion—I bear in my own body. I too have suffered. Therefore you too ought to endure much—indeed all—adversity, since you will be with Christ if you suffer with Christ and begin by your own act, in the face of adversaries, to suffer what Christ suffered." Through these words Paul reveals what he himself was suffering, how much he shared with Christ and what we also ought to suffer if we wish to live in Christ. EPISTLE TO THE GALATIANS 2.6.17.[24]

BEARING THE MARKS OF JESUS. JEROME: Anyone who after Christ's coming is circumcised in the flesh does not carry the marks of the Lord Jesus. Rather he glories in his own confusion. But the one who was flogged beyond what the law required, frequently was in prison, was beaten three times with rods, was once stoned and suffered all the other things that are written in his catalog of boasting[25]—this is the one who carries on his body the marks of the Lord Jesus. Perhaps also the ascetic today who keeps his body under control and subjects it to servitude so that he will not appear reprobate as he preaches to others may in some way carry the marks of the Lord Jesus on his own body.[26] EPISTLE TO THE GALATIANS 3.6.17.[27]

GOD'S STRENGTH PERFECTED IN WEAKNESS. GREGORY OF NYSSA: "Rejoicing in these lacerations," Paul says, "I *bear the marks of Christ in my own body.*" He readily yields to his weakness in all these misfortunes, through which the power of Christ is being perfected in virtue.[28] ORATION 12 ON SONG OF SONGS 5.7.[29]

6:18 *The Grace of Our Lord Jesus Christ*

WITH YOUR SPIRIT. CHRYSOSTOM: By this final word he has sealed the argument of the

---

[22]CSEL 81.3:68. [23]IOEP 4:101. [24]BT 1972:71 [1198A-B]. [25]2 Cor 11:23-29. [26]1 Cor 9:27. [27]Migne PL 26:438A [534]. [28]Alluding also to 2 Cor 4:10; 12:9. [29]GNO 6:366.

letter. For he does not say simply "with you," as in the other letters, but *with your spirit*. He is leading them away from corrupted things and pointing everywhere to the benevolent work of God and reminding them of the grace that they have enjoyed. By this he is able to lead them away from the legalistic error in its entirety. For the receiving of the Spirit was not for the poverty of legalism but for righteousness according to the Spirit. . . . The concluding prayer and teaching work together, serving as a double fortress. The teaching reminds them of all the gracious benefits they have enjoyed and holds them all the more firmly in the teaching of the church. And this prayer, by invoking grace and persuading them to stand fast, does not allow their spirit to fall away. HOMILY ON GALATIANS 6.18.[30]

THE GRACE OF OUR LORD. JEROME: How does the blessing refer to the letter? Not discord, not slavery to the law, not biting and railing, but the grace of the Lord Jesus Christ is asked to be "with your spirit." Not with the flesh only; not with the soul only. For having been made spiritual they have ceased to be cheaply embodied. In the Spirit both body and soul are embraced. The grace of the Lord Jesus is not given indiscriminately to all but to those who are ready to be called brothers by the apostle—faithful brothers and intimate brothers, as the word *amen*[31] signifies in Hebrew. EPISTLE TO THE GALATIANS 3.6.18.[32]

---

[30]IOEP 4:102. [31]I.e., "truly." [32]Migne PL 26:438B-C [534-35].

THE EPISTLE TO THE EPHESIANS

1:1-2 INTRODUCTORY GREETING

¹*Paul, an apostle of Christ Jesus by the will of God,*
To the saints who are also faithful^a *in Christ Jesus:*
²*Grace to you and peace from God our Father and the Lord Jesus Christ.*

a *Other ancient authorities read* who are at Ephesus and faithful

---

OVERVIEW: Paul is called by Christ as an apostle (CASSIODORUS) and elected through the Spirit (MARIUS VICTORINUS). To recall the Ephesians to their allegiance Paul calls them saints and faithful (MARIUS VICTORINUS), thus showing that faith sanctifies (AMBROSIASTER). Only faith in Christ can save (JEROME). Paul hopes to quell strife with a blessing (MARIUS VICTORINUS). Grace and peace come from the Father and the Son (AMBROSIASTER).

1a *Paul, an Apostle of Christ Jesus*

CALLED BY GOD. CASSIODORUS: Paul frequently declares that he was directly called as an apostle by the will of the Lord, so as to circumvent those who desired this honor with human presumptions. He writes to the saints and the faithful at Ephesus, adding his blessing as with the love of a father. SUMMARY OF EPHESIANS I.I.I.[1]

THE WILL OF GOD IS THE WORD OF GOD IN CHRIST THROUGH THE SPIRIT. MARIUS

VICTORINUS: When Jesus Christ elected Paul and made him an apostle, he elected him through the Spirit by the will of God or the power through whom God works his will. Let us therefore understand, as I often say, that the will of God is the very power, greatness and substance of the whole divine plenitude. Christ—that is, God's Word which was in Christ—is the will of God. Those who consider this more closely will find that God and his will are inseparable. EPISTLE TO THE EPHESIANS I.I.I.[2]

1b *To the Saints*

LOYAL TO THE NAME. MARIUS VICTORINUS: In other letters when he writes to a church and its people he does not add *to the saints and the faithful*. But now, because he desires

---

[1]Migne PL 70:1345C-D. [2]BT 1972:124 [1236B]. Cf. Jerome *Epistle to the Ephesians* 1.1.1 [Migne PL 26:443A-444B (544-45)]; and Origen *Epistle to the Ephesians* [JTS 3:235].

---

to keep them loyal to the holy Name, so that being sanctified they will not add anything superficially in excess of the Name, he calls them simply by this name: they are the faithful *in Christ*. EPISTLE TO THE EPHESIANS 1.1.1.[3]

TO THE SAINTS. AMBROSIASTER: He writes not only to the faithful but to the saints to show that they are truly faithful insofar as they have been sanctified in Christ. For a good life is worthwhile and is called saintly if it is lived in the name of Jesus. Otherwise it is polluted, because it injures the Creator. EPISTLE TO THE EPHESIANS 1.1.[4]

THE FAITHFUL IN CHRIST JESUS. JEROME: Those whom he has called saintly he also calls faithful, because faith derives from the choice of our own minds, but sanctification we receive meanwhile from the abundance of the Sanctifier, not from our own will. As for his saying *faithful in Jesus Christ*, this is aimed at drawing a distinction that should be carefully noted. For there are those who have genuine faith but not faith in Jesus Christ. Someone who returns a deposit and does not deny another's trust shows himself a faithful friend. . . . This person is indeed faithful but not *in Christ*. EPISTLE TO THE EPHESIANS 1.1.1.[5]

1:2 Grace and Peace from God Our Father and the Lord Jesus Christ

GRACE AND PEACE. MARIUS VICTORINUS: Both grace and peace remove contention. They convey the will of God. Since therefore they were in the grip of error, grace was first sought on their behalf, in order that they should know God and fully obey God and Christ, putting all trust in Christ and nothing else. . . . Then he also adds *peace from God*. The one who wills ungraciously creates severe discord. EPISTLE TO THE EPHESIANS 1.1.2.[6]

FATHER AND LORD. AMBROSIASTER: He calls God *our Father* because all things are created and restored in him. He calls Christ Lord because he redeems us, offering himself on our behalf. EPISTLE TO THE EPHESIANS 1.2.[7]

WHETHER GRACE IS FROM THE FATHER AND PEACE FROM THE SON. JEROME: It could be argued that both should be referred to both, that is, both grace and peace apply no less to God the Father than to our Lord Jesus Christ. Or it could be argued that each should be referred to each, so that grace is referred to God the Father and peace to Christ. It is more likely the latter, since the words immediately following are to the praise of the glory of God's grace. Thus the *grace* of the Father lies in his willingness to send the Son for our salvation, while the *peace* of the Son lies in the fact that we are reconciled to the Father through him. EPISTLE TO THE EPHESIANS 1.1.2.[8]

---

[3]BT 1972:125 [1236D-1237A]. [4]CSEL 81.3:71-72. [5]Migne PL 26:444A-B [545]. Sanctification comes from the will of the Sanctifier; faith does not occur without the willing of the believer. [6]BT 1972:125-26 [1237A-B]. [7]CSEL 81.3:72. [8]Migne PL 26:444B-445A [545-46].

1:3-6 THE GREAT BENEDICTION

³*Blessed be the God and Father of our Lord Jesus Christ, who has blessed us in Christ with every spiritual blessing in the heavenly places, ⁴even as he chose us in him before the foundation of the world, that we should be holy and blameless before him. ⁵He destined us in love*[b] *to be his sons through Jesus Christ, according to the purpose of his will, ⁶to the praise of his glorious grace which he freely bestowed on us in the Beloved.*

b Or before him in love, having destined us

OVERVIEW: Knowing God as Father and Son, we become blessed through Christ's mercy (AMBROSIASTER). Spiritual blessings consist in the realized promises of the gospel (THEODORET). They are conferred in full on humanity (JEROME). They make heaven visible precisely through earthly shadows (HILARY OF POITIERS). Divine love is the motive of God's predestinating will (AMBROSIASTER). The distance between sinners and God remains infinite (CHRYSOSTOM), since we are fallen beings (ORIGEN) created from nothing (JEROME). God, who demands virtue as well as faith, bestows and enables virtue (ORIGEN, CHRYSOSTOM, JEROME). God's love predestines to make us children by adoption (FULGENTIUS), so that a determinate number are saved (CHRYSOSTOM, FULGENTIUS). God desires for our sake that we should praise him in loving acknowledgment of our unmerited forgiveness (MARIUS VICTORINUS, CHRYSOSTOM). Rightly understood, Christ is God's only Son by nature (MARIUS VICTORINUS, JEROME). His virtues are loved even by those who do not pursue them (JEROME).

1:3a The God and Father of Our Lord Jesus Christ

WHY GOD AND FATHER? JEROME: Now the phrase *blessed be the God and Father of our Lord Jesus Christ* is to be read in a double sense. It first means that God is blessed as the maker of all things, this being the main clause. To this is then added "who is also the Father of our Lord Jesus Christ." It means that both *God* and *Father* are to be referred in common to our Lord. Blessed is the God of the man who has been assumed[1] and the father of him who was the Word of God with God in the beginning! Not that the assumed one is other than the Word who assumed him, but that he who is one and the same is spoken of now by sublime and now by humble titles, according to what circumstances demand. EPISTLE TO THE EPHESIANS 1.1.3.[2]

1:3b Blessed in Christ

HOW GOD IS BLESSED AND HOW GOD BLESSES US. AMBROSIASTER: He means not with an earthly but a heavenly blessing, not

---

[1]In the incarnation true humanity has been assumed and taken up by God the Son. [2]Migne PL 26:446A-B [547].

corruptible but eternal, because Christ's glory is not in earth but in heaven and in Christ. For every gift of God's grace is in Christ. If someone who despises Christ imagines that he is blessed by God, he is wrong. Yet God is blessed in one way, humans in another. There is indeed one term *blessing*, but it should be understood as is proper to the recipient. . . . God is blessed when he is extolled with due praises, but the way in which God blesses human beings is to impart to them the gift of his grace, not according to their merits but according to his mercy. EPISTLE TO THE EPHESIANS 1.3.1-2.[3]

1:3c *Spiritual Blessing in Heavenly Places*

EVERY SPIRITUAL BLESSING? JEROME: Now God has blessed us not with this or that blessing but with every blessing. It is not as though we all obtain them all at once, but singly we obtain particular ones in due time or some of the whole number. Thereby we possess their fullness through these singular blessings. He speaks not only of earthly blessings but of spiritual—there are indeed earthly blessings, as when someone has children, affluence in riches, the pleasure of honor and health. . . . But spiritual blessings are in the heavens because the earth is too small to circumscribe a spiritual blessing. EPISTLE TO THE EPHESIANS 1.1.3.[4]

WHY "IN HEAVENLY PLACES"? HILARY OF Poitiers: Since God reveals himself to be blessed in spiritual and heavenly things, it is not amid these earthly and corporeal things that one should look for that perfect blessedness of the saints. TREATISE ON

PSALM 127, CHAPTER 8.[5]

SPIRITUAL BLESSING AS HEAVENLY GIFTS. THEODORET: He has conferred on us the gifts of the Holy Spirit. He has given us the hope of resurrection, the good news of immortality, the promise of the kingdom of heaven, the dignity of sonship. These he calls the *spiritual blessings*. And he adds *in heavenly places*, because these gifts are heavenly. EPISTLE TO THE EPHESIANS 1.3.[6]

1:4a *Chosen Before the Foundation of the World*

CALLED TO PERSEVERE. AMBROSIASTER: God, foreknowing all, knew who were going to believe in Christ.[7] . . . Therefore those whom God is said to call will persevere in faith. These are the ones whom he elected before the world in Christ, so that they might be blameless before God through love—that is, so that the love of God might give them holy lives. For no one can show greater respect toward another than when he obeys in love. EPISTLE TO THE EPHESIANS 1.4.[8]

HE CHOSE US IN HIM. CHRYSOSTOM: What he means is this: The one through whom he has blessed us is the one through whom he has elected us. . . . Christ chose us to have faith in him before we came into being, indeed even before the world was founded. The word *foundation* was well chosen, to indicate that it was laid down from some great height. For great and ineffable is the height

---

[3]CSEL 81.3:72. [4]Migne PL 26:445C-D [547]. [5]Migne PL 9:708A [480]. [6]CPE 2:4. [7]Here Ambrosiaster cites Romans 8:29. [8]CSEL 81.3:73.

of God, not in a particular place but rather in his remoteness from nature. So great is the distance between creature and Creator. HOMILY ON EPHESIANS 1.1.4.[9]

OUT OF NOTHING. JEROME: Paul, wishing to show that God made all things out of nothing, ascribed to him not the "composition," the "creation" or the "making" but the *katabolē*, that is, the inception of the foundation. EPISTLE TO THE EPHESIANS 1.1.4.[10]

1:4b *Holy and Blameless Before God*

WHETHER IT IS POSSIBLE TO RECEIVE THE GRACE OF PURE HOLINESS. ORIGEN: One might ask if this is not contradicted by the prophetic saying *In your sight shall no living being be justified.*[11] . . . One may answer, taking refuge in the double meanings of prophecy, that . . . no one is in all respects and throughout his whole life justified in God's sight, since he will of course have sinned at some time. But this would not prevent some from being at times holy and blameless before him if they have become so through correction. EPISTLE TO THE EPHESIANS.[12]

ELECTED FOR HOLINESS. CHRYSOSTOM: "You have been elected," he says, *"in order to be holy and unblemished before his face."* . . . He himself has made us saints, but we are called to remain saints. A saint is one who lives in faith, is unblemished and leads a blameless life. HOMILY ON EPHESIANS 1.1.4.[13]

FAITH, VIRTUE AND LOVE TOGETHER. CHRYSOSTOM: The sanctified life is not the effect of our labors or achievements but of God's love. It is not born of love alone or of our own virtue. For if it were from love

alone, all ought to be saved. Again, if it were from our virtue his earthly appearing and the whole of his work would be unnecessary. But it is not from love alone or from our virtue but from God through God. . . . Virtue would have saved no one had there been no love. . . . For to become virtuous and to believe and to advance, this too was the work of the One who called us, even though it is something we can share. HOMILY ON EPHESIANS 1.1.5.[14]

DISTINGUISHING AN INFANT FROM A SAINT. JEROME: Between *saintly* and *unblemished* there is this difference, that one who is saintly is ipso facto understood also to be unblemished, but one who is at some point unblemished is not by that fact itself saintly. Infants, after all, are spotless because their bodies are pure and they have committed no sin; and yet they are not saintly, because sanctity is not acquired without will and effort. Moreover, he who has done no sin can be called unblemished, but the saintly person is the one who is full of virtues. EPISTLE TO THE EPHESIANS 1.1.4.[15]

NOT CHOSEN ON ACCOUNT OF OUR BEING HOLY. JEROME: It is asked how anyone can be saintly and unblemished in God's sight. . . . We must reply [that] Paul does not say he chose us before the foundation of the world on account of our being saintly and unblemished. He chose us that we might become saintly and unblemished, that is, that we who were not formerly saintly and unblemished should subsequently be so. . . . So

---

[9]IOEP 4:108. [10]Migne PL 26:446C [548]. [11]Ps 143:2. [12]JTS 3:237. [13]IOEP 4:108. [14]IOEP 4:109-10. [15]Migne PL 26:447C-D [549].

understood it provides a counterargument to one who says that souls were elected before the world came to be because of their sanctity and freedom from any sinful vice. EPISTLE TO THE EPHESIANS 1.1.4.[16]

1:5a Destined to Be His Children

OUR SONSHIP BY ADOPTION. MARIUS VICTORINUS: God in his love has predestined us to adoption through Christ. How could God possibly have Christ for his Son by adoption? . . . We speak of ourselves as heirs of God the Father and heirs through Christ, being sons through adoption. Christ is his Son, through whom it is brought about that we become sons and fellow heirs in Christ.[17] AGAINST THE ARIANS 1.2.[18]

DISTINGUISHING DESTINED FROM ORDAINED. JEROME: The former [verse] refers to those saints who did not previously exist and who before they came into being were thought of and subsequently acquired existence. This [verse] speaks of God, who was preceded by no thought or willing but always existed and never had a beginning for his existence. Therefore he rightly used the term *destined* for those who, having once not existed, subsequently acquired existence. But of the Son, that is, of our Lord Jesus Christ, he wrote *ordained* in another place also.[19] EPISTLE TO THE EPHESIANS 1.1.5.[20]

DESTINED US IN LOVE. JEROME: Christ, as we have often said already, is wisdom, justice, peace, joy, temperance and the rest. Note that the names of all these virtues are loved even by those who do not pursue them! No one is such a brazen criminal that he does not claim to love wisdom and jus-

tice. EPISTLE TO THE EPHESIANS 1.1.6.[21]

DESTINED IN LOVE. FULGENTIUS: The reason for saying *he destined us in love* is that he empowered us with his gracious love in order to predestine us. ON THE TRUTH OF PREDESTINATION 3.5.[22]

1:5b The Purpose of God's Will

DISTINGUISHING GOD'S ANTECEDENT WILL FROM GOD'S CONSEQUENT WILL. CHRYSOSTOM: Everywhere the purpose[23] or *good pleasure* means God's antecedent will.[24] Yet there is another will. For God's first [or antecedent] will is that sinners should not perish. His second or consequent will[25] is that those who become evil should perish. Hence he does not chastise them from necessity but due to their own willing. HOMILY ON EPHESIANS 1.5.[26]

GOD'S KNOWLEDGE OF THE NUMBER OF THE ELECT. FULGENTIUS: The eternal firmness and firm eternity of God's predestinating will consist not only in the ordaining of works. God also knows in advance the number of the elect. No one of that full number may lose his eternal grace, nor may any out-

---

[16]Migne PL 26:448A-B [549-50]. See introduction on this verse. [17]Christ's Sonship is by nature; our sonship is by adoption. [18]BT 1976:11 [1020C-D]. Cf. Origen *Epistle to the Ephesians* [JTS 3:237]. [19]Cf. Rom 1:4. [20]Migne PL 26:448C [550]. The eternal Son is ordained. As adopted sons the faithful are said to be destined. [21]Migne PL 26:450B [552], following Origen *Epistle to the Ephesians* [JTS 3:238]. [22]CCL 91A:525. [23]Or better: "good pleasure." [24]God's will prior to human choices to do evil. [25]God wills consequent to human choice. Hence this is often called God's consequent will, as distinguished from the primary or antecedent will of God to save all. [26]IOEP 4:109-10.

side that total attain the gift of eternal salvation. For God, who knows all things before they come to pass, is not confused about the number of the predestined, any more than he doubts the effectiveness of the works he has ordained.[27] ON THE TRUTH OF PREDESTINATION 3.6.[28]

1:6 The Praise of God's Glorious Grace

OUR ADOPTION IS HIS GLORY, HIS GRACE.
MARIUS VICTORINUS: We, being such as we are, are surrounded and held fast by vice and libidinous sin. When we are set free by him, acquitted of sin and pardoned for our sins, we are also adopted as his sons. All this is therefore to the praise of his glory and grace —his glory because he can do so much, and

his grace because he offers this to us freely. EPISTLE TO THE EPHESIANS 1.1.(4) 5-6.[29]

WHY GOD DESIRES TO BE PRAISED. CHRYSOSTOM: So that our love for him may become more fervent, he desires nothing from us except our salvation. He does not need our service or anything else but does everything for this end. One who openly expresses praise and wonder at God's grace will be more eager and zealous. HOMILY ON EPHESIANS 1.1.6.[30]

---

[27]It should be recalled that God's relation to time is different from ours. For God is contemporary with all moments of time; hence God has no difficulty grasping the future. [28]CCL 91A:525. [29]BT 1972:134 [1243A]. [30]IOEP 4:110.

1:7-10 REDEMPTION THROUGH CHRIST

[7]In him we have redemption through his blood, the forgiveness of our trespasses, according to the riches of his grace [8]which he lavished upon us. [9]For he has made known to us in all wisdom and insight the mystery of his will, according to his purpose which he set forth in Christ [10]as a plan for the fulness of time, to unite all things in him, things in heaven and things on earth.

OVERVIEW: We have been redeemed from former captivity (JEROME) by Christ's death that is worthy of our love (THEODORET), bringing freedom now (AMBROSIASTER) and a promise for future glory (CHRYSOSTOM). God has given us a special gift of divine and human knowledge (MARIUS VICTORINUS,

JEROME). God has revealed his previously hidden will for our salvation (AMBROSIASTER), though the revelation may still be from our vantage point incomplete (JEROME). Predestination is the eternal plan, the historical execution of which reveals Christ's role as Lord of creation (ORIGEN, MARIUS VIC-

TORINUS). With the complete cooperation of the Son the Father has reversed the degenerative trend of history (CHRYSOSTOM). "Uniting all things in him," or recapitulation, denotes here the summing up of all times and creatures in Christ through the Spirit (IRENAEUS, CHRYSOSTOM), restoring every creature to its original goodness (THEODORET).

1:7a Redemption Through Christ's Blood

WHAT IS REDEMPTION? JEROME: The one who is yet to be redeemed is a captive. He has ceased to be free by coming under the power of the enemy. So we are captives in this world and bound by the yoke of slavery to the principalities and powers, unable to release our hands from our chains. So we raise our eyes upward until the Redeemer arrives. EPISTLE TO THE EPHESIANS 1.1.7.[1]

THROUGH HIS BLOOD—WHAT HIS DEATH ACHIEVED. THEODORET: The death of the Lord has made us worthy of love. In shedding through him the toils of sin and being freed from slavery to the tyrant,[2] we have been drawn toward the characteristics of God's image. EPISTLE TO THE EPHESIANS 1.7.[3]

1:7b Forgiveness of Our Trespasses, According to His Grace

HOW OUR FORGIVENESS RELATES TO CHRIST'S REDEMPTIVE GRACE. ORIGEN: Forgiveness of sins follows redemption, for there would be no forgiveness of sin for anyone before redemption occurs. First then we need to be redeemed, to be no longer subject to our captor and oppressor, so that having

been freed and taken out of his hands we may be able to receive the benefit of remission of sins. Once our wounds have been healed we are called to live in accord with piety and the other virtues. EPISTLE TO THE EPHESIANS.[4]

HE SACRIFICED HIS BELOVED SON FOR THOSE WHO HATED HIM. CHRYSOSTOM: The wonder is not only that he gave his Son but that he did so in this way, by sacrificing the one he loved. It is astonishing that he gave the Beloved for those who hated him. See how highly he honors us. If even when we hated him and were enemies he gave the Beloved, what will he not do for us now? HOMILY ON EPHESIANS 1.1.8.[5]

1:8 Grace Lavished on Us

RICHES HEAPED ON US. MARIUS VICTORINUS: The riches of God are heaped upon us in that he makes us something better than we were at the beginning of our existence. EPISTLE TO THE EPHESIANS 1.1.8.[6]

1:9a Wisdom and Insight Made Known to Us

THE WISDOM AND PRUDENCE OF KNOWING CHRIST. MARIUS VICTORINUS: The whole of this wisdom and prudence consists in knowing Christ and through Christ understanding and seeing God. For whatever remaining wisdom there is in the world and whatever other wisdom of this kind there may be outside it, all wisdom and prudence is nonethe-

---

[1]Migne PL 26:450C [553], following Origen *Epistle to the Ephesians* [JTS 3:238]. [2]The adversary, the devil. [3]CPE 2:5. [4]JTS 3:238. [5]IOEP 4:112. [6]BT 1972:136 [1244B].

less empty, worthless and wretched without Christ. EPISTLE TO THE EPHESIANS 1.1.8.[7]

THE MYSTERY OF HIS GIFT. AMBROSIASTER: The pleasure of God, whose counsel cannot be changed, was to show in Christ the mystery of his will. This happened at the time when he chose that he should be revealed. Now his will was this, that he should then draw close to all who were in sin, either in heaven or in earth. God gave Christ to bring believers the gift of forgiveness of their sins through faith in Christ. EPISTLE TO THE EPHESIANS 1.9.1.[8]

PRUDENCE TOWARD THE VISIBLE, WISDOM TOWARD THE INVISIBLE. JEROME: The Stoics also hold that there is a distinction between wisdom and insight. They say, "Wisdom is the knowledge of things divine and human, insight only of that which is mortal." According to this distinction we might apply Paul's term *wisdom* to the invisible and visible and *insight* only to the visible. EPISTLE TO THE EPHESIANS 1.1.9.[9]

ALL WISDOM REVEALED BUT KNOWN IN PART AS WE ARE ABLE. JEROME: Some attentive reader might object: "If Paul knows in part and prophesies in part and now sees as through a glass darkly,[10] how is the mystery of God revealed either to him or to the Ephesians *in all wisdom and insight?*" . . . It is not that they by themselves have learned this mystery *in all wisdom and insight*, but God *in all wisdom and insight* has revealed the mystery to us, so far as we are able to grasp it. EPISTLE TO THE EPHESIANS 1.1.9.[11]

1:9b *According to God's Purpose*

WHETHER PREDESTINATION IS DISTIN-

GUISHED FROM PURPOSE. ORIGEN: We must examine the possibility that predestination and purpose differ so that purpose is presupposed in predestination. Thus, as it were, the predestination is in the thought of God and the purpose unfolds in accordance with things predestined, so that then they become realities and actualize the predestination. EPISTLE TO THE EPHESIANS.[12]

HIS PURPOSE SET FORTH IN CHRIST. MARIUS VICTORINUS: Not only has God a will, but the intention of his will is expressed in Christ. Hence all things are done through him. There is nothing in the mystery that is not done through Jesus Christ. EPISTLE TO THE EPHESIANS 1.1.9.[13]

1:10a *A Plan for the Fullness of Time*

HOW THE FULLNESS OF TIME WAS DETERMINED. CHRYSOSTOM: The *fullness of time* was the Son's appearing. When, then, God had done all through angels, through prophets and through the law, yet nothing had improved, there was a danger that humanity had come into being for nothing. It was not going merely nowhere but to the bad. All were perishing together, just like in the days of the flood but more so. Just then he offered this gracious dispensation—to ensure that creation should not have come into being for nothing or in vain. The *fullness of time* is that divine wisdom by which, at the

---

[7]BT 1972:136 [1244C-D]. [8]CSEL 81.3:74. [9]Migne PL 26:452A [554]. Accordingly, the range of the knowledge of God applies both to that which is visible and to that which is invisible, to both mortal and immortal. [10]1 Cor 13:12. [11]Migne PL 26:453A-B [555]. [12]JTS 3:240-41, followed by Jerome *Epistle to the Ephesians* 1.1.9 [Migne PL 26:452A-453D (554-56)]. [13]BT 1972:137 [1245A].

moment when all were most likely to perish, they were saved. Homily on Ephesians 1.1.10.[14]

The Coordination of the Work of the Father and the Son.

Chrysostom: See how precisely he speaks. The origin is from the Father—the design, the resolution, the first initiative. The embodied fulfillment of the design came through the Son, who is never called *servant* but always *Son*. . . . What the Father has willed in the Son is not external to his will. What the Son has done has not deprived the Father of his willing action. All is common in the relation of Father and Son. Homily on Ephesians 1.1.10.[15]

1:10b *To Unite All Things in Him*

Uniting Heavenly and Earthly Things.

Irenaeus: Thus Christ unites[16] . . . in himself all that is earthly and all that is spiritual. He unites humanity to Spirit and places the Spirit in humanity. Being himself made the fountainhead of the Spirit, Christ gives the Spirit to be the head of humanity. Thus through the Son by the Spirit we ourselves now see and hear and speak. Against Heresies 5.20.2.[17]

All Things in Christ.

Marius Victorinus: It is not all things indifferently that are restored but all things that are in Christ—both those that are in heaven and those that are on the earth but only those that are in Christ. Others are strange to him. Whatever things then are in Christ, it is these that are revitalized and rise again, whether in heaven or in earth. For he is salvation, he is renewal, he is eternity. Epistle to the Ephesians 1.1.10.[18]

What Is Meant by This Summing Up?

Chrysostom: To "recapitulate" is to join together. But let us press on closer to the fuller truth. In our customary usage a *recapitulation* is a brief summary of what has been said at great length. It is a concise expression of everything that has been detailed. That is what it is here as well. The providential ordering that has occurred over a long time, the Son has once for all *recapitulated*. Everything is summed up in him. . . . There is also another meaning: In Christ's incarnation God has given a single head to all creation, both angels and humans. Homily on Ephesians 1.1.10.[19]

Recapitulating Heaven and Earth.

Theodoret: Only God's nature needs nothing. The whole creation stood in need of his healing order of gifts. For, since the elements came into being to serve human needs, he made them subject to corruption, for he could foresee that transgression was going to make humanity mortal also. As for the unseen powers,[20] they were naturally aggrieved when they saw human beings living in wickedness. . . . By *recapitulation* he means the complete transformation of things. For through the gift given through Christ the Lord the human nature is raised anew and puts on incorruptibility. Ultimately the visible creation, delivered from corruption, will receive incorruption. The hosts of unseen powers will rejoice continually, because sorrow

---

[14]IOEP 4:114. [15]IOEP 4:114. [16]Or "recapitulates." [17]SC 153:260. [18]BT 1972:137 [1245B-C]. [19]IOEP 4:114; cf. Jerome *Commentary on Ephesians* 1.1.10 [Migne PL 26:453D-454C (556-57)]. [20]Invisible creatures; the angelic creation.

and grief and sighing have fled away. This is what the divine apostle teaches through these words; for he said not simply "heaven and earth" but *those in heaven* and *those on earth*. EPISTLE TO THE EPHESIANS 1.10.[21]

[21]CPE 2:6-7.

1:11-14 OUR INHERITANCE IN CHRIST

[11]*In him, according to the purpose of him who accomplishes all things according to the counsel of his will,* [12]*we who first hoped in Christ have been destined and appointed to live for the praise of his glory.* [13]*In him you also, who have heard the word of truth, the gospel of your salvation, and have believed in him, were sealed with the promised Holy Spirit,* [14]*which is the guarantee of our inheritance until we acquire possession of it, to the praise of his glory.*

OVERVIEW: Election is a great privilege (CHRYSOSTOM) given first to the Jews (AMBROSIASTER) and then to the new people of God. Our inheritance is sealed, secured (CHRYSOSTOM). The seal of the Spirit elicits and develops inward virtue (DIDYMUS THE BLIND). All virtue is grounded in hope (MARIUS VICTORINUS). Refuting false teachers (JEROME) Paul reminds the Ephesians that salvation is by the gospel (CHRYSOSTOM), the sure guarantee of the ultimate outcome (JEROME, THEODORET), which evokes that praise due only to God (AMBROSIASTER).

1:11 God Accomplishes All Things According to His Will

GOD'S FOREKNOWLEDGE SEES ALL THINGS BEFORE THEY OCCUR. CHRYSOSTOM: Since inheritance is a matter of fortune, not of choice or virtue, it often depends on obscure or fortuitous circumstances, overlooking virtue. It may bring to the fore those who are of no account. But notice how Paul qualifies this statement. . . . He says *have been destined,* that is, God has set us apart for himself. It is as if to say God saw us before we became heirs. The foreknowledge of God is wonderful and sees all things before they occur. HOMILY ON EPHESIANS 2.1.11-14.[1]

1:12 Living for the Praise of God's Glory

LIVING FOR THE PRAISE OF HIS GLORY. MARIUS VICTORINUS: First the believer is enabled to hope in Christ, that is, follow Christ and believe that all Christ's promises can be fulfilled. Only then will the conse-

[1]IOEP 4:114-16.

quence be that he will live for the praise of the glory of God. EPISTLE TO THE EPHESIANS 1.1.12.[2]

WE WHO FIRST HOPED. AMBROSIASTER: What he means is that God first allotted the task of preaching to those believers in Christ who were from a Jewish background. Therefore no one of Gentile background was chosen to be an apostle. It was fitting that the first preachers should be chosen from those who had previously hoped for the salvation that had been promised to them in Christ. EPISTLE TO THE EPHESIANS 1.12.[3]

1:13a The Word of Truth, the Gospel of Salvation

THE WORD OF TRUTH HEARD. JEROME: It is no small praise for the Ephesians that they have heard not preaching as such but *the word of truth*. Remember that we read in another letter[4] that there is a great distance between preaching and the word of truth. EPISTLE TO THE EPHESIANS 1.1.13.[5]

1:13b Sealed with the Promised Holy Spirit

HOW THE SPIRIT SEALS US. DIDYMUS THE BLIND: One who takes on discipline and virtue receives in his own character the seal and form of the knowledge that he puts on. So one who is made a partaker of the Holy Spirit becomes likewise spiritual and holy through disciplined fellowship with him. ON THE HOLY SPIRIT 20.[6]

OUR INHERITANCE IS SECURED. CHRYSOSTOM: By this seal God shows great forethought for humanity. He not only sets apart a people and gives them an inheritance but secures it as well. It is just as if someone might stamp his heirs plainly in advance; so God set us apart to believe and sealed us for the inheritance of future glory. HOMILY ON EPHESIANS 2.1.11-14.[7]

SEALED IN THE SPIRIT OF PROMISE. CHRYSOSTOM: What does *in the Spirit of promise* mean? That we have now received him according to his promise. There are two promises, first through the prophets[8] and finally through the Son.[9] HOMILY ON EPHESIANS 2.1.11-14.[10]

1:14a The Guarantee of Our Inheritance

GUARANTEE CONTRASTED WITH PLEDGE. JEROME: A guarantee (*arrabon*, "earnest") is not the same as a token or pledge. For a guarantee is given as an affidavit and bond for a future purchase. But a pledge . . . is an expression of a present reciprocal transaction. Thus when the money is returned the pledge is restored by the creditor to the one who has repaid the debt. . . . So from the guarantee the majestic scope of the future inheritance may be grasped. EPISTLE TO THE EPHESIANS 1.1.14.[11]

HOW GREAT THE EXPECTATION OF THE FAITH. THEODORET: He shows how great are our expectations. This grace is already being given, through which miracles were worked: the dead were raised, lepers

---

[2]BT 1972:138-39 [1246B]. [3]CSEL 81.3:75. [4]1 Cor 2:4. [5]Migne PL 26:456B-C [559]. [6]SC 386:160; translated by Jerome. [7]IOEP 4:117. [8]In the form of expectation. [9]In the form of fulfillment; cf. Joel 2:28; Acts 1:8. [10]IOEP 4:117. [11]Migne PL 26:457B-C [560-61].

cleansed and demons driven out. All of these and similar things have the status of a pledge, so it will become obvious that the faithful will enjoy in the future a much greater grace. EPISTLE TO THE EPHESIANS 1.14.[12]

1:14b To the Praise of His Glory

THE PRAISE OF HIS GLORY. AMBROSIASTER: Just as it is the glory of a doctor if he cures

many, so it is to the praise of God's glory when many are won for the faith. And so it is part of God's glory to have called the Gentiles that they might obtain their salvation through the faith promised to the Jews. The Gentiles have as a sign of their redemption and future inheritance the Holy Spirit, given at baptism. EPISTLE TO THE EPHESIANS 1.14.[13]

---

[12]CPE 2:7-8. [13]CSEL 81.3:75.

1:15-18 PAUL'S THANKSGIVING

[15]For this reason, because I have heard of your faith in the Lord Jesus and your love[c] toward all the saints, [16]I do not cease to give thanks for you, remembering you in my prayers, [17]that the God of our Lord Jesus Christ, the Father of glory, may give you a spirit of wisdom and of revelation in the knowledge of him, [18]having the eyes of your hearts enlightened, that you may know what is the hope to which he has called you, what are the riches of his glorious inheritance in the saints.

c Other ancient authorities omit your love

OVERVIEW: Paul's compliment becomes the prelude to his advice (MARIUS VICTORINUS). His prayers for the Ephesians are both a pattern for us (MARIUS VICTORINUS) and an expression of his piety (CHRYSOSTOM). The Father is Father of Christ as God and the God of Jesus as man (JEROME). God's glory is shown in its effects (CHRYSOSTOM, HILARY OF POITIERS). His revelation has already become known to the Ephesians (JEROME), who are now further inspired with zeal by Paul's prayer for them (AMBROSIASTER).

The eyes of the heart, opened by faith (JEROME, EPHRAIM THE SYRIAN), add insight to revelation (MARIUS VICTORINUS) but not without moral responsibility (JEROME).

1:15 Faith in the Lord Jesus

THE FAITHFUL LOVE ALL THE SAINTS. MARIUS VICTORINUS: He now moves on to specific exhortations for the Ephesians, and at the same time he warns them not to entertain contrary ideas. He first expresses himself generously: *having heard*, he says, *of your faith in the Lord Jesus Christ*. For this is the sum of things, this is virtue, this is the mystery, that there should be faith in Christ Jesus. This faith also encourages one to love all the saints, all who have faith in Christ and have been sanctified through him. Thus one who is faithful in Christ loves the saints. . . . "Therefore I also, having heard of your faith, love you." EPISTLE TO THE EPHESIANS 1.1.15.[1]

1:16 *Remembering Them in His Prayers*

PAUL REMEMBERS THE EPHESIANS IN HIS PRAYERS. MARIUS VICTORINUS: Every prayer that we offer up to God is made either in thanks for what we have received or in petition to receive something else. We are encouraged to pray both for ourselves and for those we love. So Paul says, "I make mention of you in my prayer." "Therefore my chief prayer is first on my account,[2] then on yours." EPISTLE TO THE EPHESIANS 1.1.16.[3]

FAITH JOINED WITH LOVE IN PRAYER. CHRYSOSTOM: Consider how many people he had in mind, whom it was hard work even to remember. All these he has remembered in his prayers, giving thanks to God as though he himself were the chief beneficiary. . . . Everywhere he joins faith and love in a remarkable union. HOMILY ON EPHESIANS 3.1.15-19.[4]

1:17a *The Father of Glory*

WHY THE GOD AND FATHER OF OUR LORD JESUS CHRIST? JEROME: It is this God of the incarnate man who is the Father of glory, wisdom and truth, who gives the Spirit of wisdom and revelation to those who believe in his Son so that they may become wise and contemplate the glory of the Lord with unveiled face.[5] When this wisdom and revelation have made them wise and opened to them the mysteries that were hidden, it follows at once that they have *the eyes of their heart enlightened*. EPISTLE TO THE EPHESIANS 1.1.15 seq.[6]

AS FATHER OF GLORY, GOD IS KNOWN BY HIS EFFECTS. CHRYSOSTOM: Glory is the name among us which denotes that which is most magnificent. *The Father of glory* means "the one who has given you these most extraordinary gifts." Through his subordinate effects his glory is revealed. Everywhere in Scripture this name is applied to God: glory. HOMILY ON EPHESIANS 3.1.15-19.[7]

GOD AND FATHER. HILARY OF POITIERS: Where Jesus Christ is, there is God, and where there is glory, there is the Father. ON THE TRINITY 11.17.[8]

1:17b *A Spirit of Wisdom and Revelation*

FOR WHAT DOES PAUL PRAY? AMBROSIASTER: The hope of their faith lies in a heavenly reward. When they truly know what the fruit of believing is, they will become more eager in acts of worship. EPISTLE TO THE EPHESIANS 1.18.1.[9]

1:18a *Enlightening the Eyes of the Heart*

---

[1]BT 1972:139-40 [1247A-B]. [2]That is, "my thanks for your love toward all the saints." [3]BT 1972:140 [1247B-C]. [4]IOEP 4:124. [5]2 Cor 3:18. [6]Migne PL 26:458D-459A [563]. [7]IOEP 4:125. [8]Migne PL 10:411A [385]. [9]CSEL 81.3:76.

THE EYES OF THE HEART. JEROME: His phrase *eyes of the heart* clearly refers to those things we cannot understand without sense and intelligence. . . . Faith sees beyond what the physical eyes see. Physical eyes are in the heads of not only the wise but the unwise. EPISTLE TO THE EPHESIANS 1.1.15 SEQ.[10]

THESE EYES HAVE BECOME OPENED AMONG THE GENTILES. EPHRAIM THE SYRIAN: The signs manifested to the external eyes of the Jews did them little good. But faith opened the eyes of the hearts of the Gentiles. HOMILY ON OUR LORD 32.[11]

1:18b The Hope to Which We Are Called

THAT YOU MAY KNOW BY INSIGHT AND REVELATION. MARIUS VICTORINUS: Let us understand that we arrive at the full mystery of God by two routes: We ourselves by rational insight may come to understand and discern something of the knowledge of divine things. But when there is a certain divine self-disclosure God himself reveals his divinity to us. Some may directly perceive by this revelation something remarkable, majestic and close to truth. . . . But when we receive wisdom we apprehend what is divine both through our own rational insight and through God's own Spirit. When we come to *know* what is true in the way this text intends, both these ways of knowing correspond. EPISTLE TO THE EPHESIANS 1.1.17-18.[12]

KNOWING THE HOPE OF RESURRECTION. JEROME: It is not without effort that we come to *know the hope of our calling and the riches of God's inheritance in the saints.* This effort in fact comes in response to that renewing gift which God himself gives in the glorious resurrection of his own Son. This gift he gives not once but continually. . . . Every day Christ rises from the dead. Every day he is raised in the penitent. EPISTLE TO THE EPHESIANS 1.1.18 SEQ.[13]

[10]Migne PL 26:459A [563]. [11]NPNF 2 13:319. [12]BT 1972:141 [1248A-B]. [13]Migne PL 26:460A [564].

1:19-23 THE RULE OF CHRIST

[19]*And what is the immeasurable greatness of his power in us who believe, according to the working of his great might* [20]*which he accomplished in Christ when he raised him from the dead and made him sit at his right hand in the heavenly places,* [21]*far above all rule and authority and power and dominion, and above every name that is named, not only in this age but also in that which is to come;* [22]*and he has put all things under his feet and has made him the head over all things for the church,* [23]*which is his body, the fulness of him who fills all in all.*

OVERVIEW: The cross ironically reveals God's incomparable power (CHRYSOSTOM, THEODORET). The human nature God assumed in the incarnation is honored by the one who assumes it, so that all humanity is exalted in the exaltation of Christ (THEODORET). Nothing remains for God to do (HILARY OF POITIERS). Sitting at the right hand of God is a metaphor for Christ's lordship (JEROME), which is all-transcending (CHRYSOSTOM), revealed in both its potentiality and its actuality (MARIUS VICTORINUS), just as he is revealed in Scripture (JEROME). Christ is the lord of all lordships (ORIGEN), transcending all that is (MARIUS VICTORINUS), possessing the whole substance of the Godhead (ORIGEN). All has been subjected to him as Creator from the foundation of time (AMBROSIASTER). This subjection, being all-encompassing (CHRYSOSTOM), is already a fact in nature, though some wills yet remain to be subdued (JEROME). The church is his body even if all do not yet obey willingly (JEROME). The risen Christ is the soul of the church (ORIGEN). The church is to Christ as body to head (CHRYSOSTOM). His exaltation is the converse of his self-emptying on the cross (MARIUS VICTORINUS). It will be consummated only at the end of time (THEODORET).

1:19 *The Immeasurable Greatness of His Power*

THE WORKING OF HIS GREAT MIGHT. CHRYSOSTOM: When the prophets had achieved nothing, nor angels nor archangels, nor the whole creation visible and invisible . . . he decided to appear himself in the flesh to show that this was a matter that re-quired divine power. HOMILY ON EPHESIANS 3.1.20-23.[1]

THE IMMEASURABLE GREATNESS OF HIS POWER. THEODORET: Since he was speaking within the limits of human language and was unable to hymn the Lord as he wished and show the greatness of his gifts, the holy apostle brings together many things under one name, striving to reveal these as much as language permits. The name "Father of glory" embraces the hope of our calling and the riches of the glory of our inheritance, the exceeding greatness of his power and the good pleasure of his will, and all that goes with it. But *the immeasurable greatness of his power* ironically now comes to mind as he thinks of the dishonor of the cross and considers how much was achieved through it. EPISTLE TO THE EPHESIANS 1.19.[2]

1:20a *Redemption Accomplished in Christ*

THIS REDEMPTION IS ALREADY ACCOMPLISHED, EVEN IF STILL IN REFERENCE TO THE FUTURE. HILARY OF POITIERS: The language of the apostle, acknowledging the power of God, refers to future things as though they have already happened. For the things which are to be performed already subsist in their fullness in Christ, in whom is all fullness. Whatever is future is so by God's provident ordering, not as if it might exist on its own. ON THE TRINITY 11.31.[3]

HUMAN NATURE HONORED. THEODORET: It

---

[1]IOEP 4:127. [2]CPE 2:9. [3]Migne PL 10:420A-B [394].

is clear that he says all this of Christ in his humanity. This is what inspires wonder. For it would hardly be remarkable to say that God sits by God if fellowship in power is a corollary of their identity of nature as Father and Son. But that the human nature assumed from us should partake of the same honor as the one who assumed him, so that no difference in worship is apparent, so that the invisible Godhead is worshiped through the visible human nature—this exceeds all wonder! The holy apostle is overwhelmed. He first sings of the exceeding greatness of his power. Then he speaks of the working of his mighty strength. Then he looks for whatever he can say that might point to the extraordinary nature of his exaltation. EPISTLE TO THE EPHESIANS 1.20.[4]

1:20b *Sitting at God's Right Hand*

UNDERSTANDING ESCHATOLOGICAL META-PHORS. JEROME: He demonstrates the power of God through a human image. It is not that a material throne is set up and God the Father is physically seated on it and has the Son seated above with him. Rather he communicates with this metaphor because we could not understand his role as incomparable governor and judge except in our own terms. . . . Being on the right or left of God is to be understood as meaning that saints are on his right but sinners on his left.[5] . . . The very word *sits* denotes the power of kingship, through which God confers benefits on those above whom he is seated. He has reined them in and has them in his service, guiding those who had previously strayed. EPISTLE TO THE EPHESIANS 1.1.21.[6]

1:21a *Above Rule, Authority, Power and Dominion*

WHETHER OTHER POWERS EXIST BESIDES GOD. ORIGEN: Under one Lord there may be many subordinate powers and lordships, who may themselves delegate a portion of their own power, some operating in this age and some in that which is to come. But none of these has an authority equal to the Son's. All authorities must be subject to his authority. All subordinate powers are rightly exercised under that of Christ, since God's power is superior to every other power. EPISTLE TO THE EPHESIANS.[7]

ABOVE ALL AUTHORITY, ABOVE ALL POWER. MARIUS VICTORINUS: Because he is the fount and the origin and the principle in everything that moves, Christ was therefore set *above all authority and above all power.* Authority is one thing, power another. Authority is expressed in action. Power is expressed in the capacity to act. A potential act may exist not as present fact but as the present possibility of something. But since Christ is himself the origin of all and is in all that is possible, he is *above all power.* Since he is the source of all acts and authority is expressed in actions, he is therefore said to be *above all authority.* EPISTLE TO THE EPHESIANS 1.1.20-23.[8]

FAR ABOVE EVERY SOVEREIGNTY. CHRYSOSTOM: He says not merely "above" but *far above.* For God is higher than the powers on high. So he led him up there, the very one who shared our lowly humanity. He led him from the lowest depth to the highest sovereignty, beyond which there is no higher

---

[4]CPE 2:10. [5]Here Jerome cites Matthew 25:33. [6]Migne PL 26:460B-461A [564-66]. [7]JTS 3:401. [8]BT 1972:145 [1250D-1251A].

honor. *Above every sovereignty*, he says: not merely compared with this or that. . . . What gnats are compared with humans, so is the whole creation compared with God. Homily on Ephesians 3.1.20-23.[9]

The Symbols of Power in the History of Israel. Jerome: Now we must ask where the apostle found these four names—*principalities, powers, forces and dominions?* From what sources did he bring them into the open? It would be dishonorable to imagine that Paul, who had been schooled in godly literature, might be quoting this from pagan sources. I therefore suggest that he has brought into the open some of the Hebrew traditions which are secret. Or better, it might have been that once he understood that the law is spiritual, he grasped a higher meaning in those things that are written in the guise of history. He could have known, for example, that there was a symbol of other powers and authorities in what is said in the books of Numbers and Kings about kings, princes, captains and leaders of tribes and ages. Epistle to the Ephesians 1.1.21.[10]

1:21b *Above Every Name That Is Named*

Above Every Name. Origen: The One who is above all by definition has no one above him. He is not temporally following after the Father but eternally from the Father. This same thing is said of the Holy Spirit, according to the Wisdom of God, when it says *the Spirit of God has filled the world.*[11] If therefore the Son of God is said to be above all and the Holy Spirit is said to contain all, while God the Father is the one far above all names, it is plainly demonstrated that the na-

ture and substance of the Trinity is one, which is above all. Commentary on Romans 7.13.[12]

That Name from Which All Naming Comes. Marius Victorinus: All names are secondary inventions. They primarily point to that which is in the created order, whether it be angels, human beings or temporal powers. By contrast only that is eternal in essence which has existence without dependency upon something else that exists, which lives by its own power. That which is eternal has no name in itself. Such "names" are added by us with our vocabulary and language. Christ receives these names from us (Son of God, divine, Spirit), yet he is still more than whatever these names convey. . . . Among names, the name that holds the chief place and that from which all names come is that which the Greeks call Being itself. But Christ is above this very being and is therefore above every name. Epistle to the Ephesians 1.1.20-23.[13]

1:22a *Putting All Things Under His Feet*

Under His Feet. Chrysostom: God set him above so as to be honored before the rest, not merely to distinguish him but to make all things his servants. Truly this is an awesome reality—that the whole power of creation should finally bow before a man in

---

[9]IOEP 4:128. [10]Migne PL 26:461A-B [566]. Contrary to those who would place "principalities, powers, forces and dominions" in a pagan or hellenistic provenance, Jerome argues on internal evidence that they are more likely from Jewish sources. [11]Wis 1:7. [12]Migne PG 14:1141; from Rufinus's Latin translation. [13]BT 1972:145-46 [1251B-C].

whom God the Word dwells. For it is possible for someone to be on high without subjects but held in peculiar honor. Here, however, it is not so, but *he has put all under his feet*. And he has not only subjected them but imposed the most extreme subjection, below which there is no other. For this reason he says *under his feet*. HOMILY ON EPHESIANS 3.1.20-23.[14]

HE RECEIVED THIS AUTHORITY BEFORE ALL THINGS. AMBROSIASTER: He says that the Father has subjected all creation to the Son, so that he may be the head and Lord of all on account of being the one through whom he made all things. He *made all things subject to him* when he generated him before all things, that through him all that had not been might come into being. EPISTLE TO THE EPHESIANS 1.23.[15]

1:22b *The Head Over All Things*

WHETHER THIS HAS ALREADY OCCURRED. JEROME: By his foreknowledge he is celebrating what is to come as though it were done already, as I explained above when he says *he has blessed us.*[16] . . . Either this interpretation, or a better one might be: If we are to take account of what has gone before, we should take this to mean that even those things whose will is not subject to him serve him because of their natural condition. So demons, Gentiles and Jews all serve him. Even if they do not freely serve Christ nor are they put under his feet, yet, because they have been created by him for good, they are unwillingly subject to his power, even if they strive against him with the volition of their free judgment. EPISTLE TO THE EPHESIANS 1.1.22-23.[17]

ALL THINGS. JEROME: Why *all things*? Why is it said that angels, thrones, dominions, powers and the other forces that were never opposed to God should be *put under his feet*? It seems obscure. But it could be said in reply that none is without sin. The *stars themselves are not clean in God's sight,*[18] and every creature dreads the advent of the Lord. . . . But another explanation refers the word *all* not to everything but only to those things that are in dispute. It is as if one says "all the citizens cried out," not meaning that there was no one in the city who was silent but that what is said of the majority covers the minority also. EPISTLE TO THE EPHESIANS 1.1.22-23.[19]

1:22c-23a *The Church Is His Body*

HOW THE CHURCH IS CHRIST'S BODY. JEROME: In the same way as a hand has many members subject to it, of which some are diseased and weak, so too our Lord Jesus Christ, being the head of the church, has as his members the whole congregation of the church, the saints and also the sinners. But the saints are in voluntary subjection to him, while the sinners are under compulsion. EPISTLE TO THE EPHESIANS 1.1.22-23.[20]

WHETHER CHRIST IS THE SOUL OF THE CHURCH. ORIGEN: The church is called the body of Christ. We inquire whether as the body is distinguished from the head so we should think of [the church] here as an organ of its Head. Or should we rather think of the head as an aspect of the body of a per-

---

[14]IOEP 4:128. [15]CSEL 81.3:78. [16]Eph 1:3. [17]Migne PL 26:462B-C [567]. [18]Job 15:15. [19]Migne PL 26:463B [568]. [20]Migne PL 26:463A [568].

son, so the whole church of Christ is Christ's body in that he ensouls it with his Godhead and fills it with his Spirit. Or perhaps it should be interpreted in another way. But even if the second is true, the more human part of it is by itself a subservient aspect of the whole body, while the divinity that gives life to the whole church is, as it were, the divine power that enlivens it. EPISTLE TO THE EPHESIANS.[21]

THE LIFTING UP OF THE CHURCH. CHRYSOSTOM: Oh, how high he has raised the church! For, as if he were lifting it by some stage machine, he has led it up to a great height and installed it on that throne. For where the head is, there is the body also. HOMILY ON EPHESIANS 3.1.20-23.[22]

1:23b The Fullness of Him Who Fills

HOW CHRIST FILLS THE CHURCH. MARIUS VICTORINUS: Christ is the fullness of the church. This entire fullness is in process of being filled up.[23] At one stage everything which is being filled is made empty. So Christ was emptied or emptied himself.[24] Having recovered all things again through the mystery of salvation and saved the full number of souls, Christ is filling all in all. EPISTLE TO THE EPHESIANS 1.1.20-23.[25]

NOTHING FURTHER IS TO BE ADDED OR RECEIVED. MARIUS VICTORINUS: All these statements about the magnificence and power of Christ have this purpose: To prove that nothing further is to be received, no other thought required to complete the revelation. The Ephesians are therefore in error if they add anything further and introduce anything from the teaching of the Jews or of

the world. EPISTLE TO THE EPHESIANS 1.1.20-23.[26]

THE CHURCH IS CALLED THE FULLNESS OF CHRIST. CHRYSOSTOM: The fullness of the head is the body and that of the body is the head. Observe how skillfully Paul writes and how he spares no word to express the glory of God. *The fullness* of the head, he says, is fulfilled through the body. The body consists of all its members. He shows Christ using each member individually, not merely all in common. For if we were not many—one a hand, one a foot, one another member—the body would not be full. Through all members, therefore, his body is made full. Then the head is fulfilled, then the body becomes perfect, when we are all combined and gathered into one. HOMILY ON EPHESIANS 3.1.20-23.[27]

WHEN WILL GOD BE ALL IN ALL? THEODORET: By *the church* he means the whole community of the faithful. This he calls the body of Christ and the fullness of the Father. This body he has filled with all gifts. He *lives in it and goes about in it,*[28] as the voice of prophecy says. But this will be more strictly so in the future life. . . . In the present life God is in all, since his nature is uncircumscribed; but he is not *all in all,*[29] since some are impious and some lawless. Yet he lives in those who fear him and who put hope in his mercy. In the next life at any rate, when mortality has ceased and immortality is conferred and sin has no place any longer, he will be all in all. EPISTLE TO THE EPHESIANS 1.23.[30]

---

[21]JTS 3:401. [22]IOEP 4:128-29. [23]Or, "is being fulfilled." [24]Cf. Phil 2:7. [25]BT 1972:147 [1252B-C]. [26]BT 1972:147 [1252C]. [27]IOEP 4:129. [28]Lev 26:11-12. [29]1 Cor 15:28. [30]CPE 2:10-11.

2:1-3 THE STATE OF THE UNREDEEMED

¹*And you he made alive, when you were dead through the trespasses and sins* ²*in which you once walked, following the course of this world, following the prince of the power of the air, the spirit that is now at work in the sons of disobedience.* ³*Among these we all once lived in the passions of our flesh, following the desires of body and mind, and so we were by nature children of wrath, like the rest of mankind.*

OVERVIEW: The body's faults alone cannot kill, as if without a soul or will (CHRYSOSTOM). Death has two meanings: the soul's separation from the body and the soul's pursuit of sin (MARIUS VICTORINUS). The world as created is not evil (TERTULLIAN). The devil has corrupted the world in his desire to have accomplices (AMBROSIASTER). Human nature has become voluntarily subject to his sway (CHRYSOSTOM). The children of disobedience are subject to the devil by choice, however, and not by their created nature (MARIUS VICTORINUS). Christians are given grace to resist him (THEODORET). Paul confesses his past transgressions (JEROME). Admonishing both immorality and heresy, Paul describes the voluntary disobedience of sinners as their sin nature (PSEUDO-AUGUSTINE), relying on scriptural precedent (GREGORY OF NYSSA) and implying that our first nature has been corrupted (AUGUSTINE), according to Scripture (GREGORY OF NYSSA).

2:1 Dead in Trespasses and Sins

DEAD IN SIN. MARIUS VICTORINUS: Death is understood in two ways. The first is the familiar definition—when the soul is separated from the body at the end of life. The second is that, while abiding in that same body, the soul pursues the desires of the flesh and lives in sin. EPISTLE TO THE EPHESIANS 1.2.1-2.[1]

THE SOUL SINS FROM CHOICE, NOT NATURE. CHRYSOSTOM: There is a distinction between the death of the body and the death of the soul. There is no reproach in the death of the body as such and hence no moral danger since there is no reproach. The body's death is merely a matter of nature, not of choice. This death had its origin in the transgression of the first human being, and thereafter it has had its subsequent effect on nature. Its release will be swift. But the death of the soul is the result of free choice. Hence it entails reproach, from which there is no easy release. It is a much weightier task to heal a deadened soul than to raise a dead body, as Paul has already shown. Yet this is what

---

[1]BT 1972:148 [1253A].

has now happened, incredible as it may be. HOMILY ON EPHESIANS 4.2.1-3.[2]

TRESPASS DISTINGUISHED FROM SIN. JEROME: [The Greeks] speak of trespass as the first step toward sin. It is when a secret thought steals in, and, though we offer a measure of collusion, it does not yet drive us on to ruin. . . . But sin is something else. It is when the collusion is actually completed and reaches its goal. EPISTLE TO THE EPHESIANS 1.2.1 SEQ.[3]

2:2a Walking in Sin, Following the Course of This World

THE COURSE OF THIS WORLD. TERTULLIAN: *Once you followed the course of this world.* World here is completely distinguishable from God. For the creature is unlike the Creator, the artifact unlike its Maker, the world unlike God. Similarly when Paul speaks of those who "follow the prince of the power of the air" he is referring not to the one God who holds sway over all the ages. For the one who presides over higher authorities is never classified by reference to one lower. AGAINST MARCION 5.17.7-8.[4]

2:2b Following the Prince of the Power of the Air

HOW THE DEVIL CORRUPTED THE WORLD. AMBROSIASTER: He indicates that the prince of power, that is, the devil, has corrupted the understanding of the world to make it depart from the one God and conceive a belief in many gods. In this way the devil made them associates in his own conspiracy, seeing that they were found to exhibit the same impiety in their denial of the one God. EPISTLE TO THE EPHESIANS 2.2.1-3.[5]

THE DEVIL AS COLLABORATOR. CHRYSOSTOM: Do you see Paul's gentleness, how he everywhere soothes his hearer and avoids burdening him? For having said that they had arrived at the extreme consequence of evil (for what else does "being dead" mean?) . . . he provides them with a collaborator, so that they themselves will not be held accountable alone for their plight but share responsibility with a powerful accomplice, the devil. HOMILY ON EPHESIANS 4.2.1-3.[6]

THE POWERS OF THE DEVIL. CHRYSOSTOM: Why does he call the devil the ruler of this world? Because virtually the whole of humanity surrendered to him. All are his voluntary and willing slaves. Few pay any heed to Christ, who promises unnumbered blessings. Rather they follow after the devil, who promises nothing but leads them all to hell. He rules in this age, where he has . . . more subjects than God, more who obey him rather than God. All but a few are in his grasp on account of their laxity. HOMILY ON EPHESIANS 4.2.1-3.[7]

2:2c The Spirit at Work in the Children of Disobedience

HOW THE SATANIC SPIRIT WORKS. MARIUS VICTORINUS: Light and dark are two things, as are truth and falsehood, goodness and wickedness. But they are not to be imagined as equal, for it is not pious to compare any-

---

[2]IOEP 4:136. [3]Migne PL 26:465C [571], following Origen *Epistle to the Ephesians* [JTS 3:403]. [4]CCL 1:714. [5]CSEL 81.3:79. [6]IOEP 4:136. [7]IOEP 4:136.

thing to God even by contraries. So we are to understand that there are two spirits, one of faith and one of disobedience. Satan and his devils have their substance from air, that is, from material reality. They derive their power in that same way, over those who think materially. The prince of that power which is in the air works through matter. He is therefore that spirit now at work through material means among the children of disobedience. He possesses their minds and has dominion over them. Therefore the one who lives *according to the course of this world* lives *according to the prince of the power of the air, of the spirit who is now at work in the children of disobedience.* EPISTLE TO THE EPHESIANS 1.2.1-2.[8]

THE CHILDREN OF DISOBEDIENCE. THEODORET: Long ago, before the Fall, a certain authority was primordially entrusted to the devil. But falling from this through wickedness he became a teacher of impiety and wickedness. Yet he does not have power over all but only over those who do not receive divine revelation. These Paul calls *sons of disobedience.* EPISTLE TO THE EPHESIANS 2.1-2.[9]

2:3a Living in the Passions of Our Flesh

THE IDOLATRY-PRONE PLEASURES OF THE FLESH. AMBROSIASTER: He is speaking of a great deception when he brings to mind the "passions of the flesh." For the pleasure of the flesh means being delighted by the visible, so that it gives the name of gods to the elements that God appointed as his means of ordering the world. But this name [God] belongs rightly to the one and only God, from whom everything derives. . . . If anyone imag-

ines that the "passions of the flesh" mean anything else, let him reflect on how the apostle led a pure life. He lived without blemish according to the righteousness of the law. But because he had persecuted the church he includes himself in the "we"—*we lived in the passions of our flesh.* For every sin, according to Paul, has something to do with the deception associated with living according to the flesh, which is the mother of all corruption. EPISTLE TO THE EPHESIANS 2.3.1-3.[10]

PAUL INCLUDES HIMSELF. CHRYSOSTOM: Paul encourages them by including himself with them. *Among these,* he says, *we all once lived.* All are included. It is not possible to say that anyone is exempted. HOMILY ON EPHESIANS 2.3.[11]

THE SINS IN WHICH WE ALL ONCE LIVED. JEROME: So that he would not appear to have exempted himself through pride when he said *your sins in which you walked,* he now adds *in which we also lived.* However, the one who says he has lived confesses past, not present, transgressions. EPISTLE TO THE EPHESIANS 1.2.1 SEQ.[12]

2:3b Following the Desires of Body and Mind

DISTINGUISHING SIN OF THE FLESH AND OF THE MIND. JEROME: There is a difference between sin of the flesh and sin of the mind. The sin of the flesh is indecency and profligacy and whatever might act as instrument

---

[8]BT 1972:148-49 [1253C-D]. [9]CPE 2:11. [10]CSEL 81.3:79-80. [11]IOEP 4:138; cf. Theodoret *Epistle to the Ephesians* 2.3 [CPE 2.12]. [12]Migne PL 26:466C [572].

to its lusts. The transgression of the mind pertains to doctrine contrary to truth and to the baseness of heretics. EPISTLE TO THE EPHESIANS 1.2.1 SEQ.[13]

2:3c By Nature Children of Wrath

THE LORD DOES NOT DIRECTLY WILL WRATH APART FROM HUMAN CHOICE. TERTULLIAN: As a Jew Paul had been one of the *children of unbelief* in whom *the devil was at work*, especially when he persecuted the church and the Christ of the Creator. On this account he says, *We were by nature children of wrath*. But he says *by nature* so that a heretic could not argue that it was the Lord who created evil. We create the grounds for the Creator's wrath ourselves.[14] AGAINST MARCION 5.17.9-10.[15]

"BY NATURE" DEFINED AS HUMAN WILLING. PSEUDO-AUGUSTINE: Undoubtedly the will passes for nature—for it is from their will, not their nature, that people are judged. Similarly all the martyrs and the justified are upright not because they were born faithful but because they were reborn so. QUESTIONS ON THE OLD AND NEW TESTAMENTS 115.11.[16]

"BY WRATH" IMPLIES BY CHOICE. GREGORY OF NYSSA: When [Scripture] speaks of *sons of men* or *sons of rams* it indicates an essential relation between the one begotten and the source of his begetting. But when it speaks of *sons of power* [as at 1 Sam 14:52]

or *children of wrath*, it asserts a connection made by choice. AGAINST EUNOMIUS 3.1.116.[17]

WHETHER SIN IS RIGHTLY SPOKEN OF AS NATURAL. AUGUSTINE: We speak of "nature" in two ways. When we are speaking strictly of nature itself we mean the nature in which humanity was originally created—after God's own image and without fault. The other way we speak of nature refers to that fallen sin nature, in which we are self-deceived and subject to the flesh as the penalty for our condemnation. The apostle adopts this way of speaking when he says *for we were by nature children of wrath, like the rest*. ON NATURE AND GRACE 81.[18]

HOW THE CORRUPTION OF OUR NATURE IS STILL RUNNING ITS COURSE. AUGUSTINE: What then is meant by this wickedness of the natural man and of those who . . . *by nature* are children of wrath? Could this possibly be the nature created in Adam? That created nature was debased in him. It has run and is running its course now through everyone by nature, so that nothing frees us from condemnation except the grace of God through Jesus Christ our Lord. ON MARRIAGE AND CONCUPISCENCE 2.20.[19]

---

[13]Migne PL 26:467A [572-73]. [14]The heresy would be to say that the Lord willed wrath apart from human choice or human nature. [15]CCL 1:714-15. [16]CSEL 50:322. [17]GNO 2:43. [18]Migne PL 44:288; citing *On Free Will* 3.54. [19]Migne PL 44:448.

2:4-10 THE MERCY OF GOD

⁴But God, who is rich in mercy, out of the great love with which he loved us, ⁵even when we were dead through our trespasses, made us alive together with Christ (by grace you have been saved), ⁶and raised us up with him, and made us sit with him in the heavenly places in Christ Jesus, ⁷that in the coming ages he might show the immeasurable riches of his grace in kindness toward us in Christ Jesus. ⁸For by grace you have been saved through faith; and this is not your own doing, it is the gift of God— ⁹not because of works, lest any man should boast. ¹⁰For we are his workmanship, created in Christ Jesus for good works, which God prepared beforehand, that we should walk in them.

OVERVIEW: Through the resurrection of Christ we are mercifully saved despite our unworthiness (AMBROSIASTER). Without exception all who are saved are saved by grace (JEROME). The faithful are already in a sense raised to heaven through the resurrection of Christ (THEODORET, JEROME) and hence are called to live accordingly (ORIGEN). Christians are not arrogant when they celebrate this salvation (AMBROSE), for their faith is not a work (FULGENTIUS) but an act of divine grace (JEROME). We can claim no credit for our conversion (CHRYSOSTOM) or subsequent good works (MARIUS VICTORINUS). We can and must do works but have no right to glory in ourselves (CHRYSOSTOM, AMBROSIASTER). God, who created us from nothing (JEROME), also wills our recreation in Christ (THEODORE OF MOPSUESTIA). Although we now fail to do good works (CYRIL OF ALEXANDRIA), God prepares both present and future works for us in which we must persevere (CHRYSOSTOM, MARIUS VICTORINUS).

2:4 God, Rich in Mercy

GOD DID NOT ORIGINALLY DESIRE THAT ANY SHOULD PERISH. AMBROSIASTER: These are the true riches of God's mercy, that even when we did not seek it mercy was made known through his own initiative. . . . This is God's love to us, that having made us he did not want us to perish. His reason for making us was that he might love what he had made, seeing that no one hates his own workmanship. EPISTLE TO THE EPHESIANS 2.4.[1]

2:5a Made Alive with Christ

HE FORMED US ANEW AS HIS MEMBERS. . AMBROSIASTER: God made us in Christ. So it is through Christ once again that he has formed us anew. We are his members; he our Head. EPISTLE TO THE EPHESIANS 2.5.[2]

---

[1]CSEL 81.3:80-81. [2]CSEL 81.3:81.

2:5b Saved by Grace

HOW GRACE SAVES. THEODORET: Since he rose we hope that we too shall rise. He himself [by his rising] has paid our debt. Then Paul explains more plainly how great the gift is: *You are saved by grace.* For it is not because of the excellence of our lives that we have been called but because of the love of our Savior. EPISTLE TO THE EPHESIANS 2.4.5.[3]

WHAT WE GIVE FOR WHAT HE BESTOWED. JEROME: The sufferings of the present time are not worthy to be compared with the future glory that will be revealed in us.[4] If so, we are saved by grace rather than works, for we can give God nothing in return for what he has bestowed on us. EPISTLE TO THE EPHESIANS 1.2.1.[5]

2:6a Raised with Christ

BELIEVE YOU HAVE RISEN WITH CHRIST. ORIGEN: What Paul is saying then is: If you believe that Christ is risen from the dead, believe also that you too have risen with him. If you believe that he sits at the Father's right hand in heaven, believe that your place too is amid not earthly but heavenly things. COMMENTARY ON ROMANS 5.8.[6]

ALREADY EXALTED. JEROME: Above he said that God raised Christ from the dead and seated him at his right hand. . . . Some may ask how God who has saved us and raised us with him has also made us sit with Christ. A simple response would be indeed that, in the light of God's foreknowledge, Paul is speaking of what is to come as though it had already been done. . . . One who understands the resurrection and the kingdom of Christ spiritually does not scruple to say that the saints already sit and reign with Christ! Just as a person may become truly holy even in the flesh, when he lives in the flesh and has his conversation in heaven, when he walks on earth and, ceasing to be flesh, is wholly converted into spirit, so he also is seated in heaven with Christ. For indeed *the kingdom of God is within us.*[7] EPISTLE TO THE EPHESIANS 1.2.1 SEQ.[8]

CHRIST SHARED OUR BODILY NATURE. THEODORET: If Christ the Lord did not share our human nature, he would have been falsely called our firstfruits. If so his bodily nature was not raised from the dead and did not receive its seat at the right hand in heaven. And if none of this occurred how can it be said that God has raised us and seated us with Christ, that is, if we have nothing by nature that belongs to him? ERANISTES 1.[9]

2:6b Sitting in Heavenly Places in Christ Jesus

NOT BY OUR OWN DESERVING. MARIUS VICTORINUS: He did not make us deserving, since we did not receive these things by our own merit but by the grace and goodness of God. . . . But all this, as he often asserts and I insist, is in Christ. For in him is the whole mystery of the resurrection, both ours and of all others. EPISTLE TO THE EPHESIANS 1.2.7.[10]

---

[3]CPE 2:12. [4]Cf. Rom 8:18. [5]Migne PL 26:468B [574]. [6] Migne PG 14:1041c; from Rufinus's Latin translation. [7]Lk 17:21. [8]Migne PL 26:468B-469A [574-75], following Origen *Epistle to the Ephesians* [JTS 3:405]. [9]Eran 89. [10]BT 1972:152 [1255C].

OUR DESTINY IS TO SIT WITH HIM. JEROME: How abundant is his grace and how multifaceted is the glory in which God has caused us to be seated and reign with Christ, after freeing us from the tribulations of the age! This is shown above all by the fact that in the ages to come he will shed his glory upon us in the sight not of some but of all rational creatures. . . . But an attentive reader might inquire: "Are you saying then that the human arena is greater than the angels and all the heavenly powers?" No. . . . Some might conceivably argue that *he made us sit with him in heavenly places* refers not to the good angels but to the bad angels, the banished angels and the prince of this world, and Lucifer who rises in the morning, over whom the saints will be enthroned with Christ. . . . But a better argument will translate [the reference to Christ's grace] as meaning that we are saved not by our own merit but by his grace and that it is a proof of greater goodness to die for sinners rather than for the just. EPISTLE TO THE EPHESIANS 1.2.7.[11]

2:7 Showing the Immeasurable Riches of Grace

IN THE COMING AGES IT WILL BE CLEAR. CHRYSOSTOM: Do not be disbelieving. You have received a proof from former events, from the head[12] and from his desire to manifest his goodness. For how otherwise could there be a revelation to us if this does not happen? This will be demonstrated in the ages to come. What now seems nonsense to unbelievers then will appear as fully sensible to everyone. We will sit with him. Nothing is more trustworthy and worthy of praise than this revelation. HOMILY ON EPHESIANS

2.7.[13]

2:8a By Grace Saved Through Faith

DARE WE CLAIM THIS PROMISE? AMBROSE: Do not rely on your own efforts but on the grace of Christ. "You are," says the apostle, "saved by grace. Therefore it is not a matter of arrogance here but faith when we celebrate: We are accepted! This is not pride but devotion." ON THE SACRAMENTS 5.4.19.[14]

WHETHER FAITH IS ITSELF FINALLY OUR WORK. JEROME: Paul says this in case the secret thought should steal upon us that "if we are not saved by our own works, at least we are saved by our own faith, and so in another way our salvation is of ourselves." Thus he added the statement that faith too is not in our own will but in God's gift. Not that he means to take away free choice from humanity . . . but that even this very freedom of choice has God as its author, and all things are to be referred to his generosity, in that he has even allowed us to will the good. EPISTLE TO THE EPHESIANS 1.2.8-9.[15]

THE ONLY WAY TO SALVATION: BY GRACE THROUGH FAITH. FULGENTIUS: The blessed Paul argues that we are saved by faith, which he declares to be not from us but a gift from God. Thus there cannot possibly be true salvation where there is no true faith, and, since this faith is divinely enabled, it is without doubt bestowed by his free generosity. Where there is true belief through true faith, true salvation certainly accompanies it.

---

[11]Migne PL 26:469A-470A [575-76]. [12]The Master, the Creator of the universe. [13]IOEP 4:139. [14]CSEL 73:66. [15]Migne PL 26:470A-B [577].

Anyone who departs from true faith will not possess the grace of true salvation. ON THE INCARNATION 1.[16]

2:8b Not Our Doing but the Gift of God

OUR OWN DOING? CHRYSOSTOM: So that you may not be elated by the magnitude of these benefits, see how Paul puts you in your place. For *by grace you are saved*, he says, *through faith*. Then, so as to do no injury to free will, he allots a role to us, then takes it away again, saying *and this not of ourselves*. . . . Even faith, he says, is not from us. For if the Lord had not come, if he had not called us, how should we have been able to believe? *For how*, he says, *shall they believe if they have not heard?*[17] So even the act of faith is not self-initiated. It is, he says, *the gift of God*. HOMILY ON EPHESIANS 2.8.[18]

2:9a Not Because of Works

NOT WORKS. MARIUS VICTORINUS: The fact that you Ephesians are saved is not something that comes from yourselves. It is the gift of God. It is not from your works, but it is God's grace as God's gift, not from anything you have deserved. Our works are one thing, what we deserve another. Hence he distinguishes the two phrases *not from yourselves* and *not from works*. Remember that there are faithful works that ought to be displayed daily in services to the poor and other good deeds. EPISTLE TO THE EPHESIANS 1.2.9.[19]

WHETHER GOD HAS FORBIDDEN WORKS. CHRYSOSTOM: God's mission was not to save people in order that they may remain barren or inert. For Scripture says that faith has saved us. Put better: Since God willed it, faith has saved us. Now in what case, tell me, does faith save without itself doing anything at all? Faith's workings themselves are a gift of God, lest anyone should boast. What then is Paul saying? Not that God has forbidden works but that he has forbidden us to be justified by works. No one, Paul says, is justified by works, precisely in order that the grace and benevolence of God may become apparent! HOMILY ON EPHESIANS 4.2.9.[20]

2:9b Lest Anyone Should Boast

ALL THANKS TO GOD. AMBROSIASTER: All thanksgiving for our salvation is to be given only to God. He extends his mercy to us so as to recall us to life precisely while we are straying, without looking for the right road. And thus we are not to glory in ourselves but in God, who has regenerated us by a heavenly birth through faith in Christ. EPISTLE TO THE EPHESIANS 2.10.[21]

2:10a We Are God's Workmanship

WHAT WE OWE OUR MAKER. JEROME: We are his creation. This means that it is from him that we live, breathe, understand and are able to believe, because he is the One who made us. And note carefully that he did not say "we are his fashioning and molding" but *we are his creation*. Molding starts with the mud of the earth, but creation from the outset is *according to the image and likeness of God*.[22] EPISTLE TO THE EPHESIANS 1.2.10.[23]

---

[16]CCL 91:313. [17]Rom 10:14. [18]IOEP 2:160. [19]BT 1972:152 [1256A-B]. [20]IOEP 2:140. [21]CSEL 81.3:82. [22]Gen 1:26-27. [23]Migne PL 26:470B-C [577].

2:10b Created in Christ Jesus for Good Works

THE SECOND CREATION IN CHRIST. THEODORE OF MOPSUESTIA: Here he is speaking not of the first but of the second creation, wherein we are re-created by the resurrection. Completely unable as we are to mend our ways by our own decision on account of the natural weakness that opposes us, we are made able to come newly alive without pain and with great ease by the grace of the One who re-creates us for this purpose. EPISTLE TO THE EPHESIANS 2.10.[24]

CREATED FOR GOOD WORKS. CYRIL OF ALEXANDRIA: Human beings choose their own way of life and are entrusted with the reins of their own intelligence, so as to follow whatever course they wish, either toward the good or toward the contrary. But our [original, created] nature has implanted in it a zealous desire for whatever is good and the will to concern itself with goodness and righteousness. For this is what we mean by saying that humanity is *in the image and likeness of God*,[25] that the creature is naturally disposed to what is good and right. DOCTRINAL QUESTIONS AND ANSWERS 2.[26]

2:10c Works Prepared by God

PREPARED BEFOREHAND? MARIUS VICTORINUS: Does Paul means "good works" in the future tense or those which we now perform? Taken either way they are good for us to walk in. They are witnesses to Christ's working in us. EPISTLE TO THE EPHESIANS 1.2.10.[27]

THAT WE SHOULD WALK IN THEM. CHRYSOSTOM: He does not say "so that we might begin" but *so that we should walk*—all the way. For walking is a metaphor that suggests continuance, extending to the end of our lives. Suppose we had to walk a road that leads to a royal city, but after having gone almost all the way we grow faint almost at the end and stop. We would then have no profit. Instead Paul says we are created "for good works."[28] HOMILY ON EPHESIANS 4.2.9.[29]

---

[24]CGPEP 6:142. [25]Gen 1:26. [26]OECT 188. For an earlier, similar comment see Cyril of Jerusalem *Catechetical Homily* 2.1, *Opera*, ed. W. K. Reischl and J. Rupp (Munich: 1848), 1:38-41. [27]BT 1972:153 [1256B-C]. [28] Hence we need grace not only sufficient now but also prepared beforehand as sufficient for all future occasions. This we already have. [29]IOEP 2:161; cf. NPNF 1 13:68.

2:11-16 THE SALVATION OF THE GENTILES

[11]*Therefore remember that at one time you Gentiles in the flesh, called the uncircumcision by what is called the circumcision, which is made in the flesh by hands—* [12]*remember that you were at that time separated from Christ, alienated from the commonwealth of Israel, and strangers to the covenants of promise, having no*

hope and without God in the world. [13]*But now in Christ Jesus you who once were far off have been brought near in the blood of Christ.* [14]*For he is our peace, who has made us both one, and has broken down the dividing wall of hostility,* [15]*by abolishing in his flesh the law of commandments and ordinances, that he might create in himself one new man in place of the two, so making peace,* [16]*and might reconcile us both to God in one body through the cross, thereby bringing the hostility to an end.*

Overview: Paul illustrates the extent of God's mercy to Gentiles (Chrysostom), whose former state was a preparation for their future spiritual state (Epiphanius), which they now possess as the true circumcision (Jerome). They were strangers to truth and the covenants (Tertullian, Marius Victorinus) and hence to God (Jerome). They are now called to accept their destiny as the true Israel (Origen) and give thanks for the love of Christ (Ambrosiaster). Only he, our Creator, can overcome the flesh (Marius Victorinus), uniting Jews and Gentiles in a new humanity (Chrysostom) by breaking down their mutual animosity (Ambrosiaster) and overcoming the barrier between sin and God (Chrysostom). The law was good in its time, though now it has been transcended (Chrysostom). Though the law's ceremonial rules are discarded (Ambrosiaster), the moral commandments must be kept in the spirit (Theodoret). A new creation is coming into being (Chrysostom) that embraces Jews and Gentiles (Theodoret). Christ is the true mediator because he alone is able to reconcile all things (Chrysostom). The new person in Christ (Tertullian) is a unity of soul and spirit (Marius Victorinus). The resurrection brings that person peace with God (Theodore of Mopsuestia). The crucified one joins himself with us to join us to God (Gregory of Nyssa), vanquishing the old enmity by taking us into his body (Chrysostom).

2:11 Gentiles in the Flesh

Remembering the Circuitous Path of Salvation. Chrysostom: Many are the evidences of God's love of humanity. God has saved us through himself, and through himself in such a special way, remembering what we were when he saved us and to what point he has now brought us. For each of these stages in itself is a great proof of his benevolence. Paul now reviews at each stage what he writes. He has already said that God has saved us when we were dead in sins and children of wrath. Now Paul shows to what extent God has raised us. Homily on Ephesians 5.2.11-12.[1]

On the Figure of Gentiles in the Flesh. Epiphanius: The phrase *Gentiles in the flesh* contrasts types of realities. The type in the flesh was awaiting the time of the spirit. The less perfect fulfillment of the circumcision is expressed in relation to its more perfect fulfillment. Panarion 42.12.3, Thirty-Sixth Refutation of Marcion.[2]

---

[1]IOEP 4:146. [2]GCS 31:178-79.

DISTINGUISHING FOUR POSSIBLE TYPES OF GENTILES AND JEWS REGARDING CIRCUMCISION. JEROME: By calling the Ephesians *Gentiles in the flesh*, he shows that in the spirit they are not Gentiles, just as conversely the Jews are Gentiles in spirit and Israelites in the flesh. Therefore the Jews and Gentiles are subject to a fourfold division: Some are circumcised in spirit and flesh, as were Moses and Aaron. . . . Some have been circumcised neither in spirit nor in flesh, as were Nebuchadnezzar and Pharaoh. . . . A third group are circumcised only in the flesh. . . . Lastly come those of whom he now speaks, . . . believers such as today we see in the whole host of believing Gentiles around the world. EPISTLE TO THE EPHESIANS 1.2.12.[3]

2:12a *Separated from Christ*

PREVIOUSLY DESTITUTE OF KNOWLEDGE OF GOD. THEODORET: He wants to show that Christ is the provider of all goods for them. "For previously," he says, "you were destitute of the knowledge of God and did not enjoy the goods promised beforehand to Israel." EPISTLE TO THE EPHESIANS 2.12.[4]

2:12b *Alienated from Israel*

TRUE ISRAEL. MARIUS VICTORINUS: The true way of Israel consists in living according to the Spirit, thinking according to the Spirit and being circumcised from unworthy desires. EPISTLE TO THE EPHESIANS 1.2.12.[5]

2:12c *Without Hope and Without God in the World*

HAVING MANY GODS BUT WITHOUT GOD.

JEROME: When he says *having no hope, without God in the world*, he does not deny that the Ephesians had many gods before they believed in Christ. His point is that one who is without the true God has no god worthy of the name. And the next phrase, *without God in the world*, is significant: The Gentiles in a sense already had God indeed in the form of anticipation, because God knew beforehand that he would have them. In God's foreknowledge they were never without God. But enmeshed in the world they were without God.[6] EPISTLE TO THE EPHESIANS 1.2.12.[7]

2:13 *Once Far Off, Now Brought Near*

FROM WHAT WERE THEY ONCE FAR OFF? TERTULLIAN: They were once far off from the Christ of the Creator, from the way of the Israelites, from the covenants, from the hope of the promise, from God himself. Once far off, the Gentiles now come close in Christ to the things that were once far off. AGAINST MARCION 5.17.12-13.[8]

NOW BROUGHT NEAR TO THE COMMONWEALTH OF TRUE ISRAEL. ORIGEN: Paul is responding to those who think that believers in Christ may enter into the commonwealth of Israel but that it is some entirely different one that has nothing in common with the history of Israel. . . . It is those who know the spiritual law and live in accordance with it who are made dwellers in the commonwealth of Israel, more so than those who are

---

[3]Migne PL 26:471D-472A [579]. [4]CPE 2:14. [5]BT 1972:154 [1257B-C]. [6]In their limited vision of the future salvation, which had not yet unfolded, they were without God. [7]Migne PL 26:472C-D [580]. [8]CCL 1:715.

Israelites in the body only. EPISTLE TO THE EPHESIANS.[9]

WHETHER ONE CAN BE FAR FROM GOD "WHO IS EVERYWHERE." JEROME: God in his entirety is everywhere. Who can be separated from him when all things are in him? . . . He is, however, said to be far away from the unrighteous, according to Proverbs [15:29]. . . . Just as far as the unrighteous are away from him, so close is he to the saints. Just when God seem to be furthest from the Ephesians, he was coming close to them by the blood of Jesus. EPISTLE TO THE EPHESIANS 1.2.13-14.[10]

BROUGHT NEAR BY THE BLOOD OF CHRIST. AMBROSIASTER: He reminds us that we were brought close to God by the blood of Christ in order to show how great is God's affection toward us, since he allowed his own Son to die. We too, enduring in faith, should not yield to despair in any of the agonies inflicted on us for his sake, knowing that what he deserves from us exceeds all that our enemies can bring upon us. EPISTLE TO THE EPHESIANS 2.13.[11]

2:14a Christ Is Our Peace

THE PEACEMAKER DESTROYS THE WALL OF PARTITION. MARIUS VICTORINUS: *Christ*, he says, *is our peace*. Elsewhere Paul calls him mediator. He interposed himself of his own accord between divided realms. Souls born of God's fountain of goodness were being detained in the world. There was a wall in their midst, a sort of fence, a partition made by the deceits of the flesh and worldly lusts. Christ by his own mystery, his cross, his passion and his way of life destroyed this wall.

He overcame sin and taught that it could be overcome. He destroyed the lusts of the world and taught that they ought to be destroyed. He took away the wall in the midst. It was in his own flesh that he overcame the enmity. The work is not ours. We are not called to set ourselves free. Faith in Christ is our only salvation. EPISTLE TO THE EPHESIANS 1.2.14-15.[12]

HOW HAVE BOTH BEEN MADE ONE? THEODORE OF MOPSUESTIA: Christ, conferring immortality on us through his resurrection, has put an end to this division [between Jew and Gentile], for there can be no circumcision of an immortal nature. CATENA 2.13.[13]

2:14b Breaking Down the Wall of Hostility

THE WALL BETWEEN JEW AND GENTILE BROKEN DOWN. AMBROSIASTER: The passion of the Savior made peace between the circumcision and the uncircumcision. For the enmity, which was between them like a wall and divided the circumcision from the uncircumcision and the uncircumcision from the circumcision, was abolished by the Savior. His command is that the Jew should not so presume on his circumcision as to reproach the Gentile, nor should the Gentile trust in his uncircumcision, that is, his paganism, so as to abhor the Jew. Both, made new, should maintain in Christ their faith in the one God. EPISTLE TO THE EPHESIANS 2.14.1.[14]

THE WALL BETWEEN GOD AND HUMANITY.

---

[9]JTS 3:405. [10]Migne PL 26:472D-473A [580]. [11]CSEL 81.3:83. [12]BT 1972:155 [1258B-C]. [13]CGPEP 6:145. [14]CSEL 81.3:83.

CHRYSOSTOM: Some say that the wall between them is that of the Jews against the Greeks, because it does not allow them to mix. I do not think so. Rather I think that the wall between them is common within both. It is the hostility proceeding within the flesh. This was the midwall cutting them off, as the prophet says, *Do not your sins stand in the midst between you and me?*[15] The midwall was the enmity that God had both toward Jews and toward Greeks. But when the law came this enmity was not dissolved; rather it increased. *For the law*, he says, *works wrath.*[16] HOMILY ON EPHESIANS 5.2.13-15.[17]

2:15a *Abolishing the Law of Commandments and Ordinances*

LAW AS FENCE. CHRYSOSTOM: The law was a fence, but this was made for our security. This is why it was called a fence, so that it might fence us in. . . . Now he has *abolished the law of commandments* through his teaching. Oh, what love of humanity! He gave us a law that we might keep it, but when we failed to keep it and deserved punishment he dissolved the law. HOMILY ON EPHESIANS 5.2.13-15.[18]

CEREMONIAL LAW NO LONGER BINDING. AMBROSIASTER: The law that he abolished was that which had been given to the Jews concerning circumcision and new moons and food and sacrifices and the sabbath. He ordered it to cease because it was a burden. In this way he made peace. EPISTLE TO THE EPHESIANS 2.15.[19]

UNDER THE GOSPEL THE TEN COMMANDMENTS STILL REMAIN FREELY TO BE OBEYED.

THEODORET: Christ dispelled the enmity between us and God. He gave his own flesh as a ransom for us. Once this was done he put an end to the things that separated you and them.[20] For this is what he means by *the law of ordinances*. He has not annulled the Decalogue. . . . For Christ the Lord himself held these up to the one who wanted to know the way to eternal life.[21] But by doctrines he meant the gospel teaching, since the realizing of full maturity lies in the responsive choices[22] of the will. . . . Yet these gospel teachings are not laid down as laws. They are a matter of free choice. What he does lay down as law is what he inscribed on nature when he created it in the beginning. EPISTLE TO THE EPHESIANS 2.14-15.[23]

2:15b *Creating One New Being*

CHRIST UNIQUELY FITTED TO CREATE A NEW HUMANITY. TERTULLIAN: He was born in a singular way from a virgin by the Spirit of God. He was born to reconcile both Gentile and Jew to God, both of whom had offended God. He reconciled them into one body through the cross. The enmity was in this way slain. This reconciliation took place in his flesh through his body as he suffered on the cross. AGAINST MARCION 5.17.15.[24]

THE NEW SPIRITUAL PERSON. MARIUS VICTORINUS: Their souls have thus been reconciled to the eternal and the spiritual, to all

---

[15]Is 59:2. [16]Rom 4:15. [17]IOEP 4:149. [18]IOEP 4:150. [19]CSEL 81.3:84. [20]Gentiles and Jews. [21]See the narrative of the encounter between Jesus and the rich young ruler (Lk 18:18-25). [22]Responsive to grace. [23]CPE 2:15A. [24]CCL 1:716.

things above. The Savior, through the Spirit, indeed the Holy Spirit, descended into souls. He thereby joined what had been separated, spiritual things and souls, so as to make the souls themselves spiritual. He has established them in himself, as he says, *in a new person*. What is this new person? The spiritual person, as distinguished from the old person, who was soul struggling against flesh. EPISTLE TO THE EPHESIANS 1.2.14-15.[25]

CREATING ONE NEW PERSON IN PLACE OF GENTILE VERSUS JEW. CHRYSOSTOM: Don't you see? The Greek does not have to become a Jew. Rather both enter into a new condition. His aim is not to bring Greek believers into being as different kinds of Jews but rather to create both anew. Rightly he uses the term *create* rather than *change* to point out the great effect of what God has done. Even though the creation is invisible it is no less a creation of its Creator. HOMILY ON EPHESIANS 5.2.13-15.[26]

A SINGLE PERSON WITH ONE HEAD. THEODORET: He has reconciled both, that is, those from Gentile and from Jewish backgrounds, in the one body that was offered on behalf of all, so that they may at last be made one body. And he has called all believers a single man because Christ our Lord is the one head, and those who have been favored with salvation fill the role of members. EPISTLE TO THE EPHESIANS 2.16.[27]

IN HIMSELF. CHRYSOSTOM: He did not pass the task of reconciliation on to another. He made himself the means of combining one with the other. This produced one wonderful result. He himself was the first instance of this reconciliation, a result greater than all

the previous creation. For that is what *in himself* means: Having assumed dominion over the Jew and then of the Greek, he himself became their mediator. He brought them together, doing away with all that estranged them. Now he has fashioned them anew through fire and water—no longer water and earth but water and fire.[28] He became a Jew when he was circumcised. Then, being cursed, he became a Greek outside the law and one more excellent than either Greek or Jew. HOMILY ON EPHESIANS 5.2.15.[29]

2:15c Making Peace

PEACE BETWEEN GOD AND SINNERS. CHRYSOSTOM: *Making peace* may mean their peace with God or with one another. . . . The focus is primarily on peace with God, as is made clear by what follows. What does he say? He has fully reconciled both to God in one body through the cross. He did not say "to some degree reconciled" but "fully reconciled." Even before this human nature was in principle reconcilable,[30] as we see in the righteous and before the law. HOMILY ON EPHESIANS 5.2.16.[31]

2:16a Reconciled to God Through the Cross

THE ENMITY IS SLAIN IN HIMSELF. GREGORY OF NYSSA: Taking up the enmity that had come between us and God on account of sins, *slaying it in himself*, as the apostle says

---

[25]BT 1972:156 [1258D-1259A]. [26]IOEP 4:151. [27]CPE 2:15. [28]Compounded no longer of the earthy but of the spiritual. [29]IOEP 4:151. [30]By faith anticipating grace even prior to its fulfillment. [31]IOEP 4:152.

(and sin is enmity), and becoming what we are, he joined the human to God again through himself. AGAINST EUNOMIUS 3.10.12.[32]

2:16b Bringing Hostility to an End

HIS DEATH ENDED THE HOSTILITY. CHRYSOSTOM: No expression could be more authoritative or more emphatic. His death, he says, killed the enmity, wounded and destroyed it. He did not give the task to another. And he not only did the work but suffered for it. He did not say that he dissolved it; he did not say that he put an end to it, but he used the much more forceful expression: He killed! This shows that it need not ever rise again.[33] How then does it rise again? From our great wickedness. So long as we remain in the body of Christ, so long as we are one with him it does not rise again but lies dead. HOMILY ON EPHESIANS 5.2.16.[34]

---

[32]GNO 2:294. [33]So long as we remain in him. [34]IOEP 4:152.

2:17-22 THE CHURCH OF CHRIST

[17]*And he came and preached peace to you who were far off and peace to those who were near;* [18]*for through him we both have access in one Spirit to the Father.* [19]*So then you are no longer strangers and sojourners, but you are fellow citizens with the saints and members of the household of God,* [20]*built upon the foundation of the apostles and prophets, Christ Jesus himself being the cornerstone,* [21]*in whom the whole structure is joined together and grows into a holy temple in the Lord;* [22]*in whom you also are built into it for a dwelling place of God in the Spirit.*

OVERVIEW: Jews were near, Gentiles far off, but neither had any access to God except through Christ's Spirit (MARIUS VICTORINUS). The one Spirit guarantees unity (CHRYSOSTOM), viewed eschatologically (JEROME). We receive an honor analogous to that of Roman citizens (AMBROSIASTER). The church is built on the concordant witnesses of both covenants (ORIGEN, MARIUS VICTORINUS, AMBROSIASTER). Christ is the foundation for both prophets and apostles (MARIUS VICTORINUS). Among the many images used of Christ (CHRYSOSTOM), that of the cornerstone expresses his foundational and unitive function (MARIUS VICTORINUS). The resultant temple is the community in which God dwells (MARIUS VICTORINUS). It includes not only angels (JEROME) but also the Ephesians themselves (MARIUS VICTORINUS).

2:17 Preaching Peace to Those Near and Far Off

JEWS WERE NEAR, GENTILES FAR OFF.
MARIUS VICTORINUS: He distinguishes *those who are far off* from *those who are near*. This refers to the Gentiles and Jews. For the Jews are obviously close and the Gentiles far off. Yet the Savior himself has brought the gospel to the Gentiles. Paul here mentions first that Christ by his advent has truly preached peace also to those who are far off, that is, the Gentiles, as is shown by many evidences. For those who come to belief from Gentile backgrounds ironically have a greater claim to be called sons than those from Jewish backgrounds. And yet, so that it may not be denied to the latter, he adds *and those who are near*. EPISTLE TO THE EPHESIANS 1.2.17.[1]

2:18 Access in One Spirit to the Father

ACCESS TO THE FATHER. MARIUS VICTORINUS: Both Jews and Gentiles *have access to the Father* through Christ himself. But how? *In one Spirit*. For the Spirit, who is one with Christ, enters into us when we believe in Christ. We then feel God's presence, know God and worship God. Thus we come to the Father in that same Spirit through Christ. No one, whether Jew or Gentile, comes to the Father except through Christ. EPISTLE TO THE EPHESIANS 1.2.18.[2]

IN ONE SPIRIT. CHRYSOSTOM: "We both" means not less to one and more to another but having access by a single grace. For he has dispelled the wrath through death[3] and made us all beloved to the Father through one Spirit. Note that *in* here means

"through." HOMILY ON EPHESIANS 6.2.17-22.[4]

FULL CONSUMMATION YET AWAITING.
JEROME: However, it should not be thought possible to achieve perfect and complete reconciliation in this world. . . . The making of the new person in Christ will be fully consummated when earthly and heavenly things have been reconciled, when we come to the Father in one Spirit and with one affection and understanding. EPISTLE TO THE EPHESIANS 1.2.15 SEQ.[5]

2:19 Fellow Citizens, Members of the Household of God

FELLOW CITIZENS ARE ONE WITH THE SAINTS. MARIUS VICTORINUS: What are we to understand by *fellow citizens with the saints*? It implies a distinction between citizens and saints. But if this is so, who are the saints and who are the citizens? *Saints* refers to the apostles, prophets and all who formerly experienced God or spoke divinely through the Spirit dwelling within them. They in some way beheld God's presence, as did Abraham, either through the flesh, through the Spirit or through both flesh and Spirit, as with all the apostles. Those who have later believed in Christ without any such special means are *fellow citizens with the saints and members of God's household*. EPISTLE TO THE EPHESIANS 1.2.19.[6]

THE ANALOGY OF CITIZENSHIP. AMBROSIASTER: Believers become "fellow citizens" in a

---

[1]BT 1972:157-58 [1260A]. [2]BT 1972:158 [1260A-B]. [3]Having dispelled the wrath of God through the death of the Son. [4]IOEP 4:156. [5]Migne PL 26:475A [583]. [6]BT 1972:158-59 [1260C-D].

way analogous to all those who desired the peace of Rome. They brought gifts and were accepted as Roman citizens, as were the people of Cilician Tarsus. Paul was a Roman citizen of that city. So too anyone who has joined himself to the Christian faith becomes a fellow citizen of the saints and a member of God's household. EPISTLE TO THE EPHESIANS 2.19.[7]

2:20 The Foundation of the Apostles and Prophets

PROPHETS AND APOSTLES SHARE IN ONE DIVINE PLAN. ORIGEN: These are fitting words to cite against those who would divide the Godhead[8] and think that the prophets belong to one God and the apostles to another. EPISTLE TO THE EPHESIANS.[9]

THE FOUNDATION FOR THE EDIFICE. MARIUS VICTORINUS: Jesus Christ and his teachings are the foundation for the apostles. The edifice built on this foundation consists in life and character and one's conduct and discipline. The primary foundation is for life; the rest of the edifice is for its adornment and edification. The primary foundation, I say, is to believe in Christ, hope in him and trust in God. This foundation is the teaching of the apostles, which is also heard in the word of the prophets. Note the order of this distinction, first apostles and then prophets. The apostles beheld [God incarnate]; the prophets received the Spirit. These are the saints mentioned above: those who saw and those who were inhabited by the Spirit. Hence the teachings of the apostles and prophets are indeed the teachings of Christ, which proclaim the foundation of all eternal hope. EPISTLE TO THE EPHESIANS 1.2.20.[10]

THE HOUSEHOLD OF GOD IS BUILT ON BOTH COVENANTS. AMBROSIASTER: This means that the household of God is built upon both the old and the new covenants. For what the apostles preached had been foretold by the prophets. In his words to the Corinthians, that *God placed in the church first apostles then prophets*,[11] he is concerned with the order of the church. But in this case he is speaking of the foundation in the prophets of old. EPISTLE TO THE EPHESIANS 2.20.[12]

2:21a The Whole Structure Joined Together

JOINED TOGETHER FROM ABOVE AND FROM BELOW. CHRYSOSTOM: See how he joins himself to us. Sometimes it is as if holding together and unifying the whole body from above. Sometimes it is as if joining the edifice from below, as if supporting the building with underpinnings and being its root. HOMILY ON EPHESIANS 6.2.17-22.[13]

THE IMPORTANCE OF THE CORNERSTONE TO THE BUILDING. MARIUS VICTORINUS: He called this stone a cornerstone not merely because it is at the corner but because is the first and most important stone. From it begins the foundation of the corner which joins and couples two things to make them one. Souls above already with Christ are united together with those that live in holiness and receive Christ in a mystery that is present. Souls below that are Christ's, in-

---

[7]CSEL 81.3:85. [8]As in Marcion's resistance to the Old Testament. [9]JTS 3:407. [10]BT 1972:159 [1261A-B]. [11]1 Cor 12:28. [12]CSEL 81.3:85-86; cf. Theodoret, CPE 2:16. [13]IOEP 4:157.

cluding those of the Gentiles, are also joined by that cornerstone, Jesus Christ. EPISTLE TO THE EPHESIANS 1.2.20.[14]

2:21b A Holy Temple in the Lord

GROWING INTO A HOLY TEMPLE. MARIUS VICTORINUS: All souls made spiritual through Christ are joined and built up into a holy temple, where God dwells. As Christ is in all and God in Christ, all are a temple of God through Christ. EPISTLE TO THE EPHESIANS 1.2.21-22.[15]

WHETHER THE ANGELS ARE WITHIN THIS EDIFICE. JEROME: It is maintained by some that the whole edifice built on the foundation of the apostles and prophets comprises not only human souls but also angelic powers, so that all equally will become the abode of God. They argue that it would be absurd if angels and all the blessed forces who serve God in heaven would have no part in this blessedness. For in this is a building, put together harmoniously, that is growing into a holy temple of God and to be an abode of God in the Spirit. EPISTLE TO THE EPHESIANS 1.2.19 SEQ.[16]

2:22 The Ephesians Also Built into the Edifice

THE EPHESIANS ARE STILL IN THE PROCESS OF BEING BUILT INTO THE EDIFICE. MARIUS VICTORINUS: As he does so often, he brings the argument back to individuals, that is, to the Ephesians. They themselves have been built into that same temple cornerstone. Here he cleverly adjusts his language to form an exhortation. They have not yet fully entered into this unity but are still being built up. There is a deficiency, and therefore he warns and exhorts them. EPISTLE TO THE EPHESIANS 1.2.21-22.[17]

---

[14]BT 1972:159-60 [1261B-C]. [15]BT 1972:160 [1261C]. [16]Migne PL 26:476B-C [584-85], probably quoting Origen. [17]BT 1972:160 [1261D].

3:1-6 THE PRISONER OF CHRIST JESUS

[1]*For this reason I, Paul, a prisoner for Christ Jesus on behalf of you Gentiles—* [2]*assuming that you have heard of the stewardship of God's grace that was given to me for you,* [3]*how the mystery was made known to me by revelation, as I have written briefly.* [4]*When you read this you can perceive my insight into the mystery of Christ,* [5]*which was not made known to the sons of men in other generations as it has now been revealed to his holy apostles and prophets by the Spirit;* [6]*that is, how the*

Gentiles are fellow heirs, members of the same body, and partakers of the promise in Christ Jesus through the gospel.

OVERVIEW: Paul is now a prisoner, which has become his permanent condition (JEROME). We must look for order in Paul's meaning rather than in his words, which skip around and leave the reader in suspense (JEROME). He alludes to the charge that he received at Damascus (AMBROSIASTER) and notes that he has expounded the mystery of the gospel discreetly (THEODORET, AMBROSIASTER). We, however, cannot expect to receive it by a similar revelation (MARIUS VICTORINUS). The old prophets had partial revelation (CHRYSOSTOM). Paul and the apostles share an identical revelation (MARIUS VICTORINUS) and pass it on to new proclaimers (THEODORET). The Gentiles are fellow heirs of Israel and Christ, cemented in one body by mutual love (JEROME).

3:1a I, Paul

HE ESTABLISHES HIS OWN AUTHORITY TO SPEAK. MARIUS VICTORINUS: It remains, after he has stated the truth that all their hope is in Christ and thus they are all being built up together in the Spirit to be the dwelling place of God—it remains, I say, that he should teach them who he himself is and whether he himself is contributing to building them up together through the gospel and can give a reason for his own authority so that they may believe him. EPISTLE TO THE EPHESIANS 1.3.1-2.[1]

THE DISJOINTED SENTENCE HAS A SIMPLE MEANING. JEROME: After a diligent search I have found nothing that answers to his prior clause. . . . For he does not say, "For this reason I, Paul, have done this or that or have taught this or that." Instead, leaving the thought in suspense, he goes on to other matters. Perhaps we ought to pardon him for what he himself has admitted when he said, *if unschooled in speech, at least not in knowledge,*[2] and look for order in his meaning rather than in his words. This can be rendered as follows: "I, Paul, in the chains of Jesus Christ and in chains for you Gentiles, have learned the mystery so that I may hand it on to you." EPISTLE TO THE EPHESIANS 2.3.1.[3]

3:1b A Prisoner for Christ Jesus

THE SOUL CONFINED IN THE BODY AS A PRISON: TWO POSSIBLE READINGS. JEROME: We often read that the body is called the prison of the soul. The soul is confined as if in a cage. Paul, for example, was constrained by the ties of the body and did not return to be with Christ so that the preaching to the Gentiles might be perfectly accomplished through him. But I grant that there are some who introduce another meaning here: Paul before his birth was predestined and sanctified from his mother's womb for the purpose of preaching to the Gentiles. For this vocation he took on the bonds of flesh. EPISTLE TO THE EPHESIANS 2.3.1.[4]

---

[1]BT 1972:160 [1262A]. [2]2 Cor 11:6. [3]Migne PL 26:477B-C [586]. [4]Migne PL 26:477D-478A [587].

145

IMPRISONED FOR YOU GENTILES. CHRYSOSTOM: This is a very emphatic statement. Not only do we not hate you; we are even imprisoned on your account! HOMILY ON EPHESIANS 6.3.1-2.[5]

3:2 The Stewardship of God's Grace

HIS STEWARDSHIP OF GRACE. CHRYSOSTOM: He is hinting at what was said about him in Damascus to Ananias, when the Lord said, *Go, for he is a chosen instrument of mine to carry my name before the Gentiles and kings and the sons of Israel.*[6] By *dispensation of grace* he means the revelation made to him. It is as if he were saying: "I did not learn it from any human. God chose to reveal it to me for your benefit, though I am only an individual." HOMILY ON EPHESIANS 6.3.1-2.[7]

3:3 The Mystery Made Known by Revelation

HIS REVELATION UNIQUE. MARIUS VICTORINUS: Paul indicates that this mystery was made known to him through revelation. From this passage it is evident that a Christian, and a very excellent Christian at that, can be brought into being solely by grace. . . . Nevertheless, the power of God dispenses grace in many ways. Others come to faith by teaching, wherein by a legitimate training process and through the commandments of the Savior a person is reborn through the Spirit and water, so as to receive the spirit of Christ, in a teaching process that is mediated from human beings and through human beings. But what happened to Paul came to him by the grace of God through revelation. Although he, in my judgment, was the only one who received this particular revelation,

God is able to reveal himself in this form or in other ways to others. EPISTLE TO THE EPHESIANS 1.3.1-2.[8]

WHY BRIEFLY? AMBROSIASTER: He indicates that he has been shown the revelation of the mystery of God, about which he says that he has written briefly, that is, precisely, according to their capacity to comprehend the wisdom of the apostle concerning the mystery of Christ. EPISTLE TO THE EPHESIANS 3.4.[9]

HAS PAUL WRITTEN OF THIS BEFORE? THEODORET: The words *I wrote a little before* do not mean, as some think, that he has written another letter. For it is not with respect to himself that he says "I have written" but with respect to the mystery. For he is referring to "the mystery made known to me by revelation, as I wrote to you a little while ago," yet it is this "about which I have just now written." For this has been his subject from the outset right up to this passage. EPISTLE TO THE EPHESIANS 3.1-4.[10]

3:5 Not Made Known in Other Generations

THE HARMONY BETWEEN PAUL'S REVELATION AND THE APOSTLES'. MARIUS VICTORINUS: He teaches that there is a perfect harmony—a complete unity and identity—between the revelations given to him and those given to the apostles. His purpose is to avoid discord and any appearance of having received by revelation something that was not given to the apostles by the living Christ.

---

[5]IOEP 4:158. [6]Acts 9:15. [7]IOEP 4:158. [8]BT 1972:161 [1262B-C]. [9]CSEL 81.3:87. [10]CPE 2:17-18.

EPISTLE TO THE EPHESIANS 1.3.5.[11]

THE PROPHETS GRASPED THE REVELATION IN PART. CHRYSOSTOM: Tell me then, what part did the prophets not fully grasp? How can Christ say later that Moses and the prophets wrote "these things about me"?[12] . . . What he is saying is that the expectation of Christ was not revealed to everyone. It "was not made known to the sons of men in other generations as it has now been revealed to his holy apostles and prophets by the Spirit." Peter, if he had not been guided by the Spirit, would never have gone to the Gentiles.[13] . . . The prophets therefore spoke but did not have complete knowledge at the time. They did not even have complete knowledge after they heard the gospel, which far exceeds human reason and common expectations. HOMILY ON EPHESIANS 6.3.3-6.[14]

NOT MADE KNOWN TO OTHER GENERATIONS. THEODORET: It was made known incrementally to the prophets of old, but not fully then as it is now. For they did not see the whole picture but wrote down words about aspects of it.[15] . . . Remember that in the apostles' day there were many who had the gift of prophecy. It is in this order that

he mentions that the revelation was known to the apostles and then to the prophets. EPISTLE TO THE EPHESIANS 3.5.[16]

3:6 The Gentiles Are Fellow Heirs

FELLOW HEIRS WITH CHRIST. JEROME: The Gentiles are fellow heirs with Israel. Put more precisely, they are fellow heirs with Christ.[17] . . . It is not that some possession is divided among us but that God himself in his fullness is our inheritance and possession. EPISTLE TO THE EPHESIANS 2.3.5 SEQ.[18]

MEMBERS OF THE SAME BODY. JEROME: Now the meaning of fellow heirs is this: Just as there are many members in one body . . . and these, though in one body, have their differences and feel their own joy and grief in turn, so those who have believed in Christ, even if they have different gifts, are bonded together in the one body of Christ. EPISTLE TO THE EPHESIANS 2.3.5 SEQ.[19]

---

[11]BT 1972:163 [1263D]. [12]Here Chrysostom cites John 5:39, 46. [13]Here Chrysostom cites Acts 11:17. [12]IOEP 4:159-60. [15]Here Theodoret cites Luke 10:24. [16]CPE 2:18. [17]Here Jerome cites Romans 8:17. [18]Migne PL 26:481A [591]. [19]Migne PL 26:481B-C [591].

3:7-13 THE MINISTRY OF THE GOSPEL

[7]Of this gospel I was made a minister according to the gift of God's grace which was given me by the working of his power. [8]To me, though I am the very least of all the saints, this grace was given, to preach to the Gentiles the unsearchable riches of

*Christ, ⁹and to make all men see what is the plan of the mystery hidden for ages in*ᵈ *God who created all things; ¹⁰that through the church the manifold wisdom of God might now be made known to the principalities and powers in the heavenly places. ¹¹This was according to the eternal purpose which he has realized in Christ Jesus our Lord, ¹²in whom we have boldness and confidence of access through our faith in him. ¹³So I ask you not to*ᵉ *lose heart over what I am suffering for you, which is your glory.*

d Or by   e Or I ask that I may not

OVERVIEW: God's power is the basis of preaching (MARIUS VICTORINUS), though the preacher must be prepared (CHRYSOSTOM). Paul's humility is genuine (JEROME) and should be a pattern for ours (CHRYSOSTOM). His ministry, a free gift from God (MARIUS VICTORINUS), is to make known what was formerly unsearchable and still remains in many ways an unsearchable mystery (JEROME, THEODORET). Paul addresses both Jew and Gentile (MARIUS VICTORINUS). He establishes the unity of creation and covenant (JEROME), both of which are dispensed through Christ (MARIUS VICTORINUS). *The church* means all believers. The manifold wisdom of God includes all of Christ's mysteries (MARIUS VICTORINUS). The angels had only partial knowledge (CHRYSOSTOM). They are now delivered from the devil (AMBROSIASTER). Concealed in Christ through all ages (MARIUS VICTORINUS), the mystery is now revealed by the inauguration of his kingdom (AMBROSIASTER). Belief and virtue based on Christ bring confidence (JEROME); therefore the Ephesians should not despair because of Paul's suffering (MARIUS VICTORINUS), which is for their glory (ORIGEN).

3:7 God's Grace Given by His Power

GRACE GIVEN BY THE WORKING OF GOD'S POWER. MARIUS VICTORINUS: Everywhere Paul reminds us that we receive God's gifts not by our own merit but by grace. Grace belongs to the giver, not to the recipient. And by adding "according to the working of his power," he also ascribes this to God, so that "if I do any work, it is God's power. For it is not my power that works in me but God's." EPISTLE TO THE EPHESIANS 1.3.7-8.[1]

PROCLAMATION REQUIRES GRACE, PREPARATION AND PRUDENT UNDERSTANDING. CHRYSOSTOM: The gift was not sufficient if he did not provide power along with it. And, great as the power was, human zeal was not sufficient either. For Paul brought three things to the task of proclamation: ready and boiling fervor, a soul prepared to bear anything whatever and prudent understanding. HOMILY ON EPHESIANS 6.3.7.[2]

3:8a The Least of the Saints

THE LEAST OF ALL THE SAINTS. JEROME: Although it is a token of humility to call oneself *the least of all the saints*, one is guilty of deceit if one conceals the truth in the heart and says something else with the tongue.

[1]BT 1972:164 [1264B-C]. [2]IOEP 4:161.

We must therefore look for an argument showing how Paul truly was *the least of all the saints* and yet did not fall from the rank of an apostle. The Lord says in the Gospel, *He who would be great among you, let him be less than all.*[3] . . . Paul demonstrates this in his actions.[4] . . . Therefore the apostle Paul was meekest of all who sought to be weak on Christ's account. . . . Because of this humility, amazing grace was given to him. In this way he became *the least of all the saints* in order to *preach the unsearchable mysteries of God.* EPISTLE TO THE EPHESIANS 2.3.8-9.[5]

PAUL'S HUMILITY. CHRYSOSTOM: Those who visit a doctor do not complete their journey simply by arriving there. They must also learn the remedy and apply the medicines. We too, having reached this point, need to do the same, by learning the great humility of Paul. . . . Paul demonstrates humility when he calls himself a blasphemer and a persecutor.[6] He describes himself as a dreadful offender on account of his former sins, which had now been canceled, . . . hence as *the least of all the saints.* He did not say "of the apostles" but of the saints who come after the apostles. HOMILY ON EPHESIANS 7.3.8-11.[7]

3:8b Grace to Preach the Unsearchable Riches of Christ

THE GRACE TO WORK. MARIUS VICTORINUS: Was work given before grace? Or did grace come before any works? That which is working is God's power. So grace had already been given. When it is said that Paul was made a minister according to the gift of God, we understand that the gift of being a minis-

ter was given before his working to make him a minister, and his being a minister is the gift and grace of God. EPISTLE TO THE EPHESIANS 1.3.7-8.[8]

UNSEARCHABLE RICHES. JEROME: *Unsearchable* and *hidden* can be given two senses. The riches were previously unable to be searched out. They are now laid open after the Lord's passion. Another sense, perhaps even better: Those things which by nature were unsearchable to humanity are the ones that have been made known by God's revelation. EPISTLE TO THE EPHESIANS 2.3.8-9.[9]

WHAT IS KNOWN IS THEIR UNSEARCHABILITY. THEODORET: The divine apostle says not only that Christ's nature is divine but also that *his riches are unsearchable.* "And how does one preach if his riches are indeed unsearchable?" "I preach this very thing," he says, "that they are unsearchable." EPISTLE TO THE EPHESIANS 3.8.[10]

3:9 Revealing the Mystery Hidden for Ages

TO ENLIGHTEN ALL. MARIUS VICTORINUS: When he speaks of making "all men see the plan" this includes both Israel and the Gentiles. Paul had doubtless received the gospel for the Gentiles. But the Jews too can see the plan if they follow and obey. EPISTLE TO THE EPHESIANS 1.3.9.[11]

---

[3]Mt 20:26. [4]Here Jerome quotes 1 Corinthians 4:9. [5]Migne PL 26:482B-C [592-93]. [6]1 Tim 1:13. [7]IOEP 4:165. [8]BT 1972:164 [1264C-D]. [9]Migne PL 26:482C [593]. [10]CPE 2:19. [11]BT 1972:165 [1265B].

THE CREATOR OF ALL WORKS THROUGH THE SON. MARIUS VICTORINUS: Christ is the only begotten Son of God, and through him all the rest are created. Through him the works of God are created, as God works in and through him. All ages of time are subsequent to Christ, being made by Christ. . . . Therefore, even though God is acknowledged as the Creator, God is nonetheless Creator through Christ. The term *Creator* therefore does not pertain simply to God as such but pertains to Christ and through Christ to God. Christ who was eternally begotten created all things in time. God worked and created all things through Christ. EPISTLE TO THE EPHESIANS 1.3.9.[12]

THE MYSTERY HIDDEN FROM AGES. JEROME: These riches of his generosity were *hidden from all past ages in God* the Creator of all. Where are Marcion, Valentinus and the other heretics who say that there is one creator of the visible world and another creator of the invisible? . . . However, the phrase *mystery hidden from the ages* could also be understood to mean that the very ages of time remained ignorant of his generosity when all spiritual and rational creatures who inhabited all previous ages remained unenlightened.[13] EPISTLE TO THE EPHESIANS 2.3.8-9.[14]

3:10a God's Wisdom Made Known Through the Church

WISDOM KNOWN THROUGH THE CHURCH. MARIUS VICTORINUS: His expression *through the church* means through all the members of God and through every soul that has put on his mysteries and has hope in him. From this we understand what has been given to humanity. The powers and principalities in heaven are learning the wisdom of God through a human mediator. EPISTLE TO THE EPHESIANS 1.3.10.[15]

WHAT CONSTITUTES THE MANIFOLD WISDOM OF GOD. MARIUS VICTORINUS: Paul briefly touches on all the parts of the mystery that we have spoken of above when he speaks of the *manifold wisdom of God*, whether this be that he sent his Son or that such great majesty assumed the form of a slave[16] or that greater gifts were given. The promises are so great: the forgiveness of sins, the promise of heaven, eternal life, glorification and our inheritance together with the same Christ in his resurrection after death and even his death itself. This is what makes up the manifold wisdom of God. EPISTLE TO THE EPHESIANS 1.3.10.[17]

3:10b Made Known to Principalities and Powers

WHAT THE ANGELS LEARN BY PREACHING. AMBROSIASTER: So abundant was God's wisdom that he not only gave this teacher (Paul) to the Gentiles but also caused the truth to become known to the angelic spirits in heaven, who are the principalities and powers. They are powers because they have more power among the other spirits and are principalities because they are the principal powers. . . . The goal of all this is that the preaching of the church should be profitable to the Gentiles also. They are called to for-

---

[12]BT 1972:165-66 [1265C-1266A]. [13]Here Jerome cites Galatians 1:4 and Ephesians 2:7. [14]Migne PL 26:482D-483A [593-94]. [15]BT 1972:166 [1266B]. [16]Phil 2:6. [17]BT 1972:167 [1266C-D].

sake their allegiance to the devil's tyranny. EPISTLE TO THE EPHESIANS 3.10.1.[18]

3:11 According to the Eternal Purpose Realized in Christ

CONCEALED PURPOSE REVEALED. MARIUS VICTORINUS: From this we see what it means to say that the mystery was concealed in God, for he adds *according to the purpose of the ages.* This means that, after certain ages had reached their destined end, the mystery was to appear through the presence of the Lord in whom it had been concealed. For it was proper for it to be revealed through the One in whom it was concealed. EPISTLE TO THE EPHESIANS 1.3.11.[19]

REALIZED IN CHRIST. AMBROSIASTER: The saving knowledge of the mystery of God is conferred upon the human race in this way: God bestows his grace on humanity as the firstfruits of Christ's coming kingdom. When Christ appeared God revealed his mystery for the salvation of humanity. EPISTLE TO THE EPHESIANS 3.12.[20]

3:12 Boldness and Confidence Through Faith in Christ

FROM WHAT IS OUR BOLDNESS AND CONFIDENCE DERIVED? JEROME: Nothing can give us such trust in God and purity of conscience[21] . . . as the Word, the truth, the wisdom and the righteousness received in Christ. . . . One who thinks in an orderly manner now has the Word and reason as the content of his faith. One who can comprehend wisdom has wisdom as the content of his faith. One who understands truth has truth as the content of his faith. One who

lives righteously now has righteousness as the content of his faith. EPISTLE TO THE EPHESIANS 2.3.12.[22]

3:13a Not Losing Heart About Paul's Suffering

DO NOT LOSE HEART. MARIUS VICTORINUS: When some hear that Paul suffers tribulations, they may grow faint in faith. To prevent this he argues, in effect: "I pray on account of what has been revealed to me that you should not grow faint through my tribulations. These tribulations I am suffering are not due to anything I have caused but rather because you are either weak in faith or now wavering, or because you are making some unnecessary additions to the faith. That is the reason I endure these trials. I am now hoping to recall you to true discipline and observance so that you will not depart from Christ, having your hope in Christ alone. For this is *your glory.*" EPISTLE TO THE EPHESIANS 1.3.13.[23]

3:13b Suffering for the Ephesians' Glory

FOR YOUR GLORY. ORIGEN: One person will say that he attaches the words *which is your glory* to the tribulations . . . another to the boldness or else to the access or the faith. For boldness [or freedom of speech] is the glory to the one who possesses it, and access can be called the glory of the one who has ac-

---

[18]CSEL 81.3:89-90. [19]BT 1972:167 [1266D-1267A]. Cf. Chrysostom *Homily on Ephesians* 7.3.8-11 [IOEP 4:167]; Theodoret *Epistle to the Ephesians* 3.10-11 [CPE 2:19-20]. [20]CSEL 81.3:91. [21]Here Jerome quotes 1 John 3:21. [22]Migne PL 26:484C-485A [595-96]. [23]BT 1972:168 [1267C-D].

cess to God and faith the glory of the one with faith. EPISTLE TO THE EPHESIANS.[24]

[24]JTS 3:409.

3:14-19 A PRAYER TO GOD

[14]*For this reason I bow my knees before the Father,* [15]*from whom every family in heaven and on earth is named,* [16]*that according to the riches of his glory he may grant you to be strengthened with might through his Spirit in the inner man,* [17]*and that Christ may dwell in your hearts through faith; that you, being rooted and grounded in love,* [18]*may have power to comprehend with all the saints what is the breadth and length and height and depth,* [19]*and to know the love of Christ which surpasses knowledge, that you may be filled with all the fulness of God.*

OVERVIEW: Human fatherhood is best understood by analogy with divine Fatherhood (JEROME). God is Father by nature; all other proximate creativity is fatherly by grace (THEODORET). Humbly bending his knees Paul worships this one creative One, the Father, who works through Christ (MARIUS VICTORINUS). Knowledge of Christ's ineffable love, displayed on the cross (AMBROSIASTER), leads spontaneously to obedience (MARIUS VICTORINUS). All this is manifested in the cross (GREGORY OF NYSSA) and fulfilled in successive revelations (GREGORY OF ELVIRA). This knowing magnifies faith (MARIUS VICTORINUS), which grows ever fuller toward knowledge of the whole, triune God (AMBROSIASTER). As spatial metaphors are cautiously applied to God they are understood spiritually by the saints (MARIUS VICTORINUS). They point to the infinity of God (AMBROSIASTER) and the ubiquity of his saving purpose (JEROME).

3:14 Bowing Before the Father

THE LOWLY BODY LANGUAGE OF SUPPLICATION. MARIUS VICTORINUS: By kneeling we demonstrate the full form of prayer and petition. So we bend our knees. We ought not merely to incline our minds to prayer but also our bodies. We do well to lower our bodies lest we create an impression of elevation or an appearance of pride. EPISTLE TO THE EPHESIANS 1.3.14.[1]

BENDING BEFORE THE FATHER. MARIUS VICTORINUS: All good working and doing occur through Christ. The spirit of Christ is that of a serving ministry. He is himself the ministry

[1]BT 1972:169 [1268A-B].

of God toward us. God does everything through him. Therefore he says, *I bend my knees to the Father.* EPISTLE TO THE EPHESIANS 1.3.14.[2]

3:15 *All Fatherhood Named from God the Father*

ALL FATHERHOOD NAMED FROM HIS FATHERHOOD. THEODORET: God is fully and truly Father; for he was not first a father and later became son but is always Father and Father by nature. The other fathers, whether bodily or spiritual, have received this name from above. . . . Paul is saying here that he is petitioning the Father of our Lord Jesus Christ, who is truly Father. He has his fatherhood not by receiving from another but himself has conferred fathering upon others. EPISTLE TO THE EPHESIANS 3.14-15.[3]

HUMAN FATHERHOOD UNDERSTOOD BY ANALOGY TO DIVINE FATHERHOOD. JEROME: Before any discussion we must note that he did not say "from whom every fatherhood in heaven and earth is born" but *from whom every fatherhood in heaven and earth is named.* For it is one thing to merit the name of *father,* another to have a natural relation [as eternal Father to all creatures]. . . . I have searched about in Scripture asking whether the word *fatherhood* is ever applied to the Gentiles. I have found nothing except the twenty-first psalm, *and all the fatherhoods of the Gentiles shall adore in his sight,*[4] and the twenty-eighth, *Give to the Lord, fatherhoods of the Gentiles, bring him the young of rams.*[5] Think by this analogy: As God exists, God allows the term *existence* to be applied to creatures as well. So we say that creatures exist and subsist, not so as to imply that they exist

in and of themselves [as God exists] but as a derived existence enabled by God. . . . According to this same argument, God allows the term *fatherhood* to be given to creatures. So by analogy to his fathering we can understand creaturely fathering. . . . Similarly, as the only good One[6] he makes others good. As the only immortal[7] One God has bestowed immortality on others. As the only true One[8] he imparts the name of truth. So also the Father alone, being Creator of all and the cause of the subsistence of all things, makes it possible for other creatures to be called fathers. EPISTLE TO THE EPHESIANS 2.3.14.[9]

WHETHER THERE IS FATHERHOOD IN HEAVEN. JEROME: We who are not of Abraham's race are called Abraham's children if we possess his faith. Similarly, I think that the angels and other invisible powers have something like princes of their own in heaven whom they rejoice to call fathers. . . . Our term *fatherhood* may now be used in the light of the awareness that God is Father of our Lord Jesus Christ. For the only begotten Son is so not by adoption but by nature. It is by adoption that creatures also are allowed to participate in fathering and hence are given the name of fathers. And remember that whatever we say of the Father and Son we say also of the Holy Spirit. EPISTLE TO THE EPHESIANS 2.3.[10]

3:16 *Strengthened Through His Spirit*

STRENGTHENED IN THE INNER MAN. MARIUS

---

[2]BT 1972:169 [1268A]. [3]CPE 2:20. [4]Ps 21:30 (Vulgate). [5]Ps 28:1 (Vulgate). [6]Cf. Mk 10:18. [7]Cf. 1 Tim 6:16. [8]Cf. Rom 3:4. [9]Migne PL 26:488A-489B [599-601]. [10]Migne PL 26:489C-D [601].

VICTORINUS: What are these *riches of the glory of God?* They are *being strengthened with might through his Spirit*, so that they may be strong against the sinful nature, the desires of the flesh and the dreadful powers of this world. This strengthening happens through the Spirit of God. But how are persons strengthened and made firm through the Spirit of God? By *Christ's dwelling in the inner man*, he says. For when Christ begins to dwell in the inner citadel of the soul, persons are made strong by might through the Spirit. In this way everything of a hostile nature is evicted. EPISTLE TO THE EPHESIANS 1.3.16-17.[11]

3:17 Christ Dwelling in Hearts Through Faith

PRAYER FOR CHRIST'S INDWELLING. AMBROSIASTER: Paul prays that believers be made more steadfast, not doubting but believing increasingly that Christ dwells in them even when they do not see him with their physical eyes. He prays that the Spirit which has been given them might infuse into them a certainty that Christ lives and is the Son of God, so that he lives by faith in their hearts. Thus when we have faith in him we behold him in our hearts. The benefit of this is that we grow more sure of his blessing. He does not desert us. He is always present through that faith in him which he guards in us. The gift of the Spirt, which is also the gift of God the Father, is given to us that he may keep us safe, to his glory. EPISTLE TO THE EPHESIANS 3.17.1-2.[12]

3:18a Power to Comprehend with All the Saints

PETITION FOR FAITH, UNDERSTANDING AND LOVE. MARIUS VICTORINUS: Since he has taught that three things tend toward maturity in Christ—faith, understanding and love—he here brings them all into a brief compass. He is now praying that God will bestow all these gifts upon the Ephesians. Note the sequence he has followed: He spoke first of faith, *that you may have Christ dwelling in the inner man in your hearts through faith*. Now he speaks of understanding by saying *so that you may comprehend with all the saints the breadth, length and depth*. Again he adds with regard to love, *to know the love that surpasses knowledge*. EPISTLE TO THE EPHESIANS 1.3.18-19.[13]

3:18b Breadth, Length, Height and Depth

WHETHER THE SAINTS COMPREHEND THESE DIMENSIONS SPIRITUALLY. MARIUS VICTORINUS: God is through all and in all, and is all things and the source of all, through whom all things come and over all. In this aspect the task of understanding is to note and know what is *the breadth, the length, the height and the depth* of divine grace. How all these exist together or may be understood to exist in God and according to these aspects requires another, higher comprehension. . . . Hence he prays finally that the Ephesians may understand them all together. And so that they will not despair through their inability to comprehend them together, he adds: *so that you may be able to comprehend with all the saints*. Therefore

---

[11]BT 1972:170 [1268C-D]. [12]CSEL 81.3:92. [13]BT 1972:171 [1269C].

the saints comprehend these things together and can expound them. EPISTLE TO THE EPHESIANS 1.3.18-19.[14]

WHETHER MEASUREMENTS CAN BE APPLIED TO GOD. AMBROSIASTER: What is meant when Paul speaks of *length and breadth and depth and height?* Think of a sphere. The length is the same as the breadth and the height the same as the depth. So too all is proportional within the immeasurable infinity of God. A sphere is enclosed in a definite manner. God, being unenclosed, not only fills all things but exceeds all things. God is not confined but has everything within himself, so that he is the only one to be reckoned infinite. We cannot sufficiently thank him for the fact that, being so great, he deigned through Christ to visit human beings when they were subject to death and sin. EPISTLE TO THE EPHESIANS 3.18.2.[15]

LIMITS OF SYMBOLIC MEASUREMENTS OF THE CREATION. JEROME: Let us think first about physical *breadth and length, depth and height* in order that we may be able to pass through these physical dimensions to their spiritual dimensions. For the sake of argument, let the physical length be that of heaven and earth, that is, of the whole world, from east to west. Let the breadth be from south to north. Let the depth be from the abyss and the infernal regions. Let the height be to all that is elevated above the heavens. But they say that the earth is round and rotates as a sphere. Roundness has no breadth and length, height and depth, but is proportional in all dimensions.[16] Hence we are necessarily forced to understand spiritually by *height* the angels and forces above and by *depth* those powers below and what

is beneath them. By *length* and *breadth* we speak spiritually of that which occupies the middle place between those above and those below. The consequence is that one draws near as a neighbor either to those things above or to those below. Whatever begins to advance one's path toward better things so as to rise to the heavenly height, that is what Paul is calling *length*. Whatever brings one to the lower things as one lapses toward vice he is calling *breadth*.[17] EPISTLE TO THE EPHESIANS 2.3.16.[18]

THE FOURFOLD FIGURE OF THE CROSS. GREGORY OF NYSSA: The divine mind of the apostle did not imagine this fourfold figure of the cross to no purpose. He knew that this figure, which is divided into four segments from the common center, represents the power and providence of the one displayed upon it. This dimensionality runs through all things. For this reason he calls each of four projections by its own name. By the height he means what is above, by the depth the underworld, by the length and breadth the intermediate domain which is under the control of his all-governing power. Hence the worship of the cross is viewed in relation to the fourfold figure of the cross. The heavenly order is symbolically paying its devotion to the Lord in the upper part, the

---

[14]BT 1972:172 [1270A-B]. [15]CSEL 81.3:93. [16]If one takes the premise that the world is round and is in constant rotation, the assumption that one single direction is up and another down is made more ambiguous and problematic. Note that the debate that accompanied the demythologizing controversy (cf. Rudolf Bultmann, Paul Tillich, J. A. T. Robinson) about whether God is "up" is deftly anticipated by Jerome in the fourth century. [17]Jerome is probably following Origen in this passage. [18]Migne PL 26:490D-491B [603].

cosmic order in the middle part and even the infernal order in the lower part. ON THE THREE DAYS.[19]

ANOTHER INTERPRETATION. GREGORY OF ELVIRA:The *height* is the measure of the majesty of the Lord. . . . The *length* is the passion of the Lord's cross, by which believers are sealed. The *breadth* is seen in Pentecost, when the Holy Spirit is coming down upon all believers. ON THE ARK OF NOAH 32.[20]

3:19a The Love of Christ Surpasses Knowledge

LOVE PASSES ALL UNDERSTANDING. MARIUS VICTORINUS:The one who knows the love that *passes all understanding* will better express the full measure of love for Christ. Paul prays that they may first know [the love of Christ] rather than do something. Doing comes from this knowing. EPISTLE TO THE EPHESIANS 1.3.18-19.[21]

KNOWING THAT WHICH SURPASSES KNOWING. AMBROSIASTER: Can any words adequately describe this mystery, that God is born as a man? That God dies for the human

race, the master for his servants, the Creator for his creation, the righteous for the unrighteous? . . . In the greatness of his majesty he became lowly to do on our behalf what was worthy of his love, so that we, insofar as we can, should join his household. EPISTLE TO THE EPHESIANS 3.19.1-3.[22]

3:19b Filled with All the Fullness of God

BEING FILLED WITH THE TRIUNE FULLNESS. AMBROSIASTER: Faith is never directed solely to the Father or solely to the Son [but to Father and Son in their relationship]. Hence he adds *that you may be filled with all the fullness of God.* Thus by confessing Christ and giving thanks to him in the same glorious terms, the same honor is reserved for the Son as for the Father. All things that come from God the Father have been restored through his Son. By this the faithful confess the divine perfection in its wholeness. EPISTLE TO THE EPHESIANS 3.19.4.[23]

---

[19]GNO 9:299-302. The likely source is Origen; cf. Jerome *Epistle to the Ephesians* 2.3.16 [Migne PL 26:290A-292A (602-4)]. [20]CCL 69:154. [21]BT 1972:172 [1270B-C]. [22]CSEL 81.3:93-94. [23]CSEL 81.3:94.

3:20-21 DOXOLOGY

[20]*Now to him who by the power at work within us is able to do far more abundantly than all that we ask or think,* [21]*to him be glory in the church and in Christ Jesus to all generations, for ever and ever. Amen.*

Overview: Paul builds this benediction upon his supplication (Marius Victorinus). God's wisdom is superior to ours (Ambrosiaster). His glory is eternal (Jerome). We adore him everlastingly (Theodoret).

3:20 God Is Able to Do Abundantly

Able to Do Far More Abundantly.
Marius Victorinus: He says in effect: "I pray that you will do these things and understand these things. If, however, anyone is able to do more and more abundantly and go beyond these things—that is, beyond what I ask or understand—praise be to him. Yet whoever does more abundantly will receive this ability through the same power that works within us all, namely, through the power of God and Christ our Lord." Epistle to the Ephesians 1.3.20-21.[1]

The Father's Governing Power at Work Within Us. Ambrosiaster: He is praying to God the Father that we might know better what is expedient for us, and what had better not be asked for, and when something should be given, and how much of it and exactly what we really need. He prays that God himself might fittingly govern those who believe in him by his own providence and power. Epistle to the Ephesians 3.21.[2]

3:21 Glory in the Church and in Christ Jesus

Glory Forever. Jerome: This glory does not extend over the present time only, as if terminating in the age to come. Rather it extends throughout all generations and all ages. It is eternally ineffable. It abides, develops and increases. Epistle to the Ephesians 2.3.20-21.[3]

Glory in All Generations. Theodoret: God is to be worshiped both in the present life and in the next. Having thus revealed God's goodness to them, he proceeds to urge them on to the particular virtues. Epistle to the Ephesians 3.20-21.[4]

---

[1]BT 1972:173 [1270D-1271A]. [2]CSEL 81.3:94. [3]Migne PL 26:492C [605]. [4]CPE 2:22.

4:1-6 PAUL'S PETITION

[1]I therefore, a prisoner for the Lord, beg you to lead a life worthy of the calling to which you have been called, [2]with all lowliness and meekness, with patience, forbearing one another in love, [3]eager to maintain the unity of the Spirit in the bond of peace. [4]There is one body and one Spirit, just as you were called to the one hope that belongs to your call, [5]one Lord, one faith, one baptism, [6]one God and Father of us all, who is above all and through all and in all.

OVERVIEW: Paul alludes to his own bonds (JEROME) to humble the temptation to pride that may accompany the lavish gifts of the Spirit (THEODORET). The fundamental virtue of humility (CHRYSOSTOM) is enhanced by other virtues (MARIUS VICTORINUS) and is perfected by long-suffering (CHRYSOSTOM). Service in love is true freedom, beautiful and not oppressive, uniting people of all races (CHRYSOSTOM). The term *one body* expresses the relation between Christ and the church (JEROME). The one Spirit is inseparable from the living body (CHRYSOSTOM). The church has one hope because there is one kingdom (JEROME). Idolatrous washings cannot be called baptism (AMBROSE). Threefold immersion celebrates the Trinity (JEROME). The baptismal confession is implicit in the three prepositions: *of, through* and *in*—of the Father, through the Mediator, in the Spirit (AUGUSTINE, AMBROSIASTER). God contains all things (GREGORY OF NYSSA), transcending local confinement (ORIGEN).

4:1a *A Prisoner of the Lord*

PRISONER OF THE LORD. JEROME: Those who love Christ follow him. They are bonded with him in the ties of love. There is also another explanation [i.e., Origen's], which it is the reader's prerogative to accept or not: Suppose what is called here *the prison* is the body. Because Paul has taken on the body for the ministry of the gospel, he is consequently said to be in bondage to Christ. EPISTLE TO THE EPHESIANS 2.4.1.[1]

CONTENT WITH HIS BONDS ON CHRIST'S ACCOUNT. THEODORET: When Paul recalls his chains his intent is to encourage his hearers to rise above their own infirmities to moral excellence. It is as if he were saying: "Remember that it is in relation to you that I am in prison. Suppose I had refused to preach. I would have been free of all this." In this poignant way the divine apostle elicits sympathy, for he is more content with his chains on Christ's account than a king with his crown. EPISTLE TO THE EPHESIANS 4.1.[2]

4:1b *A Life Worthy of the Calling*

THE TEMPTATION OF PRIDE MAY ACCOMPANY THE GIFTS OF THE SPIRIT. THEODORET: They were enjoying the gifts of the Spirit. They were performing miracles, speaking in many tongues and experiencing much prophetic activity. But all this was prone to boggle their minds. Therefore it is about these that he first gives them advice. EPISTLE TO THE EPHESIANS 4.1.[3]

4:2 *Lowliness, Meekness, Patience*

LOWLINESS THE FOUNDATION OF VIRTUE. CHRYSOSTOM: How is it possible to "walk worthily" with "all lowliness"? Meekness is the foundation of all virtue. If you are humble and are aware of your limits and remember how you were saved, you will take this recollection as the motive for every excellent moral behavior. You will not be excessively impressed with either chains or privileges. You will remember that all is of grace and so walk humbly. . . . *With all lowliness*, he says, not in words only or even in deeds but more

---

[1]Migne PL 26:493A [606]. [2]CPE 2:22. [3]CPE 2:22.

so in the very manner and tone of your voice. And not meek toward one person and rude toward another but humble toward everyone, whether enemy or friend, great or small. HOMILY ON EPHESIANS 9.4.1-3.[4]

DISTINGUISHING LOWLINESS, MEEKNESS AND PATIENCE. MARIUS VICTORINUS: He speaks of several forms of forbearance, each of which prevents them from being carried away or proud. Lowliness is first, then meekness. Lowliness consists in having a humble mind. Meekness is a curb on pride and cruelty. Patience consists in bearing any adverse circumstance that may befall them. With lowliness and meekness they learn not to be afraid to suffer. With patience they learn how to respond if they must suffer. EPISTLE TO THE EPHESIANS 1.4.2-4.[5]

FORBEAR ONE ANOTHER. JEROME: Anyone who understands what it is to *forbear one another in love* will understand that this is a precept appropriate to the faithful. It is not indeed saints[6] who have any need to *forbear one another*. Rather it is those in the earlier stages of Christian life, who being human are still under the control of some passion. Nor is it strange that this should be said to the Ephesians. Among them there were surely some who still had to bear patiently with others. EPISTLE TO THE EPHESIANS 2.4.2.[7]

4:3 Maintaining the Unity of the Spirit

THE UNITY OF THE SPIRIT IN THE BOND OF PEACE. CHRYSOSTOM: In the body it is the living spirit that holds all members together, even when they are far apart. So it is here. The purpose for which the Spirit was given was to bring into unity all who remain sepa-

rated by different ethnic and cultural divisions: young and old, rich and poor, women and men. HOMILY ON EPHESIANS 9.4.1-3.[8]

THIS BOND IS BEAUTIFUL, NOT OPPRESSIVE. CHRYSOSTOM: Again he uses the metaphor of bonding. We have left it behind, and now it comes running back to us. Beautiful was Paul's bond; beautiful too is this [bond of peace among Christians], and the former arises from the latter. Bind yourselves to your brethren. Those thus bound together in love bear everything with ease. . . . If now you want to make the bond double, your brother must also be bound together with you. Thus he wants us to be bound together with one another, not only to be at peace, not only to be friends, but to be all one, a single soul. Beautiful is this bond. With this bond we bind ourselves together both to one another and to God. This is not a chain that bruises. It does not cramp the hands. It leaves them free, gives them ample room and greater courage. HOMILY ON EPHESIANS 9.4.1-3.[9]

4:4a One Body and One Spirit

THE PAST, PRESENT AND FUTURE ONENESS OF THE CHURCH. CHRYSOSTOM: What is this one body? They are the faithful throughout the world—in the present, in the past and in the future. . . . The body does exist apart from its enlivening spirit, else it would not be a body. It is a common human metaphor to say of things that are united and have coherence that they are one body. So we too

---

[4]IOEP 4:201. [5]BT 1972:174 [1271B-C]. [6]The faithful set apart for life in Christ. [7]Migne PL 26:494A-B [607]. [8]IOEP 4:202. [9]IOEP 4:202.

take the term *body* as an expression of unity. HOMILY ON EPHESIANS 10.4.4.[10]

ONE BODY, ONE SPIRIT. JEROME: His words *one body and one Spirit* can be taken most simply to mean the one body of Christ, which is the church. Or it could refer to the humanity of the Lord, which he assumed from the Virgin. . . . Yet indeed the one body can also refer to life and the works that are called in Greek "the practical life." These are distinguished from the oneness of the Spirit in the heart that finds its unity in contemplation. EPISTLE TO THE EPHESIANS 2.4.3-4.[11]

4:4b Called to the One Hope

THE KINGDOM AND ITS CONSUMMATION. JEROME: If the Father's house has many mansions, how are we to say that we are called to one hope? One reply is that the one hope of the calling is the kingdom of God. It is as though we were to speak of the one house of God or say that in one house are many mansions.[12] . . . Or again, this subtler meaning may be implied: at the end and consummation of all things everything is to be restored to its original condition, when we are all made one body and formed anew into a perfect man. EPISTLE TO THE EPHESIANS 2.4.3-4.[13]

4:5 One Lord, One Faith, One Baptism

IDOLATROUS WASHINGS ARE NOT BAPTISM. AMBROSE: There are many kinds of baptism, but *one baptism* is the cry of the apostle. Why? There are so-called baptisms among unbelievers, but they are not baptisms. They are washings but cannot be baptisms. ON

THE SACRAMENTS 2.1.2.[14]

ONE LORD, ONE FAITH, ONE BAPTISM. JEROME: There is one Lord and one God, because the dominion of Father and Son is a single Godhead. The faith is said to be one because we believe similarly in Father, Son and Holy Spirit. Baptism is one. We are all baptized in the same way in the name of the Father, Son and Holy Spirit. We are immersed three times so that the sacrament of the Trinity may be apparent. . . . There is one baptism in the Spirit, in water and in fire. EPISTLE TO THE EPHESIANS 2.4.5-6.[15]

4:6a One God and Father of All

WHETHER FATHER OF ALL OR SOME. ORIGEN: He is *God and Father of all* by being the God but not the Father of some and both God and Father of others. It is as if, picking out ten men of whom five were someone's sons and five his slaves, one said, "this is the lord and father of all ten." EPISTLE TO THE EPHESIANS.[16]

4:6b God Is Above, Through and in All

GOD TRANSCENDS LOCAL CONFINEMENT. ORIGEN: It is impossible to speak of any parts or division in the incorporeal, but he is *in all and through all and above all* . . . insofar as he is understood as either Wis-

---

[10]IOEP 4:207. [11]PL 26:495A-B [608]. [12]Cf. Jn 14:2. [13]Migne PL 26:495B-C [608-9]. [14]CSEL 73:26. [15]Migne PL 26:496B-C [610]; no doubt following Origen, as the same thought occurs in Marius Victorinus *Epistle to the Ephesians* 1.4.5-6 [BT 1972:174-75 (1272 A-C)]. Cf. Didymus the Blind *On the Holy Spirit* 100 [SC 386:238]. [16]JTS 3:413.

dom or Word or life or truth, an interpretation which undoubtedly excludes all local confinement. ON FIRST PRINCIPLES 4.4.31.[17]

A PHYSICAL ANALOGY TO A SPIRITUAL TRUTH. ORIGEN: Here is a physical analogy to a spiritual truth: We can agree that the sun is *above all* things on earth. But by its rays it might be said at the same time to be *through all*. And insofar as the power of its light penetrates everywhere, it could also be said to be *in all*. It is in this way, I think, that God's majesty is denoted by the phrase *above all*. God's all-sufficiency is denoted in the words *through all*. It also belongs to the power of God to penetrate into all, so that because of his being in all no one is entirely void of him. EPISTLE TO THE EPHESIANS.[18]

SUCCINCT THEOLOGY. GREGORY OF NYSSA: One God contains all and guides all as is fitting and is in all. This one saying of Paul suffices by itself to express everything succinctly, when he says that God is *over all and through all and in all*. REFUTATION OF EUNOMIUS'S "CONFESSION OF FAITH" 169.[19]

IN THE FAITHFUL BY THE SPIRIT. AMBROSIASTER: God the Father owes his existence to no one. Hence he is declared to be *over all* and *through all*. He is *through all* in the sense that all things come from him. Necessarily he will be *over all* the things that come from him. And God is *in all*, that is, dwelling in all the faithful. For he is in us by our confession, because we confess him, and he has given us his own Spirit, through which without doubt he is dwelling in us. He is not in the same sense dwelling in unbelievers who deny that he is the Father of Christ. EPISTLE TO THE EPHESIANS 4.5.1-2.[20]

FROM THE FATHER, THROUGH THE SON, IN THE SPIRIT. AUGUSTINE: Those who read very closely recognize the Trinity in this passage. Paul writes of God the Father "who is above all and through all and in all."[21] All things are *from God*, who owes his existence to no one. All things are *through him*, as though to say through the Mediator. All things are *in him*, as though to say in the One who contains them, that is, reconciles them into one. ON FAITH AND THE CREED 19.[22]

---

[17]GCS 22:353; Rufinus's Latin translation. [18]JTS 3:413. [19]GNO 2:383. [20]CSEL 81.3:96. [21]Rom 11:36. [22]Migne PL 40:192. See Jerome *Epistle to the Ephesians* 2.4.5-6 [Migne PL 26:496A-497B (609-11)] for another trinitarian interpretation.

4:7-16 THE GIFTS OF CHRIST

[7]*But grace was given to each of us according to the measure of Christ's gift.* [8]*Therefore it is said,*

"*When he ascended on high he led a host of captives,*

and he gave gifts to men."
⁹*(In saying, "He ascended," what does it mean but that he had also descended into the lower parts of the earth?* ¹⁰*He who descended is he who also ascended far above all the heavens, that he might fill all things.)* ¹¹*And his gifts were that some should be apostles, some prophets, some evangelists, some pastors and teachers,* ¹²*to equip the saints for the work of ministry, for building up the body of Christ,* ¹³*until we all attain to the unity of the faith and of the knowledge of the Son of God, to mature manhood, to the measure of the stature of the fulness of Christ;* ¹⁴*so that we may no longer be children, tossed to and fro and carried about with every wind of doctrine, by the cunning of men, by their craftiness in deceitful wiles.* ¹⁵*Rather, speaking the truth in love, we are to grow up in every way into him who is the head, into Christ,* ¹⁶*from whom the whole body, joined and knit together by every joint with which it is supplied, when each part is working properly, makes bodily growth and upbuilds itself in love.*

OVERVIEW: To draw the Ephesians toward the servant life (MARIUS VICTORINUS) Paul explains to them the diversity of gifts (CHRYSOSTOM). Christ delivered us from captivity to the devil (JEROME), receiving gifts in heaven that he might send them to us (JEROME, PSEUDO-ATHANASIUS). To show the humble way, Christ descended to death and captivity (CHRYSOSTOM), though these could not hold him (AMBROSIASTER). From this humbling he ascended beyond the visible (JEROME) to fill the whole universe (MARIUS VICTORINUS).

With the Father and the Spirit the Son disposes the gifts within his house (JEROME, DIDYMUS THE BLIND). The ordering of gifts reflects both the history of the apostle's times (CHRYSOSTOM) and the structure of the church (AMBROSIASTER). The church has distinct roles for prophets and evangelists (MARIUS VICTORINUS), though those of shepherd and teacher may be combined (JEROME). These offices under Christ's headship (AMBROSIASTER) will remain until the life of glory (THEODORET), when all the faithful will become mature in virtue (JEROME, CHRYSOSTOM), partaking in Christ Jesus as the perfection of human nature (AMBROSIASTER, JEROME).

Confessing his own defects (JEROME), the apostle characteristically proposes love as the remedy (THEODORET). It is a love that cannot be divorced from truth (AMBROSIASTER). Christ unites the church through his Spirit, analogous to the brain and nerves joining the whole body together. Christ rules the church through his Spirit (CHRYSOSTOM). The members partake of the increase of the body proportionally through the distribution of gifts (CHRYSOSTOM, JEROME).

4:7 Grace Given According to the Measure of Christ's Gift

DIFFERING GIFTS OFFERED TO EACH ONE.

Marius Victorinus: In counseling humility, meekness, etc., he sets forth the reason why each person is called to patience and forbearance. Grace has been given to each of us according to the measure in which Christ grants it. Since therefore different people have different gifts, there is no cause for envy or refusal. One should not grieve over what another has, nor should any refuse to give what grace he has received. If therefore Christ grants according to the measure of the grace given to each, we should all embrace one another in love, bearing everything with forbearance and patience, with meekness and humility. Epistle to the Ephesians 1.4.7.[1]

Countering Resentment Toward the Diversity of Gifts. Chrysostom: With the Ephesians as with the Corinthians and many others, this subject has been a constant temptation to arrogance, despondency or envy. For this reason he uses the simile of the body everywhere. . . . Pay attention to what he says. He does not say "according to each one's faith," so that he may not induce despondency in those who have not received the great gifts. Rather what does he say? *According to the measure of Christ's gift.* "The truly capital things," he says, "are common to all: baptism, salvation by faith, having God as Father and partaking of the same Spirit. If someone has more in grace, feel no resentment, for his task is greater too." . . . What does *according to the measure* mean? It does not mean according to our own merit, for if so then no one would have received what he has received. But of his gift we have all received. Why has one received more, another less? This, he says, means nothing, but it is a matter of indifference,

since each person contributes to the work of upbuilding. Homily on Ephesians 11.4.4-7.[2]

4:8 Leading Captives, Giving Gifts to Humanity

He Led Captivity Captive. Jerome: We believers in Christ, having been gathered from the Gentiles, had been taken captive by the devil, though we were creatures of God. We were sold out to the demonic powers. Into this circumstance our Lord Jesus Christ came bearing the baggage of captivity, as Ezekiel says,[3] and, covering his head so that his adversaries would not know him,[4] preaching remission to those who had been taken captive and release to those held in chains. . . . After Christ freed us, we were snatched out of an old captivity into a new freeing captivity [to Christ], as he led us with him into heaven. Epistle to the Ephesians 2.4.8.[5]

Does Paul Misquote the Psalm? Jerome: It was a nice touch for Paul to write here that Christ gave gifts to humanity, when what is written in Psalm 68 is that *he received gifts among humanity.*[6] Why this difference? Since in the psalm the act had not yet occurred but was promised in the future, the phrase was accordingly *he received.* But the apostle is seeing this as a promise earlier given and later fulfilled. At this time of writ-

[1]BT 1972:175 [1272C-D]. [2]IOEP 4:215. [3]Ezek 12:2-7. [4]Ezek 12:6-7. [5]Migne PL 26:498A-B [612]. [6]Ps 68:18 (RSV): "Thou didst ascend the high mount, leading captives in thy train, and receiving gifts among men" (LXX, Ps 67:18). Prior to the promised salvation event he received gifts from humanity; after it he gave gifts to humanity. Hence the change of the psalm's language recognizes this distinction in time.

ing, Christ has already made the gift and churches have been established throughout the whole world. Accordingly he is said to have already given to humanity rather than received gifts among humanity. EPISTLE TO THE EPHESIANS 2.4.8.[7]

THE GIFTS WERE GIVEN TO US. PSEUDO-ATHANASIUS: The Word was not in need and did not come into being, nor were humans able to give these gifts to themselves. But through the Word they have been given to us. For these reasons they were given to us after being given to him. For his purpose in becoming a man was that, having been given to him, they might be passed on to us. AGAINST THE ARIANS 4.6.[8]

4:9 Ascent and Descent

NOT AN ASIDE. CHRYSOSTOM: Do not suppose when you hear this that he has changed the subject. For his design here is just the same as in the epistle to the Philippians. When he was exhorting them there to be humble he showed them Christ.[9] So he does also here too, showing that even Christ descended to the lowest parts of the earth. HOMILY ON EPHESIANS 11.4.9-10.[10]

DESCENT INTO THE ABODE OF THE DEAD. CHRYSOSTOM: The *lower parts of the earth* here means death, by a human metaphor.[11] . . . And why does he mention this region here? What sort of captivity is he speaking of? That of the devil. He has taken captive the tyrant, the devil and death, the curse and sin. HOMILY ON EPHESIANS 11.4.9-10.[12]

HE DESCENDED IN ORDER TO ASCEND. AMBROSIASTER: The truth incarnate is that he is

said to have descended in order to ascend, unlike humans, who have descended in order to remain there. For by decree they were held in the lower world. But this decree could not hold the Savior. He has conquered sin. Therefore, after his triumph over the devil, he descended to the heart of the world, so that he might preach to the dead, that all who desired him might be set free. It was necessary for him to ascend. He had descended to trample death underfoot by the force of his own power, then only to rise again with the former captives. EPISTLE TO THE EPHESIANS 4.9.[13]

4:10a He Who Descended Also Ascended

THE PLAIN SENSE DISTINGUISHED FROM THE SPIRITUAL SENSE OF THE ASCENSION. JEROME: Could he possibly have passed through and beyond all the heavens and all the supernal regions and the heavenly orbits which philosophers call the spheres to take his place in the highest heaven, in its topmost location? Or should we rather believe that, transcending and spurning everything corporeal and contemplating the eternal, he has taken his place *above* the heavens, that is, above all that is visible? I think this the better opinion. Therefore the Son of God descended to the lower parts of the earth and ascended above all the heavens, so that he might fulfill not only the Law and the Prophets but also certain hidden dispensations

---

[7]Migne PL 26:498B [612-13]. [8]OSA 226. It is generally agreed that the fourth of the Athanasian orations against the Arians is spurious. [9]Phil 2:7-11. [10]IOEP 4:216. [11]Here Chrysostom cites Genesis 44:29. [12]IOEP 4:216-17. [13]CSEL 81.3:97-98.

which only the Father knew. He also descended to the lower parts and ascended to heaven, so that he might bring fulfillment to those who were in those regions, so far as they were able to receive. From this we know that before Christ descended and ascended everything was void and in need of his fullness. EPISTLE TO THE EPHESIANS 2.4.10.[14]

4:10b Filling All Things

NOTHING LACKING. MARIUS VICTORINUS: Nothing in the cosmos is left untouched by Christ. He indeed descended to the lower parts of the earth and ascended above all the heavens. What heavens? Some say three, some more[15] . . . but what does it matter? Christ, who ascended, ascended above all the heavens, however many. For eternity is now presently reigning in heaven and incorruptible life. All things there live by the Spirit. This reordering did not occur, however, until the descent of Christ. Once the mystery [of the cross] had been accomplished, all these received salvation after the passion and ascent of Christ and have been perfected. For this is what he means by adding *so that he might fulfill all*, that is, make them perfect and full, with nothing lacking. . . . Surely this could not be understood to infer that he fulfilled his mission on earth but set nothing right in the heavens and perfected nothing there. EPISTLE TO THE EPHESIANS 2.4.10.[16]

4:11a Apostles, Prophets, Evangelists

PROPHETS THEN AND NOW. MARIUS VICTORINUS: The name *prophets* is given to those who, having received the Spirit of God, spoke beforehand of Christ and his ad-

vent. These were the prophets who "were until Christ."[17] But after he arrived, was there no reason for any further prophecy? What prophets does Paul speak of here? It is obviously those who being full of the Spirit spoke of God after his coming, continuing to expound the divine teaching. EPISTLE TO THE EPHESIANS 2.4.11.[18]

GIFT OF THE EVANGELIST DISTINGUISHED FROM OTHER GIFTS. MARIUS VICTORINUS: There are five ways of speaking about the Scriptures: speaking in tongues, speaking in revelation, speaking in knowledge, speaking in prophecy, speaking in teaching. . . . But there is another thing apart from these. It is being an evangelist. This means to relate what Christ did and announce that Christ himself is to be worshiped. EPISTLE TO THE EPHESIANS 2.4.11-12.[19]

JESUS HIMSELF ORDERS THE HOUSE OF HIS MINISTRY. DIDYMUS THE BLIND: This is a house set up and ordered by Jesus. . . . He does not do this in a casual manner. It is with the utmost discrimination and discretion: One is assigned to the rank of an apostle, one to the place of a prophet, others to look after the flock of Christ and to work at the divine instruction of others for those saints who are prepared to learn. ON ZECHARIAH 1.228.[20]

WHETHER THE ORDER OF THE TERMS IMPLIES PRECEDENCE. CHRYSOSTOM: *First apostles*, because these had all the gifts. *Then*

---

[14]Migne PL 26:499B-C [614], probably following Origen. [15]Here Victorinus cites 2 Corinthians 12:1-2. [16]BT 1972:178 [1274B-D]. [17]Cf. Mt 11:13. [18]BT 1972:179 [1275A-B]. [19]BT 1972:179 [1275B]. [20]SC 83:310.

prophets, for there were some who were not apostles but were prophets, like Agabus. *Third, evangelists,* those who did not travel everywhere but merely preached the gospel, like Priscilla and Aquila. *Shepherds and teachers* means all those in positions of trust. Are these shepherds and teachers of less account? Certainly it seems that those who are stationary and reside in a single place, like Timothy and Titus, [are of less account] than those who go about the world preaching the gospel. But on another reading we cannot from this passage deduce subordination and precedence but from a different letter. Homily on Ephesians 11.4.11-12.[21]

Whether These Gifts Are to Be Understood as Ecclesiastical Offices. Ambrosiaster: *Apostles* are bishops, while *prophets* are interpreters of the Scriptures. . . . Even if they are not elders they can nonetheless preach the gospel without a chair, as Stephen and Philip are recorded to have done. *Shepherds* may be readers, who nourish the people who hear them by their readings. . . . *Masters* may refer to the healers in the church who constrain and chastise those who are troubled. Or they may be those who were accustomed to hearing the readings and imparting them to children, as was the Jewish custom. Their tradition was passed on to us but has by now become obsolete through neglect. Epistle to the Ephesians 4.12.1-2.[22]

The Gifts of the Father Are Inseparably the Gifts of the Son. Jerome: From this passage Paul clearly confirms the divinity of the Father and Son. What Christ is here said to have bestowed [as in his first letter to the Corinthians] is nothing less than

the gift of God.[23] . . . Failing to understand this, Sabellius confused the Father and the Son, not grasping that, though distinguishable, they work together with single intent. Epistle to the Ephesians 2.4.11-12.[24]

4:11b *Pastors and Teachers*

The Shepherd Should Be a Teacher. Jerome: It is not to be supposed that as with the first three . . . he has allotted different offices to shepherds and teachers. For he does not say "some shepherds, some teachers" but *some shepherds and teachers,* meaning that he who is a shepherd should at the same time be a teacher. No one in the church, even a saintly person, should take to himself the name of shepherd unless he can teach those whom he feeds. Epistle to the Ephesians 2.4.11-12.[25]

4:12 *Equipping the Saints for Ministry*

The Work of Ministry. Ambrosiaster: He says that the church's order has been so formed as to join the human race together in the profession of unity, so that all may be in Christ, having Christ as their single head, that is, as the source of life. Epistle to the Ephesians 4.12.6.[26]

4:13a *Unity of the Faith, Knowledge of the Son of God*

Until All People Attain the Unity of

---

[21]IOEP 4:218. [22]CSEL 81.3:98-99. [23]Cf. 1 Cor 12:28. [24]Migne PL 26:499D-500A [614-15]. [25]Migne PL 26:500B [615], contradicting Marius Victorinus *Epistle to the Ephesians* 2.4.11-12 [BT 1972:179-80 (1275B-D)]. [26]CSEL 81.3:100-101.

FAITH. JEROME: We must ask: Who are the *all* whom he speaks of as *coming together in the unity of faith*? Does he mean all the people of God or all saints? Or rather all who are capable of reason? He seems to me to be speaking of all the people of God because there are so *many winds of doctrine* blowing about them. When these blasts and billows are aroused, people in general are carried here and there by diverse errors, uncertain of their course. EPISTLE TO THE EPHESIANS 2.4.13.[27]

WHEN WILL THIS UNITY BE ATTAINED? THEODORET: In the future life we shall attain perfection. But in the present life we need all the help we can get from the apostles, the prophets and our teachers. EPISTLE TO THE EPHESIANS 4.13.[28]

4:13b To Maturity

TOWARD MATURITY. CHRYSOSTOM: By *maturity* he means here the perfecting of conscience. For a grown man stands firm while young boys' wits are tossed about. So it is with the faithful. We mature until we attain the unity of the faith, that is, until we are all found to share a single faith. For this is unity of faith when we are all one, when we all alike acknowledge our common bond. Until then we must labor. If you have received the gift of upbuilding others, be sure that you do not overthrow yourself by envying someone else's gift. HOMILY ON EPHESIANS 11.4.13.[29]

TO THE MEASURE OF THE STATURE OF THE FULLNESS OF CHRIST. AMBROSIASTER: He exhorts them to strive to attain to the perfecting of faith, the essence of which is to hold fast to Christ as true and perfect God. Do not measure him by some human measure.

Measure yourself by regarding him as perfect God in the fullness of his deity. When he refers to a *mature man* he does not mean a span of years or physical stature but a maturation into the full understanding of the divinity of the Son of God. EPISTLE TO THE EPHESIANS 4.13.[30]

RESURRECTED MATURITY. JEROME: According to the traditions of the church and the apostle Paul, our resurrection will *be into a mature man and the stature of the fullness of Christ*. This is the state in which the Jews claim that Adam was created and in which we have read that the Lord rose. LETTER 108.25.3-4.[31]

4:14 Carried About with Every Wind of Doctrine

WHETHER PAUL IS SPEAKING FROM HUMILITY OR CONSCIENCE. JEROME: Was Paul referring to himself as one who was tossed to and fro and drifting? According to one view, he was saying this in humility, aware that we see in part and know in part.[32] He is aware of how far he is from perfect knowledge and bursts into an expression of his own awareness. If so, anyone who might think himself to be humble should look to Paul as an example.[33] . . . But another will respond to this that, by comparison with the majority, the apostle had already reached *mature manhood*, even though he still might be here regarded as an infant in relation to those eternal blessings that are stored up for the saints. . . . The exposition must proceed very

---

[27]Migne PL 26:501A-B [616]. [28]CPE 2:25. [29]IOEP 4:218-19. [30]CSEL 81.3:101. [31]CSEL 55:343-54. [32]1 Cor 13:9. [33]Cf. 1 Cor 13:11.

carefully after this to meet the possible claim that the apostle really is speaking in humility when he prays that we *may no longer be children, drifting and carried away in different directions by every blast of doctrine....* Maybe it is out of good conscience and not some false humility that Paul is confessing his own limitations. For he was a man of acute and sharp intellect.... He could see that there was often in the manner of speaking on both sides some distorted motives, such that there seemed to be so much truth in contrary assertions as to cause doubt in the listener. Thus, as a human being and still in his fragile little body, he was at times carried about by every wind of doctrine, though he was not cast against the rocks. EPISTLE TO THE EPHESIANS 2.4.13.[34]

4:15 *Speaking the Truth in Love*

SPEAKING IN LOVE. AMBROSIASTER: Considering the love of Christ by which he loved us and gave himself up for us, we should make everything subject to him, knowing that he is the author of life for all. This is the truth. We are to be subject to him as members of the body are to the head. Others, either through error or through malice, may not confess that Christ is the head of everything or that everything is created from him by the Father's will. But we who adhere to the wholeness of faith ought nonetheless to take pains with all care and devotion that we bring no harm to this faith but rather to uphold it. We do this by remaining steadfast in this affirmation, so as to constrain the talk of depraved minds armed against the truth. EPISTLE TO THE EPHESIANS 4.15.[35]

WITHOUT PRETENSE. THEODORET: This he also says in the letter to the Romans: *Let love be without pretense.*[36] In his letter to the Corinthians he speaks of *unpretending love.*[37] Here also he calls upon them to act with genuine love and through this to increase the riches of the excellence of their life in the Lord himself. EPISTLE TO THE EPHESIANS 4.15.[38]

4:16a *The Whole Body, Joined and Knit Together*

THE ANALOGY OF THE BRAIN AND NERVES JOINING THE WHOLE BODY TOGETHER. CHRYSOSTOM: Paul has not explained himself clearly due to his desire to say everything at once. But what he is saying is based on this metaphor: Just as the spirit comes down from the brain, passes through the nerves and communicates with the senses, so it makes sense of the whole body. Its communication is not to all the members equally but according to the capacity of each member to receive. It gives more to that member more able to receive and less to that member able to receive only so much. So it is with Christ. The spirit is like a root. The souls of persons depend upon Christ as members. Each member depends on his providential distribution of gifts. The supply of spiritual gifts occurs according to a due proportion, as each member effects the increase of the body. HOMILY ON EPHESIANS 11.4.15-16.[39]

KNIT TOGETHER. CHRYSOSTOM: To *join and knit together* requires the exercise of great care. For the condition of the body is a sub-

---

[34]Migne PL 26:501C-502A [617-18]. [35]CSEL 81.3:102. [36]Rom 12:9. [37]2 Cor 6:6. [38]CPE 2:25. [39]IOEP 4:220.

tle matter, not something simple. When one thread is misplaced, the pattern is lost. It is with this sort of subtlety that you must be united with the body so as to maintain your own place. If you leave it you are not united and do not receive the Spirit. HOMILY ON EPHESIANS 11.4.15-16.[40]

4:16b Built Up in Love

BODILY GROWTH INCREASES THROUGH THE PROPORTIONAL DISTRIBUTION OF GIFTS. CHRYSOSTOM: One might say that the whole body receives increase as each member partakes of the distribution of gifts proportionally. In this way . . . the members, receiving the distribution in accordance with their own capacities, are thus increased. The Spirit, flowing abundantly from above, comes into contact with all the limbs and distributes according to the ability of each one to receive, thus "enabling bodily growth." HOMILY ON EPHESIANS 11.4.15-16.[41]

EACH PART WILL BE RESTORED TOGETHER. JEROME: This entire upbuilding, by which the body of the church increases cell by cell, is being accomplished through the mutual love of one for another. . . . This does not imply that to each member will be distributed the same level of maturity. It is an error to assume, for example, that all human beings will be formed anew into angels. Rather every member will be perfected according to its own distinctive measure and function. Humanity, which has been expelled from paradise, will be restored to the cultivation of paradise again. EPISTLE TO THE EPHESIANS 2.4.16.[42]

---

[40]IOEP 4:220. [41]IOEP 4:220. [42]Migne PL 26:502D-503C [618-20]. Jerome is probably refuting Origen in this passage.

4:17-24 EXHORTATION TO NEW LIFE

[17]*Now this I affirm and testify in the Lord, that you must no longer live as the Gentiles do, in the futility of their minds;* [18]*they are darkened in their understanding, alienated from the life of God because of the ignorance that is in them, due to their hardness of heart;* [19]*they have become callous and have given themselves up to licentiousness, greedy to practice every kind of uncleanness.* [20]*You did not so learn Christ!—* [21]*assuming that you have heard about him and were taught in him, as the truth is in Jesus.* [22]*Put off your old nature which belongs to your former manner of life and is corrupt through deceitful lusts,* [23]*and be renewed in the spirit of your minds,* [24]*and put on the new nature, created after the likeness of God in true righteousness and holiness.*

Overview: In exercising admonition the teacher must yield human words over to the Lord (Chrysostom). Moral callousness begins with unawareness of future life (Ambrosiaster). Persons remain responsible for their own callousness (Chrysostom). Paul shows how the minds of the Gentiles became subject to futility (Origen). It was not that God's own works became vain, but human works did (Chrysostom) through hardness of heart and lack of remorse (Theodoret).

Our illusions have been corrupted though inordinate desire (Chrysostom). To overcome this death we must learn of Christ (Marius Victorinus). In Jesus alone the truth of God has appeared (Jerome, Ambrosiaster) as truly God and truly man (Jerome). Debilitated by sin (Jerome), we must become renewed through baptism (Origen), changing not our physical but our spiritual nature, putting off that which belongs to our former life (Tertullian). Only then do we avoid an otherwise inevitable corruption (Chrysostom). Only then are we enlightened in spirit (Origen, Jerome). Christ himself is this new nature (Gregory of Nyssa). By him the spirit of our minds is being renewed (Jerome). The new creation is a great work (Jerome) and the very end for which we were made (Marius Victorinus).

4:17a Affirming and Testifying in the Lord

The Teacher Hands Over His Human Words to the Lord. Chrysostom: It is the duty of the teacher to instruct and restore the souls of his disciples. This occurs not only by counsel and teaching but by awakening fear and handing them over to God. For when the words spoken by human beings are taken as if from fellow servants and lack the power to reshape the soul, it then becomes necessary to hand our very words over to the Lord. This is what Paul does here. Homily on Ephesians 12.4.17.[1]

4:17b Living in Futility of Mind

How Their Minds Became Subject to Futility. Origen: Consider what Paul calls *futility of mind*. This occurs when someone has a mind but does not use it for contemplation, instead surrendering it to captivity under Satan. Palestinian Catena on Psalm 118.37.[2]

Not God's Works but Ours Became Empty. Chrysostom: What is meant by *the futility of their minds*? It is being preoccupied with futile things. This is what the Preacher in Ecclesiastes referred to when he said: *Vanity of vanities, all is vanity*.[3] But someone might say, "if these things are all vain and vanity, why have they come into being? If they are God's works, how are they vain?" And there is great debate about this. But listen, beloved: he did not say that the works of God are vain, far from it! . . . *Vanity of vanities* refers to splendid houses, enormous and inflated wealth, herds of slaves strutting about the market, conceit, vainglory, arrogance and boastfulness. All these things are vain. Such things are not created by God but are of our own creating. Why are they vain? They lead to nothing good. Homily on Ephesians 12.4.17.[4]

---

[1]IOEP 4:227. [2]SC 189:254-55. This passage is attributed to Origen in the edition of M. Harl, SC 190:607. [3]Eccles 1:2. [4]IOEP 4:227.

4:18 *Alienated from the Life of God*

INSENSIBLE HARDNESS OF HEART. THEO-
DORET: By *hardness of heart* he means a complete lack of remorse. When parts of the
body are hardened they feel no sensation, as
though they were completely dead. This
may happen to the heart. EPISTLE TO THE
EPHESIANS 4.18.[5]

4:19a *Callousness and Licentiousness*

**GIVING THEMSELVES UP TO LICENTIOUS-
NESS.** AMBROSIASTER: They have lost their
moral compass through lack of hope in a future life. Living now as if they had no future,
they pollute their own lives with the foulest
behaviors. They refuse to submit themselves
to the most elementary requirement of faith,
which brings their pleasure-seeking into accountability in relation to the future life. It is
this future life that these people declare to
be ridiculous. Hence they pretend to have a
right to debauch themselves. They covet the
goods of others with ravenous greed, as
though there were no life whatever after this
little space. EPISTLE TO THE EPHESIANS 4.19.[6]

**THEY ARE RESPONSIBLE FOR THEIR CAL-
LOUSNESS.** CHRYSOSTOM: If the cause of
their licentiousness is ignorance, why reproach them? Why not just inform them?
For the one who is ignorant should not
justly be punished or reproached but taught
what he does not know. But how quickly
Paul takes away from them this easy excuse:
*They have become callous and given them-
selves up to licentiousness, greedy to practice
every kind of uncleanness*. . . . He shows
here that the cause of their hardening was
their own voluntary way of life. Their way of

life arose freely out of their own laxity and
lack of remorse. HOMILY ON EPHESIANS
13.4.17-19.[7]

4:19b *Practicing Uncleanness*

GREEDY TO SIN. THEODORET: At first their
sickness was lawlessness. Then it became indulgence. Having slipped then into a lawless
way of life, they gradually came to suffer
from lack of remorse. Finally they ventured
out toward every sin without fear, living the
life of corruption beyond indulgence. This is
what he means by *becoming greedy to practice every kind of uncleanness*.[8] EPISTLE TO
THE EPHESIANS 4.19.[9]

4:20 *You Did Not So Learn Christ!*

LEARNING CHRIST TO OVERCOME DEATH.
MARIUS VICTORINUS: To believe in Christ is
to obtain immortality and receive eternal
life. For he himself is life. He himself is light.
He himself is eternity. He himself is the one
who overcomes death. He has by overcoming death overcome us too through the fulfilled mystery of salvation. EPISTLE TO THE
EPHESIANS 2.4.20-21.[10]

4:21a *Hearing About and Being Taught in Christ*

**PRACTICING WHAT WE WERE TAUGHT IN
CHRIST.** AMBROSIASTER: It is Christ himself
who teaches us about himself! When we are
"taught in him" we learn who he is, how
great we should reckon him to be and what

---

[5]CPE 2:27. [6]CSEL 81.3:104. [7]IOEP 4:235. [8]Here Theodoret cites Romans 1:27. [9]CPE 2:27. [10]BT 1972:184
[1278C].

hope is in him. We learn "in him" what sort of people believers ought to be. Any one who has "learned Christ" knows that he rose from the dead to be the pattern for the faithful. He teaches that there is great hope after this death for those who love God. EPISTLE TO THE EPHESIANS 4.21.[11]

ASSUMING YOU HAVE HEARD. JEROME: If all who seem to hear Christ did indeed hear him, the apostle would never had said this to the Ephesians. They were those to whom he had already revealed the promises of Christ. Why would he then say conditionally: *if indeed you have heard him?* To know Christ is the same thing already as knowing virtue. To hear of Christ rightly is the same as being attentive to all the virtues: wisdom, justice, temperance, fortitude and the other names by which Christ is called. Therefore if anyone has indeed heard and learned Christ, he would not be living *in the futility of his mind* nor *be darkened in understanding* nor be *alienated from the life of God.* He would already have practical knowledge, since his ignorance would have been dispelled, his darkness illuminated and every blindness lifted from the eyes of his heart. EPISTLE TO THE EPHESIANS 2.4.20.[12]

4:21b Truth Is in Jesus

IN JESUS THE TRUTH OF GOD HAS APPEARED. JEROME: On the one hand the name *Jesus* refers to the man who was assumed by the Word, the man born from the Virgin.[13] . . . Then again it refers to the Word of God: *for to us there is one Lord Jesus Christ, through whom are all things.*[14] . . . When Paul says *as truth is in Jesus* he is speaking of the temple of God in which God the

Word dwells. The Word was made flesh and dwelt among us.[15] God is the Word. As life dwells in him, so he also is life.[16] . . . In this same way the Son too may be called the truth, and truth may be said to dwell in him. In saying this we do not separate God the Word from the humanity he assumed. The man he assumed is not someone else. According to our understanding of certain passages we give different titles to him whom we believe to be the one Son of Man and Son of God, both before and after the virgin birth. . . . In none of the patriarchs, in none of the prophets, in none of the apostles did truth reside as it did in Jesus. For others know in part and prophesy in part and see *as through a glass darkly.*[17] In Jesus alone the truth of God has appeared. He confidently asserts *I am the truth.*[18] EPISTLE TO THE EPHESIANS 2.4.21.[19]

4:22a Put Off the Old Nature

THE OLD NATURE IS PUT OFF. ORIGEN: The "old man"[20] includes all born as earthly men in their old nature.[21] It is this "old man," this ancient condition of humanity, that is put off in Christ. Although his body continues he nonetheless undergoes a change to new life engendered by living baptism. What he was has been "put off." His old life is renewed by the holy water and the copious mercy of the anointing. He becomes new rather than old, whole rather than corrupt, fresh rather than enfeebled, an infant rather

---

[11]CSEL 81.3:104. [12]Migne PL 26:506A [622-23]. [13]Here Jerome cites Luke 1:31 and John 4:6. [14]1 Cor 8:6. [15]Jn 1:14. [16]Here Jerome cites John 5:26. [17]1 Cor 13:9, 12. [18]Jn 14:6. [19]Migne PL 26:506C-507A [623-24]. [20]The literal translation of "old nature." [21]Cf. 1 Cor 15:45.

than an old man, eternal rather than ephemeral. On Psalm 91.12-13.[22]

Put Off That Which Belongs to Your Former Way of Life. Tertullian: The apostle clearly identifies the old man. For he says *put off the old man which belongs to your former manner of life*, not with respect to the decay of any substance. For he is telling us to put away not the flesh but those things that he has elsewhere shown to be oriented to the fleshly way of life, indicting not the body as such but its works. On the Resurrection of the Dead 45.6.[23]

The Old Nature Aged by Wickedness. Jerome: The *old nature* whom he tells them to put off has, in my opinion, been aged by wickedness. For, going constantly astray in his former way of life and in the desires of waywardness and acting like a beast in works of corruption, he himself suffers corruption and decay. . . . But the Word of God kills in such a way as to make the dead one come alive. He then seeks the Lord whom he did not know before his death. He does not corrupt but kills the old man.[24] . . . As the outer man decays the inner man is renewed. Epistle to the Ephesians 2.4.22.[25]

4:22b *Corrupt Through Deceitful Lusts*

Lusts Deceive. Chrysostom: As his lusts become corrupt, so does he himself. How do his lusts become corrupt? Everything is finally dissoved in death. Remember the psalm that says "in that very day" [of his death] "his thoughts perish." "Beauty departs. It dies and decays at the approach of illness or old age. So does bodily vigor. Even luxury itself does not afford the same com-

fort in old age." Pleasures often are destructive. They end up being not really pleasures but bitterness and deceit and pretense, like a theatrical illusion. Homily on Ephesians 13.4.22.[26]

4:23 *Renewed in the Spirit of One's Mind*

The Mind Renewed. Origen: As there are many spirits, each has its proper abode. There is a spirit proper to your mind. When your mind is detoxified and expels confusions, the spirit of your mind renews you by taking up its dwelling within you. Epistle to the Ephesians.[27]

The Spirit of Our Mind. Jerome: We are not being renewed in our thinking process apart from the renewal of our spirits. Nor are we renewed in our spirits without thinking. We are being jointly renewed *in the spirit of our mind.* Hence as we sing psalms in the spirit, so we also sing them in our thoughts. As we pray in the spirit, so we also pray in our thoughts. The renewal of *the spirit of our mind* means that when the thought is clear and pure . . . then the spirit is rightly joined to it. They are so coupled as if by a cohesive glue that we no longer speak simply of spirit but of *the spirit of our mind.* Epistle to the Ephesians 2.4.23-24.[28]

4:24 *Putting On the New Nature*

---

[22]CCL 69:215, from the translation of Gregory of Elvira. [23]CCL 2:982. [24]Here Jerome cites Deuteronomy 32:39, Psalm 78:34 and 2 Corinthians 4:16. [25]Migne PL 26:507C-508A [624-25]. [26]IOEP 4:237. [27]JTS 3:419. [28]Migne PL 26:508B-C [625-26].

CREATED AFTER THE LIKENESS OF GOD.
MARIUS VICTORINUS: He is calling us to live as one whose thoughts come from the Spirit, who is himself once again becoming the spiritual man created by God. We are to live in the likeness of God, just as God intended when he said: *Let us make humanity in our own image and likeness.*[29] Admittedly God has no face or physical aspect. God is Spirit. So we too have been created according to God, to think according to the Spirit and thus to allow nothing to drag us down to worldly and unworthy thoughts. EPISTLE TO THE EPHESIANS 2.4.23-24.[30]

THE CLOTHING OF THE BAPTIZED. CHRYSOSTOM: When one is already clothed, how is it said that one must further "put on" a new nature? New clothing was once put on in baptism. The new clothing now being put on is the new way of life and conduct that flows from baptism. There one is no longer clothed by deceitful desires but by God's own righteousness. HOMILY ON EPHESIANS 13.4.24.[31]

PUTTING ON THE NEW NATURE. GREGORY OF NYSSA: There is but one garment of salvation, namely, Christ. Hence the "new man" created in God's likeness is none other than Christ. One who has put on Christ has thus put on the new person created in God's likeness. AGAINST EUNOMIUS 3.1.52.[32]

THE NEW PERSON IS CREATED. JEROME: The metaphors of creating and establishing are never spoken of in Scripture except in great works. The world is created. A city is established. But observe that a house, however grand it may be, is more commonly said to be built than established or created. Note then that it is a great work of God when it is said that *the new person is created by God in Christ.* This creature towers over the other creatures. This creature alone is said to have been established in the same way as the world was established, from *the beginning of God's ways,*[33] when all the elements first came into being. EPISTLE TO THE EPHESIANS 2.4.23-24.[34]

---

[29]Gen 1:26. [30]BT 1972:185 [1279B]. [31]IOEP 4:240. [32]GNO 2:22. [33]Prov 8:22. [34]Migne PL 26:509A-B [627].

4:25-32 THE DUTIES OF THE NEW LIFE

[25]*Therefore, putting away falsehood, let every one speak the truth with his neighbor, for we are members one of another.* [26]*Be angry but do not sin; do not let the sun go down on your anger,* [27]*and give no opportunity to the devil.* [28]*Let the thief no longer steal, but rather let him labor, doing honest work with his hands, so that he may be able to give to those in need.* [29]*Let no evil talk come out of your mouths, but only such as is good for edifying, as fits the occasion, that it may impart grace to those who hear.* [30]*And do not grieve the Holy Spirit of God, in whom you were sealed*

for the day of redemption. [31]*Let all bitterness and wrath and anger and clamor and slander be put away from you, with all malice,* [32]*and be kind to one another, tenderhearted, forgiving one another, as God in Christ forgave you.*

OVERVIEW: Telling the truth is a sign of regeneration (AMBROSIASTER). Lying is a fatal vice that signals death (AUGUSTINE). We have a special duty to one another as fellow members of the body (THEODORET) to speak the truth (JEROME). Evil talk is another source of anger (CHRYSOSTOM) that brings the faith into disrepute (AMBROSIASTER). Wherever we harbor anger against one another the devil gains an easy entrance (AMBROSIASTER, CHRYSOSTOM), which he will quickly turn to advantage (ORIGEN). We ourselves remain responsible for what we allow the devil to do in us (MARIUS VICTORINUS). Bitterness and wrath lead to anger so as to breed worse sins (JEROME). It is useless to cherish them secretly (CHRYSOSTOM), bear malice (AMBROSIASTER) or neglect the edifying virtues (CHRYSOSTOM). Theft is a common sin (JEROME) but forgivable to those who mend their ways (MARIUS VICTORINUS). It often stems from idleness (THEODORET) and is best overcome by honest toil for the sake of others (MARIUS VICTORINUS, AMBROSIASTER). Be ready for ordinary occasions for edifying speech (CHRYSOSTOM). It is our everyday faults and vices (MARIUS VICTORINUS) that grieve the Spirit (CHRYSOSTOM). The good conscience must be tended and kept spotless (JEROME). When we consider Christ the commands to kindness and forbearance become easier to fulfill (JEROME, CHRYSOSTOM).

4:25a *Let Everyone Speak Truth*

CREATED FOR TRUTH, WE MUST TELL THE TRUTH. AMBROSIASTER: Since we have been *created in truth and righteousness* and reborn in baptism, in order to remain in it we are instructed to put away lying altogether. Hold fast to the truth. Do not cheat your brother in any way. Being members of one body, support one another's causes in turn. EPISTLE TO THE EPHESIANS 4.25.[1]

FIRST WE MUST PUT AWAY LYING. AUGUSTINE: It is written, *The mouth that lies destroys the soul.*[2] . . . Therefore the apostle puts truth telling in the first place when he commands us to put off the *old nature*, under which name all sins are understood, saying *therefore, putting off lying speak the truth.* ON LYING 6.[3]

TREAT THE NEIGHBOR AS WE WISH HIM TO BECOME. AUGUSTINE: Let no one mistake this. The apostle is not giving us room to tell a lie to those who are not yet members of Christ with us. The point of the saying is that each of us should consider everyone as we wish him to become, even if he has not become so. . . . We ought to deal with a person in such a way that he will cease to be an outsider. Regard him as your neighbor already, rather than as an outsider. It may be that, because of the fact that he is not yet a partaker of our faith and sacraments, certain truths must be concealed from him. But that

---

[1]CSEL 81.3:105-6. [2]Wis 1:11. [3]Migne PL 40:491-92.

is no reason for telling him falsehoods. On Lying 15.[4]

4:25b Members One of Another

Members One of Another Speak the Mystery of God's Truth to One Another. Jerome: To be members one of another points to a great mystery. He is speaking of those who are very close to us in faith. For people are not generally considered *members one of another*. But the faithful indeed are members of the faithful. Christians are members of the body of Christ. We are members with the saints who embody purity of heart and consummate goodness. . . . Hence we are being instructed to speak intimately of the truth of this mystery with the neighbor—to speak of the fullness of God's truth. Epistle to the Ephesians 2.4.25.[5]

The Eyes Warn the Feet of Danger. Theodoret: It would be extremely perverse, since we belong intimately to one another, to say things that are not true. For this is not the way the body functions. The eyes, for example, when they see cliffs and steep caverns, instantly report them to the feet so that they may turn aside and protect the whole body from harm. Epistle to the Ephesians 4.25.[6]

4:26a Being Angry but Not Sinning

How These Two Precepts Interrelate. Chrysostom: Note Paul's persistent wisdom. He speaks first to prevent our sinning. If we do not listen, he does not abandon us. His role as a spiritual father does not allow him to give up on us easily. It is like the doc-

tor who tells the sick person what he must do. If the patient refuses to hear him, he does not write him off. Rather he continues to care for him by giving him further persuasive counsel. So too does Paul. He has already said, *Do not lie*. But suppose anger should arise from lying. He then deals with this. What does he say? *Be angry and do not sin*. It is better not to grow angry at all. But if one ever does fall into anger he should at least not be carried away by it toward something worse. Homily on Ephesians 14.4.25-27.[7]

The Double Sense of Anger. Jerome: This is taken from the fourth psalm,[8] as I am sure no one doubts. It may seem contrary to what is said of anger elsewhere, that we must put away all anger.[9] . . . It is an oversimplified interpretation that does harm, especially when people imagine that the constraints against anger are being here relaxed. It is not only among us but among philosophers too that anger is spoken of in a double sense. Anger emerges first when we are understandably aroused by a natural stimulus after being wounded by an injury. Or it arises when, after the impulse has abated and our rage has been restrained, the mind is capable of judgment but nonetheless we find ourselves desiring vengeance upon the one who is thought to have inflicted the wound. In this [verse] Paul is speaking of the first kind of anger. He is allowing to us as vulnerable humans that in the face of some undeserved event we may be moved to some level of annoyance, as if a light breeze

---

[4]Migne PL 40:527. [5]PL 26:509C-510B [627-28]. [6]CPE 2:28, following Chrysostom *Homily on Ephesians* 14.4.25-27 [IOEP 4:245]. [7]IOEP 4:246. [8]Ps 4:4. [9]Col 3:8.

were disturbing the serenity of the mind. But on no account are we to be carried into swelling rapids by the impulse of rage. EPISTLE TO THE EPHESIANS 2.4.26.[10]

4:26b *Not Letting the Sun Go Down on One's Anger*

DO NOT LET THE SUN LEAVE YOU AS ENEMIES, LEST ANGER INCREASE OVERNIGHT. CHRYSOSTOM: Do you wish to have your fill of anger? One hour, or two or three is enough for you. But do not let the sun go down and leave you both as enemies. It was God's goodness that did not leave us in anger. He did not let us part in enmity. He shed his light upon those of us who were sinners. So when evening is coming on, be reconciled. Quell the evil impulses while they are fresh. For if night overtakes you, the next day will not be enough time to extinguish the further evil which has been increasing overnight. HOMILY ON EPHESIANS 14.4.25-27.[11]

4:27 *Giving No Opportunity to the Devil*

HOW THE DEVIL GAINS ENTRY. ORIGEN: He is showing us how an opportunity is being given to the devil by these acts and desires. Once he has entered our body, he takes full possession of us. Or if he cannot take full possession, he at least pollutes the soul, having stuck his flaming darts into us unawares. At times these pierce us with a wound that goes goes down very deep. At other times we are merely temporarily inflamed. But it is indeed seldom that these burning darts are easily extinguished. They find their place to wound. ON FIRST PRINCIPLES 3.2.4.[12]

FREE PERSONS REMAIN RESPONSIBLE FOR WHAT THEY ALLOW THE DEVIL TO DO. MARIUS VICTORINUS: The devil can do nothing to us unless we ourselves willingly allow him to do so. This is true in all our acts. Thus we are masters of our own will; otherwise we would deserve no good return for our good acts and no punishment for our bad acts. The devil's opportunity arises from our own vice. EPISTLE TO THE EPHESIANS 2.4.27.[13]

THE OPPORTUNITY ANGER GIVES TO THE DECEIVER. AMBROSIASTER: An angry mind will necessarily think evil thoughts, as the devil desires. If the devil finds a mind ready for evil and slipping toward it, he deceives the person who was created for life. The thought, you see, is human. But the devil completes it. EPISTLE TO THE EPHESIANS 4.27.[14]

4:28a *No Longer Stealing*

PERSISTING IN SIN. MARIUS VICTORINUS: Sin does not consist in simply committing sin but persisting in it. If so, there is always a place for repentance. There is a place for correction. So the apostle says: *let the one who has stolen not steal again.* This should be applied not only to stealing but also to all sin. Anyone who has sinned in any way is now called not to sin again. EPISTLE TO THE EPHESIANS 2.4.28.[15]

---

[10]Migne PL 26:510B-C [628], following Origen *Epistle to the Ephesians* [JTS 3:420]. [11]IOEP 4:246. [12]GCS 22:252, from Rufinus's Latin translation. Cf. Jerome *Epistle to the Ephesians* 2.4.27 [Migne PL 26:511B-512A (629-30)]. [13]BT 1972:187 [1281A-B]. [14]CSEL 81.3:106-7. [15]BT 1972:188 [1281B].

The Subtle Temptation of Theft.
Jerome: Those who live in the midst of this life's intense business appear to be forced, for the sake of food and necessary provisions, to buy and sell certain things and to seek unfair profit from business. It is difficult even for those who have been set free from the other passions—namely fornication, idolatry, adultery and murder—to escape being caught by this subtle vice. Epistle to the Ephesians 2.4.28.[16]

4:28b *Doing Honest Work*

Honest Work. Theodoret: Idleness is a major source of sin. So it is reasonable for Paul to set honest work over against it. The text contrasts theft, which is an evil work, with honest labor, which is a good work. Epistle to the Ephesians 4.28.[17]

4:28c *Giving to Those in Need*

Restore to the Poor What Was Taken Unworthily. Ambrosiaster: Paul exhorts them not to return to their past vices and sins. He wants them to behave as new persons. What good is it to be called new if our evil deeds prove us to be still gripped by our old nature? The Christian is commanded not merely to avoid stealing but more so to care actively for the poor through his own hard work. Hence by commitment to good works he may restore what he formerly stole. We are not to be praised for refusing to steal. What makes one praiseworthy is to give of one's own to the needy. Epistle to the Ephesians 4.28.[18]

4:29a *Not Speaking Evil*

One Does Not Live Well Who Speaks

Evil. Ambrosiaster: To the servant of God, all things appear to have some aspect of good. This does not stain his purity in any respect. What use is it to have a clean life and a foul mouth? The Lord says that everyone will be justified or condemned by his own words.[19] One who speaks ill cannot be thought to live well. Many vices are implied in speaking ill of another, whether this means talking basely or disparaging the good of another or telling deceitful tales or lies. All these are repugnant. But good and sober reports are gratifying to those who hear them. They set an example. God is glorified in such words, which build up faith in Christ. Epistle to the Ephesians 4.29.[20]

Labor from the Hands, Not Evil Talk from the Mouth. Chrysostom: What is *corruption*? It is what he elsewhere calls *idleness*: detraction, insult, facetiousness. This is how Paul trims away the roots of anger, by reducing lying, theft and even unseasonable speech. Homily on Ephesians 14.4.29.[21]

A Good Word Gives Grace to the Hearer. Jerome: A *good word* is one that serves to build upon the occasion, communicating grace to the hearers because it teaches them to pursue virtues and shun vices. An *evil word* is one that prompts them to sin and rather drives them headlong into disaster. . . . Whenever we say what is not in season or inappropriate for the context, or that which does not contribute to the good of the hearers, an evil word proceeds from our mouth. . . . Even if we do no direct harm, yet

---

[16]Migne PL 26:512A-B [630-31]. [17]CPE 2:28-29. [18]CSEL 81.3:107. [19]Mt 12:37. [20]CSEL 81.3:107-8. [21]IOEP 4:249.

we are not thereby building up. We shall pay the penalty of an evil word. EPISTLE TO THE EPHESIANS 2.4.29.[22]

4:29b Edifying Words

UPBUILDING SPEECH. CHRYSOSTOM: This means: "whatever edifies your neighbor, say this and nothing more." . . . Say *only such as is good.* The flood of words is vast. Paul is right to charge us to use language carefully. He gives us a pattern for doing this. Of what then are we to speak? *Whatever edifies,* he says. Why? *So the one who hears may be grateful to you.* Suppose your brother has committed fornication. Do not lord it over him. Do not gloat. That will not help your brother but damage him. It is as if you were driving a nail into him. If you counsel him, do so in a gracious manner. Show him how to keep his mouth clean. Teach him not to disparage anyone. Make his instruction your first concern. Then you have rendered him a great service. And if you speak with him about abstinence, discretion and alms, all these things soothe his soul, and he will give great thanks to you. HOMILY ON EPHESIANS 14.4.29.[23]

4:30a Not Grieving the Holy Spirit of God

AN ARROGANT WORD GRIEVES THE SPIRIT. CHRYSOSTOM: This is a particularly awful and fearful saying. It reminds us of what he said to the Thessalonians: *Whoever disregards this disregards not man but God.*[24] . . . If you say an arrogant word, if you strike your brother, you have not merely hurt him but have grieved the Spirit. He contrasts such arrogance with the benevolence of God in order to sharpen the admonition. HOMILY

ON EPHESIANS 14.4.30.[25]

HOW THE SPIRIT GRIEVES FOR US. AMBROSIASTER: The Holy Spirit rejoices in our salvation not for himself, since he has no lack of blessedness. But if we have disobeyed the Spirit, we have grieved the Spirit. His work in us is cut short, just when he wishes us to belong to life. Yet he is not grieved in such a way as to suffer in a literal sense. For God the Spirit is invisible and not subject to physical suffering. When Paul says the Spirit is "grieved," he speaks metaphorically on our account to show that the Spirit leaves us to our own self-will when we have, so to speak, wounded him by despising his admonitions. EPISTLE TO THE EPHESIANS 4.30.[26]

4:30b Sealed for the Day of Redemption

THE SEAL OF THE SPIRIT. JEROME: That we have been "sealed" with the Holy Spirit means that both our spirit and our soul are impressed with God's own seal, signifying that we belong to him. By this we receive in ourselves that image and likeness in which we were created at the outset. . . . You are sealed so that you may be preserved to the end. You may show that seal on the day of redemption, pure and unblemished and not damaged in any part. You are thereby ready to be counted with those who are redeemed. EPISTLE TO THE EPHESIANS 2.4.30.[27]

4:31a Putting Away Bitterness, Wrath, Anger, Clamor and Slander

---

[22]Migne PL 26:513A-514A [632]. [23]IOEP 4:249. [24]1 Thess 4:8. [25]IOEP 4:250. [26]CSEL 81.3:108. [27]Migne PL 26:514B [632]; partly following Origen *Epistle to the Ephesians* [JTS 3:555-56].

Putting Away Slander. Origen: People who insult others are said to slander or blaspheme against those whom they insult. . . . One blasphemes when one makes a true doctrine appear false or a false one true, especially when one speaks of God or matters pertaining to God. Epistle to the Ephesians.[28]

Distinguishing These Five Terms. Marius Victorinus: He adds five terms briefly at the end—*bitterness, wrath, anger, clamor, slander*. Then at the very end he has added the summarizing phrase *with all malice*. Bitterness consists in envying and speaking ill of others and similar actions. Wrath consists in the lust for vengeance and punishment. Anger is the impulse of a mind boiling over and upheaving beyond what is reasonable. Clamor is a kind of insane, uncontrolled utterance. And blasphemy is wicked thought or speech that attacks God and is primarily directed against God. Epistle to the Ephesians 2.4.31.[29]

Types of Aggression. Jerome: Wrath is the outspewing of indignation in the mind when anger overflows. Bitterness and wrath are varieties of anger. Anger desires vengeance after rage has been subdued. Anger wishes to harm the one by whom it believes itself injured. . . . Vengeance wants to return evil to the one it considers guilty of injury. A Christian ought not to return evil for evil but *overcome evil with good*.[30] Epistle to the Ephesians 3.4.31.[31]

Putting Away Bitterness. Chrysostom: All this bitterness is not merely to be cleansed but to be *put away* altogether. Why should anyone try to contain it or hold it in? Why

keep the beast of anger around so as to have to watch it constantly? It is possible to banish it, to expel it and drive it off to some mountain place. Homily on Ephesians 15.4.31.[32]

4:31b *With All Malice*

Why Add Malice? Ambrosiaster: Some repress anger and clamor yet still remain mischievous. Paul therefore adds that these should be entirely done away, along with all malice. Such mischief consists not only in blasphemy but in putting on a face of peace while holding on to discord within the soul. Epistle to the Ephesians 4.31.[33]

4:32 *Kind, Tenderhearted, Forgiving*

After Cutting Weeds, Plant Good Seeds. Chrysostom: Tell me what good it is to weed a garden if we do not plant good seed. . . . Sow good habits and dispositions. To be free from a bad habit does not mean we have formed a good one. We need to take the further step of forming good habits and dispositions to replace what we have left behind. Homily on Ephesians 16.4.31-32.[34]

The Value of Forgiveness. Chrysostom: *Patience* means practicing forgiveness. To give patience is a far greater gift than to give money. The one who gives money to one who asks of him does indeed do a fine and admirable deed, but such a gift touches only the body. Spiritual gifts touch the soul with

---

[28]JTS 3:557. [29]BT 1972:189 [1282A-B]. [30]Rom 12:17-21. [31]Migne PL 26:516B-D [636-37], partly following Origen, JTS 3:557. [32]IOEP 4:255. [33]CSEL 81.3:109. [34]IOEP 4:265.

redemption. Hence one who forgives does good both to his own soul and to that of the one who has received forgiveness. Homily on Ephesians 16.4.31-32.[35]

The Risk of Forgiving. Chrysostom: Paul's words contain a great mystery. "For," he says in effect, "God took a chance in forgiving you. He placed his own Son in jeopardy. To forgive you he even sacrificed his Son. But you have received forgiveness time after time, at no risk or expense, yet you do not forgive." Homily on Ephesians 17.4.32—5.2.[36]

Gentleness Overcomes Bitterness. Jerome: Paul wants us to be gentle, approachable people, people who have left anger, bitterness, wrath and slander behind. If we are merciful and serene, taking the initiative in reaching out to others, our very approachability will overcome the shyness and fear of those for whom we reach out. Epistle to the Ephesians 3.5.1.[37]

---

[35]IOEP 4:266. [36]IOEP 4:269. [37]Migne PL 26:517C-D [637-38].

5:1-5 THE IMITATION OF GOD

[1]*Therefore be imitators of God, as beloved children.* [2]*And walk in love, as Christ loved us and gave himself up for us, a fragrant offering and sacrifice to God.*

[3]*But fornication and all impurity or covetousness must not even be named among you, as is fitting among saints.* [4]*Let there be no filthiness, nor silly talk, nor levity, which are not fitting; but instead let there be thanksgiving.* [5]*Be sure of this, that no fornicator or impure man, or one who is covetous (that is, an idolater), has any inheritance in the kingdom of Christ and of God.*

Overview: The more God loves us and the more mature we are, the more we strive to reflect his goodness (Chrysostom, Jerome). Love is the foundation of all virtue (Chrysostom). Christ remains our pattern, even to death (Jerome). He is one with the father (Theodoret), even in his sacrifice (Marius Victorinus), and we must be one with him in self-denial (Chrysostom). No sin is trivial, whether it emerges out of affection or appetite (Chrysostom, Origen, Ambrosiaster). A saint reveals faith in both conduct and conscience (Jerome, Marius Victorinus). Foolish as they are (Jerome), sins of speech lead to much worse sins (Chrysostom). They are to be overcome by giving thanks to God constantly (Marius Victorinus). Though some sins are not even to be named among the saints (MARIUS VIC-TORINUS), all sins are resisted (JEROME). Love of money is worship of a creature (AMBROSIASTER), which is idolatry (THEODORET).

5:1 *Imitators of God*

HAVING BEEN ADOPTED, ACT AS BELOVED CHILDREN. CHRYSOSTOM: You are called to imitate God, to become like God. This can happen when you are reconciled with him. . . . Paul then adds another splendid incentive: You are to act *as beloved children*. He is saying, in effect: "You have another reason for imitating him, not only to receive good but also to be fittingly called his own children." . . . Not all children imitate their father, but those who know themselves to be beloved act like *beloved children*. HOMILY ON EPHESIANS 17.4.32-5.2.[1]

WHETHER IT IS POSSIBLE FOR HUMANS TO IMITATE GOD. JEROME: When he wrote to the Corinthians, indeed, he said *be imitators of me*[2] . . . for though they could not instantaneously become imitators of Christ, it was still a great thing for them if they could be imitators of the imitator. But to the Ephesians, since they are those to whom he has revealed such great mysteries, he neither says "be imitators of me" nor "be imitators of Christ" but *be imitators of God*. This does not imply that it is less to be an imitator of Christ than of God, for Christ is God. . . . Admittedly much that God has done we humans can hardly be said to imitate. But in the way that he is merciful to all and rains on good and bad, so we may pour out mercy upon all we meet. When we do this, we shall be beloved children. We shall be imitating

either Paul or, as I rather think, God himself. EPISTLE TO THE EPHESIANS 3.5.1.[3]

5:2a *Walk in Love*

AS CHRIST LOVED YOU, SO YOU LOVE. CHRYSOSTOM: See how love is the foundation of everything. Where love is present there is no anger, no passion, no railing, no blasphemy. All this is put away. Now he states his chief point: How have you become a child? Because you have been reconciled. On the same basis on which you have received so great a privilege, offer this same gift to others. . . . And as the Lord has loved you, so you love your neighbor. Even if you are not able to do that completely, you must do it according to your ability. HOMILY ON EPHESIANS 17.4.32—5.2.[4]

AS HE GAVE HIMSELF UP FOR US. JEROME: Who is it that truly walks in love? The one who, for the salvation of others, contends against sin to the point of shedding blood, so as even to give up his soul for them. That is the one who *walks in love*, imitating Christ. EPISTLE TO THE EPHESIANS 3.5.2.[5]

TO IMITATE THE FATHER, LOVE LIKE THE SON. THEODORET: Here too he reveals the equality of the Father and the Son. For having called them to be imitators of God, he then urges the same pattern with respect to the Son. The Father has bestowed forgiveness. The Son has loved us and gave up his life for us. EPISTLE TO THE EPHESIANS 5.2.[6]

---

[1]IOEP 4:270; cf. Theodoret *Epistle to the Ephesians* 5.1 [CPE 2:30]. [2]1 Cor 11:1. [3]Migne PL 26:518B-D [639]. [4]IOEP 4:271. [5]Migne PL 26:519A [639]. [6]CPE 2:30.

5:2b A Fragrant Offering and Sacrifice to God

THE AROMA OF SWEETNESS. MARIUS VIC-TORINUS: As Father and Son are of one substance, so too they are one in will. . . . The Son offered himself to the Father that through this mystery of his sacrifice all things might be made new by his Spirit. In this way he himself is the aroma of sweetness. EPISTLE TO THE EPHESIANS 2.5.2.[7]

HOW WE IMITATE HIS SACRIFICE. CHRYSOSTOM: You spare your friends. He spared his enemies. . . . He suffered on his enemies' behalf. This is the fragrant offering, the acceptable sacrifice. If you suffer for your enemies as a fragrant offering, you too become an acceptable sacrifice, even if you die. This is what it means to imitate God. HOMILY ON EPHESIANS 17.4.32-5.2.[8]

5:3a Impurity and Covetousness Repudiated

FORNICATION AND IMPURITY DISTINGUISHED. ORIGEN: *Fornication* in the strict sense is consorting with prostitutes. *Impurity* is the generic name, in the maelstrom of our bodily existence, not only for adultery and pederasty but also all the other inventions of sexual licentiousness in all their many and diverse practices. *Greed* can be taken either straightforwardly or, as I have established [with regard to 1 Thess 4:4-6], in the sense of *adultery*. EPISTLE TO THE EPHESIANS.[9]

COVETOUSNESS NOT TRIVIAL. AMBROSIASTER: What a grave sin is covetousness, though we gloss over it when compared with fornication and uncleanness. We treat covetousness as a minor fault when in fact it is a grave matter. No one can be a saint in whom is found any of these things that he forbids. EPISTLE TO THE EPHESIANS 5.3.[10]

MURDER AND ADULTERY DISTINGUISHED. CHRYSOSTOM: He has already spoken of the bitterest affection, which is wrath. Next he passes on to lust, which comes after wrath, as we see in the law of Moses, who first says *You shall not murder*, which springs from wrath, and then *You shall not commit adultery*, which springs from lust.[11] For just as bitterness, clamor and every evil, including blasphemy and the like, belong to the anger-prone, passionate nature, so do fornication, impurity and covetousness belong to the lust-prone, appetitive nature. Just as he earlier prohibited clamorous disorder because it is a vehicle of anger, so he now prohibits filthy and loose talk, because it is a vehicle of lust. HOMILY ON EPHESIANS 17.5.3.[12]

5:3b What Is Fitting Among Saints

SOME SINS NOT EVEN TO BE NAMED AMONG THE SAINTS. MARIUS VICTORINUS: The name, the mind and the conscience of the saints demand that the tongue itself should be an agent of holiness. If a person who is holy in his ways speaks unnecessarily of abominable behaviors, he may harbor sin. Even speaking of them may show how well acquainted he is with vices better left unspoken. EPISTLE TO THE EPHESIANS 2.5.3.[13]

---

[7]BT 1972:190-91 [1283A-B]. [8]IOEP 4:271. [9]JTS 3:559. [10]CSEL 81.3:111. [11]See Ex 20:13-14; Deut 5:17-18. [12]IOEP 4:271. [13]BT 1972:191 [1283B-C].

PREOCCUPATION WITH SIN. JEROME: Even one who is in fact free of fornication is not holy if he remains mentally preoccupied with some uncleanness or with the avaricious pursuit of the pleasures that have once delighted him. EPISTLE TO THE EPHESIANS 3.5.3-4.[14]

5:4a *Fitting Speech*

SILLINESS NOT UPBUILDING. CHRYSOSTOM: Let there be no obscenities, either in word or deed, that might quench the flame of the spirit.[15] For words often lead the way to actions. Then, in order that it may not appear that he is a spoilsport or too austere, Paul gently shows that he is not an opponent of playfulness. For he qualifies this instruction by explaining its reason: You are not to indulge in that form of silly talk that is *not befitting* to this community. Better to offer thanksgiving than to spew out such talk. What good is it if you make an unbefitting witticism? All you have done is raise a laugh. Tell me, does the shoemaker use any instrument that does not befit his trade? Would he purchase a tool that does not contribute to his craft? Of course not. Similarly, that which is of no use to our purpose is nothing to us. . . . Inordinate levity may easily open the door to blasphemy, and the blasphemer heaps up countless other evils for himself. HOMILY ON EPHESIANS 17.5.4.[16]

DISTINGUISHING SILLINESS AND LEVITY. JEROME: The "silly talk" to which Paul refers occurs not only among those who tell dirty jokes to get a cheap laugh. He is also referring to those who put on frivolous airs and to those who manipulate whoever they are trying to please. There is another kind of silly talk that occurs among those reckoned to be the intellectuals of the age who, when disputing on matters of natural science, imagine that they have fully comprehended the sands of the shore, the drops of ocean, the extent of heavens and the minuteness of earth. . . . Note that *levity* follows *silly talk.* The intent here is to speak of frivolous and inappropriate stories. The difference between silliness and levity is this: silliness has nothing in it that is wise or worthy of the human heart. Levity devolves from a clever mind and deliberately seeks out certain words, be they witty, vulgar, obscene or facetious, in a jocularity the sole aim of which is to get a laugh. EPISTLE TO THE EPHESIANS 3.5.3-4.[17]

5:4b *Let There Be Thanksgiving*

THE ALTERNATIVE TO UNNECESSARY TALKATIVENESS. MARIUS VICTORINUS: Having said what should be the case, he adds what must above all be the case, which is this, that we should *give thanks*—to God, without doubt, but also to other people. Hence he uses the term *thanksgiving* without qualification. EPISTLE TO THE EPHESIANS 2.5.4.[18]

5:5a *Who Inherits the Kingdom of God?*

WHETHER SOME SINS ARE MORE SERIOUS. MARIUS VICTORINUS: Since he has listed three sins first, then added another three, his instruction requires him to explain that the first three are more serious, seeing that he has said that these first three[19] are not

---

[14]Migne PL 26:519B-C [640]. [15]Here Chrysostom quotes 1 Corinthians 5:1. [16]IOEP 4:272. [17]Migne PL 26:519C-520A [640-41]. [18]BT 1972:191 [1283D-1284A]. [19]Fornication, sexual impurity and covetousness.

even to be named among the saints. EPISTLE TO THE EPHESIANS 2.5.5.[20]

WHETHER WORDS SAID IN JEST CONDEMN Us. JEROME: Are those merely guilty of silliness and inordinate levity to be kept out of the kingdom of God? Are they excluded on the same basis as those sins that he has marked off specially[21]? It would seem a cruel sentence not to pardon the weakness of human frailty, so that our words condemned us even when said in jest. . . . Yet in making this distinction [between lesser and more serious sins] we are not making excuses for silliness and levity. They do not exclude from the kingdom. But they are not negligible and remind us that just as *the Father has many mansions*[22] and *one star differs from another in glory*,[23] so too will it be in the resurrection of the dead. EPISTLE TO THE EPHESIANS 3.5.5.[24]

5:5b Covetousness Linked with Idolatry

THE IDOLATROUS HEART OF COVETOUSNESS. AMBROSIASTER: To teach us that covetousness is such a dangerous thing he calls it

idolatry, no sin being greater than this. But why is covetousness called *idolatry?* Idolatry usurps the honor of God and claims it for the creature. The holy name of God, which belongs solely to the Creator, is thereby applied to creatures. Covetousness is viewed on a level with idolatry because the covetous person similarly usurps for himself what belong to God and hides them away. Covetousness withholds the resources offered by God for the common use of all. It hoards them to itself so that others may not use them. EPISTLE TO THE EPHESIANS 5.5.1.[25]

YOU CANNOT SERVE GOD AND MAMMON. THEODORET: Paul also makes this point in his letter to the Corinthians.[26] He speaks of covetousness as idolatry, reminding us of the Lord's saying: *No one can serve two masters; and you cannot serve God and Mammon.*[27] EPISTLE TO THE EPHESIANS 5.5.[28]

---

[20]BT 1972:192 [1284A]. [21]Fornication, sexual impurity and covetousness. [22]Jn 14:2. [23]1 Cor 15:41. [24]Migne PL 26:521A-B [642]. [25]CSEL 81.3:112. [26]1 Cor 6:10-11. [27]Mt 6:24. [28]CPE 2:31.

5:6-14 DARKNESS AND LIGHT

[6]*Let no one deceive you with empty words, for it is because of these things that the wrath of God comes upon the sons of disobedience.* [7]*Therefore do not associate with them,* [8]*for once you were darkness, but now you are light in the Lord; walk as children of light* [9]*(for the fruit of light is found in all that is good and right and true),* [10]*and try to learn what is pleasing to the Lord.* [11]*Take no part in the unfruitful works of*

darkness, but instead expose them. [12]*For it is a shame even to speak of the things that they do in secret;* [13]*but when anything is exposed by the light it becomes visible, for anything that becomes visible is light.* [14]*Therefore it is said,*

"*Awake, O sleeper, and arise from the dead,*
and Christ shall give you light."

OVERVIEW: We must not belittle our sins (CHRYSOSTOM) or forget what the kingdom requires of us (MARIUS VICTORINUS). Paul's pastoral method constantly combines admonition and encouragement (CHRYSOSTOM). The light of grace is always dispelling the darkness of sin (AMBROSIASTER). Christ himself is rightly called the good, the true and the right (ORIGEN, JEROME), which transforms bitterness, covetousness and false pleasure (CHRYSOSTOM). Scripture and Spirit show us how to discern God's holy will (THEODORET, AMBROSIASTER), which calls forth fruits, not barren works (JEROME). One who undertakes to admonish the wicked (CHRYSOSTOM) must first acknowledge his own limits (JEROME). The counseling and admonition of sins are crucial services to those entrapped in sin (MARIUS VICTORINUS). Insensitivity to sin is death (AMBROSIASTER) even for Christians (CHRYSOSTOM). In some cases Paul's admonitions are taken from unknown Christian sources (THEODORET) and in other cases are supplied by himself (JEROME).

5:6a Deceived with Empty Words

HOW EMPTY WORDS LEAD ASTRAY.
CHRYSOSTOM: There are always people among us who want to diminish the force of words. When Paul clearly says that covetousness is idolatry, they immediately argue that this is an exaggerated saying and in this way compromise all the commandments. It is to these that the blessed Paul is alluding when he writes to the Ephesians, *Be sure of this, that no one who is covetous, that is, an idolater, has any inheritance in the kingdom. Empty words* are words that are for a moment attractive but in no way are proved by deeds. They become a flimsy deceit. HOMILY ON EPHESIANS 18.5.5-6.[1]

5:6b God's Wrath on the Children of Disobedience

THE CHILDREN OF DISOBEDIENCE. MARIUS VICTORINUS: These people he calls *children of disobedience;* for there are many who make light of the promise of a heavenly kingdom. . . . They disbelieve; they have no faith. The wrath of God comes upon the children of disobedience. Disobedience is epitomized by the devil they serve. Therefore they are said to be his children. EPISTLE TO THE EPHESIANS 2.5.6.[2]

5:7-8a Not Associating with the Disobedient

PAUL'S PASTORAL METHOD INTERMIXES ADMONITION AND ENCOURAGEMENT. CHRYSOS-

---

[1]IOEP 4:276. [2]BT 1972:192 [1284C].

TOM: Note the balanced way in which he exhorts them. First he approaches them from the viewpoint of Christ, saying "love one another and do no wrong to anyone." Then he approaches them from the viewpoint of their punishment and Gehenna . . . reminding them of their previous wickedness, as if to say "remember what you were and what you have become." HOMILY ON EPHESIANS 18.5.7-8.[3]

THE LIGHT OF GRACE DISPELS THE DARKNESS OF SIN. AMBROSIASTER: *Once you were darkness* suggests ignorance. No one sees clearly in shadows. The ignorance referred to is disbelief, harking back to pagan days. Those who lived in darkness have been drawn to faith by the grace of God, which has been brought to light, that is, truth. Things that exist are made apparent in the light. Paganism remains deluded as with covered eyes they celebrate their own mysteries as if in the shadows of a cave. EPISTLE TO THE EPHESIANS 5.8.[4]

5:8b *Walking as Children of Light*

YOU ARE LIGHT IN THE LORD. JEROME: The darkness is being turned into light. There is not, as some heretics argue, a nature so alienated that it cannot receive salvation. . . . Those who receive salvation—the righteous —are *the light of the world.*[5] Those who refuse, the unrighteous, are in consequence called *darkness.* . . . The difference and distance between one and the other is clearly seen by their own fruits. EPISTLE TO THE EPHESIANS 3.5.8.[6]

5:9 *The Fruit of Light*

ALL THAT IS RIGHT AND TRUE. ORIGEN:

Where there is goodness there is righteousness. Where there is truth there you will find righteousness. For both goodness and truth belong to God alone. So righteousness is always found with him and no other. EPISTLE TO THE EPHESIANS.[7]

COUNTERING BITTERNESS, COVETOUSNESS AND FALSE PLEASURE. CHRYSOSTOM: When Paul says *in all goodness* he is directing this against those who are wrathful and bitter. When he says *and in all that is right* he is speaking against covetousness. When he says *and in all that is true* he speaks against false pleasure. The fruit of the light is evidenced not in the vices he has already spoken of[8] but in their opposites. HOMILY ON EPHESIANS 18.5.9-10.[9]

CHRIST HIMSELF IS RIGHTLY CALLED THE GOOD, THE TRUE AND THE RIGHT. JEROME: Christ himself is rightly called goodness, righteousness and truth. He is goodness in that he gives grace to those who believe in him, not according to their works but according to his mercy. He is himself righteousness in that he gives to each what he deserves. He is himself truth in that he is the one who knows the causes of all creatures and all things. EPISTLE TO THE EPHESIANS 3.5.9.[10]

5:10 *Learn What Is Pleasing to God*

LEARNING WHAT DELIGHTS GOD. AMBROSI-

---

[3]IOEP 4:277. [4]CSEL 81.3:113. [5]Mt 5:14. [6]Migne PL 26:523B-C [645]. [7]JTS 3:562. Origen is writing against Marcion in this passage. He is followed by Jerome *Epistle to the Ephesians* 3.5.9 [Migne PL 26:524A (646)]. [8]Wrath, covetousness and sexual impurity. [9]IOEP 4:277. [10]Migne PL 26:524A [646].

ASTER: From the abundance of his holiness and goodness it is possible to know what works delight God.[11] . . . In his holiness we are purified. In his mercy we are brought to full and perfect righteousness. EPISTLE TO THE EPHESIANS 5.10.[12]

LEARNING THROUGH WORD AND SPIRIT. THEODORET: You share in the Word. You have received the grace of the Holy Spirit. Now you are made able to discern what is pleasing to God. EPISTLE TO THE EPHESIANS 5.10.[13]

5:11 Expose the Works of Darkness

LIGHT EXPOSES DARKNESS. CHRYSOSTOM: He has said, *you are light*. Light exposes what takes place in darkness. Insofar as you are light your goodness shines forth. The wicked are not able to hide. Their actions are illuminated as though a lamp were at hand. HOMILY ON EPHESIANS 18.5.11-13.[14]

DISTINGUISHING WORKS FROM FRUITS. JEROME: Paul uses the term *fruits* in the case of the Spirit, *works* in the case of the sin nature.[15] . . . In the present case he indeed is saying that the works of darkness are unfruitful. Those who do these works share an association with darkness. EPISTLE TO THE EPHESIANS 3.5.11.[16]

EXPOSING UNFRUITFUL WORKS. JEROME: No one is prepared to admonish sinners except one who does not deserve to be called a hypocrite [as with the account in Lk 6:42]. . . . Only those prophets who were themselves unpolluted by any stain of sin were in a position to upbraid others for their wrongdoing. From this we learn that the one who

is in the best position to reprimand is the one who cannot himself rightly be reprimanded in turn. EPISTLE TO THE EPHESIANS 3.5.11.[17]

5:12 A Shame to Speak of Secret Things

SOME UNFRUITFUL WORKS SHAME EVEN THOSE WHO SPEAK OF THEM. MARIUS VICTORINUS: If it is shameful even to speak of these things in secret, it is fairly plain that these people were doing wicked things, things too depraved even to talk about. EPISTLE TO THE EPHESIANS 2.5.12.[18]

5:13 Light Exposes Shameful Things

COMBAT WITH LIGHT THOSE MOST SHAMEFUL THINGS DONE IN SECRET. MARIUS VICTORINUS: Having instructed them also to counsel all those who are doing ill, he next shows what a great service this is. For admonition makes those sins manifest. It puts them in the light. For the one who admonishes shows how important is the behavior he illumines. In doing this he is in effect illuminating the evil to show its consequences. When the one who commits evil understands this, the shadows are dispelled, and he enters the light. EPISTLE TO THE EPHESIANS 2.5.13.[19]

5:14 "Awake, O Sleeper"

FROM WHAT SOURCE IS THIS QUOTED?

---

[11]Here Ambrosiaster cites Luke 6:36. [12]CSEL 81.3:114. [13]CPE 2:31. [14]IOEP 4:278. Cf. Theodoret *Epistle to the Ephesians* 5.11-13 [CPE 2:31-32]. [15]Gal 5:19. [16]Migne PL 26:524B-C [646]. [17]Migne PL 26:524C-D [646-47]. [18]BT 1972:194 [1285C]. [19]BT 1972:194 [1285C].

JEROME: The one who is content with a simple answer will say indeed that Paul must have read this phrase in some arcane prophet or in the writings called apocryphal. He then brought the text into the open, as he manifestly does in other places—not to substantiate the apocryphal texts but in the same way that he makes use of verses elsewhere from Aratus, Epimenides and Menander to substantiate what he says on other occasions. . . . Someone less content with this simple answer might argue that the apostle said this as an exhortation to penitence. It is as if he were assuming the voice of the Holy Spirit. For my part, scanty as my knowledge is, I have nowhere found this written after diligently scouring all the editions of the ancient Scriptures and the texts of the Hebrews themselves. EPISTLE TO THE EPHESIANS 3.5.14.[20]

THE METAPHORS OF SLEEPING AND DEATH. AMBROSIASTER: By *sleep* he signifies a stupor of the mind. The sleepers are lost from the true path. This estrangement is a kind of death, from which he calls them to rise that they may repent and acknowledge the truth, which is Christ. Thus the faithless and

vicious, steeped as they are in mud without hope of life, are called to rise and come out and have a share in life with Christ, so as to pass from the shadows out to the light and from death to life. EPISTLE TO THE EPHESIANS 5.14.[21]

ADDRESSED ALSO TO BELIEVERS WHO SLEEP IN SIN. CHRYSOSTOM: He is not speaking only to unbelievers. For there are many believers, no less than unbelievers, who remain still trapped in various sins. There are indeed some who do so all the more. Therefore it was necessary to call these to *awake*, etc. HOMILY ON EPHESIANS 18.5.14.[22]

ITS SOURCE UNKNOWN. THEODORET: It is to be noted that this testimony is not scriptural, for we nowhere find it in the canonical text. Some interpreters have argued that those who were favored with spiritual grace were writing psalms. The apostle himself hints at this when he says in his letter to the Corinthians, *each of you has a psalm.*[23] EPISTLE TO THE EPHESIANS 5.14.[24]

---

[20]Migne PL 26:525B-C [647-48]. [21]CSEL 81.3:115. [22]IOEP 4:279. [23]1 Cor 14:26. [24]CPE 2:32.

5:15-20 ABSTINENCE FROM SIN

[15]*Look carefully then how you walk, not as unwise men but as wise,* [16]*making the most of the time, because the days are evil.* [17]*Therefore do not be foolish, but understand what the will of the Lord is.* [18]*And do not get drunk with wine, for that is debauchery; but be filled with the Spirit,* [19]*addressing one another in psalms and*

hymns and spiritual songs, singing and making melody to the Lord with all your heart,
[20]always and for everything giving thanks in the name of our Lord Jesus Christ to
God the Father.

Overview: We must be wise in our dealings with unbelievers (Ambrosiaster), for the times are not our own. They mostly belong to the wicked (Chrysostom). We must strive to make all time God's time (Jerome). God wills moderation (Ambrosiaster) so that others will respect us (Ambrosiaster) and flagrant sins will be avoided (Chrysostom). To be drunk with the Spirit is to be truly sober (Ambrose). The faithful are called to be filled with the Spirit and to practice the types of singing commended in the Psalter (Chrysostom, Jerome), using the mind (Chrysostom) but not neglecting the voice (Ambrosiaster). Even in adversity Christians can thank God (Jerome) because they know Christ as their Redeemer (Ambrosiaster).

5:15 Not as Unwise but as Wise

Prudence Required Amid Unjust Civil Authority. Ambrosiaster: Paul has previously ordained that false and vicious lives be exposed by the servants of God. He now adds a qualifier: they are to be exposed in a careful manner to avoid scandal. The faithful must be prudent in their conduct among the faithless, especially at a time when the faithless hold dominion, trusting in an unholy ruler. If then a Christian encounters a troubler who is turbulent and angry, he should be cautious in his presence so as not to incite him to blaspheme or raise a storm. He will utter his words where occasion offers. Epistle to the Ephesians 5.15.1.[1]

5:16 The Days Are Evil

Redeeming the Time. Chrysostom: His motive for giving this counsel is not to urge them to be more crafty or underhanded. Rather he is saying: "The times do not belong to you. Now you are migrants and expatriates, strangers and foreigners. Do not seek honors. Do not seek glory, authority or retribution. Bear all things. Only by patience will you redeem the time. Pay whatever is required, all that they desire." Homily on Ephesians 18.5.15-17.[2]

God's Creation of Time Itself Not Evil. Chrysostom: When Paul says *the days are evil* he does not mean that they are created evil or that they are by their very nature evil. Rather he says this of the troubling events that occur in time. We are in the habit of saying, "I have had a terrible day." But that does not imply that the day of itself is intrinsically terrible. Rather it refers to what has occurred in the day. Some of the things that occur in it are good, as they are enabled by God. Some are bad, because they are brought about by evil willing. Therefore it is we humans who are the authors of the evils that occur in time. Only on this basis are the times called evil. Homily on Ephesians 18.5.15-17.[3]

---

[1]CSEL 81.3:115. [2]IOEP 4:287. Cf. Theodoret *Epistle to the Ephesians* 5.15-16 [CPE 2:32]. [3]IOEP 4:287.

AVOID CONSTANT CHANGE. JEROME: Christ, the Sun of Righteousness, has risen. Rise up from the sleep of the age. Walk cautiously and prudently. Cast off folly. Take hold of wisdom. In this way you will be able to avoid changing yourself constantly as you walk through the vicissitudes of the times. Rather you will find a unity within yourself even amid the diversity of the times. EPISTLE TO THE EPHESIANS 3.5.16.[4]

5:17 Understand the Will of the Lord

THE WILL OF THE LORD. AMBROSIASTER: Do what you have to do with moderation. This is the will of the Lord. Do not allow commotion and din or discord with bad feeling to give rise to estrangement. So Paul adds these words to what he has said about his wish that the servants of God should admonish wrongdoing. EPISTLE TO THE EPHESIANS 5.17.[5]

5:18a Maintain Sobriety

THE DUTY OF SOBRIETY. AMBROSIASTER: It is good conduct that strikes fear in the wrongdoer. Only one who is sober is prepared to counsel another realistically and with confidence. The person being counseled feels less resentment when he knows how good is the actual conduct of the one who admonishes him. But where there is intoxication there is also debauchery, and debauchery causes base deeds. Therefore it is our duty to be sober, so that the requirements of good conduct may be observed. EPISTLE TO THE EPHESIANS 5.18.[6]

WINE GIVEN TO GLADDEN, NOT INTOXICATE. CHRYSOSTOM: Immoderate indulgence makes one rash, passionate, prone to stumbling, anger and severity. Wine was given to gladden us, not for intoxication. HOMILY ON EPHESIANS 19.5.18.[7]

5:18b Be Filled with the Spirit

SPIRIT-FILLED, NOT WINE-FILLED. AMBROSE: One drunk with wine sways and stumbles. But one who is filled with the Spirit has solid footing in Christ. This is a fine drunkenness, which produces even greater sobriety of mind. ON THE SACRAMENTS 5.3.17.[8]

THE HOLY SPIRIT ENTERS THE HOUSE RIGHTLY SWEPT CLEAN FOR HIM. CHRYSOSTOM: Be ready for the Spirit's filling. This happens only when we have cleansed our souls of falsehood, anger, bitterness, sexual impurity, uncleanness and covetousness. It happens only when we have become compassionate, meek and forgiving to one another, only when facetiousness is absent, only when we have made ourselves worthy. Only then does the Spirit come to settle within our hearts, only when nothing is there to prevent it. Then he will not only enter but also fill us. HOMILY ON EPHESIANS 19.5.19-21.[9]

5:19a Sing Psalms, Hymns and Spiritual Songs

TO BE FILLED WITH THE SPIRIT, LEARN TO SING PSALMS. CHRYSOSTOM: Do you wish to be happy? Do you want to know how to spend the day truly blessed? I offer you a

---

[4]Migne PL 26:527A-B [649-50], probably following Origen. [5]CSEL 81.3:116. [6]CSEL 81.3:116-17. [7]IOEP 4:288. [8]CSEL 73:65. [9]IOEP 4:290.

drink that is spiritual. This is not a drink for drunkenness that would cut off even meaningful speech. This does not cause us to babble. It does not disturb our vision. Here it is: Learn to sing psalms! Then you will see pleasure indeed. Those who have learned to sing with the psalms are easily filled with the Holy Spirit. But if you sing only the devil's songs you will soon find yourself filled with an unclean spirit. HOMILY ON EPHESIANS 19.5.19-21.[10]

PSALMS, HYMNS AND SPIRITUAL SONGS. JEROME: Our hymns declare the strength and majesty of God. They express gratitude for his benefits and his deeds. Our psalms convey this gratitude also, since the word *Alleluia* is either prefaced or appended to them. Our psalms properly belong to the domain of ethics, teaching us what is to be done and avoided. The domain of the psalms is the body as an instrument of grace. But the domain of the spiritual canticles is the mind. As we sing spiritual canticles we hear discourses on things above, on the harmony of the world, on the subtly ordered concord of all creatures. These spiritual songs help us express our meaning more plainly for the sake of simple folk. It is more with the mind than with the voice that we sing, offer psalms and praise God. EPISTLE TO THE EPHESIANS 3.5.19.[11]

5:19b Make Melody to the Lord

SING WITH HEARTS ENGAGED. CHRYSOSTOM: *Making melody to the Lord* means paying attention while you are singing. It means not letting your mind drift. Those who in singing do not offer this deep attention to God are merely mouthing psalms, uttering words, while their hearts are preoccupied elsewhere.

HOMILY ON EPHESIANS 19.5.19-21.[12]

SINGING FROM THE HEART. AMBROSIASTER: If we are living well, we are always being filled with the Holy Spirit so as to confess and extol the gift of God. The Holy Spirit loves this way of life. This is especially expressed in songs, that praise may be sung to God by every tongue. If the Spirit is dwelling within someone, he is always meditating on the Spirit. It is not only his lips that burst forth but his heart. EPISTLE TO THE EPHESIANS 5.19.[13]

5:20 Give Thanks in All Things

WHAT IT MEANS TO GIVE THANKS IN CHRIST'S NAME. AMBROSIASTER: We are told to give thanks to God for all his gifts. For God has stooped low to adopt us through Christ his own Son, through whom we know God. We have learned that God, being Spirit, is to be adored in the Spirit. So we submit ourselves to one another out of reverence for Christ, who commanded us to pursue humility. EPISTLE TO THE EPHESIANS 5.21.[14]

EXTOL GOD ALWAYS AND IN EVERYTHING. JEROME: Paul now calls us to *give thanks always and in everything*. This is to be understood in a double sense, both in adversity and in good times. . . . In this way the mind rejoices and bursts out in gratitude to God, not only for what we think good but for what troubles us and happens against our will. . . . It is obvious that generally we are called to give thanks to God for the sun that

---

[10]IOEP 4:289. [11]Migne PL 26:528B-C [651-52], probably following Origen. [12]IOEP 4:289. [13]CSEL 81.3:117. [14]CSEL 81.3:117.

rises, for the day that goes by and for the night that brings rest . . . for the rains that come, for the earth that brings forth fruit and for the elements in their course. . . . Finally, we are thankful that we are born, that we have being, that our wants are sufficiently taken care of in the world, as if we lived in the house of an extremely powerful family patriarch, knowing that whatever is in the world has been created on our account. In this way we give thanks when we are grateful for the benefits that come to us from God. All these things, however, the heathen also does, and the Jew and the publican and the Gentile. But the second sense of giving thanks is seen in the special gift of Christians to give thanks to God even in seeming adversity. . . . Those who are saintly in their own eyes are prone to give thanks to God because they have been released from dangers and afflictions. But according to the apostle the greater virtue is to give thanks to God precisely amid those very dangers and afflictions. EPISTLE TO THE EPHESIANS 3.5.20.[15]

[15]Migne PL 26:529A-D [652-53].

5:21-27 HUSBANDS AND WIVES

[21]*Be subject to one another out of reverence for Christ.* [22]*Wives, be subject to your husbands, as to the Lord.* [23]*For the husband is the head of the wife as Christ is the head of the church, his body, and is himself its Savior.* [24]*As the church is subject to Christ, so let wives also be subject in everything to their husbands.* [25]*Husbands, love your wives, as Christ loved the church and gave himself up for her,* [26]*that he might sanctify her, having cleansed her by the washing of water with the word,* [27]*that he might present the church to himself in splendor, without spot or wrinkle or any such thing, that she might be holy and without blemish.*

OVERVIEW: True marriages are in Christ (JEROME). They bring relationships into social harmony (CHRYSOSTOM). Marriage partners are to be acquiescent to each other as if to the Lord (JEROME). Meekness characterizes the whole of the Christian life (JEROME), excepting the case in which one is given an unjust command (THEODORET). The simile of the body endears wives to husbands and husbands to wives (THEODORET). It astutely defines the church's relation to Christ (JEROME). The analogy between Christ and the church has limitations, however, since husband and wife are of the same nature (AMBROSIASTER). Much is asked of husband, even more than is asked of the wife—readiness to die for the other (THEODORET, CHRYSOSTOM). Christianity, like marriage, is exclusive in its bonds. There is only one church that Christ loves, not two (CYPRIAN). Husband and wife are cleansed by the same bath of regeneration in baptism and ongoing repentance (AUGUSTINE). As the bride is made holy in faithful baptism (MARIUS VICTORINUS), so does Christ adorn the church (CHRYSOSTOM). So it is said that one spouse washes and cleanses another spouse through water by the Word (MARIUS VICTORINUS). Each looks for inward rather than outward beauty in the other (CHRYSOSTOM).

5:21 Subject to One Another

CHRISTIAN LEADERS VIEW THEMSELVES AS SERVANTS. JEROME: Let bishops hear this, let priests hear, let every rank of learning get this clear: In the church, leaders are servants. Let them imitate the apostle.... The difference between secular rulers and Christian leaders is that the former love to boss their subordinates whereas the latter serve them. We are that much greater if we are considered least of all. EPISTLE TO THE EPHESIANS 3.5.21.[1]

SUBMISSIVENESS EXCEPT TO UNLAWFUL COMMANDS. THEODORET: We must not be submissive to those who command us to act unlawfully. But to those who call us to live with piety, we must be subject to one another. Having laid down this general law of obedience, Paul next advises the Ephesians in detail on their duties to another. EPISTLE TO THE EPHESIANS 5.21.[2]

5:22 Wives Subject to Husbands, As to the Lord

BE SUBJECT AS IF TO THE LORD. JEROME:

The union of Christ and the church is holy. So is the proper union of husband and wife holy. Just as a congregation of heretics, however, cannot rightly be called the church of Christ and cannot have Christ as its head, so it is that a union between husband and wife cannot be truly called holy if there is a disregard for the way of life taught by Christ. EPISTLE TO THE EPHESIANS 3.5.22-23.[3]

5:23 An Analogy of Headship

THE SWEET FRAGRANCE OF HARMONY IN MARRIAGE. CHRYSOSTOM: When they are in harmony, and their children are being reared well and their household is in good order, their neighbors will smell the sweet fragrance of harmony, along with all their friends and relatives. But if the contrary is true, everything is overturned and thrown into confusion. HOMILY ON EPHESIANS 20.5.22-24.[4]

FLESH DISTINGUISHED FROM BODY. JEROME: Note that the church is never called the flesh but always the body of Christ. Whatever lives according to the flesh must necessarily be embodied. That is true. But it is not true that whatever is body is consequently living according to the flesh. EPISTLE TO THE EPHESIANS 3.5.22-23.[5]

THE PURPOSE OF THE ANALOGY. THEODORET: The apostle has been very constrained in setting forth this analogy [of the husband as the head of the wife, as Christ is

---

[1]Migne PL 26:530A-C [653-54]. [2]CPE 2:33. [3]Migne PL 26:530D-531A [654]. [4]IOEP 4:300. [5]Migne PL 26:531B [655].

the head of the church, his body]. Its purpose is to encourage women to respect men and to implant in men an affection for their wives. EPISTLE TO THE EPHESIANS 5.22-23.[6]

5:24 The Church and Christ, Wives and Husbands

THE LIMITS OF THE ANALOGY: WOMAN AND MAN SHARE THE SAME NATURE. AMBROSIASTER: Here is Paul's analogy: As the church takes its beginning from Christ and therefore is subject to him, so too does woman take hers from the man and is subject to him.[7] There is a crucial difference, however, between Christ and the church as opposed to man and woman. The essential difference is that the woman is of the same nature as the man. The church, on the other hand, can participate in Christ in name but not in nature. EPISTLE TO THE EPHESIANS 5.24.[8]

ONLY THOSE REARED IN PIETY WILL UNDERSTAND. THEODORET: As one who is giving instruction to the pious, Paul here adds the words *subject in all things*. It is evident from this analogy that he is speaking essentially to the pious, to those well trained in religious life. None of those reared in piety would think of putting their own affairs before God. EPISTLE TO THE EPHESIANS 5.24.[9]

5:25 Loving as Christ Loved the Church

THERE IS ONLY ONE SPOUSE THAT CHRIST LOVES. CYPRIAN: There is only one church that Christ loves. It is this church alone that is being cleansed by his washing. LETTER 69.2.3.[10]

THE HUSBAND'S READINESS TO GIVE HIS

LIFE FOR HIS WIFE. CHRYSOSTOM: Have you noted the measure of obedience? Pay attention to love's high standard. If you take the premise that your wife should submit to you, as the church submits to Christ, then you should also take the same kind of careful, sacrificial thought for her that Christ takes for the church. Even if you must offer your own life for her, you must not refuse. Even if you must undergo countless struggles on her behalf and have all kinds of things to endure and suffer, you must not refuse. Even if you suffer all this, you have still done not as much as Christ has for the church. For you are already married when you act this way, whereas Christ is acting for one who has rejected and hated him. So just as he, when she was rejecting, hating, spurning and nagging him, brought her to trust him by his great solicitude, not by threatening, lording it over her or intimidating her or anything like that, so must you also act toward your wife. Even if you see her looking down on you, nagging and despising you, you will be able to win her over with your great love and affection for her. HOMILY ON EPHESIANS 20.5.25.[11]

5:26 Cleansed by the Washing of Water by the Word

IN WHAT SENSE IT IS SAID THAT ONE SPOUSE WASHES AND CLEANSES ANOTHER SPOUSE. MARIUS VICTORINUS: Here we take

---

[6]CPE 2:33. [7]Cf. 1 Tim 2:13. [8]CSEL 81.3:117-18. The analogy is limited in that the woman is of the same nature as the man, whereas the church is not of the same nature as Christ. The church participates not directly in Christ's nature as such but in Christ's redemptive work, hence in his name. [9]CPE 2:33. [10]CCL 3c:473. [11]IOEP 4:302.

the church to mean every believer and everyone who has received baptism. The believer is brought to faith by the washing in water and the invocation of the Word. But how is this applied to a husband's conduct toward his wife? This is not entirely clear. One possible view is that the mystery of baptism is being rehearsed in this metaphor. On the other hand, if we refer this to the endurance of the husband, which entails his giving himself for the wife and bearing and suffering all that is hers, even sharing in all that she endures, she is being cleansed with water and the Word—that is, she is being purified in the Lord's sight when he renders her pure and by his endurance makes her ready to be sanctified by washing and the Word. EPISTLE TO THE EPHESIANS 2.5.25-26.[12]

5:27 Holy and Without Blemish

THE BRIDE IS MADE HOLY IN FAITHFUL BAPTISM. MARIUS VICTORINUS: What Christ is accomplishing [in baptism] is that the church should be *holy and spotless*. It is *holy* in that it has been cleansed by the washing of water by the Word. It is *spotless* in that it is without spot or wrinkle. EPISTLE TO THE EPHESIANS 2.5.27.[13]

IN FAITHFUL BAPTISM CHRIST ADORNS THE CHURCH WITH GLORY. CHRYSOSTOM: By what *word* is she *washed? In the name of the Father, and of the Son and of the Holy Spirit.*[14] He did not simply bathe her; he adorned her, making her glorious, having no spot or wrinkle or anything lacking. Let us too seek that sort of beauty, and grace will make us able to refract it. The husband does not seek from the wife something she does not have to give. For you see the pattern: the church has received everything from Christ. HOMILY ON EPHESIANS 20.5.27.[15]

HUSBAND AND WIFE ARE CLEANSED BY THE SAME BATH OF REGENERATION IN BAPTISM AND ONGOING REPENTANCE. AUGUSTINE: By the same bath of regeneration[16] and water of sanctification all sins of the redeemed are cleansed and healed, not only those which are pardoned at this time in baptism but also those that are subsequently contracted by human infirmity or ignorance. ON MARRIAGE AND CONCUPISCENCE 1.38.[17]

---

[12]BT 1972:197 [1287C-D]. [13]BT 1972:197 [1288A]. [14]Mt 28:19. [15]IOEP 4:303. [16]Cf. Tit 3:5. [17]Migne PL 44:435.

5:28-33 THE GREAT MYSTERY

[28]Even so husbands should love their wives as their own bodies. He who loves his wife loves himself. [29]For no man ever hates his own flesh, but nourishes and cherishes it, as Christ does the church, [30]because we are members of his body. [31]"For this reason a man shall leave his father and mother and be joined to his wife, and the two shall

become one flesh." [32]*This mystery is a profound one, and I am saying that it refers to Christ and the church;* [33]*however, let each one of you love his wife as himself, and let the wife see that she respects her husband.*

OVERVIEW: Paul now turns to the moral implications of husbands loving their wives as Christ loved the church and loving their wives as their own bodies (CHRYSOSTOM, AUGUSTINE). Unlike Marcion he commends the body and even the flesh (DIDYMUS THE BLIND, TERTULLIAN), which God loves as its Creator (PSEUDO-AUGUSTINE). The infirm flesh is to be cared for (DIDYMUS THE BLIND), not cut off (CHRYSOSTOM). As we bear with the defects of our own bodies, so do we bear with infirm members of Christ's church (CHRYSOSTOM, THEODORET). In Genesis 2:24 Adam and Eve prefigure Christ and the church (JEROME). Paul stresses the inviolability of marriage (THEODORET). He justifies spiritual interpretations of Scripture (DIDYMUS THE BLIND) and does not try to exhaust the meaning of the analogy (JEROME), which applies both to Christ (AUGUSTINE) and to the soul (FULGENTIUS). Nonetheless, even though his incarnation and passion are the mysteries signified here (METHODIUS), wedlock itself is both sacred (AUGUSTINE) and a symbol of divine providence (TERTULLIAN). Love coexists with reverence in an ordered home (MARIUS VICTORINUS, CHRYSOSTOM).

5:28 How Husbands Should Love Their Wives

SO OUGHT HUSBANDS LOVE. CHRYSOSTOM: Has he moved on to a greater image and a more vivid illustration? No, but to something more homely and plainer, with a differ-

ent justification. Now he takes up the argument from a moral point of view, saying *so ought husbands love their wives.* HOMILY ON EPHESIANS 20.5.28.[1]

HUSBANDS LOVE THEIR WIVES AS THEIR OWN BODIES. AUGUSTINE: The example proceeds to wives from the church and to husbands from Christ. . . . He urges the husbands on the basis of something inferior, namely, their own body, not only from the superior, that is, their Lord. ON CONTINENCE 23.[2]

5:29 Nourishing and Cherishing One's Flesh

THE ERROR OF MARCION HINGED ON HATRED OF THE FLESH. TERTULLIAN: *No one, he says, hates his own flesh*—excepting only Marcion, obviously—*but he nourishes and cherishes it, as Christ does the church.* But you [Marcion] are the only one who hates it, since you deprive it of resurrection. So you also hate the church. But Christ loved the flesh, as seen in his love for the church. The point is that as no man hates his own flesh so he does not hate his own wife but indeed acts to preserve, honor and crown her. AGAINST MARCION 5.18.9.[3]

NO ONE HATES HIS OWN FLESH. DIDYMUS THE BLIND: When the apostle asks *whoever*

---

[1]IOEP 4:304-5. [2]Migne PL 40:364. [3]CCL 1:719.

hated his own flesh? what is meant by *flesh?* Flesh is to be taken care of, *nourished and fostered. Flesh* here refers to the body yoked to the rational soul, as is clear [from the previous verse]. ON ZECHARIAH 1.169.[4]

THE HEALTHY MEMBER OF THE BODY DOES NOT CUT OFF THE LAME MEMBER. CHRYSOSTOM: It is all too evident that our bodies have many defects. One is lame, one has crooked feet, another a withered hand, each a weakness in a different member. Nevertheless the person does not complain or cut off the defect. Rather he often treats it better than the other members—and all this quite reasonably, since it is his own. HOMILY ON EPHESIANS 20.5.31.[5]

GOD, WHO MADE THE BODY, LOVES IT. PSEUDO-AUGUSTINE: The purpose of God cannot be undone, nor can anyone make a better provision than God already has. God made the body. No workman loves another's work better than his own. Hence the apostle says *no one hates his own flesh.* QUESTIONS ON THE OLD AND NEW TESTAMENTS 127.31.[6]

5:30 Members of Christ's Body

TO BE A MEMBER OF CHRIST'S BODY IS TO BE FASHIONED FROM HIM. THEODORET: Just as Eve was fashioned from Adam, so were we from Christ the Lord.[7] We are buried with him in baptism. We rise with him. We eat his body and drink his blood [in the Eucharist]. EPISTLE TO THE EPHESIANS 5.30.[8]

5:31a Leaving One's Father and Mother

EVE PREFIGURES THE CHURCH AS MOTHER OF ALL THE FAITHFUL. JEROME: The same al-

legorical interpretation applies both to Christ and to the church, that Adam is to prefigure Christ and Eve the church. For *the last Adam was made a lifegiving spirit.*[9] Just as the whole human race is born from Adam and his wife, so the whole multitude of believers has been born of Christ and the church. EPISTLE TO THE EPHESIANS 3.5.31.[10]

IN THE INCARNATION THE SON LEFT THE FATHER AND CLEAVED TO HUMANITY, BECOMING ONE FLESH WITH THE CHURCH. AUGUSTINE: If Christ cleaved to the church so that they became one flesh, in what way did he *leave* his Father? In what way did he *leave* his mother? He left his Father in the sense that, when he was in the form of God he . . . emptied himself, assuming the form of a slave.[11] . . . That means that he left the Father, not by deserting him or withdrawing from him but by coming to humanity in a lowly form in which he temporarily divested his glory with the Father. TRACTATE ON THE GOSPEL OF JOHN 9.10.[12]

5:31b Becoming One Flesh

AS ONE CHILD COMES OUT OF TWO. THEODORET: You are to respect the first law [of creation], he says in effect, which was laid down along with the fashioning of the woman and implanted in human nature. . . . This is the fruit of marriage: One child comes of two partners. The apostle, having recalled the holy requirement of marriage [that the two shall become one flesh], shows that this is illustrated also in the spiritual

---

[4]SC 83:282. [5]IOEP 4:307. [6]CSEL 50:413. [7]See Gen 2:21-23. [8]CPE 2:34-35. [9]1 Cor 15:45. [10]Migne PL 26:535B [660]. [11]Phil 2:6-8. [12]Migne PL 35:1463.

marriage. He not only demonstrates it but virtually shouts it out. EPISTLE TO THE EPHESIANS 5.31.[13]

5:32a *A Profound Mystery*

THE HIGHER MYSTERY. DIDYMUS THE BLIND: We find frequently in the writings of the blessed Paul principles conducive to a higher (anagogic)[14] interpretation. This is evident when he writes *This mystery is a profound one, and I am saying that it refers to Christ and his church.* ON GENESIS 102.[15]

HUMILITY REQUIRED IN INTERPRETING PASSAGES THAT POINT TO PROFOUND MYSTERY. JEROME: Gregory of Nazianzus, a very eloquent man and outstandingly versed in the Scriptures, used to say while discussing this passage with me: See how great the promise in this passage is! The apostle, interpreting it as an analogy of Christ and the church, does not himself even profess to have expounded it as the dignity of the idea demanded. He is in effect saying: "I know that this analogy is full of ineffable promises. It requires a divine heart in its interpretation. But in the weakness of my understanding I can only say that in the meantime it should be interpreted as Christ in relation to the church. Nothing is greater than Christ and the church. Even all that is said of Adam and Eve is to be interpreted with reference to Christ and the church." EPISTLE TO THE EPHESIANS 3.5.32.[16]

CLEAVING TO CHRIST IS LIKE CLEAVING TO A SPOUSE IN WEDLOCK. FULGENTIUS: Any soul that cleaves faithfully to Christ is like a wife living faithfully with her husband. Even in chaste wedlock she may grieve the mind of her husband. But she preserves the faith of the marriage bed with chaste purity. Prudently and temperately she orders the husband's household. Even while she falls short of meeting his needs she lives chastely and faithfully with him. Though human infirmity often causes her to transgress against him, conjugal chastity makes her cleave with pleasure to her husband. ON THE INCARNATION 41.[17]

5:32b *The Mystery Refers to Christ and the Church*

GREAT MYSTERIES IN THE EYES OF THE APOSTLES ARE SMALL IN THE EYES OF HERETICS. TERTULLIAN: Small in the eyes of heretics[18] but great in the eyes of the apostles are the Creator's works. Of just such a great mystery the apostle speaks when he says: *But I speak of Christ and the church.* He says this to confirm the mystery, not to undermine it. He shows us that the mystery was prefigured beforehand by the One who is the author of the mystery. AGAINST MARCION 5.18.10.[19]

CHRIST WILLINGLY DIED FOR HIS SPOUSE, THE CHURCH. METHODIUS: The apostle's aim was not amiss when he compared the first condition of Adam with that of Christ. It is a perfectly accurate analogy: the church is generated from Adam's bones and flesh.[20] For her sake the Word left his Father in heaven. He came down to be bonded with this woman, the church. Then he fell into

---

[13]CPE 2:35. [14]Leading up to, that is, words leading up to mystery. [15]SC 233:240-41. [16]Migne PL 26:535D-536A [661]. [17]CCL 91:346. [18]Tertullian is struggling here against Marcion's dualism, which did not adequately grasp the goodness of the body. [19]CCL 1:719. [20]Cf. Gen 2:23.

the sleep of his passion. He willingly died for her. . . . He did this to make her ready for the blessed seed[21] which he himself sows secretly in her, which she cherishes in the depth of her soul. The seed is sown that the church might receive it and fashion it like a woman, to bring forth and foster excellence. SYMPOSIUM 3.8.71.[22]

WHETHER THE GREATER MYSTERY IS THE RELATION OF CHRIST AND THE CHURCH OR MAN AND WOMAN. AUGUSTINE: The apostle speaks of *a great mystery* in the relation of Christ and the church. That which is great in respect of Christ and the church may seem less auspicious in the relation between husbands and wives. But in marriage it still represents the mystery of an inseparable bond. ON MARRIAGE AND CONCUPISCENCE 1.23.[23]

5:33a Loving One's Wife as Oneself

THE SAME PRECEPT APPLIED TO THE EPHESIANS. MARIUS VICTORINUS: Already he has given instructions generally to men concerning their wives and to women concerning their husbands. He now applies the same principles specifically to the Ephesians. . . . He has added the connecting word *however*. This shows that even as Christ and the church are one body, so are husband and wife one flesh. The husband's maxim is to love his wife as if she were his own flesh. EPISTLE TO THE EPHESIANS 2.5.33.[24]

5:33b Respecting One's Husband

HOW LOVE AND RESPECT REINFORCE EACH OTHER. CHRYSOSTOM: How, one may say, is there to be love when there is respect?[25] Love is most powerfully present when accompanied by respect. For what she loves she also reveres, and what she reveres she also loves. She reveres him as the head and loves him as a member of the whole body. God's purpose in ordering marriage is peace. One takes the husband's role, one takes the wife's role, one in guiding, one in supporting. If both had the very same roles, there would be no peace. The house is not rightly governed when all have precisely the same roles. There must be a differentiation of roles under a single head.[26] HOMILY ON EPHESIANS 20.5.33.[27]

---

[21]The analogy is that Christ loved the church by coming to her in her fallen form to be bonded with her as flesh, as Adam's flesh. For this reason he left his father and cleaved to her, even died for her. The seed is the new life that emerges in human history as a result of this union. [22]GCS 27:35-36. [23]Migne PL 44:427. [24]BT 1972:199 [1289C]. [25]Literally "reverence." [26]The household cannot be rightly ordered or governed on the basis of undifferentiated roles, wherein each voice claims absolute parity without respect for functional differences. [27]IOEP 4:308.

6:1-9 DIRECTIONS TO CHILDREN AND SLAVES

^{1}*Children, obey your parents in the Lord, for this is right.* ^{2}*"Honor your father and mother"* *(this is the first commandment with a promise),* ^{3}*"that it may be well with you and that you may live long on the earth."* ^{4}*Fathers, do not provoke your children to anger, but bring them up in the discipline and instruction of the Lord.*

^{5}*Slaves, be obedient to those who are your earthly masters, with fear and trembling, in singleness of heart, as to Christ;* ^{6}*not in the way of eyeservice, as menpleasers, but as servants*^{f} *of Christ, doing the will of God from the heart,* ^{7}*rendering service with a good will as to the Lord and not to men,* ^{8}*knowing that whatever good any one does, he will receive the same again from the Lord, whether he is a slave or free.* ^{9}*Masters, do the same to them, and forbear threatening, knowing that he who is both their Master and yours is in heaven, and that there is no partiality with him.*

f Or slaves

OVERVIEW: We are called to submit in the Lord to those who gave us birth (CHRYSOSTOM), whether life is viewed according to the order of natural birth or spiritual birth (AMBROSIASTER, JEROME). Good instruction from parents prompts obedience in children (CHRYSOSTOM). Tempting diversions must be avoided (JEROME). Evangelical freedom might otherwise tend to inspire rebellion (AMBROSIASTER) were it not that all service is an honor for Christians (CHRYSOSTOM). The Christian community is obedient within the secular orders (THEODORET). Obedience within worldly orders is viewed as obedience to Christ (AMBROSIASTER). In obedience to Christ slaves are set free (CHRYSOSTOM), a master is transformed (AMBROSIASTER) and benevolence is put into practice (JEROME). There must be no dishonesty among Christian servants (THEODORET, CHRYSOSTOM). Slavery is only a temporary institution (CHRYSOSTOM), having no durable standing in the created order. It is only an artifact of a passing social order (THEODORET).

6:1 Obeying Parents in the Lord

THE SEQUENCE COMES TO CHILDREN.
CHRYSOSTOM: Paul has spoken first about the husband, second about the wife; now he moves along this path to children. The husband is responsible for the wife.[1] Both the husband and the wife are responsible for the children. He speaks to children in an infant voice. He is well aware that if husband and wife are well disposed according to the commands he has laid down, there will be little difficulty in eliciting the cooperation of children. But what if the parents command fool-

---

[1] Or "responsible to care for the wife," which is not an absolute or unchecked authority but mutual accountability or responsibility based on mutuality of interests, as Chrysostom has previously explained.

ish things? Generally parents do not command foolish things. But if they should, the apostle has a remedy when he says that parents are to be obeyed *in the Lord*. They are to be obeyed in whatever way they are not offending against God. HOMILY ON EPHESIANS 21.6.1-3.[2]

THE JUSTICE OF OBEDIENCE TO ONE THROUGH WHOM ONE EXISTS. AMBROSIASTER: This law is given to children: Since their parents are the enablers of their existence, they are to obey them. The principle is that they reverence those through whom they exist. EPISTLE TO THE EPHESIANS 6.2.[3]

SUBMIT IN THE LORD TO THOSE WHO GAVE US BIRTH. JEROME: It is not clear whether this saying means that children are to obey their "parents in the Lord" or that in the Lord children are to obey their parents. I take it both ways. We are to obey those parents who gave birth to us in the Lord, as through Paul and the apostles they were spiritually born, and do what they say. And we should submit in the Lord to our own parents, from whom we were born according to the flesh, performing all their commands that are not contrary to the Lord's will. EPISTLE TO THE EPHESIANS 3.6.1.[4]

THE INTENTIONAL SEQUENCE OF THESE INJUNCTIONS. THEODORET: The order in which he gives his injunctions is worthy of admiration. For first he has given laws to husbands and wives, for marriage comes before childbirth. Then he tends to fathers and children, for childbirth is the fruit of marriage, since it is only after the birth that one is called a father and one called son. Finally he has set forth his instructions to servants

and masters. This arises from the social environment, as distinguished from those arrangements that come about under the laws of nature. Thus, having given all these specific injunctions, he once again gives them a common one. EPISTLE TO THE EPHESIANS 6.9.[5]

6:2 Honoring One's Parents

PARENTING IS IN THE SECOND TABLE OF THE LAW. AMBROSIASTER: Because the first four commandments pertain to God, it is implied that they are contained in the first table. The second table pertains to humans, that they should honor their parents, not murder, not commit adultery, not steal, not bear false witness and covet none of their neighbors' goods. These six commandments are viewed as written on the second table. EPISTLE TO THE EPHESIANS 6.3.2.[6]

THE FIRST COMMANDMENT WITH A PROMISE. JEROME: A promise is attached to this commandment. . . . It is found in the Decalogue. It is the first command in the second table of the law. It was given to the people as they were leaving Egypt. EPISTLE TO THE EPHESIANS 3.6.1.[7]

6:3 Being Well, Living Long

A SPIRITUAL INTERPRETATION OF THE PROMISE. JEROME: What is promised in hon-

---

[2]IOEP 4:321. [3]CSEL 81.3:120. [4]Migne PL 26:537B-C [662-63], following Origen *Epistle to the Ephesians* [JTS 3:568]. [5]CPE 2:37. [6]CSEL 81.3:120. [7]Migne PL 26:537D-538A [663-64], following Origen *Epistle to the Ephesians* [JTS 3:569].

oring one's father and mother is not intended for the Jews alone, nor was it intended as an outright financial exchange. . . . For there surely have been many who, even while being obedient to their parents, died abruptly. Others who have been irreverent to their parents have reached extreme old age. . . . Rightly interpreted the command looks for the land that the Lord promises to Israel. It is offered to those who have left the spiritual Egypt. It calls us to patience as we traverse the vast and terrible wilderness of this life, as we overcome great challengers whom the Lord strikes down and as we enter into the Judea that flows with milk and honey. EPISTLE TO THE EPHESIANS 3.6.1.[8]

6:4a Not Provoking Children to Anger

DO NOT PROVOKE. CHRYSOSTOM: He does not say, "Love your children." Nature itself takes care of this by implanting this in us even against our will. So that interpretation would be superfluous. Instead, what does he say? *Do not make your children angry*. So many parents do this. They do this by depriving them of their portion of the inheritance and their promises, by oppressing them with burdens, by treating them not as though they were free but as slaves. HOMILY ON EPHESIANS 21.6.4.[9]

6:4b The Discipline and Instruction of the Lord

TRACING THE MOTIVE OF OBEDIENCE BACK TO ITS SOURCE. CHRYSOSTOM: Then he explains the all-important thing about parenting: how children are to be brought to obedience. He traces the motive of obedience back to its source and fountain. He has

already shown how the husband's behavior elicits the wife's obedience when he spoke primarily to the husband, advising him to draw her to him by the bonds of love. Similarly here also he shows how the parents' behavior elicits the children's obedience, saying *Rear them in the instruction and discipline of the Lord*. Do you see how, when the spiritual motives are present, the physical effects will follow along? Do you want your son to be obedient? Rear him from the outset in the teaching and discipline of the Lord. Never regard it as a small matter that he should be a diligent learner of Scriptures. HOMILY ON EPHESIANS 21.6.4.[10]

EDUCATE CHILDREN IN CHRISTIAN DOCTRINE. JEROME: Instead of asking parents to give their children a fancy education in secular literature, instead of making them read comedies and recite the obscene writings of the theater, he asks the Ephesian laypersons, many of whom, as is common in a population, were engaged in the ordinary occupations of this life, that they should *educate their children in every doctrine and counsel of the Lord*. Overseers and elders ought to take note of this. EPISTLE TO THE EPHESIANS 3.6.4.[11]

6:5a Obedience to Earthly Masters

THE WITNESS OF OBEDIENCE TO GRACE. AMBROSIASTER: Christianity promises the kingdom of heaven only to those who believe, in order that they will not feel human

---

[8]Migne PL 26:538C-539B [664-65], following Origen *Epistle to the Ephesians* [JTS 3:569]. [9]IOEP 4:323. [10]IOEP 4:323. [11]Migne PL 26:540A-C [666].

pride on meriting this. Our faith is by grace, which is exalted to a higher plane than works. Only faith avails. On this gracious premise we are ordered to discharge all that is due to earthly masters. This will have the effect of inciting all the more the minds of unbelievers toward the worship of God. They will see by our behavior that our religion is both righteous and humble. Then, as masters see their slaves become more educated and more faithful in rendering service, they will see with what light reins true religion exercises governance in human affairs. So, when servants for their part notice the increased kindness of their masters, they will be similarly moved to more avid faith. EPISTLE TO THE EPHESIANS 6.5.1.[12]

WHY PAUL DID NOT OMIT THIS INJUNCTION. THEODORET: It was necessary for Paul to offer instructions for slaves. They were present everywhere in the church, which contains all classes and strata of human society, both men and women, parents and children, slaves and masters, rich and poor, governors and the governed. EPISTLE TO THE EPHESIANS 6.5.[13]

6:5b With Singleness of Heart, as to Christ

THE BROTHER OF SERVANTS. CHRYSOSTOM: Paul instructs those virtuous servants who contribute so much to the organization and protection of the household. He does not overlook them. Though their instruction comes last, because they are last in dignity and rank, he addresses them at great length. He does not speak to them as children but in a far more advanced manner. He does not make this-worldly promises to them but points directly to the world to come. He in-

structs them to love wisdom. In this way he raises up and soothes their wounded souls. He counsels them not to grieve that they have less status or honor than others. Their brief earthly submission is for a time only. Whatever power their masters might have remains transient and brief and subject to the vulnerabilities of the flesh. All that is carnal is fleeting. It is *in fear and trembling* that they are learning obedience. He does not call for the same kind of reverence from the servant as from the wife, who is called to reverence her husband. Rather he heightens the expression in saying that it is *in sincerity of heart* that they are to serve, *as if serving Christ!* He is speaking concisely here. Just what are you saying, blessed Paul? Here is one who has become the brother of servants, living himself the servant life, as they live. He is their brother, facing the same limitations, contributing to the same body. His servanthood is understood in relation to the Son of God. He is not his own master. He has entered into the life of the serving Son. Out of this assumption he calls them to *be obedient to earthly masters with fear and trembling!* Why? He is in effect saying: "How much more powerful is the ministry to those who are already servants, more than to those who are free men. How much easier do they learn the life of obedience in their reverence for God." They are not entering into a lower status but into the highest status when they learn how to yield to their neighbor, how to become meek and how to be humble. HOMILY ON EPHESIANS 22.6.5-8.[14]

6:6 Doing the Will of God from the Heart

---

[12]CSEL 81.3:121. [13]CPE 2:36. [14]IOEP 4:331.

SERVING GOD THROUGH SERVICE TO PERSONS. AMBROSIASTER: It is on account of their reverence for God that they are called to demonstrate here and now their faithful and just service to persons. As they serve God by their service to earthly masters, they look toward the day of judgment, when all will be requited and all brought to final justice. EPISTLE TO THE EPHESIANS 6.8.[15]

IN SERVING FREELY FROM THE HEART ONE IS NO SLAVE. CHRYSOSTOM: Serving Christ comes *from the heart* and *with good will*. The goal is not merely to serve sincerely and do nothing wrong. It is rather to serve with all one's might. Paul does not call servants simply to do what is barely due but to serve abundantly out of ardor, not from necessity. Serve on principle and by choice, not under compulsion. If you serve freely in this way you are not a slave. If your service comes from your free choice, from good will, from the soul and on account of Christ, you are no slave. HOMILY ON EPHESIANS 22.6.5-8.[16]

6:7 Rendering Service with Good Will

GOOD WILL AS TO THE LORD. AMBROSIASTER: This conduct may also tend toward the salvation of the master. They will see that their slaves through the grace of God have become faithful ministers. This is no small thing. They will then come to praise God's grace as well. EPISTLE TO THE EPHESIANS 6.8.[17]

6:8 Receiving Good from the Lord

REGARDLESS OF SOCIAL LOCATION, WHATEVER GOOD ONE DOES WILL COME TO THE LORD'S ATTENTION. CHRYSOSTOM: Regrettably it is the way of many unbelieving masters

to feel no shame when they fail to keep faith. They do not give any just return to their slaves for their obedience. Paul comes to comfort these servants. They should not look for retaliation but be fully confident about their ultimate compensation. Those who receive benefits but make no just payment to their servants are putting themselves in debt to God, ultimately. If your master receives good from you but does not treat you fairly, you do well to serve him all the more earnestly. You have all the more compensation stored up finally. For God is watching these transactions. Your time of compensation will come. HOMILY ON EPHESIANS 22.6.5-8.[18]

THE CATEGORIES OF SLAVERY AND MASTERY BELONG ONLY TO THIS LIFE, NOT FUTURE LIFE. THEODORET: He shows that slavery and mastery are categories that are confined to this present life. When we pass on from here, these distinctions will no longer apply. There nothing will be based on social status, such as slave or master, but on virtue and vice. EPISTLE TO THE EPHESIANS 6.8.[19]

6:9a Masters, Forbear Threatening

THE MASTER HAS A MASTER. JEROME: Serving is to be done *in singleness of heart*. One is called to *do the will of God* and to do it *with a good will*, that is, with benevolence from the heart. Everyone will finally receive just judgment from the Lord for whatever good he has done. If he has served as a lowly one in the household, he will be judged

---

[15]CSEL 81.3:122. [16]IOEP 4:332. [17]CSEL 81.3:122. [18]IOEP 4:332-33. [19]CPE 2:37.

justly according to his responsibility. The master of the household is not to be overbearing, not quick to punish. He should know that he too has a master in heaven who will judge justly, who will judge fairly according to our own willing, who will judge by deeds, not status. EPISTLE TO THE EPHESIANS 3.6.9.[20]

6:9b No Partiality with the Heavenly Master

SLAVERY BEGOTTEN BY SIN. CHRYSOSTOM: Society arrangements, like laws made by sinners, acknowledge these distinctions of classes.[21] But we are all called to accountability before the law of the common Lord and Master of all. We are called to do good to all alike and to dispense the same fair rights to all. God's law does not recognize these social distinctions. If anyone should ask where slavery comes from and why it

has stolen into human life—for I know that many are keen to ask such things and desire to learn—I shall tell you. It is avarice that brought about slavery. It is acquisitiveness, which is insatiable. This is not the original human condition. Remember that Noah had no slave, nor Abel nor Seth nor those after them. This horrid thing was begotten by sin. It does not come from our earliest ancestors. We pay our ancestors no respect by blaming them. We have insulted nature by this system. Note how Paul connects everything to the idea of headship. As to the woman he says to the husband: *love her.*[22] As to children he says to parents: *you are to rear them in the instruction and discipline of the Lord.*[23] As to slaves he can only say: *knowing that you too have a Lord in heaven.* In this light be benign and forgiving.[24] HOMILY ON EPHESIANS 22.6.9.[25]

---

[20]Migne PL 26:542C [668-69]. [21]Masters and slaves. [22]Eph 5:25. [23]Eph 6:4. [24]Cf. Eph 6:5-9. [25]IOEP 4:334.

6:10-17 THE ARMOR OF GOD

[10]*Finally, be strong in the Lord and in the strength of his might.* [11]*Put on the whole armor of God, that you may be able to stand against the wiles of the devil.* [12]*For we are not contending against flesh and blood, but against the principalities, against the powers, against the world rulers of this present darkness, against the spiritual hosts of wickedness in the heavenly places.* [13]*Therefore take the whole armor of God, that you may be able to withstand in the evil day, and having done all, to stand.* [14]*Stand therefore, having girded your loins with truth, and having put on the breastplate of righteousness,* [15]*and having shod your feet with the equipment of the gospel of peace;* [16]*besides all these, taking the shield of faith, with which you can quench all the*

flaming darts of the evil one. ¹⁷*And take the helmet of salvation, and the sword of the Spirit, which is the word of God.*

OVERVIEW: The faithful must arm themselves with Christ, trusting in God's inconceivable might (CHRYSOSTOM, JEROME) to defend themselves against the subtle stratagem of evil powers (THEODORET, CHRYSOSTOM). This is a different kind of warfare, involving an alternative understanding of the cosmos (JEROME). The spirits rule not the natural order but within the wills of fallen humanity (THEODORET), which has fallen disastrously of its own choice (ORIGEN) and now must undertake a battle in the air (JEROME). The Old Testament speaks allegorically of the forthcoming day of battle (ORIGEN, JEROME), which will test our virtues to their limit (AMBROSIASTER). The faithful are girdled about by truth (CHRYSOSTOM). Righteousness, which must always accompany faith (MARIUS VICTORINUS), defends us like a breastplate (JEROME). Our feet must carry abroad the promised gospel (MARIUS VICTORINUS, THEODORET), which will bring peace both to the nations and to us (CHRYSOSTOM, JEROME). Faith, the chief of virtues (MARIUS VICTORINUS), assures us of God's providence (THEODORET) and thus acts as a shield against temptation (CHRYSOSTOM). Christ, as our helmet, protects our inward affections (JEROME). The Word of God is the sword of the Spirit (MARIUS VICTORINUS), by which we put the devil to flight (THEODORET, JOHN CASSIAN).

6:10 *Be Strong in the Lord*

THE STRENGTH OF HIS MIGHT. ORIGEN: To be *strong in the Lord* is to be strengthened in word and wisdom and the contemplation of truth. All these qualities are encompassed in the titles applying to Christ. The greatest of these is the strength of his might, which is stronger than all human virtues combined. Moral corruption lacks power in his presence. This one virtue, being strong in the Lord, is inconceivably powerful. Those who are wise in these matters call it the strength of his might. It has some analogy with bodily might but far exceeds it. This strength is beautiful, as a strong body is beautiful. EPISTLE TO THE EPHESIANS.[1]

THE CLIMAX. CHRYSOSTOM: This is the rhetoric Paul always employs when he is about to conclude his discourse. Did he not already indicate at the very beginning that every person's house is a bit like a military camp? Now you see he has drawn up every regiment ready for battle. He is ready to arm them and lead them into the struggle. HOMILY ON EPHESIANS 22.6.10.[2]

6:11 *The Whole Armor of God*

THE DEVIL'S WILES. CHRYSOSTOM: The enemy does not make war on us straightforwardly or openly but by his *wiles*. What are the devil's *wiles*? They consist in trying to capture us by some shortcut and always by deceit. . . . The devil never openly lays temptation before us. He does not mention idolatry out loud. But by his stratagems he

---

¹JTS 3:570. ²IOEP 4:335.

presents idolatrous choices to us, by persuasive words and by employing clever euphemisms. HOMILY ON EPHESIANS 22.6.11.[3]

CHRIST HIMSELF AS THE ARMOR OF GOD.
JEROME: From what we read of the Lord our Savior throughout the Scriptures, it is manifestly clear that the whole armor of Christ is the Savior himself. It is he whom we are asked to *put on*. It is one and the same thing to say *Put on the whole armor of God* and "Put on the Lord Jesus Christ." Our belt is truth and our breastplate is righteousness. The Savior is also called both *truth* and *righteousness*.[4] So no one can doubt that he himself is that very belt and breastplate. On this principle he is also to be understood as the *preparation of the gospel of peace*. He himself is the *shield of faith* and the *helmet of salvation*. He is the *sword of the Spirit*, because he is the Word of God, living and efficacious, the utterance of which is stronger than any helmet and sharp on both sides.[5] EPISTLE TO THE EPHESIANS 3.6.11.[6]

WHO MUST FIGHT IN THIS BATTLE? THEODORET: In ordinary battles the generals do not arm women or children or the aged. But our general, Christ the Lord, distributes this royal armory to all alike. He then teaches them the stratagems of the devil. This is what he means by the devil's *wiles*. EPISTLE TO THE EPHESIANS 6.11.[7]

6:12a Contending Against Principalities

IT IS NOT FLESH AND BLOOD THAT DECEIVE. JEROME: The battle is not against flesh and blood or ordinary temptations. The scene is the war of flesh against spirit. We are being incited to become entrapped in the works of the flesh.[8] . . . But this is not merely a physical temptation. It is not merely the inward struggle against flesh and blood as such. Rather Satan has cleverly transformed himself into an angel of light. He is striving to persuade us to regard him as a messenger of goodness. This is how he throws his full might into the struggle. He employs deceptive signs and lying omens. He sets before us every possible ruse of evil. Then, when he has so ensnared us that we trust him, he says to us, "Thus says the Lord." This is not flesh and blood deceiving us. It is not a typical human temptation. It is the work of principalities and powers, the ruler of darkness and spiritual wickedness. EPISTLE TO THE EPHESIANS 3.6.11.[9]

6:12b Against Powers and Rulers of This Present Darkness

PAUL'S UNIQUE TERM: WORLD RULERS OF THIS PRESENT DARKNESS. JEROME: We have elsewhere read the expression "world rulers" nowhere in the Old or the New Testament —only here. Paul the apostle employs this name because it was necessary for him, in addressing the Ephesians, to apply new terms to new and invisible subjects. EPISTLE TO THE EPHESIANS 3.6.11.[10]

THE AUTHORITY OF THE WORLD RULERS.
THEODORET: Paul calls them *world rulers* not because they have received authority to rule from God but because they have made

---

[3]IOEP 4:336. [4]Cf. Jer 23:6; Jn 14:6. [5]Here Jerome cites Hebrews 4:12. [6]Migne PL 26:543A-B [669]. [7]CPE 2:38. [8]Cf. Gal 5:19-21. [9]Migne PL 26:544B-C [671], following Origen *Epistle to the Ephesians* [JTS 3:571]. [10]Migne PL 26:547D-548A [675].

captive loose-living people as their willing slaves. The holy apostle has imitated the best sort of general. Wishing to drive out the unfit from his army, the astute general describes to them the exceptional courage of the enemy. EPISTLE TO THE EPHESIANS 6.12.[11]

6:12c *Spiritual Hosts of Wickedness in Heavenly Places*

HOSTS OF WICKEDNESS. ORIGEN: From what ancient Scripture is Paul drawing when he speaks of *the spiritual hosts of wickedness in the heavenly places?* My conjecture is that it comes out of the narratives written in Israel about wars and particular combats, like those of David and Goliath, and about the battles of the children of Israel against their enemies. . . . In each of these narratives there is some implication of the vanquishing and overcoming of demonic spiritual powers. EPISTLE TO THE EPHESIANS.[12]

INIQUITY IN HIGH PLACES. ORIGEN: Some spiritual creatures have sinned in heaven. It is against these that we now struggle, *against the spirits of iniquity in high places.* They first sinned in heaven. Now they are doing it again on earth. PALESTINIAN CATENA ON PSALM 118.119.[13]

WHETHER DEMONS COULD RESIDE IN THE SAME HEAVEN WITH GOD. JEROME: *Hosts of wickedness in heavenly places?* This does not mean that demons dwell in heaven but that the air above has received this name, as birds who fly through the air are called *fowls of heaven.*[14] . . . It is indeed impious to suppose that the spirits of wickedness in the heavens occupy the same heaven of which God says,

It is my throne.[15] EPISTLE TO THE EPHESIANS 3.6.11.[16]

6:13 *Being Able to Stand*

WHAT IS MEANT BY "THE EVIL DAY." JEROME: The *evil day* may arguably signify the present time. . . . But the better interpretation is that *to stand in the evil day* is a reference to the final consummation and judgment. Then the devil, our enemy and our adversary, will struggle to keep us in his clutches. Who will be freed from him? One who understands what is said of the poor and needy: *the Lord will deliver him in the evil day.*[17] . . . Still another interpretation, however, expounds this more simply: The Ephesians are now being encouraged to prepare for future temptations and persecutions. Paul the apostle in his prophetic spirit saw them as coming at a later time. They are being counseled to do anything they can that might enable them to stand in the faith of the gospel and not to lapse under persecution. EPISTLE TO THE EPHESIANS 3.6.13.[18]

THE WHOLE ARMOR OF GOD. AMBROSIASTER: We are waging war against the fiercest of enemies. He is skilled in every deceit. We must therefore keep on the lookout, with all circumspection and care, that wherever they test our resistance they will find us protected and ready. . . . Against earthly foes the body must be strengthened with food and the mind aroused by drink to become bold

---

[11]CPE 2:38. [12]JTS 3:572. [13]SC 189:378-81. Attributed to Origen in the edition of M. Harl, SC 190:705. [14]Dan 4:12. [15]Is 66:1. [16]Migne PL 26:547B-C [675]. [17]Ps 41:1. [18]Migne PL 26:549A-550B [676-78]. For the last interpretation see Theodoret *Epistle to the Ephesians* 6.13 [CPE 2:39].

enough to fight back. So against the spiritual weapons of iniquity we must fight spiritually. But our weapons must be sobriety and abstinence, that, having been imbued with the Holy Spirit, we may vanquish the unclean, warring spirits. EPISTLE TO THE EPHESIANS 6.17.1-2.[19]

6:14a Girding One's Loins with Truth

WHY BEGIN WITH THE GIRDLE? CHRYSOSTOM: The first art in tactics is to know how to stand firmly. From this firmness all else follows. . . . He is not speaking here of a literal girdle. He is setting in contrast, by this metaphor, the soldier who is slack and dissipated in his appetites, who lets his thoughts creep on the ground. . . . He speaks here of the loins. Just like the keel of a ship the loins are the central balancing support of our whole body. They are a kind of foundation. All is built up from them. . . . The girdle is used in combat to bind and hold together this foundation of ours. That is why we are also girdled when we run. It secures the strength within us. HOMILY ON EPHESIANS 23.6.14.[20]

6:14b Putting On the Breastplate of Righteousness

RIGHTEOUSNESS LIVES BY FAITH. MARIUS VICTORINUS: Faith lives in righteousness. Faith remains the fountain of all the virtues, as Paul has often stated. Righteousness is not as strong as faith because *righteousness lives by faith*.[21] But the effect of righteousness is accomplished by faith. So in this battle we must strive toward righteousness. Faith is proven to be true faith when we live righteously. Then faith is seen to be useful

to us, as the righteousness that accompanies faith is useful. EPISTLE TO THE EPHESIANS 2.6.13-14.[22]

WHY IS IT CALLED A BREASTPLATE? JEROME: One who has put on a sturdy breastplate is difficult to wound. Especially well-protected are those essential parts of the body upon which life depends. So put on the breastplate. Strap it together by iron rings and insert the hooks in their place. One protected by such a breastplate of righteousness will not be like a vulnerable stag that receives the arrow in his liver. He will not lapse into rage or lust. Rather he will be protected, having a clean heart, having God as the fashioner of his breastplate, since he fashions the whole armor for every one of the saints. EPISTLE TO THE EPHESIANS 3.6.14.[23]

6:15 Shod with the Equipment of the Gospel of Peace

WHAT IS THE SIGNIFICANCE OF FEET? MARIUS VICTORINUS: The gospel is to be carried abroad. It is to be preached among the nations. Wherever, then, it is preached, it must be heard. But so that all may hear, one must use one's feet to travel. And so do we travel with haste and urgency. EPISTLE TO THE EPHESIANS 2.6.15.[24]

HAVING SHOD YOUR FEET WITH THE EQUIPMENT OF THE GOSPEL OF PEACE. JEROME: It is asked whether he says *the gospel of peace* to distinguish it from another gospel. Or is it

---

[19]CSEL 81.3:123-24. [20]IOEP 4:344-45. [21]Hab 2:4; Rom 1:17. [22]BT 1972:201 [1290D-1291A]. [23]Migne PL 26:550D-551A [679]; this follows Origen *Epistle to the Ephesians* [JTS 3:573]. [24]BT 1972:202 [1291B].

rather the distinguishing property of the gospel that it may be called *the gospel of peace*? If anyone therefore has peace, he is shod with the gospel of Christ. With this footwear he is prepared to walk. Being prepared, however, he does well not to imagine himself already perfect. Rather he merely is prepared to press on and by pressing on hopes to arrive at the goal. EPISTLE TO THE EPHESIANS 3.6.15.[25]

ONLY BY BATTLING THE DEMONIC DO WE RECEIVE PEACE WITH GOD. CHRYSOSTOM:

This war against the demonic puts an end to the previous war against God. As we are making war with the devil, we are making peace with God. Have no fear, beloved, the victory is already won. This is the good news. HOMILY ON EPHESIANS 24.6.14-17.[26]

HOW LOVELY ARE THE FEET OF THOSE WHO BRING GOOD NEWS. THEODORET: Your footwear is not put on in order that you may walk about foolishly but to accomplish the course of the gospel. In this way you will receive the prophetic blessing: *How lovely on the mountains are the feet of him who brings good news.*[27] EPISTLE TO THE EPHESIANS 6.15.[28]

6:16 *Taking the Shield of Faith*

THE CAPITAL VIRTUE. MARIUS VICTORINUS:
He returns to that capital virtue, the shield of faith. It contains all the other virtues and brings them all to fulfillment. Unless we are armed with this shield we will not have the strength to battle courageously and resist all these deadly powers. But with the protection of faith we repel all these blows and whatever attacks come from the whole host of powers. EPISTLE TO THE EPHESIANS 2.6.16.[29]

THE SHIELD OF FAITH. THEODORET: In place of a shield you are to have faith. For this shield is the insignia of God's governance. This shield opens up to you the prizes of war, the eulogies of the victors, the crowns of heroes. All this quenches the *fiery darts of the evil one*. EPISTLE TO THE EPHESIANS 6.16.[30]

QUENCHING FIERY DARTS. CHRYSOSTOM: By *his darts* Paul means both temptations and perverse desires. He calls them fiery because that is the nature of the appetite. Faith is capable of commanding hosts of demons. How much more is faith capable of ordering the passions of the soul? HOMILY ON EPHESIANS 24.6.14-17.[31]

6:17a *Taking the Helmet of Salvation*

THE HELMET GUARDS THE HEAD. MARIUS VICTORINUS: It is Christ indeed who is the author of salvation. He is our head. He descended to us and redeemed us by his own mystery. It is he indeed who guards the heads of the faithful. Therefore he is the *helmet of salvation*. He is the Word by which the adverse powers are overcome and taken captive.... Christ, who is the Word of God, was sent to overcome all corruption and wickedness and even death itself. It is in this sense that Paul refers to *the sword of the Spirit, the Word of God*. EPISTLE TO THE EPHESIANS 2.6.17.[32]

THE HELMET OF SALVATION. JEROME: Because of this helmet of salvation all the senses in our head remain intact. It espe-

---

[25]Migne PL 26:551C [679]. [26]IOEP 4:352. [27]Is 52:7. [28]CPE 2:39. [29]BT 1972:202 [1291C]. [30]CPE 2:40. [31]IOEP 4:353. [32]BT 1972:203 [1292B].

cially protects the eyes. Solomon in Ecclesiastes[33] notes that *the eyes of the wise are in the head.* Paul understood the importance of headship. He knew why the eyes are located in the head. If Christ is the head of a person of faith and *the eyes of the wise are in the head,* it follows that all our senses, mind, thought, speech and counsel (if, that is, we are wise) are in Christ. Epistle to the Ephesians 3.6.17.[34]

6:17b *Taking the Sword of the Spirit*

The Sword of the Spirit. John Cassian: This is the sword that for our health spills the noxious blood that animates the matter of our sins, cutting out and excising whatever it finds in our soul that is carnal or

earthly and, once it has made us dead to vices, causing us to live to God and flourish in spiritual virtues. Conferences 20.8.11.[35]

The Word of God in Us. Theodoret: By *the sword of the Spirit* he means the activity of the Spirit. This is the *Word of God.* This means that just as God fashioned all by the Word, so the most Holy Spirit effects all that has to do with our salvation. With this sword the spiritual person rebukes the devil, and the devil flees.[36] Epistle to the Ephesians 6.17.[37]

---

[33]Eccles 2:14. [34]Migne PL 26:552A-B [680]. [35]CSEL 13:565, citing Abbot Pinuphius. [36]Here Theodoret cites James 4:7. [37]CPE 2:40.

6:18-24 PRAYERS FOR PAUL AND THE SAINTS

[18]*Pray at all times in the Spirit, with all prayer and supplication. To that end keep alert with all perseverance, making supplication for all the saints,* [19]*and also for me, that utterance may be given me in opening my mouth boldly to proclaim the mystery of the gospel,* [20]*for which I am an ambassador in chains; that I may declare it boldly, as I ought to speak.*

[21]*Now that you also may know how I am and what I am doing, Tychicus the beloved brother and faithful minister in the Lord will tell you everything.* [22]*I have sent him to you for this very purpose, that you may know how we are, and that he may encourage your hearts.*

[23]*Peace be to the brethren, and love with faith, from God the Father and the Lord Jesus Christ.* [24]*Grace be with all who love our Lord Jesus Christ with love undying.*

Overview: We are at war (Theodoret). We call for the king himself to attend the battle (Chrysostom). We enter the battle with fervent prayer (Marius Victorinus) that issues from a pure conscience (Ambrosiaster). All pray for all (Marius Victorinus). Let the inner man pray in the spirit, whether he prays aloud or not (Marius Victorinus). Paul asks the Ephesians to pray for him that he may have both insight and boldness (Ambrosiaster). Though he has a new revelation to preach (Jerome), he is suffering novel indignities (Ambrosiaster) and therefore needs encouragement (Marius Victorinus). The commendation of Tychicus will endear him to the Ephesians (Ambrosiaster, Jerome). It illustrates Paul's humility and solicitude (Marius Victorinus). Hoping to quell the discords of the Ephesians (Marius Victorinus) Paul prays for the peace that comes with faith and love (Ambrosiaster, Jerome). He blesses those who have true love for Christ (Theodoret), warning them against unseemly associations (Chrysostom) and promising them an eternal reward (Marius Victorinus).

6:18a Pray at All Times

The Inner Man Is Praying in Spirit Even When Not Praying Aloud. Marius Victorinus: This means that we should not say or utter particular words or recite them in our prayers as though they were premeditated or written down. We are to pray *in the spirit* and *at all times*. Let your deep affections enter into your praying. The inner spirit, that is, the inner man, is making his prayer with intense desire. He is praying all the time, so that even when he is not praying aloud he is still praying in the spirit. Epistle to the Ephesians 2.6.18.[1]

Distinguishing Prayer and Petition.

Marius Victorinus: When he says *through every prayer and petition*, I think he has this distinction in mind: It is a prayer when we speak the praises of God and recount his great works and when we give thanks and worship him. It is a petition when we pray to God either to pardon our sins or to offer his grace to us. Epistle to the Ephesians 2.6.18.[2]

With a Clean Conscience. Ambrosiaster: Insofar as our conduct is right we are rightly prepared for the Holy Spirit to abide in us. Hence we are more ready to obtain what we request. This therefore is what it means to pray in the Spirit at all times. We are directing our prayer to God with a clean conscience and sincere faith. One who prays with a polluted mind prays only in the flesh, not in the spirit. Epistle to the Ephesians 6.20.1.[3]

Calling Upon the King. Chrysostom: See how clever this blessed author is. He has armed them with the utmost protection. So now what remains? Only to call on the king and urge him to extend his hand. Homily on Ephesians 24.6.18-20.[4]

6:18b Making Supplication for the Saints

With All Perseverance. Marius Victorinus: Some might think that the phrase *at all times* means only the daytime. But, so that he could amplify the force of *at all times*, what does he say? *With all persever-*

---

[1]BT 1972:204 [1292C-D]. [2]BT 1972:204 [1292D-1293A]. [3]CSEL 81.3:124. [4]IOEP 4:354.

ance. This calls us to a certain persistent disposition of the mind. We do not pray as if we were asleep. This is what some sound like who pray by reciting or reading familiar phrases or uttering them routinely from memory. EPISTLE TO THE EPHESIANS 2.6.18.[5]

SUPPLICATION FOR ALL THE SAINTS. MARIUS VICTORINUS: The saints themselves, with the bishops and apostles and elders, are called to pray on behalf of the faithful and the catechumens and all the other members of the body. It is typical of Paul to make mention of the whole people of God in prayer. He also calls upon the whole people of God to pray on behalf of their leaders, bishops and saints, and then he adds: *Pray for me too*. EPISTLE TO THE EPHESIANS 2.6.18-19.[6]

KEEP ALERT. THEODORET: Those who have wars continually pressing on them do not even sleep. Therefore the holy apostle tells them under conditions of battle to keep awake and pray constantly, not giving in to the pains of the body but to bear them with the utmost fortitude. EPISTLE TO THE EPHESIANS 6.18.[7]

6:19a *Praying for Paul*

THOSE WHOM HE ADMONISHED HE NOW ASKS FOR PRAYERS. MARIUS VICTORINUS: Isn't this wonderful? From those whom he himself has just now admonished, those whom he has instructed, to whom he has preached the gospel, he now asks for help. He is asking them for their prayers. He goes on to explain what he is asking them to pray for: *that utterance may be given to me*. His prayer is definite and specific, that a particular profit may accrue. EPISTLE TO THE EPHESIANS 2.6.18-19.[8]

HE REQUESTS PRAYER FOR FULL AND BOLD UTTERANCE. AMBROSIASTER: He exhorts them to pray for him in two ways: first that his thoughts may be filled by the Spirit for the full declaration of the mystery, and second that he may be given a faculty of bold utterance in proclaiming it. EPISTLE TO THE EPHESIANS 6.20.2.[9]

6:19b *Boldly Proclaiming the Mysteries of the Gospel*

ONLY WITH PURITY OF HEART IS THE MOUTH OPENED BOLDLY. ORIGEN: Boldness of speech is a possibility only and always for those who have a heart that does not condemn them[10] . . . and therefore the one who boldly makes known the mysteries is rare, because those who have boldness before God are rare. EPISTLE TO THE EPHESIANS.[11]

LET THE TREASURIES BE OPENED. JEROME: This is to be understood as if he said, "Let the treasuries be opened. Let the promises hidden from ages be revealed. Let the Spirit enter to bring forth those things that have been concealed." That this is indeed the meaning of this passage . . . is clarified by what follows: *in confidence*, he says, *to make known the mystery of the gospel*. EPISTLE TO THE EPHESIANS 3.6.20.[12]

---

[5]BT 1972:204 [1293A-B]. [6]BT 1972:205 [1293B-C]. [7]CPE 2:40. [8]BT 1972:205 [1293C]. [9]CSEL 81.3:125. [10]Here Origen cites 1 John 3:21-22. [11]JTS 3:575. [12]Migne PL 26:553A [681], following Origen *Epistle to the Ephesians* [JTS 3:574].

6:20a *An Ambassador in Chains*

AMBASSADOR IN CHAINS. AMBROSIASTER: This prayer God hears gladly. The apostle is being despised. God's own mission is under challenge. So God will certainly not withhold his gifts from one who is upholding God's own cause. Custom and law forbid the infliction of harm on human ambassadors. So would it not be presumptuous and rash to bring on the ambassadors of God not only harm but death? EPISTLE TO THE EPHESIANS 6.20.3.[13]

6:20b *Asking for Boldness to Speak*

PETITION FOR BOLDNESS. MARIUS VICTORINUS: *Boldly* means "so that I may not fail to accomplish it fully and that my chains may not so work on my mind as to prevent my accomplishing it, the task of expounding the mystery, as I ought." EPISTLE TO THE EPHESIANS 2.6.20.[14]

6:21a *Making Known Who Paul Is and What He Is Doing*

THAT YOU MAY KNOW. AMBROSIASTER: Through Tychicus the Ephesians would learn how the apostle is faring, and he would ascertain how things are going in Ephesus. There was no doubt in their minds that the apostle's actions were godly. But the people at Ephesus needed to know more detail about how he was acting in response to idolatrous charges and ploys. And from the Ephesians Paul needed to know whether or not they were growing. EPISTLE TO THE EPHESIANS 6.22.[15]

WHY TYCHICUS WAS SENT TO EPHESUS. JEROME: This might be understood in two ways: Either Tychicus was sent to Ephesus to announce to them that Paul's chains had become famous in the whole praetorium and his imprisonment had been profitable to the faith of the gospel . . . or Tychicus was sent to tell them more about Paul's life and daily work, of which they were not aware, so as to give them a clearer pattern of how to live. EPISTLE TO THE EPHESIANS 3.6.21-22.[16]

6:21b *Tychicus Will Tell Everything*

THE BELOVED BROTHER. AMBROSIASTER: So that they might be happy to obey and listen to Tychicus Paul calls him a most beloved brother and a useful servant of God. EPISTLE TO THE EPHESIANS 6.22.[17]

MINISTER IN THE LORD. MARIUS VICTORINUS: Note that Tychicus is described not as a minister to Paul but as a minister in the Lord with regard to the gospel and the mystery. EPISTLE TO THE EPHESIANS 2.6.21.[18]

6:22 *Sent for This Purpose*

SENT FOR THIS VERY PURPOSE. MARIUS VICTORINUS: Tychicus is sent to give the Ephesians instructions not on his own accord. Rather he was sent by Paul for this purpose. Such was Paul's concern for them and his desire that they should be well informed. EPISTLE TO THE EPHESIANS 2.6.22.[19]

6:23 *Peace and Love with Faith*

TO OVERCOME DISCORD. MARIUS VICTOR-

---

[13]CSEL 81.3:125. [14]BT 1972:206 [1294A]. [15]CSEL 81.3:125. [16]Migne PL 26:553C-554A [682-83]. [17]CSEL 81.3:125. [18]BT 1972:206 [1294B]. [19]BT 1972:206 [1294C].

INUS: The last part of the letter is a petition. His prayer and desire is for peace to the brethren, also love and then faith. For above he has already noted that there was discord among them. Now he adds thanks to those who display faith and who love our Lord Jesus Christ. Thus all is concluded with peace against discord, love eliciting concord and faith in God. EPISTLE TO THE EPHESIANS 2.6.23-24.[20]

HOW PEACE, LOVE AND FAITH ARE INTERCONNECTED. AMBROSIASTER: He prays for peace, which is the door of love, to be with the family of God. Having come into this family through the peacemaking of God, he prays that they may abide in the love that comes from faith. For this faith is the gift of God the Father and our Lord Jesus Christ. EPISTLE TO THE EPHESIANS 6.23.[21]

WITH FAITH. CHRYSOSTOM: In saying *peace be to the brethren and love with faith*, he speaks comprehensively. He does not speak simply of love as such or faith as such but love with faith. He means either this or that they are to have a faith that will make them confident about good things to come. The *peace* is toward God and so is the *love*. For where there is peace there also will be love. This love is always *with faith*, for there is no good in love without faith. Love cannot even exist without faith. HOMILY ON EPHESIANS 24.6.23.[22]

HOW PEACE ENCOURAGES FAITHFUL LOVE. JEROME: There are many gifts bestowed by God the Father and our Lord Jesus Christ, but of all these peace has a crucial place. This peace passes all understanding. It pre-

serves the body and mind of the saints. It is a certain serenity and tranquillity of a mind at rest. It is protected from the universal storm and maelstrom of perturbations. So also is *love with faith*, which at the same time is given to us by God the Father and the Holy Spirit, so that we may love God from the whole heart and our neighbor as ourselves. EPISTLE TO THE EPHESIANS 3.6.23.[23]

6:24 Grace Be with All Who Love Our Lord Jesus Christ

WITH LOVE UNDYING. MARIUS VICTORINUS: He adds *with love undying*, or in imperishability. For his prayers are not only for the present life but for the coming one as well, which is contained in the hope and promise of Christ. EPISTLE TO THE EPHESIANS 2.6.23-24.[24]

GRACE BE WITH ALL WHO LOVE. THEODORET: Grace is not simply bestowed indiscriminately upon all but on those who love the Lord and especially upon those who, as well as loving, keep his life-giving laws. Let us keep them also. By keeping them our love for him will be confirmed. EPISTLE TO THE EPHESIANS 6.24.[25]

FROM ROME. THEODORET: The letter to the Ephesians was written from Rome by the hand of Tychicus. EPISTLE TO THE EPHESIANS 6.24.[26]

---

[20]BT 1972:206-7 [1294C-D]. [21]CSEL 81.3:126. [22]IOEP 4:361-62. [23]Migne PL 26:554A-B [683]. [24]BT 1972:207 [1294D]. [25]CPE 2:41-42. [26]CPE 2:42.

The Epistle to the Philippians

1:1-2 THE GREETING

¹*Paul and Timothy, servants*ᵃ *of Christ Jesus,*
*To all the saints in Christ Jesus who are at Philippi, with the bishops*ᵇ *and deacons:*
²*Grace to you and peace from God our Father and the Lord Jesus Christ.*

a Or slaves b Or overseers

OVERVIEW: Paul describes himself as a servant of Christ without mentioning his special place as an apostle (CHRYSOSTOM, AMBROSIASTER). He calls all true believers *saints* (THEODORET, AMBROSIASTER). He blesses the bishops and deacons at Philippi who have assisted him (CHRYSOSTOM, THEODORET), affirming the harmony between God the Father and Christ the Lord (AMBROSIASTER).

1:1a Servants of Christ Jesus

DISREGARDING HIS APOSTOLIC STATUS. AMBROSIASTER: He keeps silence about his status as an apostle. He is writing to people who already know who he is and have an informed opinion of him. He suppresses his dignity. He declares his lowly state,[1] because the one who confesses Christ as Lord is all the more free and has salvation. EPISTLE TO THE PHILIPPIANS 1.1.1.[2]

SLAVE OF CHRIST, FREE FROM SIN. CHRYSOSTOM: He calls himself a slave and not an apostle. This is a great honor, to be *a slave of*

Christ—not merely to be called a slave but to be one. One who is a *slave of Christ* is truly free from sin. If he is truly a slave of Christ, he is not a slave in any other realm, since then he would not be a slave of Christ but only half so. HOMILY ON PHILIPPIANS 2.1.1-2.[3]

1:1b To the Saints at Philippi

TO ALL THE SAINTS. AMBROSIASTER: He writes to the saints in his customary manner, but his intent is to write to those who are *saints in Christ Jesus*, specifically those who confess that he is divine and human. . . . He is not writing to those who by their own deceptions suppress the truth. EPISTLE TO THE PHILIPPIANS 1.1.1.[4]

TO THE BAPTIZED AND THEIR SHEPHERDS. THEODORET: He sends his news to everyone, both those who have been deemed worthy of

---

[1]A servant; literally, a "slave." [2]CSEL 81.3:129-30. [3]IOEP 5:7. [4]CSEL 81.3:130.

ordination and those who are shepherded by them. By *those who are holy* he means those who have worthily received holy baptism. EPISTLE TO THE PHILIPPIANS 1.1-2.[5]

WITH THEIR BISHOPS AND DEACONS. THEODORET: He applies the term *bishops* to presbyters, for at that time they had both names.[6] . . . And it is clear that he makes this assumption here also. For he joins the deacons to the bishops, making no mention of the presbyters. Furthermore, it was not possible for many bishops to be shepherds to one city. So it is clear that he is calling the presbyters *bishops*; yet in this same letter he calls the blessed Epaphroditus their apostle,[7] . . . and thus he indicates plainly that he was entrusted with an episcopal function because he had the name of an apostle. EPISTLE TO THE PHILIPPIANS 1.1-2.[8]

WHY HE ADDRESSES THE CLERGY IN PHILIPPI AND NOT ELSEWHERE. CHRYSOSTOM: Nowhere else does Paul write specifically to the clergy—not in Rome, in Corinth, in Ephesus or anywhere. Rather he typically writes jointly to all who are holy, faithful and beloved. But in this case he addresses specifically the bishops and deacons. Why? Because it was they who had borne fruit and they who had sent Epaphroditus to him. HOMILY ON PHILIPPIANS 2.1.1-2.[9]

1:2 *Grace and Peace from God Our Father and Our Lord Jesus Christ*

THE HARMONY BETWEEN GOD THE FATHER AND CHRIST THE LORD. AMBROSIASTER: It is evident that while God is called *Father*, Christ Jesus is called *Lord*. Does it not then appear that the Lord does not possess equal dignity with the Father? That might seem true in the world of human beings, but between God the Father and Christ the Lord there is complete harmony.[10] EPISTLE TO THE PHILIPPIANS 1.2.[11]

---

[5]CPE 2:44. [6]Here Theodoret cites Acts 20:28 and Titus 1:5. [7]Here Theodoret cites Philippians 2:25. [8]CPE 2:44-45. Cf. Chrysostom *Homily on Philippians* 2.1.1-2 [IOEP 5:7-8]. [9]IOEP 5:8. [10]Here Ambrosiaster cites John 17:6. [11]CSEL 81.3:130.

1:3-11 PAUL'S LOVE FOR THE PHILIPPIANS

[3]*I thank my God in all my remembrance of you,* [4]*always in every prayer of mine for you all making my prayer with joy,* [5]*thankful for your partnership in the gospel from the first day until now.* [6]*And I am sure that he who began a good work in you will bring it to completion at the day of Jesus Christ.* [7]*It is right for me to feel thus about you all, because I hold you in my heart, for you are all partakers*

with me of grace, both in my imprisonment and in the defense and confirma-
tion of the gospel. ⁸For God is my witness, how I yearn for you all with the
affection of Christ Jesus. ⁹And it is my prayer that your love may abound more
and more, with knowledge and all discernment, ¹⁰so that you may approve
what is excellent, and may be pure and blameless for the day of Christ, ¹¹filled
with the fruits of righteousness which come through Jesus Christ, to the glory
and praise of God.

OVERVIEW: Paul points to the great responsibility of these church leaders, calling them to modesty (CHRYSOSTOM) and to complete dependence upon God (AUGUSTINE). He praises their faith (THEODORET) and declares his high opinion of them and affection for them (AMBROSIASTER). Grace shows forth through suffering (CHRYSOSTOM, THEODORET). As he reminds them of Christian essentials, he calls them to the special blessings of Christian purity (CHRYSOSTOM, THEODORET).

1:3 Thanking God in All Remembrance of Them

GIVING THANKS THAT THE CLERGY HAVE REMAINED UNCORRUPTED. THEODORET: Paul praises God every time he remembers the clergy of Philippi, who received the proclamation of the gospel cordially and have remained uncorrupted up to the present. EPISTLE TO THE PHILIPPIANS 1.3-5.[1]

1:4 Making His Prayer with Joy

ALWAYS IN EVERY PRAYER. CHRYSOSTOM: I both glorify God and offer prayers for you. The fact that you are already advancing in excellence does not prevent my praying further for you. HOMILY ON PHILIPPIANS 2.1.4.[2]

1:5 Partnership in the Gospel

MY COMPANIONS IN PREACHING. CHRYSOSTOM: Here he gives them a great testimonial, a truly great one and such as one might give to apostles and evangelists. "The fact that you have been put in charge of one city," he says, "does not mean that you care for that one alone, but you do everything so as to become partakers of my labors wherever I am. It is as though you are with me everywhere as my coworkers and companions in preaching. Not once, twice or three times but on all occasions, from the time when you believed until now, you have shown the zeal of apostles.". . . For the care of the saints is no small thing. It is indeed a great one, for it makes you partakers of the blessings laid up for them. HOMILY ON PHILIPPIANS 2.1.5.[3]

1:6 Bringing to Completion a Good Work

GOD WHO BEGINS A GOOD WORK IN US WILL COMPLETE IT. CHRYSOSTOM: See how he teaches them to be modest. Having just given them a superb testimonial, in order that they should not feel down and out as

---

[1]CPE 2:45. [2]IOEP 5:9. [3]IOEP 5:9.

human beings are so apt to feel, he immediately teaches them to refer both the past and the future—everything—to Christ, who will bring to completion what he has begun in them. He does not take away anything from their achievement, for he has said, *I rejoice because of your fellowship*, obviously pointing to their own very high level of accountability. But he does not imply that the achievement was theirs alone. Rather it was primarily God's work in them. HOMILY ON PHILIPPIANS 2.1.6.[4]

THROUGH THE COOPERATION OF GRACE AND WILL. AUGUSTINE: God can work in our acts without our help. But when we will the deed, he cooperates with us.[5] ON GRACE AND FREE WILL 32.[6]

1:7a Holding Them in His Heart

THE GROUNDS OF PAUL'S CONFIDENCE. AMBROSIASTER: Paul had always found the Philippians to be immovable in their devotion to God. He knew how straight and unwearied their course was. He knew they were worthy to share in his own joy. People who share the same faith have good reason to rejoice together in the hope of future immortality and glory. EPISTLE TO THE PHILIPPIANS 1.7.[7]

1:7b Partakers of Grace

IN PRISON PAUL REMEMBERS. CHRYSOSTOM: His longing for them is a great longing indeed. For he *has them in his heart*. Within the very walls of his prison cell he affectionately remembers the Philippians. This is no small form of praise. The love of this saint springs not from personal preferences but

from good judgment and upright thinking. . . . It is wonderful that he has them in his heart in his imprisonment. Even *in my defense* before the judgment seat, he says, you did not slip from my memory. HOMILY ON PHILIPPIANS 2.1.7.[8]

PARTNERS IN GRACE AMID AFFLICTION. THEODORET: His praise for them is strong. He calls them *partners in grace*. But by *grace* he is referring to his sufferings, as is made clear in what he goes on to teach, that *it has been granted to you that for the sake of Christ you should not only believe in him but also suffer for his sake*.[9] EPISTLE TO THE PHILIPPIANS 1.7.[10]

1:7c Imprisonment and the Confirmation of the Gospel

HOW HIS CHAINS CONFIRM HIS TESTIMONY. CHRYSOSTOM: His chains are without doubt a *confirmation of the gospel*. How? Because if he had refused the bonds, he would have been seen as a deceiver. But the one who endures everything, including persecution and imprisonment, shows that he does not suffer them for any human reason but on account of God, who rights the balance. . . . See how absolutely he turns everything on its head. For what others might view as a weakness or reproach, this he calls *confirmation*. HOMILY ON PHILIPPIANS 2.1.7.[11]

1:8a God Witnesses to Paul's Yearning

---

[4]IOEP 5:11. [5]Cf. Phil 2:13. [6]Migne PL 44:900-901. [7]CSEL 81.3:131-32. [8]IOEP 5:12. [9]Phil 1:29. [10]CPE 2:46. [11]IOEP 5:12-13.

WHY HE CALLS GOD TO WITNESS. AMBROSI-ASTER: He calls God to witness that his deep affection for them may be understood. One who feels so deeply about something is ready to call God as his witness to underscore his feeling. Through this he inspires a corresponding love in them for himself. For it is in being loved that we feel love. He therefore loves all these partners not with a human desire but in the love of Christ, not merely with emotional affection but with spiritual affection. They share with him in the knowledge of the mystery of God and the incarnation of the Lord Jesus Christ. EPISTLE TO THE PHILIPPIANS 1.8.[12]

1:8b *With the Affection of Christ Jesus*

THE DEPTH OF HIS AFFECTION. CHRYSOSTOM: Since he had said that they had fellowship with him, in order that they would not suppose that he longed for them for this reason and not simply for their own sake, he therefore adds *in the bowels of Christ*.[13] What does this mean? It means "in accord with the deep affection we have for Christ, because you are faithful, because you love Christ, because your love stands in accord with Christ." But he does not say "love" but uses the warmer term *bowels*, as if he had "become as a father to you through kinship with Christ." . . . "I cannot," he says in effect, "express in words the greatness of my longing. It is not even possible to articulate. Therefore I leave it to God to know, who dwells in the heart." But suppose he had just been flattering them—would he then have called God to witness? That would not have been safe. HOMILY ON PHILIPPIANS 3.1.8-11.[14]

1:9a *That Love May Abound*

ABOUNDING IN LOVE UNCEASING. CHRYSOSTOM: There is no end to such love. Anyone who is loved so deeply, loved in this way, wishes to be loved all the more. There is no measure to love. One who loves and is loved in return does not wish that love to stop but to increase. HOMILY ON PHILIPPIANS 3.1.8-11.[15]

1:9b *With Knowledge and Discernment*

DISCERNING WHAT IS USEFUL. AMBROSIASTER: He wishes, with God's assistance, to pour into them pure Christian doctrine, that their faith will be firm and that they will see clearly all the vast implications of their faith. He wants them to be able to distinguish what is useful from what is useless. He prays that they may adorn the teaching of the Lord with works of righteousness, producing the fruit of immortality to bring about an abundance of good things. This will be the glory of the apostle to the Gentiles. EPISTLE TO THE PHILIPPIANS 1.11.[16]

1:10 *Approving What Is Excellent, Being Pure and Blameless*

APPROVE WHAT IS EXCELLENT. CHRYSOSTOM: He prays that they will not receive any corrupted doctrine under the pretense of love. HOMILY ON PHILIPPIANS 3.1.8-11.[17]

1:11a *Filled with the Fruits of Righteousness*

---

[12]CSEL 81.3:132. [13]The literal translation of *affection*. [14]IOEP 5:17. Cf. Theodoret *Epistle to the Philippians* 1.8.2 [CPE 2:46]. [15]IOEP 5:18. [16]CSEL 81.3:132. [17]IOEP 5:18. Cf. Theodoret *Epistle to the Philippians* 1.9-10 [CPE 2:46].

FILLED WITH FRUITS. CHRYSOSTOM: Along with good teaching he prays that they might have an upright life, and not simply upright but truly filled with the fruits of righteousness. He is not speaking here of a kind of uprightness or virtue that tries despairingly to grow without Christ. HOMILY ON PHILIPPIANS 3.1.8-11.[18]

GOD GLORIFIED BY THE FRUITS OF RIGHTEOUSNESS. THEODORET: Enjoy these gifts! Keep your faith uncontaminated! Present the fruit of righteousness to God, so that God will be celebrated by all. EPISTLE TO THE PHILIPPIANS 1.11.[19]

1:11b *The Glory and Praise of God*

[18]IOEP 5:18. [19]CPE 2:46-47.

1:12-18 GOOD NEWS AND FALSE TEACHERS

[12]*I want you to know, brethren, that what has happened to me has really served to advance the gospel,* [13]*so that it has become known throughout the whole praetorian guard[c] and to all the rest that my imprisonment is for Christ;* [14]*and most of the brethren have been made confident in the Lord because of my imprisonment, and are much more bold to speak the word of God without fear.*

[15]*Some indeed preach Christ from envy and rivalry, but others from good will.* [16]*The latter do it out of love, knowing that I am put here for the defense of the gospel;* [17]*the former proclaim Christ out of partisanship, not sincerely but thinking to afflict me in my imprisonment.* [18]*What then? Only that in every way, whether in pretense or in truth, Christ is proclaimed; and in that I rejoice.*

c *Greek* in the whole praetorium

OVERVIEW: The gospel is becoming known (AMBROSIASTER) precisely through Paul's imprisonment (THEODORET). Despite the dangers caused by insincere and false preaching (AMBROSIASTER), Paul's fortitude is giving his brothers and sisters much confidence (THEODORET, CHRYSOSTOM). The motive of preaching for some has been envy and rivalry (CHRYSOSTOM), for others good will and love (MARIUS VICTORINUS). But God is making good use even of their bad intentions (MARIUS VICTORINUS). Against their will the enemies of truth cooperate with truth (THEODORET). This cannot become an excuse for heresy or deceit (THEODORET). Some may preach the truth without themselves standing in the truth (AUGUSTINE).

1:12 *Advancing the Gospel*

WHAT HAS HAPPENED TO ME. THEODORET: In their great concern for Paul the Philippians had sent the blessed Epaphroditus to help him. For this reason he writes to comfort them in return. He wants to show that the chains that bind him have themselves become the instruments of salvation to many. By *the progress of the gospel* he means the multitude of believers. EPISTLE TO THE PHILIPPIANS 1.12-13.[1]

1:13a The Gospel Known to the Praetorian Guard

THE GOSPEL BECOMING KNOWN. AMBROSIASTER: His imprisonment for Christ's sake is becoming known. This is his distinctive honor. Now others who love him may rejoice with him. EPISTLE TO THE PHILIPPIANS 1.17.1.[2]

1:13b Imprisonment for Christ

ALL THE REST. AMBROSIASTER: Who are *all the rest?* The whole of Jewry, in addition to all the churches of the Gentiles. The former still has precedence, since to them the promise was first made. EPISTLE TO THE PHILIPPIANS 1.17.1.[3]

1:14a Confidence in the Lord Because of Paul's Imprisonment

THE EFFECT OF MY IMPRISONMENT. THEODORET: "My chains," he says in effect, "have themselves become the source of courage to the others. They can easily see that I bear adversity with joy. So they come to preach the divine gospel fearlessly." EPISTLE TO THE PHILIPPIANS 1.14.[4]

CONFIDENT IN THE LORD. CHRYSOSTOM: "It is confidence *in the Lord*, not in me as such, that is elicited by my chains. As others take courage from my bonds, so do I. As I become the cause of confidence to others, much more does this have an effect within myself." Note how Paul, even in speaking of great things, remains aware of the tendency toward pride and does not cease to enjoin modesty. HOMILY ON PHILIPPIANS 3.1.14.[5]

1:14b Boldness to Speak the Word of God

SPEAKING WITHOUT FEAR. AMBROSIASTER: His constancy inspires others to be fearless in preaching. They are learning by the apostle's example that God is present to watch over those who love him. This itself has an effect upon the misguided brethren who have been preaching the Word of God as if from envy, prompted not by confidence or love of God but by competitiveness. EPISTLE TO THE PHILIPPIANS 1.17.2.[6]

1:15 Motives for Preaching

SOME PREACH FROM ENVY. CHRYSOSTOM: After the imprisonment of the apostle many unbelievers became so bold as to try to excite a fierce persecution from the emperor. So they apparently also started preaching Christ in their own way, but only in order that the emperor's anger might be increased. Thus, they imagined, by the spread of the preaching the whole of his anger would fall on Paul's head. So from Paul's imprisonment two lines of action have sprung. First, those

---

[1]CPE 2:47. [2]CSEL 81.3:133. [3]CSEL 81.3:133. [4]CPE 2:47. [5]IOEP 5:20. [6]CSEL 81.3:133-34.

of good will took great courage from it. The other party appeared to be preaching Christ but was really hoping for Paul's destruction. These are the ones who were *preaching Christ from envy and rivalry*. In effect he is saying: "Those who envy my reputation and constancy and wish for my death work as rivals." Or: "Wishing to be honored themselves, they were trying to use my reputation as leverage." By contrast the others are preaching *through good will*, without any hypocrisy and with the utmost zeal. HOMILY ON PHILIPPIANS 3.1.15.[7]

1:16a *Preaching Out of Love*

DISTINGUISHING PREACHING FROM ENVY, FROM GOOD WILL, FROM LOVE AND FROM EVIL MOTIVES. MARIUS VICTORINUS: Some preach Christ *from envy* because of their malice and contentiousness. What they feel is simply envy. They do not preach Christ in a holy and decent manner but merely in order to heap up grief upon me and increase my trial and sorrow. They want to flaunt their delight in my bondage. . . . Others preach not with the motive of adding further grief to my bonds but to claim the glory of preaching for themselves. Meanwhile the faithful preach Christ *through good will* in sincere belief, not out of envy but because what they believe is good. It is the gospel. So while some are preaching Christ in insolence, to bring punishment and tribulation on me, others are preaching from love. They remain dear to me. They do not insult me because I am in this state for the defense of the gospel. EPISTLE TO THE PHILIPPIANS 1.15-17.[8]

1:16b *For Defense of the Gospel*

COMMANDED TO PREACH. CHRYSOSTOM:

What does he mean by saying *I am put here for the defense of the gospel?* "Even those who preach out of envy are helping me prepare for the account I must give to God. How so? Having been appointed to preach," he says, "I am going to submit a reckoning and defend the work that I was appointed to do. My vindication will be easy because there are many who have been rightly instructed and have faith. But even those who preach out of envy inadvertently demonstrate how it is possible to do a good work even when one's motive is not good." HOMILY ON PHILIPPIANS 5.1.16.[9]

1:17 *Proclaiming Christ Out of Partisanship*

INSINCERE PREACHING. TERTULLIAN: What is skewed among those who *proclaim Christ out of partisanship* is their temperament and their motive, not the content of their proclamation. Paul exposes these bad tempers as the sole cause of their disunity, but these bad tempers apparently do not have a bad effect on the mysteries of the faith. There is still only one Christ and one God. This does not change, regardless of what motives may come into play in preaching him. So Paul is able to say that *it is nothing to me whether Christ be preached on a pretext or in truth; Christ is proclaimed.* What really matters is the one who is preached, whether through pretentiousness or in true faith. When Christ is preached *in truth* he is being preached faithfully. The rule of truth remains what it is, regardless of who preaches

---

[7]IOEP 5:2; cf. Theodoret *Epistle to the Philippians* 1.15 [CPE 2:47]. [8]BT 1972:72-73 [1197C-1198D]. [9]IOEP 5:21.

it—better or worse, there is but one truth. Meanwhile the conduct of preachers varies. Some preach truly, single-mindedly. Others preach insincerely, with affectations. AGAINST MARCION 5.20.1.[10]

HIS RESPONSE NOT MALICIOUS. CHRYSOSTOM: Note Paul's wisdom. He does not hurl around scurrilous accusations. He calmly describes what has come to pass. . . . Though the aim and motives on which they acted were corrupted, still the preaching itself was not corrupted. And the preaching of Christ occurred despite it all. HOMILY ON PHILIPPIANS 3.1.1.[11]

1:18 In Every Way Christ Is Proclaimed

THE WELCOME OUTCOME. MARIUS VICTORINUS: The outcome is very welcome to me: They preach about Christ. They speak Christ's name. They confess that he is God and the Son of God, even if in a different spirit. For by this celebration, exertion and activity, Christ is proclaimed by all. So I too obtain my wish, which is that Christ should be proclaimed. And if that is so, they are wrong to imagine that they have cast me into grief. EPISTLE TO THE PHILIPPIANS 1.18.[12]

PREACHING THE TRUTH WITHOUT BEING IN THE TRUTH. AUGUSTINE: There were in the times of the apostles some who were preaching truth but not in truth, that is, not in a true spirit. Of these the apostle says that their proclamation was not pure but was preached through *envy and rivalry*. Even though they were tolerated who proclaimed the truth without purity of mind, they were not praised, as if to assume that they were preaching with a pure mind. So Paul says of them that, whether in pretense or in truth, Christ is proclaimed. Yet he certainly does not imply that Christ may now be denied in order to be later proclaimed. ON LYING 16.[13]

PREACHING GOOD THINGS POORLY. THEODORET: Even against their will, Paul shows, the enemies of truth inadvertently cooperate with truth. Some are foolish enough to think that this can also be said about heresies. They ought to have perceived that the holy apostle's statement here is not an imperative sentence but a declarative one. He did not say "Let it be preached" but *It is being preached*. Moreover, he does not condemn those people for preaching bad things but for preaching good things poorly, being led not by reverence for God but by partisanship. EPISTLE TO THE PHILIPPIANS 1.18.[14]

---

[10]CCL 1:723-24. [11]IOEP 5:22. [12]BT 1972:73-74 [1199A-B]. [13]Migne PL 40:527. [14]CPE 2:48, following Chrysostom *Homily on Philippians* 3.1.8 [IOEP 5:22-23].

1:19-26 PAUL'S CHOICE TO REMAIN

[19]*Yes, and I shall rejoice. For I know that through your prayers and the help of the Spirit of Jesus Christ this will turn out for my deliverance,* [20]*as it is my eager expectation and hope that I shall not be at all ashamed, but that with full courage now as always Christ will be honored in my body, whether by life or by death.* [21]*For to me to live is Christ, and to die is gain.* [22]*If it is to be life in the flesh, that means fruitful labor for me. Yet which I shall choose I cannot tell.* [23]*I am hard pressed between the two. My desire is to depart and be with Christ, for that is far better.* [24]*But to remain in the flesh is more necessary on your account.* [25]*Convinced of this, I know that I shall remain and continue with you all, for your progress and joy in the faith,* [26]*so that in me you may have ample cause to glory in Christ Jesus, because of my coming to you again.*

OVERVIEW: Even that which is unworthily proclaimed may yet attest the truth (MARIUS VICTORINUS). Assured of the future, Paul humbly seeks the prayers of the Philippians (CHRYSOSTOM). He knows that he will be vindicated even in death (CHRYSOSTOM) and will magnify Christ either by miraculously escaping death or by steadfastly enduring it (MARIUS VICTORINUS). To prove that he is master of adversity (AMBROSIASTER) he enjoins detachment from life without negating its creaturely values (AMBROSE, CHRYSOSTOM, MARIUS VICTORINUS). By speaking of a choice he indicates his discernment and control over his own future (MARIUS VICTORINUS, CHRYSOSTOM). He reminds us of the soul's origin and destiny (AMBROSE, ORIGEN). He teaches patience in the face of death (TERTULLIAN). By remaining alive Paul brings good to many at his own expense (AMBROSIASTER, THEODORET). His decision reveals his benevolence toward the Philippians (MARIUS VICTORINUS, CHRYSOS-

TOM) and is supported by a true prediction (THEODORET). The glory of the Philippians is to exult in Christ (MARIUS VICTORINUS). The more they improve, the more he rejoices (CHRYSOSTOM).

1:19a Rejoicing

EVEN THAT WHICH IS UNWORTHILY PRO-CLAIMED MAY YET ATTEST THE TRUTH. MARIUS VICTORINUS: It may seem that he had been rather rash and daring in his willing and joyful acceptance of the fact that Christ was being proclaimed in any fashion, even by the unscrupulous, even through insolence and envy. But in all this he was relying on the assurance and benevolence of God, confident of what will come to be by the grace of Christ through his Spirit. EPISTLE TO THE PHILIPPIANS 1.19-20.[1]

---

[1]BT 1972:74 [1199B-C].

1:19b *Through Prayers and the Help of the Spirit*

YOUR PRAYERS IN THE SPIRIT AIDED MY DELIVERANCE. CHRYSOSTOM: Behold this blessed man's utter humility! Here is the seasoned competitor! The crown was already to be his. He had passed through a thousand exploits. This was Paul. What more could one say? And yet he humbly asks for the prayers of the Philippians, that his deliverance may be ensured through their supplication. This is the very one whose deliverance has repeatedly been proven through his thousands of exploits! HOMILY ON PHILIPPIANS 4.1.18-20.[2]

1:20a *Not Ashamed*

MY DEATH WILL NOT BRING SHAME. CHRYSOSTOM: "Whether I live or die," Paul says, "Christ will be magnified. How? Either through life, because he delivered me, or through death, because even death itself could not persuade me to deny him, since he has given me such readiness that he has made me stronger than death. . . . So even death will bring me not shame but great gain. Why? Because I am not immortal, but I shall shine all the more brightly than if I were so. It is one thing for an immortal creature to despise death, another thing for one who is mortal. Thus it would be no shame to me if I died right now. But I shall not." HOMILY ON PHILIPPIANS 4.1.18-20.[3]

1:20b *Christ Will Be Honored in My Body*

CHRIST MAGNIFIED IN MY BODY. MARIUS VICTORINUS: "Christ is being magnified in my body, now as always, even when my body, subjected to all punishments, bears them all and preaches Christ unceasingly, not terrified by punishments and not giving way under all the tribulations." He explains the alternatives before him by adding: "Whether by life or by death: If I overcome my trials by endurance, Christ will be proclaimed. Or if I die under my punishments, he will be proclaimed all the more. All will recognize that I was not terrified by punishments or by death. In the gospel I will either live out my life beyond these punishments or bear these punishments right up to death. In any case I will have persevered in the preaching of the gospel." EPISTLE TO THE PHILIPPIANS 1.19-20.[4]

1:21 *To Live Is Christ; To Die Is Gain*

NEITHER DEATH NOR TORTURE IS PUNISHMENT IF CHRIST IS LIFE. MARIUS VICTORINUS: It is not death itself that is gain, but to die in Christ. Life is Christ. The one who has hope in him is always alive, both now and forever. . . . Therefore they achieve nothing, whether they hand me over to death or to tortures in life. Neither alternative harms me. Life under torments is no punishment for me, since Christ is my life. And if they kill me, that too is no punishment for me, since Christ for me is life and to die is gain. EPISTLE TO THE PHILIPPIANS 1.21.[5]

READINESS TO DIE IF CHRIST BE PREACHED. AMBROSIASTER: What others had contrived for his death proved to be life for him. This

---

[2]IOEP 5:29. [3]IOEP 5:31. [4]BT 1972:75 [1200A-B]. [5]BT 1972:75-76 [1200B-D].

is life: if Christ is preached. He is fully prepared to meet death so that this can be accomplished. He knows that a great blessing will be given to him for his prayer and constancy. Clumsy malice will continue to work against him in ignorance. To trample down the malevolence of those who were laying snares against his life under a covering of deceit, he bears patient witness. He is fortified by the protection of God. EPISTLE TO THE PHILIPPIANS 1.21.1-2.[6]

TO LIVE IS CHRIST. AMBROSE: It seems that for him death would be profitable and life would be more a penalty. For this reason Paul says *for me to live is Christ, to die is gain.* The death of the body is nothing amid the spirit of life. So we too are ready to die with Christ that we may live with him. ON THE DEATH OF HIS BROTHER 2.40.[7]

1:22a *Life in the Flesh Means Fruitful Labor*

HIS LABORS CONTINUE. MARIUS VICTORINUS: He said above *Christ is life for me,* but it was not clear then what life he meant, whether in the flesh or life after death. So now he adds these words pointing directly to this life in the flesh: *If it is to be life in the flesh, that means fruitful labor for me.* "What is this fruit of my labor? My labor is the gospel I preach. Its fruit is to bring many to the hope of life and salvation as they in due course begin to have hope in Christ and put faith in the gospel." EPISTLE TO THE PHILIPPIANS 1.22.[8]

HE IS NOT BELITTLING THIS LIFE. CHRYSOSTOM: One must not suppose that he is demeaning this life. He is not saying that since

there is nothing good for us here, we might as well do away with ourselves. Not at all. There can be profit even here, if we live not toward this life finally but toward that other. HOMILY ON PHILIPPIANS 4.1.22.[9]

1:22b *Not Knowing Which to Choose*

EITHER CHOICE AFFIRMED. MARIUS VICTORINUS: I do not know which to choose. If I should die, death is gain and Christ is life for me, and I come to him indeed when I die here in the flesh. But if I should continue to live here in the flesh, the fruit of my labor will be to proclaim Christ and preach his gospel. EPISTLE TO THE PHILIPPIANS 1.22.[10]

WHETHER HE WAS MASTER OF HIS OWN DEPARTURE. CHRYSOSTOM: Here he divulges a great mystery: he thought that the time of his departure was in his own power. Where there is choice, there we have power. *Yet,* he says, *which one I shall choose I do not yet know.* If he would ask this grace of God, either would appear to be within his power. . . . Behold the affection of this blessed man! By this he comforts them when they see that even his departure is within his own power. This happens only by the dispensation of God. HOMILY ON PHILIPPIANS 4.1.22-23.[11]

1:23 *Desiring to Be with Christ*

MY DESIRE IS TO DEPART. ORIGEN: In expressing such a desire he knew that when he returns to Christ he will know more plainly the causes of all that is happening on earth.

---

[6]CSEL 81.3:134-35. [7]CSEL 73:270. [8]BT 1972:76 [1200D-1201A]. [9]IOEP 5:34-35. [10]BT 1972:76 [1201A]. [11]IOEP 5:35.

He will then know more of what constitutes his own humanity, his soul, his mind, his spirit. He will then know more of what the Spirit is enabling and what grace it is that is being given to those who are faithful in the Holy Spirit. ON FIRST PRINCIPLES 2.11.5.[12]

ACCEPTING DEATH WITH EQUANIMITY. TERTULLIAN: Impatience is a bad omen for our hope. It puts our faith in doubt. We wound Christ when we do not accept with equanimity his calling people away, treating them as though they were to be pitied. "I long," says the apostle, "to be taken up and be with Christ." How much better is the wish that he expresses! ON PATIENCE 9.4-5.[13]

BETTER TO BE WITH CHRIST. AMBROSE: From him we come, by his own power we are created, and to him we return. So *it is much better to be with Christ.* ON ABRAHAM 2.5.22.[14]

DEPARTURE AS REST FOR THE SOUL. AMBROSE: What does this *departure* mean but the dissolution and torpor of the body, while the soul for its part is turned toward its rest and made free, if it be faithful, *to be with Christ?* ON THE BENEFIT OF DEATH 3.8.[15]

1:24 Living Is Necessary on Their Account

MORE NECESSARY ON YOUR ACCOUNT TO REMAIN. AMBROSIASTER: He admits that it might be much easier to be dissolved and be with Christ. But nonetheless he knows that it is necessary for him to remain in the flesh for the benefit of the faithful, so that their glory may abound in the Lord and all may

praise the Lord when they see him again. They will thereby increase their knowledge and become more deeply grounded in faith. How great was his affection for the believers, that he does not choose what he says would be much better for himself. Rather he wants what is more profitable to many, in the assurance that what conduces to the benefit of many will also please the Lord. EPISTLE TO THE PHILIPPIANS 1.26.2.[16]

1:25 Remaining and Continuing with Them

I SHALL CONTINUE. MARIUS VICTORINUS: Truly like a father, like a servant of God, he has renounced that one of his two desires which was to be more profitable to himself alone, namely, that he should now depart and be with Christ. . . . He says *I shall remain,* and he adds the stronger form *I shall continue.* This means: "I shall stay until the completion, that is, the completion of your progress, so that you may obtain grace. Thus when you present your faith, you may receive grace from God." EPISTLE TO THE PHILIPPIANS 1.25.[17]

REMAINING WITH YOU. CHRYSOSTOM: He brings them into his confidence by explaining his reasoning: "It is absolutely necessary that I remain, and not only remain but remain with you. . . . If so, then I remain for your sake. But take care that you do not put my fidelity to shame." HOMILY ON PHILIPPIANS 5.1.22-26.[18]

---

[12]GCS 22:188; from Rufinus's Latin translation. [13]CCL 1:309-10. [14]CSEL 32.1:579. [15]CSEL 32.1:709. [16]CSEL 81.3:136. [17]BT 1972:77 [1201C]. [18]IOEP 5:42.

HIS PREDICTION CAME TRUE. THEODORET: In saying *I know that I shall remain and continue with you all* he means: "I know that I shall escape the present danger, so as to be once again a source of profit and encouragement to you. So you will have received what you desire." This prediction indeed came true. For he escaped the anger of Nero on the first occasion, as he shows in his letters to the blessed Timothy.[19] . . . From Rome he went to Spain and took the gospel to them also, then returned and was only later beheaded. EPISTLE TO THE PHILIPPIANS 1.25.[20]

1:26 Giving Cause to Glory

YOUR GLORY IS TO EXULT IN CHRIST. MARIUS VICTORINUS: This means: "Your glory will abound in me.[21] For I will be pre-sent to see how your glory exults and abounds in Christ. I will see how you love Christ, how you serve Christ and how you rejoice in your service to Christ." EPISTLE TO THE PHILIPPIANS 1.26.[22]

THAT YOUR BOAST MAY ABOUND. CHRYSOSTOM: What does he mean, *that your boast may abound?* All there was to glory in was their being established in the faith. This is what it means to boast in Christ, to live rightly. . . . He means "so that I may have more to boast of in you. . . . As you improve, I have more to boast of." HOMILY ON PHILIPPIANS 5.1.22-26.[23]

---

[19]Here Theodoret cites 2 Timothy 4:16-17 and Acts 28:30. [20]CPE 2:50. [21]Literally, "Your boast may abound for me." [22]BT 1972:77 [1201D-1202A]. [23]IOEP 5:42.

1:27-30 EXHORTATION TO RIGHTEOUSNESS

[27]*Only let your manner of life be worthy of the gospel of Christ, so that whether I come and see you or am absent, I may hear of you that you stand firm in one spirit, with one mind striving side by side for the faith of the gospel,* [28]*and not frightened in anything by your opponents. This is a clear omen to them of their destruction, but of your salvation, and that from God.* [29]*For it has been granted to you that for the sake of Christ you should not only believe in him but also suffer for his sake,* [30]*engaged in the same conflict which you saw and now hear to be mine.*

OVERVIEW: Paul is trying to avert the effects of pride (THEODORET). The singular corrective is good conduct that comes from life in Christ (CHRYSOSTOM, MARIUS VICTOR-INUS). He refrains from promising to return (CHRYSOSTOM). He hopes to drive away any fear that might detract from the Philippians' salvation, since fearlessness is a work of God

(MARIUS VICTORINUS). He calls them to stand in one spirit and fight with the faith of the gospel (MARIUS VICTORINUS). God's grace is present in suffering to chasten and to raise them (CHRYSOSTOM, AMBROSIASTER).

1:27a A Manner of Life Worthy of the Gospel of Christ

WORTHY OF THE GOSPEL. MARIUS VICTORINUS: The summing up of one's whole life for a Christian is this, to conduct oneself according to Christ's gospel, to announce his grace steadily both to oneself and others, to have hope in him, to do all that one does according to his commands. For this is what it means to *conduct oneself in a manner that is worthy of Christ's gospel.* A person can live honestly and uprightly, but this is not adequate to Paul's meaning. Rather we are to conduct ourselves according to Christ's gospel regardless of what happens and to do so in a worthy manner, living according to Christ's precepts and doing what Christ wants. EPISTLE TO THE PHILIPPIANS 1.27.[1]

ONLY DO THIS ONE THING. CHRYSOSTOM: All that he has said is for this single purpose, to exhort them to live a life worthy of the gospel. . . . What does *only* mean? This is the one thing looked for, and nothing else. Where this is, no hurt can befall us. HOMILY ON PHILIPPIANS 5.1.27.[2]

WHETHER GREAT VIRTUE IS TEMPTED TO PRIDE. THEODORET: Paul did not write this without reason. He was aware that certain people had started to think too highly of themselves. This was indeed due to the high excellence of their own virtue. For this rea-

son he advises them toward concord and harmony, to live a life worthy of the gospel. EPISTLE TO THE PHILIPPIANS 1.27-28.[3]

1:27b Present or Absent, He May Hear of Them

WHETHER ABSENT OR PRESENT. CHRYSOSTOM: He does not imply by saying this that he is changing his mind or that he is not going to come. Rather he is saying whether he comes or not, regardless of what comes to pass, they may stand firm even in his absence. HOMILY ON PHILIPPIANS 5.1.27.[4]

1:27c Standing Firm, Striving for the Faith

STAND IN ONE SPIRIT. MARIUS VICTORINUS: There is one Spirit that prevails when we believe the gospel wisely and live in accordance with it. This is why he calls them to *stand firm in one Spirit.* The soul's task is to overcome contrary feelings in the body. Therefore he in effect is calling them to *stand in one Spirit and fight together with one soul with the faith of the gospel.* EPISTLE TO THE PHILIPPIANS 1.27.[5]

1:28 Fearing Nothing from Opponents

FEARLESSNESS A WORK OF GOD. MARIUS VICTORINUS: This work of fearlessness is part of his explanation of what it means to conduct oneself worthily according to Christ's gospel: Never be terrified, whether by adversaries or anything else. . . . For this

---

[1]BT 1972:77-78 [1202A]. [2]IOEP 5:43. [3]CPE 2:51. [4]IOEP 5:43. [5]BT 1972:78 [1202B].

very condition of being courageous tends toward our salvation. It deals a death blow to our adversaries. Yet this too is a work of God, lest we should think it part of our own work that our not being terrified should be a cause of our salvation. "For this too is of God," he says, "just as I have often told you that all things come about through the will, the mercy and the grace of God." EPISTLE TO THE PHILIPPIANS 1.28.[6]

1:29 Believing in Christ and Suffering for Christ's Sake

BE READY TO SUFFER FOR HIS SAKE. MARIUS VICTORINUS: It was therefore within his purpose that he gave to us the gift of trusting in him. This was an incomparable gift. It is only by faith in him that we are blessed with so great a reward. We are to believe in such a way as to be ready to suffer for him. EPISTLE TO THE PHILIPPIANS 1.29.[7]

THE SPECIAL GIFT TO THOSE WHO LOVE CHRIST. AMBROSIASTER: Although he extols the grace of Christ on many occasions, he offers a special kind of honor to the Philippians in this passage. He says: "God has allowed you to suffer for Christ." He does not propose this distinction to any but true lovers of Christ. His paradoxical reasoning is that this gift[8] is given to you for Christ! This means that God the Father gives this special gift to lovers of his Son. Why? That their blessings might increase correspondingly through their participation in suffering on Christ's behalf. Paul speaks as one who himself has received this gift. EPISTLE TO THE PHILIPPIANS 1.30.[9]

THE GIFT WHOLLY OF GOD BUT NOT DENY-

ING FREE WILL. CHRYSOSTOM: He speaks of the gift of faith as if it were already granted. It is not given unilaterally from God but in a way that we can take a share in it. Even here the greater part of the share comes from God. But this gift is not given in such a way as to circumvent or overcome free will. Rather it is given to make us humble and rightly disposed. HOMILY ON PHILIPPIANS 5.1.29.[10]

GRACE BOTH BEGINS AND CONTINUES. JOHN CASSIAN: Not only the beginning of our conversion but also the continuance of it through the endurance of suffering for it are gifts given to us by the Lord. CONFERENCES 3.15.2.[11]

1:30 Engaged in the Same Conflict

WE ARE ENGAGED IN THE SAME STRUGGLE. MARIUS VICTORINUS: This is our struggle. This is our contest, our contention and our goal. This it is that leads to the crown and the palm of victory: To do all things for him, to suffer all things for him and not to turn away. You, he says, are now engaged in the same conflict which you saw and now hear to be mine. It is a conflict that implies chains, prison and all the deadly hazards that Paul has suffered. "So my sufferings," he says, "are confirmed in you by two things: what you hear and what you see." EPISTLE TO THE PHILIPPIANS 1.30.[12]

THEY BEAR HIS TRIBULATION. CHRYSOS-

---

[6]BT 1972:78-79 [1202C-D]. [7]BT 1972:79 [1203A]. [8]Suffering with Christ. [9]CSEL 81.3:137-38. [10]IOEP 5:44. [11]CSEL 13:87; citing Abbot Pahpnutius. [12]BT 1972:79 [1203A-B].

TOM: Again he encourages them. He shows them that they are engaged in the very same struggle that Paul himself is engaged in. Everywhere they undergo the same struggles and contests. They are united with him in bearing these tribulations with him. "These are trials that you not only have heard about but," he says, "are also *seeing.*" HOMILY ON PHILIPPIANS 5.1.30.[13]

---

[13]IOEP 5:44-45.

2:1-5 THE RULE OF LOVE

[1]*So if there is any encouragement in Christ, any incentive of love, any participation in the Spirit, any affection and sympathy,* [2]*complete my joy by being of the same mind, having the same love, being in full accord and of one mind.* [3]*Do nothing from selfishness or conceit, but in humility count others better than yourselves.* [4]*Let each of you look not only to his own interests, but also to the interests of others.* [5]*Have this mind among yourselves, which is yours in Christ Jesus.*

OVERVIEW: Paul pleads with the Philippians to have the mind of Christ (CHRYSOSTOM). If they obey what he is saying, their hopes will become realities (AMBROSIASTER). They are called to be united in the same love and of the same mind (MARIUS VICTORINUS). Christ elicits this love, which in turn produces the sympathies of a spiritual fellowship that tends toward unity (MARIUS VICTORINUS). Paul desires that unity in love to be complete (CHRYSOSTOM). He shows how knowledge produces love and how the two cooperate to bring about an increasing unity (MARIUS VICTORINUS). All kinds of ambition, whether from one's own volition or constraint of others, must be avoided (MARIUS VICTORINUS), as well as the temptation to become a slave to popularity (CHRYSOSTOM). The antidote is to put the interests of others before your own (MARIUS VICTORINUS). You must count others better than yourself, not merely saying this but being assured of it (CHRYSOSTOM). The lowly way of Christ enlivens our faith (CHRYSOSTOM), inculcating humility and service (MARIUS VICTORINUS).

2:1a Encouragement in Christ

IF OBEYED, THESE INJUNCTIONS WILL BECOME REALITIES. AMBROSIASTER: These things that he enumerates will, as he shows, be proved realities if the injunctions that he has given below are obeyed: They are of one

233

mind and humble in spirit, not provoking one another but rejoicing in love. If so, the apostle's joy in them may be complete. EPISTLE TO THE PHILIPPIANS 2.4.2.[1]

PLEADING FOR THEIR HIGHEST INTERESTS.
CHRYSOSTOM: See how this blessed man pleads with the Philippians concerning the things that are to their own advantage. For when he is counseling them about concord, the cause of all good things, what does he say? See how elegantly, how energetically he speaks, with what fellow feeling! *If there is any encouragement in Christ*. It is as though he were saying: "If you take comfort in Christ and if you take any account of me, if you have any thought for me personally, if you have received any good from me, listen to this carefully." We use this way of speaking when we are making a request about a matter that we take to have the highest priority. HOMILY ON PHILIPPIANS 6.2.1-4.[2]

2:1b Love, Participation in the Spirit, Affection and Sympathy

HOW THESE TERMS CORRELATE. MARIUS VICTORINUS: When we are in the midst of ills and labor under the ills of the world, if we have mutual love for one another, God will be our *consolation in love*. "If, therefore," he says, "there is this consolation in love, so that, because I love you, you console me in the midst of my ills, make my joy complete." . . . He has done well to put [the Spirit] third. For the first is to be called in Christ, the next to have love. But when both are true and they have already been called in Christ and enjoy the consolation of loving and being loved, without doubt the fellowship of the Spirit is there. . . . The church be-

comes one body when those who have been called are bound to one another in the love of Christ, when they are bound also in the Spirit and have the same *affection and sympathy*. The *affection* corresponds to the calling in Christ and the fellowship of the Spirit, the *sympathy* to the consolation of love. EPISTLE TO THE PHILIPPIANS 2.1-4.[3]

2:2a Completing Paul's Joy

BEING OF THE SAME MIND. MARIUS VICTORINUS: Remember that God is one, his Son is one and his Holy Spirit is one, and all three are one. If so, then we too ought to be one in our thoughts, so as to *be of the same mind* with the one God. Then it follows that we are to *have the same love*. To be of the same mind pertains to knowledge, while to have the same love pertains to discipline, to the conduct of life. EPISTLE TO THE PHILIPPIANS 2.2-5.[4]

COMPLETE MY JOY. CHRYSOSTOM: He does not want this exhortation to appear to be addressed to those who have failed in their duty. So he does not say "give me joy" but *complete my joy*. That is as if to say: "You have already begun to flourish. You have already pursued peace as I wish. Now I long for you to reach the highest levels of maturity in faith." HOMILY ON PHILIPPIANS 6.2.1-4.[5]

2:2b Being in Accord and of One Mind

HAVING THE SAME LOVE. MARIUS VICTORINUS: What does he mean by *the same*

---

[1]CSEL 81.3:138-39. [2]IOEP 5:50. [3]BT 1972:80 [1203D-1204B]. [4]BT 1972:82 [1205A]. [5]IOEP 5:51.

love? That you should have the same love for another that the other has for you, not a divided love but a love embedded in life in Christ. Then he adds *in full accord and of one mind.* He seems to me to be underscoring what he has said above but in a reversed order. *In full accord* corresponds to *the same love. Of one mind* refers to the previous phrase: *being of the same mind.* Yet there is something more nuanced in this pair than in the previous one. For *being of the same mind* and *of one mind* differ only slightly. Both pertain to knowledge. *Being of the same mind* suggests a knowledge that is not yet established, yet its capacity of knowing may be seen to be the same. . . . *Being of the same mind* seems to be still a continuing process. It is the way *to* life. But *having the same love* is the way *of* life to which that knowing leads.[6] EPISTLE TO THE PHILIPPIANS 2.2-5.[7]

2:3a *Doing Nothing from Ambition or Conceit*

BANISH AMBITION. MARIUS VICTORINUS: *Do nothing,* he says, *through ambition.* For many are either prone toward ambitiousness of their own accord or moved toward ambitiousness through others. All these kinds of ambition are to be banished. There is to be no inordinate ambition, whether voluntary or constrained, since both are vicious. Some rush into this ambition through speculation; others are naturally of such temper as to be ambitious. So he advises: *do nothing through ambition.* EPISTLE TO THE PHILIPPIANS 2.2-5.[8]

ENSLAVED TO POPULARITY. CHRYSOSTOM: *Selfishness* is the cause of all sorts of evils.

From it come strife and rivalry. From these come jealousy and contentiousness. Out of this that love grows cool when we are in love with human glory and become enslaved to the honors of popularity. One cannot be both a slave to popularity and a true servant of God. HOMILY ON PHILIPPIANS 6.2.1-4.[9]

2:3b *Counting Others Better Than Oneself*

COUNT OTHERS BETTER. CHRYSOSTOM: If you accept that such and such a person is better than you and persuade yourself of this, not only saying it but being fully assured of it, you also will happily see him honored. And if you happily give him honor, you will not be disturbed to see him honored by others. HOMILY ON PHILIPPIANS 6.2.1-4.[10]

2:4 *Looking to Others' Interests and One's Own*

AS ONE BODY, THE INTERESTS OF OTHERS BECOME MY OWN INTEREST. MARIUS VICTORINUS: If we think only of ourselves, we may act for our own benefit and bother only with our own affairs, our hope, our own deliverance. But this is not enough. We are truly acting for ourselves if we also have a concern for others and strive to be of benefit to them. For since we are all one body, we look out for ourselves when we look out for others. EPISTLE TO THE PHILIPPIANS 2.2-5.[11]

2:5 *The Mind That Was in Christ Jesus*

---

[6]The way to life is having the same mind. The way of life is having the same love. [7]BT 1972:82 [1205B-C]. [8]BT 1972:82-83 [1205C-D]. [9]IOEP 5:52. [10]IOEP 5:52. [11]BT 1972:83 [1206B-C].

**THE MIND YOU ARE TO HAVE AMONG YOUR-
SELVES.** MARIUS VICTORINUS: Above he has
given two injunctions, first that they should
delight in humility, then that they should
think not only of their own affairs but of
those of others. Then he says, *Have this
mind among yourselves that was in Christ Jesus.* Which of these two then do we take to
have been manifested in Christ Jesus? One
or the other or both? For the first, his humility, is manifest, since Christ humbled himself and assumed the character of a slave.
But the second injunction could be here as
well, since he bore this for others and
thought of others rather than of himself.
EPISTLE TO THE PHILIPPIANS 2.6-8.[12]

THE MIND THAT WAS IN JESUS CHRIST.
CHRYSOSTOM: Our Lord Jesus Christ, when
urging his disciples to undertake great
works, makes himself an example.[13] . . . This
too the blessed Paul does, bringing Christ before their eyes when he urges them to practice humility. . . . For nothing so sustains the
great and philosophic soul in the performance of good works as learning that through
this one is becoming like God. HOMILY ON
PHILIPPIANS 7.2.5-8.[14]

---

[12]BT 1972:84-85 [1207A-B]. [13]Here Chrysostom cites Matthew 5:12. [14]IOEP 5:57-58.

2:6-9 THE HYMN TO CHRIST

[6]*Who, though he was in the form of God, did not count equality with God a thing
to be grasped,* [7]*but emptied himself, taking the form of a servant,*[d] *being born in the
likeness of men.* [8]*And being found in human form he humbled himself and became
obedient unto death, even death on a cross.* [9]*Therefore God has highly exalted him
and bestowed on him the name which is above every name.*

d Or slave

OVERVIEW: This passage is of fundamental
importance for Christology, then as now.
The comments made upon it were numerous. It is more useful to illustrate the consensus of the Fathers from as many sources as
possible rather than to make an arbitrary selection from this abundance. In this passage
the arrangement is not chronological but the-
matic. Here are some of the questions that
arise from each verse: Does the passage imply that Christ was ever less than God
(2:6a)? What sort of robbery might he have
attempted (2:6b)? What did it mean that he
emptied himself (2:7a)? Did he take the ap-

pearance or the actuality of a slave (2:7b)? Was he human or merely in human likeness (2:7c-d)? What is involved in his humiliation (2:8)? Who is he that has been exalted (2:9a)? What is the name above every name (2:9b-c)?

WHAT THE HYMN AS A WHOLE TELLS US. EPIPHANIUS: You see that he reveals Christ to be a man but not merely so, since he is the mediator of God and humanity. . . . He is trueborn God by nature with respect to his Father, but with respect to humanity he is Mary's trueborn son by nature, begotten without the seed of a man. ANCORATUS 44.[1]

2:6a Being in the Form of God

PROOF OF HIS FULL DIVINITY AS THE FORM OF GOD. NOVATIAN: If Christ were only a man, he would have been said to have been "in the image of God," not in the form of God. We know that humanity was made in the image, not the form, of God. ON THE TRINITY 22.2.[2]

COUNTERING THE NEO-ARIANS. GREGORY OF NYSSA: He did not say "having a nature like that of God," as would be said of [a man] who was made in the image of God. Rather Paul says being in the very form of God. All that is the Father's is in the Son. ANTIRRHETICUS AGAINST APOLLINARIUS.[3]

CHRIST IS THE FORM OF GOD. MARIUS VICTORINUS: God is the very principle of life. God is being itself. God contains life as a principle of life and so also understanding. But life and understanding are in a sense the form and image of what exists. What most

truly exists is God. God is being itself, as many agree, and more so that which is above existence. The form of existence is motion, understanding and life. . . . Christ is said to be the form of God because Christ is life, consciousness and understanding. EPISTLE TO THE PHILIPPIANS 2.6-8.[4]

THE FORM OF GOD IS HIS ESSENCE. GREGORY OF NYSSA: The form of God is absolutely the same as the essence. Yet when he came to be in the form of a slave, he took form in the essence of the slave, not assuming a naked form for himself. Yet he is not thereby divorced from his essence as God. Undoubtedly when Paul said that he was in the form of God, he was indicating the essence along with the form. AGAINST EUNOMIUS 3.2.147.[5]

BEFORE HE EMPTIED HIMSELF. ORIGEN: First one may contemplate him existing in his primary form, that of God, before he emptied himself. One will then see the Son of God not yet having come forth from him, the [incarnate] Lord not yet having proceeded from his place. But then compare the preexistent state of the Son with that which resulted from his assuming the form of a slave when he emptied himself. You will then understand how the Son of God came forth and came to us and as it were became distinguishable from the One who sent him. Yet in another way the Father did not simply let him go but is with him and is in the Son as the Son is in the Father. COMMENTARY ON JOHN 20.18.[6]

---

[1]GCS 25:54-55. [2]CCL 4:55 [127]. [3]GNO 3.1:159. [4]BT 1972:85 [1207B-C]. [5]GNO 2:100. [6]COJG 2:61.

Being God He Took the Form of a Slave. Athanasius: What clearer and more decisive proof could there be than this? He did not become better from assuming a lower state but rather, *being God*, he *took the form of a slave. . . .* If [as the Arians think] it was for the sake of this exaltation that the Word came down and that this is written, what need would there be for him to humble himself completely in order to seek what he already had? Against the Arians 1.40.[7]

He Was Not Slave Before He Was Lord. Epiphanius: Suppose that when he became a slave he ceased being truly Lord. How then could it be said that in his coming the one who was *in the form of God took the form of a slave?* Ancoratus 28.[8]

Suppose the Consequences of the Opposite, That the Form of God Is Not the Being of God. Theodoret: But if [the Arians] think the *form of God* is not the being of God, let them be asked what they think is the *form of a slave. . . .* If the form of a slave is the being of a slave, then the form of God is God. . . . Furthermore, let us recognize also that the apostle uses the example of Christ as a lesson in humility. . . . If the Son was not equal to the Father but inferior, he did not obey in humility—he merely fulfilled his station. Epistle to the Philippians 2.6.[9]

The Son Stamped by the Character of the Father. Gregory of Nyssa: The one *in the form of God* was not stamped by any character other than the Father's, being *a character of the Father's substance.*[10] But the *form of God* is the same as his essence. For when he came to be in the *form of a slave* he

was formed into the essence of the slave, not taking to himself a naked form or one divorced from the essence, but the essence is signified along with the form. So beyond all doubt the one who said that Christ was in the form of God indicated the essence through the form. Against Eunomius 3.2.147.[11]

Whether He Existed Before Mary. Chrysostom: How can the wretched [Sabellius] say that Christ's existence began from Mary? This implies that before this he did not exist. But Paul says that *being the form of God he took the form of a slave. . . .* The form of a slave is truly a slave and nothing less. So too the form of God is truly God and nothing less. Paul did not write that he was in process of coming to be in the form of God; rather *being in the form of God*, hence truly divine. This is as much as to say *I am that I am.*[12] Homily on Philippians 7.2.5-8.[13]

The Form of God Is Nothing Less Than God. Ambrosiaster: When he dwelt among humans he appeared as God by his acts and works. *For the form of God* differs in nothing from God. Indeed, the reason for his being called the form and image of God is to make it apparent that he himself, though distinguishable from God the Father, is everything that God is. . . . His works revealed his form. Since his works were not those of a human, he whose work or form was that of God was perceived to be God. For what is *the form of God?* Is it not shown by the evidences given of his divinity—by his raising of the dead, his restoration of hearing to the deaf, his cleans-

---

[7]OSA 41-42. [8]GCS 25:37. [9]CPE 1:52. [10]Heb 1:3. [11]GNO 2:100. [12]Ex 3:14; Jn 8:58. [13]IOEP 5:59-60.

ing of lepers? EPISTLE TO THE PHILIPPIANS
2.6—2.8.5.[14]

**DISTINGUISHING *SON OF MAN* AND *SON OF
GOD*.** EUSEBIUS OF CAESAREA: [Paul] acknowledged Christ and no other to be the Son of
God. The flesh that Christ assumed was
called *the form of a slave* and *son of man*.
But as to that birth which, unknown to all,
was from the Father and before all ages, he
was Son of God. ON THE THEOLOGY OF THE
CHURCH 1.2.[15]

THE TRUE GREATNESS OF CHRIST. LUCIFER
OF CAGLIARI: It was he who was and is and
always shall be in the form of the Father, the
true Son, immutable and unchangeable because he is God and the all-powerful Son of
the Almighty, who nonetheless deigned to
lower himself for our salvation, so that he
might cause us to rise even as we lay pros-
trate. ON DYING FOR THE SON OF GOD 12.[16]

THE NEED TO RECEIVE THE LIKENESS.
METHODIUS: Being in the image of God, [hu-
manity] still needed to receive the likeness.[17]
The Word, having been sent into the world
to perfect this, first of all took on our own
form, even though in history it has been
stained by many sins, so that we for our
part, on whose account he bore it, should be
once again capable of partaking in his divine
nature. Hence it is now possible for us to receive God's likeness. Think of a skilled
painter painting a likeness of himself on a
surface. So we may now imitate the same
characteristics that God himself has displayed in his becoming a human being. We
hold these characteristics before us as we go
in discipleship along the path he set out. His
purpose in consenting to put on human flesh

when he was God was this: that we, upon
seeing the divine image in this tablet, so to
speak, might imitate this incomparable artist.
SYMPOSIUM 1.4.24.[18]

2:6b *Equality with God Not Counted a Thing to Be Grasped*

EQUAL TO GOD. AUGUSTINE: God who is
eternally wise has with him his eternal Wisdom [the Son]. He is not in any way unequal to
the Father. He is not in any respect inferior. For
the apostle too says *who, when he was in the
form of God, thought it no robbery to be equal
with God.*[19] ON FAITH AND THE CREED 5.[20]

EQUAL, NOT SIMILAR. MARIUS VICTORINUS:
What does this mean—*being equal to God?*
It means that he [the Son] is of the very
same power and substance [as the Father].[21]
. . . It is in this sense therefore that Christ
was equal to God. Note that Paul did not
say Christ was "similar to God," for that
would imply that Christ possessed some acci-
dental likeness to the substance of God but
not that he was substantially equal.[22] . . .
Thus Christ is the form of God. The form of
God is the substance of God. The form and
image of God is the Word. The Word is forever with God.[23] The Word is of one substance with the Father, with whom from
the beginning it remains forever the Word.
AGAINST THE ARIANS 1.21-22.[24]

HE ELECTED HUMILITY. THEODORET: Being

---

[14]CSEL 81.3:139-41. [15]GCS 14:63. [16]CCL 8:293. [17]Cf.
Gen 1:26. [18]GCS 27:12-13. [19]A more literal translation
than "equality . . . not a thing to be grasped." [20]Migne PL
40:184. [21]Here Victorinus cites Ephesians 3:18. [22]Here
Victorinus cites Genesis 1:26 regarding the likeness of humanity to God. [23]Jn 1:1-2. [24]BT 1976:53-55.

God, and God by nature, and having equality with God, he thought this no great thing, as is the way of those who have received some honor beyond their merits, but, hiding his merit, he elected the utmost humility and took the shape of a human being. EPISTLE TO THE PHILIPPIANS 2.6-7.[25]

WHETHER HUMILITY IS LACK OF POWER. CHRYSOSTOM: When someone who has the power to think great thoughts humbles himself, that one is humble. But when his humility comes from impotence, that is not what you would call humility.... It is a humility of a greater sort to refrain from *seizing* power, to be *obedient to death*. HOMILY ON PHILIPPIANS 7.2.5-8.[26]

THE EQUALITY NOT ELICITED BY ROBBERY. MARIUS VICTORINUS: It would be a kind of robbery if two things were not equal by nature but were forced to be made equal or made equal through some accident. It therefore shows great confidence and bespeaks the very nature of divinity when Paul says of Christ that he did not think it robbery to be equal with God yet did not consider this equality something he had to fortify. AGAINST THE ARIANS 1.23.[27]

TO GOD BELONGS DEITY BY NATURE. CHRYSOSTOM: Suppose someone commits a robbery and grabs something that does not belong to him. Wouldn't he be inclined to hold on to it tightly, to grasp it and not lay it aside for fear of losing it? But suppose someone else possesses an estate by nature. He would not have any fear of losing it. He would not then be afraid to descend temporarily from his estate of dignity. He would know that he would suffer no loss, because it belongs

to him naturally.... We are human beings. We are not divine by nature. We do not possess goodness by nature. But to God divinity belongs by nature.... His dominion was not acquired by seizure but was natural. It was not the gift of another but always stable and secure. HOMILY ON PHILIPPIANS 8.2.5-11.[28]

HIS EQUALITY SHOWN NOT A ROBBERY BUT A RIGHT. AMBROSIASTER: Knowing that he is *in the form of God*, he committed no theft.... Rightly, then, he equaled himself with God. For the one who *thinks robbery* is the one who makes himself equal to another whose inferior he is. EPISTLE TO THE PHILIPPIANS 2.6.[29]

THE LOGIC OF THE EQUALITY. EUSEBIUS OF VERCELLI: You must choose one of two paths. Either there is a single inequality in the two [divine Father and divine Son] or there is a single equality in the glory of divinity itself. For no one is either greater or less than his own form.... This singular equality is seen not only in the concord of their willing together. It is rather in their very deity, since the form of equality is in no way divided into parts. Where there is one equality there is no discord. Where there is one equality neither is prior to the other. Neither is posterior nor subordinate, since there is no distinction in the united equality, which is the fullness of divinity. ON THE TRINITY 3.4, 7.[30]

THE EQUALITY INDIVISIBLE. AUGUSTINE: Wherein lies the Son's equality? If you say in greatness, there is no equality of greatness in

---

[25]CPE 2:52. [26]IOEP 5:62-63. [27]BT 1976:56. [28]IOEP 5:72-73. Cf. Chrysostom *On the Equality of the Father and the Son* [SC 396:272-75]. [29]CSEL 81.3:139. [30]CCL 9:32-33.

one who is less eternal. And so with other things. Is he perhaps equal in might but not equal in wisdom? Yet how can there be equality of might in one who is inferior in wisdom? Or is he equal in wisdom but not equal in might? But how can there be equality of virtue in one who is inferior in power? Instead Scripture declares more simply *he thought it not robbery to be equal.* Therefore every adversary of truth who is at all subject to apostolic authority must admit that the Son is in some one respect at least the equal of God. Let him choose whichever quality he might wish, but from that it will appear that he is equal in all that is attributed to divinity. ON THE TRINITY 6.5.[31]

THE EQUALITY AS A PROOF OF HIS ETERNITY. CHRYSOSTOM: Now equality is not predicated of one subject, for that which is equal must be equal to something. Do you see how the existence of two subjects is affirmed, not two mere names without real significance? Do you hear how the Only-Begotten existed before the ages? HOMILY ON PHILIPPIANS 7.2.5-8.[32]

EQUALITY AS A PROOF OF HIS DIVINITY. PSEUDO-AUGUSTINE: If therefore he thought it no robbery to assert his equality with God, he demonstrated that he was the true Son of God. No one could be God's equal without being truly God. QUESTIONS ON THE OLD AND NEW TESTAMENTS 97.2.[33]

EQUALITY DISTINGUISHED FROM HUMILITY. FULGENTIUS: While the whole Word came to us when *the Word was made flesh,*[34] the whole remained with the Father in Spirit, equal to the Father, from whom he is eternally begotten yet made less by the gracious

assumption of flesh so that he could be visible to us. And by this the Lord from the Lord remained Lord *in the form of God.* In order that he might come to slaves he received *the form of a slave* from his handmaid.[35] ON THE INCARNATION 21.[36]

EQUALITY AS SHARED POWER. QUODVULTDEUS: He did not rob, because who he was, he was by nature. Thus the omnipotence of the Father was in the Son and the omnipotence of the Son in the Father. The Father is never without the Son nor the Son without the Father. ON THE CREED 1.3.14-15.[37]

THE SON'S REMEMBRANCE OF HIS IDENTITY. NOVATIAN: He never either compared or opposed himself to God the Father. He remembered [throughout his earthly ministry] that he was from the Father. ON THE TRINITY 22.5.[38]

THE ECONOMY OF THE INCARNATION. AUGUSTINE: These things are said partly on account of the economy by which the Son assumed humanity . . . partly because the Son owes to the Father his existence and also owes to the Father indeed his equality or parity with the Father. The Father, however, owes to no one his being, whatever he is. ON FAITH AND THE CREED 18.[39]

2:7a Christ Emptied Himself

THE EMPTYING THROUGH OBEDIENCE. HILARY OF POITIERS: To assume *the form of a slave* he *emptied himself* through obedi-

---

[31]Migne PL 42:926-27. [32]IOEP 5:60. [33]CSEL 50:172. [34]Jn 1:14. [35]Mary, the handmaid of the Lord. [36]CCL 91:331. [37]CCL 60:311. [38]CCL 4:55 [128]. [39]Migne PL 40:191.

ence. He emptied himself, that is, from the *form of God*, which means *equality with God*. ON THE TRINITY 8.45.[40]

THE EMPTYING COMMENSURATE WITH OUR NATURE. GREGORY OF NYSSA: And even the word *emptied* clearly affirms that he was not always as he appeared to us in history. . . . He *emptied himself,* as the apostle says, by contracting the ineffable glory of his Godhead within our small compass. In this way *what he was* remained great and perfect and incomprehensible, but *what he assumed* was commensurate with the measure of our own nature. ANTIRRHETICUS AGAINST APOLLINARIUS.[41]

THE EMPTYING INVOLVED NO LOSS OF GODHEAD. AUGUSTINE: He is said to have *emptied himself* in no other way than by taking the form of a servant, not by losing the form of God. For that nature by which he is equal to the Father in the form of God remained immutable while he took our mutable nature, through which he was born of the Virgin. CONTRA FAUSTUM 3.6.[42]

WHETHER HE HIMSELF CHANGED WHEN HE EMPTIED HIMSELF. AUGUSTINE: He *emptied himself* not because as eternal Wisdom he underwent change. For as eternal Wisdom he is absolutely changeless. Rather without changing he chose to become known to humanity in such a humble form. ON FAITH AND THE CREED 18.[43]

THE EMPTYING CONCEALED HIS DIGNITY. THEODORE OF MOPSUESTIA: By *emptying* the holy Scripture signifies becoming of no account, just as in Corinthians Paul speaks of faith as if it had been made of no account,

or emptied of significance, if Christ be not raised.[44] So *our preaching has been made empty* means that it is of no account and futile. . . . Thus the phrase *he emptied himself* means that he did not yet reveal himself. Assuming the form of a slave, he concealed that dignity which was his. So he was deemed by onlookers to be what he seemed. EPISTLE TO THE PHILIPPIANS 2.2.[45]

THE EMPTYING HIDES BUT DOES NOT CURTAIL THE DIVINITY IN HIM. GREGORY OF ELVIRA: We do not believe that he was so emptied that he himself as Spirit became something else. Rather he, having put aside for this time the honor of his majesty, put on a human body. Only by assuming human form could he become the Savior of humanity. Note that when the sun is covered by a cloud its brilliance is suppressed but not darkened. The sun's light, which is suffused throughout the whole earth, penetrating all with its brilliant splendor, is presently obscured by a small obstruction of cloud but not taken away. So too that man, whom our Lord Jesus Christ put on, being our Savior, which means God and the Son of God, does not lessen but momentarily hides the divinity in him. ON THE FAITH 88-89.[46]

THE EMPTYING AS AN EXPRESS IMAGE OF HIS GLORY. ORIGEN: The Son, *emptying himself* of his equality with the Father and showing us a way of knowing him, was made an express image of his substance,[47] so that we who were unable to see the glory of pure light that inhered in the great-

---

[40]Migne PL 10:270A-B. [41]GNO 3.1:159. [42]Migne PL 42:218. [43]Migne PL 40:191. [44]1 Cor 15:14. [45]CGPEP 6:259. [46]CCL 69:244. [47]Heb 1:3.

ness of his divinity might, through that which was made *splendor* for us, find a way of contemplating the divine light through the sight of that splendor. ON FIRST PRINCIPLES 1.2.8.[48]

THE EMPTYING PASSIVE BUT VOLUNTARY. CYRIL OF ALEXANDRIA: He let himself be *emptied*. It was not through any compulsion by the Father. He complied of his own accord with the Father's good pleasure. DIALOGUES ON THE TRINITY 1.[49]

THE EMPTYING UNCOERCED. FAUSTINUS: If he *therefore emptied himself, assuming the form of a slave*, he was not coerced but was of his own accord made the Son of Man, existing as God's equal in the form of God. Therefore you have the Son expressing in himself the faith proper to humans. ON THE TRINITY 17.[50]

THE EMPTYING AS AN ASSUMPTION OF THE BODY. ORIGEN: In *emptying himself* he became a man and was incarnate while remaining truly God. Having become a man, he remained the God that he was. He assumed a body like our own, differing only in that it was born from the Virgin by the Holy Spirit. ON FIRST PRINCIPLES 1, PREFACE 4.[51]

THE EMPTYING AS AN ASUMPTION OF FLESH. CYRIL OF ALEXANDRIA: What sort of *emptying* is this? To assume the flesh, even in the form of a slave, a likeness to ourselves while not being like us in his own nature but superior to the whole creation. Thus he humbled himself, descending by his economy into mortal bounds. ON THE UNITY OF CHRIST.[52]

THE EMPTYING AS AN ASSUMPTION OF HUMANITY. MARIUS VICTORINUS: We must understand this *emptying himself* to consist not in any loss or privation of his power but in the fact that he lowered himself to the basest level and condescended to the meanest tasks. By fulfilling these he momentarily emptied himself of his power. Assuming flesh and human form and likeness, he suffered, died and fulfilled all the things that belong to humanity. EPISTLE TO THE PHILIPPIANS 2.6-8.[53]

THE EMPTYING AS A LESSON IN HUMILITY. AMBROSIASTER: Christ, therefore, knowing himself to be *in the form of God*, showed himself equal to God. But in order to teach the law of humility when the Jews were binding him, he not only refrained from resistance but *emptied himself*, that is, withheld his power from taking effect, so that in his humiliation he seemed to be weakened as his power lay idle. EPISTLE TO THE PHILIPPIANS 2.8.1.[54]

THE EMPTYING CONSISTENT WITH TRANSCENDENCE. PSEUDO-DIONYSIUS THE AEROPAGITE: Even in this he has what is supernatural and superessential, not only because he underwent no change or confusion in his communion with us, suffering no detriment to his exceeding fullness from his ineffable emptying but because also—the newest of all new things—he was supernatural even while in our natural condition. He was above the realm of essences while being in

---

[48]GCS 22:38; from Rufinus's Latin translation. [49]Migne PG 75:693A [405]. [50]CCL 69:313. [51]GCS 22:10; from Rufinus's Latin translation. [52]Migne PG 75:1301B [742]. [53]BT 1972:86 [1208B]. [54]CSEL 81.3:140.

the realm of essences. He possessed our properties from us in a manner superior to ourselves. ON THE DIVINE NAMES 2.10.[55]

THE EMPTYING CONSISTENT WITH OMNIPOTENCE. HILARY OF POITIERS: Remaining *in the form of God*, he *took the form of a slave*, not being changed but *emptying himself* and hiding within himself and being made empty within his own power. He tempered himself to the form of the human state as far as was necessary to ensure that the weakness of the assumed humility would not fail to bear his immeasurable power. He went even so far as to tolerate conjunction with a human body. Just this far did his goodness moderate itself with an appropriate degree of obedience. But in making himself empty and restraining himself within himself, he did nothing detrimental to his own power, since even within this lowliness of his self-emptying he nonetheless used the resources of the evacuated power within him. ON THE TRINITY 12.48.[56]

THE EMPTYING NECESSARY FOR FULL HUMANITY. MARIUS VICTORINUS: How could he possibly have taken only human form and not human substance? For he put on the flesh and was in the flesh and suffered in the flesh. This is the mystery and the means of our salvation. . . . What therefore does it mean, *he emptied himself*? That the universal Logos was not universal in his actual being as the *logos* of the flesh and becoming flesh. Therefore he did not merely pretend to become a man but became a man. AGAINST THE ARIANS 1.22.[57]

THE EMPTYING A PROOF OF FULL INCARNATION. CYRIL OF ALEXANDRIA: By this alone let the difference between the divinity and humanity in him be perceived. For Godhead and humanity are not the same in natural quality. Otherwise how has the Word, being God, been *emptied*, having let himself fall among lesser beings such as ourselves? But when we speculate on the mode of incarnation the human mind inevitably sees two things commingled by an inexpressible and unconfused union yet in no way divides the united elements but believes and firmly accepts that there is one from both, who is God, Son, Christ and Lord. LETTER TO ACACIUS 14.[58]

THE EMPTYING ENABLES HUMAN NATURE TO ACCOMMODATE GOD'S REVELATION. GREGORY OF NYSSA: The Godhead is emptied so that the human nature may accommodate it. What is human, on the other hand, is made new, becoming divine through mingling with the divine. AGAINST EUNOMIUS 3.3.67.[59]

RECEIVING AS MUCH AS NATURE COULD HOLD. GREGORY OF NYSSA: He *emptied himself*, as the Scripture says, so that as much as nature could hold it might receive. ANTIRRHETICUS AGAINST APOLLINARIUS.[60]

HUMAN NATURE MADE ABLE TO RECEIVE. GREGORY OF NAZIANZUS: Since he is emptied on our account when he came down (and by emptying I mean as it were the reduction and lessening of his glory) he is for this reason able to be received. ORATION 37.2.[61]

---

[55]PTS 33:135. [56]Migne PL 10:431C-432A [405-6]. [57]BT 1976:54. [58]OECT 50. [59]GNO 2:131. [60]GNO 3.1:123. [61]SC 318:276.

**THE EMPTYING A RESTORATION OF OUR NA-
TURE BY HIS HUMILITY.** EUSEBIUS OF VER-
CELLI: How then did he *empty himself?*
When the *form of God accepted the form of
a slave,* when he who is preeminently the
Lord deigned to take on himself what belongs to a slave. The Word was made flesh
by bearing and doing what was beneath him
in his indulgence and compassion toward us.
All that he possessed by nature is emptied
into this his person. Having been made obedient as a man in the true *fashion of humanity,* he has restored to our nature by his own
humility and obedience what had perished
through disobedience in Adam. ON THE
TRINITY 10 (9).57.[62]

**THE SOVEREIGNTY TEMPORARILY UNDER
SUBMISSION.** NOVATIAN: The sovereignty of
the divine Word temporarily submitted to
assume a man and for a season *humbled himself* and abased himself, not exercising his nature through his powers, while he bore the
man that he had assumed. He *emptied himself* when he bowed to injuries and slanders,
when he heard unspeakable insults and suffered indignities. ON THE TRINITY 22.8-9.[63]

2:7b *Taking the Form of a Servant*

**HIS SERVANTHOOD NOT FROM A NATURAL IN-
FERIORITY.** CHRYSOSTOM: If it were through a
natural inferiority that he undertook to bear
the form of a slave,[64] this would not be an instance of humility. Yet Paul makes excellent
use of this example as an exhortation precisely
to humility. ON THE EQUALITY OF THE FA-
THER AND THE SON, HOMILY 10.[65]

HE ASSUMED WHAT HE WAS NOT. GRE-
GORY OF NYSSA: The one who says that he

took the form of a slave—and this form is
flesh—is saying that, being himself something else according to his divine form, something else in his nature, he assumed the
servile form. ANTIRRHETICUS AGAINST
APOLLINARIUS.[66]

THE SLAVERY AS GOD'S INSTRUMENT. CLEM-
ENT OF ALEXANDRIA: God did all things
through him. Therefore he is also said to
have *taken the form of a slave.* It is not only
the flesh of the slave that he assumed but
the very nature of a slave that he assumed.
He became a slave so that he could share human suffering in the flesh. EXCERPTS FROM
THEODOTUS 19.4-5.[67]

TAKING THE FORM OF A SLAVE. AMBROSIAS-
TER: He is said not to have *taken* the form of
God but to have *been* in the form of God.
What he is said to have *taken* is the form of
a slave when he was humbled like a sinner.
People become slaves through sin, like Ham
the son of Noah, who first received the title
of slave through his own actions.[68] His *taking the form of a slave* was not simply his becoming human but his profound identification
with sinners, voluntarily *taking the form of a
slave.* EPISTLE TO THE PHILIPPIANS 2.8.2.[69]

**YET HIS SLAVERY INVOLVED NO ACTUAL
SIN.** AUGUSTINE: The Son humbled himself,
taking the form of a slave. But meanwhile he
remained above any slavery because he had
no stain of sin. ON THE GRACE OF CHRIST
AND ON ORIGINAL SIN 2.(28).33.[70]

---

[62]CCL 9:144. [63]CCL 4:56 [129-30]. [64]"Slave" is a better
translation than is "servant." [65]SC 396:272-74. [66]GNO
3.1:159. [67]GCS 17:113. [68]Gen 9:20-27. [69]CSEL 81.3:140.
[70]Migne PL 44:402.

THE SLAVERY DID NOT INDICATE A DEFECT OF POWER. LEO THE GREAT: He *assumed the form of a slave* without the stain of sin, enhancing the human without diminishing the divine. That *emptying* by which the invisible One offered himself to be seen and the Creator and Lord of all things elected to be one among mortals was a sovereign act of stooping in majestic pity, not a defect of power. EPISTLE 28 TO FLAVIAN 3.[71]

THE SLAVERY OF THE SON ENDS THE SLAVERY OF SIN. AUGUSTINE: The Lord Jesus Christ came in flesh and, having *accepted the form of a slave, became obedient even to death on the cross.* He has no other purpose than that by this dispensation of his most merciful grace he might give life to those who have become, as it were, members of his body. He is their head in order to obtain for them the kingdom of heaven. This he did to save and set free. He redeemed and enlightened those who had formerly been consigned to the death of sin. They had been languishing in slavery, captivity and darkness under the power of the devil, the prince of sinners. ON WHAT IS DUE TO SINNERS 1.39.[72]

THE SLAVERY EXEMPLIFIES HUMILITY. AMBROSIASTER: *Taking the form of a slave.* He indeed was taken captive, bound and driven with blows. His obedience to the Father took him even as far as the cross. Yet throughout he knew himself to be the Father's Son, equal in divine dignity. Yet he did not make a display of this equality. Rather he willingly subjected himself. This patience and humility he teaches us to imitate. We are to refrain from making a display of our claims to equal dignity, but even more so we are called to lower ourselves into service as we follow the example of our Maker. EPISTLE TO THE PHILIPPIANS 2.8.1-2.[73]

THE TRIUNE GOD NOT EXHAUSTED IN THIS SLAVERY. GREGORY OF NYSSA: The Word who appeared in the flesh was the same as the Word that was with God.[74] But the earthly flesh he assumed was not the same as the Godhead[75] until this too was changed into Godhead, so that necessarily some attributes belonged to God the Word, others to the form of a slave. AGAINST EUNOMIUS 3.3.62.[76]

THE WILL OF THE FATHER AND THE SON WAS VOLUNTARY. MARIUS VICTORINUS: The Son was sent by the Father and fulfills the Father's will. The mystery stated here is that it was by his own will that he came and assumed the form and image of a slave. . . . The Father is in the Son and the Son in the Father. . . . So what the Father willed the Son also willed, and what the Son willed the Father willed. EPISTLE TO THE PHILIPPIANS 2.6-8.[77]

HIS PARTICIPATION IN SLAVERY IS AN EXPRESSION OF HIS DIVINE COMPASSION. EUSEBIUS OF CAESAREA: Read the record of his compassion. It pleased him, being the Word of God, to *take the form of a slave.* So he willed to be joined to our common human condition. He took to himself the toils of the members who suffer. He made our human maladies his own. He suffered and toiled on our behalf. This is in accord with

---

[71]TF 208; cf. *Sermon* 2.2, 14.5; *Epistle* 124.7,165.8. [72]Migne PL 44:131. [73]CSEL 81.3:140. [74]Jn 1:1. [75]Rather it was the flesh of the Son. [76]GNO 2:130. [77]BT 1972:85-86 [1207D-1208B].

his great love of humankind. DEMONSTRA-TION OF THE GOSPEL 10.1.22.[78]

THE UNITY OF THE DIVERSE APOSTOLIC TESTIMONY. THEODORET: See how the varied attestors agree. The Evangelist says *the Word became flesh*.[79] The apostle says that he, being in the form of God, *came to be in the form of a man*.[80] The Evangelist says *he pitched his tent among us*. The apostle says *he took the form of a slave*. The Evangelist says *we saw his glory, as of the only begotten of the Father*. The apostle speaks of One *who being in the form of God thought it no robbery to be equal with God*. In a word, both teach the same: that, being God and the Son of God, and clothed in the Father's glory and having the same nature and power as his Begetter, the One who *in the beginning was with God and was God*[81] and wrought the creation *took the form of slave*. ERANISTES 1.[82]

2:7c Being Born

REJECTED INTERPRETATIONS. CYRIL OF AL-EXANDRIA: If we take him simply and solely to be a man made from a woman, how could he be said to be in the *form* equal to the Father? If only a man, how could he have the fullness that would make sense of his being *emptied*? What height could he have occupied before that he might be said to have *humbled himself*? How did he *come to be in the likeness of men* if he was already so by nature? SCHOLIUM 12 ON THE INCARNATION OF THE ONLY BEGOTTEN.[83]

THE MANHOOD EXPRESSES NOT A CHANGE IN GOD HIMSELF BUT DEVELOPMENT IN THE DIVINE ECONOMY OF HIS REVELATION. HILARY OF POITIERS: Note well the breath-

taking economy by which the Son assumed flesh: Through the obedience of the one who was in the form of God [and] was emptying himself of the form of God, [he] was born as a man. In doing so he took a new nature upon himself! This occurred not by a loss of his power and nature but by an assumption of a new condition. . . . Though he retained the power of his nature as God, he was in much of his earthly ministry temporarily relinquishing his exercise of the power of his nature as God as he walked as a man. The effect of this economy of order was this: The Son in his entirety, namely, as both man and God, was now, through the indulgence of the Father's will, in union with the nature of the Father. This is what occurred to God the Son: that he became a man. ON THE TRINITY 9.38.[84]

2:7d In the Likeness of Humanity

NOT FROM THE BEGINNING INVESTED WITH THAT LIKENESS. GREGORY OF NYSSA: He says of the Son that he has *come to be in the likeness and form of men*. If he *came to be* in this likeness, this obviously implies that he was not invested with it from the beginning. Before coming to be in that likeness he was not fashioned according to some corporeal pattern. For no embodied form could become the pattern for what is previously not embodied. ANTIRRHETICUS AGAINST APOLLI-NARIUS.[85]

IN HUMAN LIKENESS. CHRYSOSTOM: What does it mean to be *in a human likeness*? Does it mean that his appearance was merely a fan-

---

[78]GCS 23:450. [79]Jn 1:14. [80]Phil 2:7. [81]Jn 1:1. [82]Eran 89-90. [83]Migne PG 75:1383 [786]. [84]Migne PL 10:309A-310A [286]. [85]GNO 3.1:159.

tasy? This would be something merely similar to[86] a human and not made in the *likeness of a man*. For to be made in *the likeness of a man* is to be a man. . . . So what does it mean, *in a human likeness?* With few exceptions he had all our common human properties. The exceptions: He was not born from sexual intercourse. He committed no sin. These properties he had which no human being has. He was not only human, which is what he appeared to be, but also God. . . . We are soul and body, but he is God, soul and body. For this reason Paul says *in the form*—and so that when you hear of his emptying you may not suppose that he underwent change, degradation and some sort of annihilation of his divinity. Rather remaining what he was he assumed what he was not. Becoming flesh, he remained the Word of God. So it is in this respect that he is *in the likeness of men*, and for this reason he says *and in form*. His nature was not degraded, nor was there any confusion [of the two natures], but he entered a *form*. HOMILY ON PHILIPPIANS 8.2.5-11.[87]

NOT A PHANTOM. MARIUS VICTORINUS: It is not as though Paul was in the slightest uncertain about Christ's identity that he said Christ was *found in human likeness*. He did not say *in human likeness* as though our Lord maybe was not truly a man but a phantom. Rather he was found in human likeness while still being God yet at the same time being truly a man in the flesh, with a physical human body that he had assumed. EPISTLE TO THE PHILIPPIANS 2.6-8.[88]

NOT A MAN ONLY, THOUGH HE APPEARED TO BE. THEODORET: He says of the divine Word that, being God, he was not seen to be

God but wore a human appearance. Yet the words *in the likeness of men* are appropriate to him, for the nature that he assumed was truly human, and yet he was not [merely] a man, though he at first glance appeared to be only a man. EPISTLE TO THE PHILIPPIANS 2.6-7.[89]

THE METAPHOR OF CLOTHING INADEQUATE. AUGUSTINE: He did not take on his humanity in the simple way that a person puts on clothes, as something exterior to him. Rather he took on human form in a manner inexpressibly more excellent and more intimate than that. The apostle has made it sufficiently clear what he meant by *He was made to appear in human likeness*. He was not exhaustively reduced to being a man. He rather assumed the true human estate when he put on the man. ON DIVERSE QUESTIONS 73.[90]

NOT ONE OF MANY. CHRYSOSTOM: He carefully uses the phrase *in human likeness*. For Christ was not one of the many but *as* one of the many. God the Word did not degenerate into a man. His essence as God did not change. Rather he appeared like a man, not deluding us with a phantom but instructing us in humility. HOMILY ON PHILIPPIANS 8.2.5-11.[91]

2:8a Being Found in Human Form

NO REASON FOR SAYING "FOUND IN HUMAN FORM" UNLESS HE WAS GOD. AMBROSIASTER: Why is he *found in human form*, if not because he was also God? Before he allowed

---

[86]*Simulacrum*, that which is simulated as human, as opposed to that which has been made in the form of a human. [87]IOEP 5:74-77. [88]BT 1972:87 [1208D]. [89]CPE 2:52. [90]Migne PL 40:85. [91]IOEP 5:77.

himself to descend he was always seen in the power of God. But having subsequently been made weak he was *found in human form?* . . . And the reason for saying *like* is to indicate that he was also God. EPISTLE TO THE PHILIPPIANS 2.8.5-6.[92]

THE FORM OF GOD INVISIBLE. GAUDENTIUS: He added *being found in human form* because the form of God, which is properly God himself, has never been seen by anyone. TREATISE 19, ON THE PRIORITY OF THE FATHER 28.[93]

THE MANHOOD NONETHELESS REAL. TERTULLIAN: Suppose the terms *figure* (or *image* or *fashion*), *likeness* and *form* referred merely to a phantom. There would then have been no substance to Christ's humanity. But in this case *figure, likeness* and *form* all point to the reality of his humanity. He is truly God, as Son of the Father, in his figure and image. He is truly man, as the Son of Man, found in the figure and image of man. It is noteworthy that elsewhere Paul calls Christ the *image of the invisible God.*[94] And indeed he had a reason for saying *found,* meaning that Christ was most certainly a man; for what is found surely must exist. Just as he was found to be God in power, so too he was a man in flesh. The apostle would not have declared him to become obedient to death if he had not been constituted of a mortal substance. Still more plainly does this appear when he adds the heavily laden words *even unto the death of the cross.* For he would not exaggerate the atrocity in extolling his power in a conflict which he knew to have been imaginary or a mere fantasy. In that case Christ would rather have eluded the cross than experienced it. There would then have

been no virtue in his suffering but only an illusion. AGAINST MARCION 5.20.4-5.[95]

HIS HUMANITY AS REAL AS HIS DIVINITY. BASIL OF CAESAREA: It is apparent that the Lord accepted natural feelings to confirm that his humanity was real and not illusory, but the feelings that come from wickedness, all those that besmirch the purity of our lives, he repudiated as being unworthy of his unsullied Godhead. LETTER 261.[96]

2:8b *Christ Humbled Himself*

THE HUMILIATION VOLUNTARY. THEODORET: His humbling was not undertaken as a slave in relation to a master's command. Rather he willingly undertook the saving work on our behalf. He obeyed as a son, not as a slave. EPISTLE TO THE PHILIPPIANS 2.8.[97]

THE HUMILIATION HONORABLE. CHRYSOSTOM: He honored the Father all the more, not that you may honor him less but that you may marvel all the more. Here we learn that he is truly a son who honors his father more than all else. No one could have honored God the Father more than God the Son. The measure of his sublimity corresponds with the depth of his humility. HOMILY ON PHILIPPIANS 8.2.5-11.[98]

HIS HUMILIATION DEMONSTRATES HIS VOLUNTARILY DIVESTED MAJESTY. HILARY OF POITIERS: Humility is hard, since the one who humbles himself has something magnificent in his nature that works against his low-

---

[92]CSEL 81.3:141. [93]CSEL 68:171. [94]Col 1:15. [95]CCL 1:724-25. [96]LCL 4:80; cf. 4:345. [97]CPE 2:53. [98]IOEP 5:78.

ering. The one who becomes obedient, however, undertakes the act of obedience voluntarily. It is precisely through the act of humbling that he becomes obedient. ON THE TRINITY 11.30.[99]

HIS HUMBLING BECOMES OUR EXAMPLE.
CYRIL OF ALEXANDRIA: He *humbled himself*, according to the Scriptures, *taking on himself the form of a slave*. He became like us that we might become like him. The work of the Spirit seeks to transform us by grace into a perfect copy of his humbling. FESTAL LETTER 10.4.[100]

2:8c He Became Obedient

SALVATION THROUGH OBEDIENCE. ORIGEN: He *was made obedient even to death*. His obedience teaches us that we too cannot obtain salvation except through obedience. By this means he has reconstituted the laws of ruling and being ruled, so much so that he *has put all his enemies under his feet*.[101] ON FIRST PRINCIPLES 3.5.6.[102]

2:8d He Was Obedient unto Death

THE DEATH STILL MORE HONORABLE.
CHRYSOSTOM: It was a great thing—ineffably great—that he became a slave. But to undergo death was much greater. Where can anything be found more paradoxical than this? This death was the most shameful of all, the most accursed. And he in death appeared to be a reprobate. This was not an ordinary death.[103] HOMILY ON PHILIPPIANS 8.2.5-11.[104]

THAT NONE MAY FEAR DEATH. AUGUSTINE: He humbled himself, being made obedient even unto death, even death on a cross, so

that none of us, though being able to face death without fear, might shrink from any kind of death that human beings regard as a great disgrace. ON FAITH AND THE CREED 11.[105]

2:8e Death on a Cross

HE PUT DEATH TO DEATH. EPIPHANIUS: The Word tasted death once on our behalf, the death of the cross. He went to his death so that by death he might put death to death. The Word, becoming human flesh, did not suffer in his divinity but suffered with humanity. ANCORATUS 92.[106]

2:9a God Has Exalted Him

WHETHER THE DIVINE NATURE WAS EXALTED. THEODORET: Even to the most inattentive it is obvious that the divine nature needs nothing. He did not become human by being raised up from lowliness. Rather he abased himself from the utmost height. He did not receive what he did not have before but received as a man what he possessed as God. EPISTLE TO THE PHILIPPIANS 2.9.[107]

HIS HUMANITY EXALTED. PSEUDO-VIGILIUS: It is not in his divine nature that the Son is said to have been exalted by the Father. Rather the one who was exalted and received *the name above every name* is the one who appeared by taking flesh from the Virgin's womb, to be born as God and man. AGAINST VARIDMADUS THE ARIAN 30.[108]

---

[99]Migne PL 10:419C [394]. [100]SC 392:230. [101]1 Cor 15:25. [102]GCS 22:277. [103]Cf. Deut 21:23; Gal 3:13. [104]IOEP 5:78. [105]Migne PL 40:187. [106]GCS 25:113. [107]CPE 2:53. [108]CCL 90:42.

THE SON OF MAN EXALTED. ORIGEN: It was not the Word of God who needed or received exaltation. For the Word was in the beginning exalted with the Father. It was the Son of Man who was exalted from lowliness. This exaltation occurred when he had glorified God in his death. COMMENTARY ON JOHN 32.25.[109]

THE DYING ONE EXALTED. GAUDENTIUS: *Therefore,* he says, *God exalted him.* But who was it that was exalted? Evidently the one who underwent the torture of the cross and death. It was not God himself, who is always on high throughout. TREATISE 19, ON THE PRIORITY OF THE FATHER 29.[110]

WHAT WAS HUMBLED WAS EXALTED. ATHANASIUS: That *God has highly exalted him* does not imply that the essential nature of the Word at long last became exalted. For God the Son is and always was equal to God the Father. The exaltation is of the humanity. . . . The text says *he humbled himself* with reference to the assumption of the flesh. So too it says *he exalted him* with reference to the flesh. It was the human race that needed this, because of the humiliation of its flesh and because of its consequent death. Thus the Word who is immortal and the image of the Father *has taken the form of a slave* and suffered death on the cross as a man for our sake. He did this in order that he might thus present himself as an offering to the Father. It is thus as a man that he is said to have been exalted for our sake. Hence all of us die in Christ and through his death may again be exalted in Christ himself. AGAINST THE ARIANS 1.41.[111]

WHAT IS EXALTED IS THAT WHICH WAS MADE LOW. GREGORY OF NYSSA: It is obvious that the highest is in need of no exaltation. Only what is lowly can be lifted to the exalted state, becoming now what it was not before. Being united to the Lord the human nature is lifted up to share in his divinity. What is exalted is that which has been lifted up from lowliness. ANTIRRHETICUS AGAINST APOLLINARIUS.[112]

NO INJURY TO THE GODHEAD. CHRYSOSTOM: Having said that he became a man, Paul is not afraid thereafter to predicate lowly things of him, knowing that this predication of lowly things does the Godhead no injury. It is to Christ's human nature that they apply. HOMILY ON PHILIPPIANS 8.2.5-11.[113]

TEACHING US HUMILITY. AMBROSIASTER: He shows what and how much his humility deserved, so that we, trampling down our boastfulness, might find ourselves all the more humble. EPISTLE TO THE PHILIPPIANS 2.11.1.[114]

2:9b *The Name Bestowed*

IT COULD NOT BE GIVEN ADOPTIVELY. AMBROSIASTER: Scripture says that the gift was given to him who *emptied himself,* who *took the form of a slave,* who was *made to appear as a man,* who was *obedient to the Father.* But if it was a mere man and nothing else who was obedient to God the Father, what is remarkable about that? . . . His name is not above every name unless he is so by his

---

[109]COJG 1:199. [110]CSEL 68:171. [111]OSA 42. [112]GNO 3.1:161. [113]IOEP 5:78. [114]CSEL 81.3:142.

very nature. A titular name rests solely on usage, not on the nobility of one's nature. The creation does not bend its knees for a titular God but for the real God. EPISTLE TO THE PHILIPPIANS 2.11.6-8.[115]

THE ERROR OF THOSE WHO SAY HIS GLORY CONSISTS IN BEING WORSHIPED BY US. CHRYSOSTOM: Those who teach falsely imply that his glory lies in his name itself. The inference is that his glory consists entirely in his being worshiped by us. The implication is that he would not be glorious until he received our worship. Is this all his glory means? Those who think this way are far from the greatness of God. HOMILY ON PHILIPPIANS 8.2.5-11.[116]

2:9c *The Name Above Every Name*

THIS IS THE NAME OF GOD. NOVATIAN: He received *the name that is above every name*, which we must certainly understand as nothing other than the name of God. For it belongs to God to be above all. So it follows that the name that is above all belongs to him who is above all, namely, God. ON THE TRINITY 22.10.[117]

THE PHRASE CONVEYS INEFFABILITY. GREGORY OF NYSSA: God is *above every name*. The only proper way to name God is as above every name. God exceeds every operation of the intellect. God cannot be contained in any nominal definition. This is a sign to us of God's incommunicable greatness. AGAINST EUNOMIUS 2.587.[118]

WHETHER HE HAD THIS NAME FOREVER. PSEUDO-AUGUSTINE: None of the faithful doubt that the Son of God was begotten in perfect reception of all that belongs to the character of God. The Son received all the attributes of divinity in being born from God the Father. It was then that he received *the name that is above all names*, that is, that he should be called what the Father is called. Nothing different is predicated of him with regard to the future, since he has all things before him. So he was born for the re-creation and restoration of all these. Seeing that order and reason demand that every knee should bow to the name of the Father, the Father bestowed this name upon the Son because of the salvation he was to perform. This name was bestowed when he begot the Son. The Father begot him that he might enjoy the same honor as the Father himself. QUESTIONS ON THE OLD AND NEW TESTAMENTS, APPENDIX 39.[119]

STILL EQUALLY GOD WHEN ASSUMING HUMANITY. GAUDENTIUS: The *name that is above every name* is God. It is not given to God in order that he should become God. For God the Son was the Word in the beginning with the Father. But the man assumed by the Son takes on his mission. In this way the Son of God, who had always existed, remains still equally God when joined to the humanity that he received from the Virgin. TREATISE 19, ON THE PRIORITY OF THE FATHER 29.[120]

HIS HUMANITY NEVER SEVERED FROM HIS DIVINITY. FULGENTIUS: Through the Son human nature was redeemed. It was human nature that he undoubtedly came to redeem.

---

[115]CSEL 81.3:144-45. [116]IOEP 5:79-80. [117]CCL 4:56 [130]. [118]GNO 1:397. [119]CSEL 50:441. [120]CSEL 68:171-72.

It was this human nature that the Son took up into the unity of his person. And because his humanity is never sundered from the Son of God, it therefore rules in heaven and earth over all angels and all humanity. ON THE INCARNATION 12.[121]

WHETHER THE NAME WAS GIVEN HIM AT BIRTH. AMBROSIASTER: Some argue that *the name which is above every name* was given only to his humanity. In no way could this be so. For it is not possible that God should lack those things that he once had. For God, even while assuming humanity, remained God. EPISTLE TO THE PHILIPPIANS 2.11.4.[122]

THE GREATNESS OF THE NATURE OF HUMANITY. NESTORIUS: There must be two natures, that of the divinity and that of the humanity. The divinity has emptied itself into the likeness of a servant. The humanity, in the likeness of a servant, has been raised into *the name which is above all names.* . . . This in fact is what summarizes the chief greatness of the nature of humanity. Christ remains in the nature of humanity. It is he who accepts *a name that is more excellent than all names.* He does this neither in consequence of moral progress nor in consequence of knowledge and faith. Rather he accepts that it has come about that humanity should be transformed in his image and his person. In this way humanity becomes by exaltation what God is, the name which is above all names. THE BAZAAR OF HERACLEIDES 58, 61.[123]

WHETHER THE NAME IS AN ETERNAL REALITY NEWLY REVEALED. MARIUS VICTORINUS: He received *the name that is above every name.* He received this name because of his

saving word, because of the mystery of his passion, where death was vanquished by the very death of Christ. Through this grace he received *the name*. It was at that point that the name rightly accrued to him. But the reality to which the name pointed was already given before. The Word, the very power of God, did not become real for the first time only when it entered flesh. Rather it possessed its reality as the power, wisdom, action and work of God from the outset, when it was called the Word and when it indeed was the Word. It is that same Word that has now put on flesh . . . that has received the title of Son, which title is above every name. EPISTLE TO THE PHILIPPIANS 2.9-11.[124]

WHETHER THE NAME SIGNIFIES PROGRESS IN THE WORD. AMBROSIASTER: It is not assumed here that the Son of God was lacking or imperfect before *the name that is above every name* was given to Christ. . . . Even before his passion he showed himself equal to God, as I have stated. Hence it is clear that he was born perfect, for he is seen to have possessed all things from the beginning. He was born in the fullness of divinity for the very purpose of doing all that he was destined to perform. So he had already received the gift before he performed the things that he was born to do. It therefore seems that the gift of God, which consists in his being Son, was that his name should be *above every name*, which consists in his being God. EPISTLE TO THE PHILIPPIANS 2.11.2.[125]

---

[121]CCL 91:322. [122]CSEL 81.3:143. [123]G. R. Driver and L. Hodgson, trans. (Oxford: Clarendon, 1925), pp. 55-58**. [124]BT 1972:89 [1210C-D]. [125]CSEL 81.3:142.

The Name Makes Jesus Our Judge. Euse-bius of Caesarea: That [saving sacrifice] which no human or angelic or divine power had yet endured he accepted for the sake of our salvation. Therefore upon him alone the Father has bestowed the name that is above every name, committing to him the judgment of all. Commentary on Isaiah 2.(53).63.5-6.[126]

---

[126]GCS 56:388.

2:10-11 THE NAME OF JESUS

[10]*That at the name of Jesus every knee should bow, in heaven and on earth and under the earth,* [11]*and every tongue confess that Jesus Christ is Lord, to the glory of God the Father.*

Overview: Jesus is worshiped as God in the unity of his divine-human being (Gauden-tius). His humanity is penetrated by his divinity and vice versa through the communication of idioms (Gregory of Nyssa). He who rightly worshiped the Father now receives our worship (Cyril of Alexandria). Every kind of creature now reveres him. Even the angelic spirits bow metaphorically (Origen). Christ now sits as ruler as first-born from the dead (Gregory of Nyssa). This demonstrates that Christ is God (Theodoret). The Father is glorified through the salvation of humanity (Atha-nasius).

2:10a *Every Knee Should Bow*

He Who Has Assumed the Worshiping Nature Is Himself Worshiped. Cyril of Alexandria: He worships as one who has assumed the worshiping nature of human-ity.[1] It is this same One who is now wor-shiped as transcending the worshiping nature of humanity. He is now known to be God. Scholium 34 on the Incarnation of the Only-Begotten.[2]

The One God-Man Is Worshiped. Gaudentius: This means that after the mys-tery of the passion and the triumph of the as-cension he who was wholly the Son of God with that which he had consented to be for our sakes, while remaining in the glory of God the Father (which means of course in the divinity of his own nature), should be adored by all the powers in heaven, on earth and below. Treatise 19, On the Priority of the Father 30.[3]

---

[1]E.g., Jn 4:22. [2]Migne PG 75:1407C [797]. [3]CSEL 68:172.

THE EXALTED ONE BECOMES LOWLY SO THAT THE LOWLY ONE MAY RECEIVE THE FRUITS OF HIS EXALTATION. GREGORY OF NYSSA: This name has become superior to every name. His divinity is such that it cannot be adequately manifested merely through verbal signs, no matter how exalted they are. As the exalted One comes to be in the lowly, so the lowly One may receive in return the properties of the exalted. ANTIRRHETICUS AGAINST APOLLINARIUS.[4]

WORSHIP DUE TO ONE WHO IS GOD BY NATURE. CYRIL OF ALEXANDRIA: God the Word inhabited as his own temple the body taken from the woman. In this body lived a rational soul. God remade it into his own glory. On this account the holy Scripture declares that worship is proper only to the one who is God by nature. This is what Paul means when he writes that *at the name of Christ Jesus every knee shall bow*. FESTAL LETTER 8.6.[5]

2:10b *In Heaven, on Earth and Under the Earth*

DISTINGUISHING IN HEAVEN, ON THE EARTH AND UNDER THE EARTH. ORIGEN: From a single beginning come many differences and varieties in creation. All these are now being recalled once again, synoptically in this text. They are now being viewed in relation to God's goodness made known through the obedience of Christ. They are being drawn into a unity by the Holy Spirit. Everything is moving toward a common end, which corresponds to the goodness of the beginning. This means all those *in heaven and earth and the lower regions*, who, *bowing the knee at the name of Jesus*, have declared through this very act the tokens of their subjection. In these three appellations the whole universe is indicated. All things issue from one origin. They have been driven by their own motions in diverse ways. They are to be allotted different levels of blessedness in accord with their own willing. ON FIRST PRINCIPLES 1.6.2.[6]

WHETHER INCORPOREAL POWERS LITERALLY BOW. ORIGEN: We should not understand this carnally, so as to suppose that even the heavenly bodies, which he says bend their knees, do this with fleshly limbs. ... What spirit has knees? But the bending of the knees indicates that all is in subjection and observes the worship of God. COMMENTARY ON ROMANS 9.41.[7]

FIRSTBORN. GREGORY OF NYSSA: The One who once came into the world has now become the Firstborn from the dead, both of brothers in faith and of all creation. He will return to the world as judge of all the world in righteousness, as the prophet declares, when it will become clear. The name of *Firstborn*, which he assumed first on our behalf, will not be cast away in in those last days. Every knee will bow at the name of Jesus. He is above every name. The whole company of angels worships this One who has been called the Firstborn. They all rejoice in the restoration of humanity, whom he has restored to their original grace by becoming

---

[4]GNO 3.1:161. [5]SC 392:106. [6]GCS 22:79-80; from Rufinus's Latin translation. [7]Migne PG 14:1243C. Cf. Jerome *Epistle to the Ephesians* 1.2.13-14 [Migne PL 26:472D-473B (580-81)], on Eph 2:14.

the Firstborn among us. AGAINST EUNOMIUS 3.2.48.[8]

2:11a Every Tongue Will Confess Christ Is Lord

CHRIST IS LORD. THEODORET: *Every tongue* stands for every people. But if the confession of Christ as Lord is a glorification of the Father, it is clear that those who call him a creature and a slave deface the glory of the Father also. In these few words, however, the divine apostle has subdued every heresy, among those who blaspheme the divinity of the Only-Begotten, and those who deny his humanity and those who misconstrue the hypostatic union of the two natures. EPISTLE TO THE PHILIPPIANS 2.11.[9]

2:11b The Glory of God the Father

HUMANITY RE-CREATED. ATHANASIUS: The glory of the Father is that the human race not only was created but was re-created when lost. It was given life once again when dead, so as to become a renewed temple of God. For the powers in heaven also, the angels and the archangels, worship him and now worship the Lord *in the name of Jesus.* This joy and exaltation belongs to human beings, because the Son of God, having himself become a human being, is now worshiped. The heavenly powers are not offended when they behold all of us being led into our heavenly abode as we share in his body. This could not have happened in any other way. It happened only because, *being in the form of God and taking the form of a slave, he humbled himself,* agreeing to assume our bodily condition *even to death.* AGAINST THE ARIANS 1.42.[10]

---

[8]GNO 2:68. [9]CPE 2:53-54. [10]OSA 43-44.

2:12-13 WORKING OUT OUR SALVATION

[12]*Therefore, my beloved, as you have always obeyed, so now, not only as in my presence but much more in my absence, work out your own salvation with fear and trembling;* [13]*for God is at work in you, both to will and to work for his good pleasure.*

OVERVIEW: Paul appeals to Christ's pattern of service (THEODORET) as the pattern of the Philippians' service, which is being tested by his absence (CHRYSOSTOM). It is through fear and trembling (CHRYSOSTOM) that he points to the mystery and inspires their zeal (MARIUS VICTORINUS). He emphasizes God's activity in them to assuage their fear (CHRYSOSTOM) and

---

forestall pride (AUGUSTINE). We remain the doers of our own actions (AUGUSTINE), but willing itself is a gift of God (ORIGEN). Only the bad will is truly ours (AUGUSTINE), while God assists continually the good will in willing further good (CHRYSOSTOM).

2:12a As You Have Always Obeyed

PRAISE JOINED WITH EXHORTATION. CHRYSOSTOM: Our admonitions are best accompanied by praises. Only in this way are they welcomed. So we call those we are exhorting to that level of zeal of which they are capable of exhibiting. For they become welcome when we call those whom we are exhorting to compete with themselves. This is what Paul does here, and note how wisely. *So, my beloved*, he says. He does not say simply *you obey*. Rather he first praises them and says *just as you have always obeyed*, as if to say, "I am urging you to imitate not others but yourselves." HOMILY ON PHILIPPIANS 9.2.12-16.[1]

AS YOU HAVE ALWAYS OBEYED. THEODORET: "Looking at this example," he says, "you have conceived a greater zeal for your own salvation, notwithstanding my absence. For this reveals the excellence of your goal, that it is not to please your teacher but out of eagerness for good things that you undertake this admirable labor." EPISTLE TO THE PHILIPPIANS 2.12.[2]

2:12b In Paul's Presence or His Absence

OBEDIENCE IN HIS ABSENCE. CHRYSOSTOM: "At that time you seemed to be doing everything for the sake of honoring and respecting me, but now no longer. If then it proves that

you now continue, it is proved then also that you did it not for my sake but for God's." HOMILY ON PHILIPPIANS 9.2.12-16.[3]

2:12c Working Out Salvation

DISTINGUISHING FEAR AND TREMBLING. MARIUS VICTORINUS: The *fear* is to be referred to the soul, the *trembling* to the body. But it is a great mystery, which we should lay to heart when we hear it, that by taking thought and showing concern for others we work out our own salvation all the more and furthermore that it is in our power to work out salvation for ourselves. EPISTLE TO THE PHILIPPIANS 2.12-13.[4]

AMID REVERENCE FOR GOD. CHRYSOSTOM: What do you want? Tell us. Not "that you should hear me" but that *with fear and trembling you should work out your own salvation*. For without fear no one can accomplish anything noble or remarkable.... If the goods of life cannot be attained without fear, how much more true is this of spiritual ones? For tell me, whoever learned letters without fear? Who became skilled in a craft without fear? But if the devil does not best us there but only lethargy oppresses us, we needed all that fear merely to overcome our natural lethargy. Here, where the war is so great and impediments so many, how can we be saved without fear? HOMILY ON PHILIPPIANS 9.2.12-16.[5]

2:13a God Is at Work in You

GOD WORKS IN YOU. CHRYSOSTOM: And

---

[1]IOEP 5:86-87. [2]CPE 2:55. [3]IOEP 5:87. [4]BT 1972:91 [1211C-1212A]. [5]IOEP 5:87.

when he says *with fear and trembling* see how he assuages the pain of it. For what does he say? *It is God who works in you.* "Do not be afraid," he says, "because I said *with fear and trembling.* I did not say it to make you give up, thinking virtue impossible of attainment, but so that you may carry on, so that you may not collapse." HOMILY ON PHILIPPIANS 9.2.12-16.[6]

FREE WILL NOT UNDERMINED. AUGUSTINE: We should not suppose, because he said, *For it is God that works in you both the willing and the doing,* that he has taken away free will. For if that were so he would not have said above *Work out your own salvation with fear and trembling.* For when he bids them work, it is agreed that they have free will. But they are to work with fear and trembling so that they will not, by attributing the good working to themselves, be elated by the good works as though they were their own. ON GRACE AND FREE WILL 21.[7]

2:13b *To Will and to Work*

HOW OUR WILLING AND WORKING IS FROM GOD. ORIGEN: Some say, "If willing is from God and working is from God, then whether we will evil or do evil, that is from God, and in that case we have not free will." ... To this one must reply that the apostle's words do not mean that willing evil is from God or that willing good is from God, and likewise with our working well or ill. Rather it is willing in general and performance in general. For just as our being animals and our being human are things we have from God, so is willing in general as, so to speak, is motion in general. ON

FIRST PRINCIPLES 3.1.19.[8]

GOD AUGMENTS OUR WILLING AS WE WILL. CHRYSOSTOM: If you have the will, then he works the willing. Do not be afraid or weary. He gives us both zeal and performance. For when we will, he will henceforth augment our willing. HOMILY ON PHILIPPIANS 9.2.12-16.[9]

WITHOUT GRACE THERE IS NO GOOD WILL. AUGUSTINE: It is not that the will or the deed is not ours, but without his aid we neither will nor do anything good. ON THE GRACE OF CHRIST 26.[10]

GOD STRENGTHENS OUR WILL TO DO GOOD. AUGUSTINE: It is certain that when we do a deed, the deed, is ours; but he is the one who makes us do the deed by giving us strength fully sufficient to carry out our will. ON GRACE AND FREE WILL 32.[11]

GRACE ASSISTS IN WILLING. AUGUSTINE: It is not in God's power that anyone should be forced against his will to do evil or good but that he should go to the bad, according to his own deserts, when God abandons him. For a person is not good if he does not will it, but the grace of God assists him even in willing. It is not without cause that it is written, *God is the one who works in you to will and do, of his own good will.* ON TWO LETTERS OF PELAGIUS 1.36.[12]

---

[6]IOEP 5:88. [7]Migne PL 44:894. [8]GCS 22:230-34; see *Philocalia* 21 [PO 158]. [9]IOEP 5:89. [10]Migne PL 44:373. [11]Migne PL 44:900-901. [12]Migne PL 44:567.

2:14-18 THE BLAMELESS LIFE

¹⁴Do all things without grumbling or questioning, ¹⁵that you may be blameless and innocent, children of God without blemish in the midst of a crooked and perverse generation, among whom you shine as lights in the world, ¹⁶holding fast the word of life, so that in the day of Christ I may be proud that I did not run in vain or labor in vain. ¹⁷Even if I am to be poured as a libation upon the sacrificial offering of your faith, I am glad and rejoice with you all. ¹⁸Likewise you also should be glad and rejoice with me.

OVERVIEW: The prohibition of grumbling is a compliment, implying that they are capable of great virtue if they avoid this seminal vice (CHRYSOSTOM). We cannot yet be perfect (JEROME), but amid all insults we can shine as stars (CHRYSOSTOM) for the benefit of others (CHROMATIUS OF AQUILEIA). Our present duty is good conduct based on Scripture as read through Christ (CHRYSOSTOM, MARIUS VICTORINUS). Paul dwells upon the magnitude and benign effect of Christ's death (THEODORET), teaching them to love (MARIUS VICTORINUS) and to rejoice in the sacrifices of the faithful (MARIUS VICTORINUS, CHRYSOSTOM).

2:14 Without Grumbling or Questioning Do All Things

WITHOUT GRUMBLING. CHRYSOSTOM: Do you see how he teaches them not to grumble, saying that murmuring belongs to slaves who know nothing and have no sense? For what son murmurs, tell me, when toiling in his father's affairs, seeing that he toils also in his own? HOMILY ON PHILIPPIANS 9.2.12-16.[1]

THE GRUMBLER IS UNGRATEFUL. CHRYSOS-TOM: When one does something voluntarily and not under compulsion, why grumble? It is better to do no work than to do it with grumbling, for the very thing that we do is destroyed. Or do you not see that in our own homes we often say, "Better that this be not done than done with grumbling"? And many times we choose to be deprived of a service rather than put up with grumbling. For grumbling is terrible, yes, a terrible thing; it is akin to blasphemy. . . . The grumbler is ungrateful to God, and one who is ungrateful to God is a blasphemer. HOMILY ON PHILIPPIANS 9.2.12-16.[2]

2:15a Children of God Without Blemish

WHETHER PRESENT OR FUTURE. JEROME: He says not "you are" but *so that you may be,* deferring it to the future and not asserting it as a present fact, to show that here there is toil and struggle and there the rewards of toil and virtue. DIALOGUE AGAINST THE PELAGIANS 3.13.[3]

---

[1]IOEP 5:91. [2]IOEP 5:91. [3]CCL 80:116.

2:15b Shining as Lights in the World

YOU SHINE AS LIGHTS IN THE WORLD.
CHRYSOSTOM: Do you do something good
but grumble? Why? Is there any constraint
upon you? "I know," he says, "that many of
your neighbors influence you to complain,"
for this is what he hints at when he says *in
the midst of a wicked and perverse generation.* But the way to excite wonder is to suffer no such thing even under provocation.
For the stars too shine in darkness yet suffer
no diminution of their own beauty, but instead they shine all the brighter. HOMILY ON
PHILIPPIANS 9.2.12-16.[4]

DISPELLING THE DARKNESS. CHROMATIUS
OF AQUILEIA: With the very light of truth
we are to illumine those who are caught in
the shadows of error, dispelling the night
of ignorance. . . . If we do not do this, it
will be apparent that our infidelity has, as
it were, concealed and overshadowed the
benefits of this needful light, to our own
perdition as well as that of others. TRAC-
TATE 19.3.2-3.[5]

2:16 Holding Fast the Word of Life

HOLD FAST THE WORD OF LIFE. MARIUS
VICTORINUS: "I have glory through you because you possess *the word of life*"—that is,
because you know Christ, who is the Word
of life, *because what was made in Christ was
life.*[6] Therefore Christ is the Word of life.
From this we perceive how great is the
profit and glory of those who correct the
souls of others. EPISTLE TO THE PHILIP-
PIANS 2.16.[7]

THE WORD OF LIFE. CHRYSOSTOM: It means

those who hold that they are going to live
and are among the saved. See what immediate prizes he sets before them: "The stars,"
he says, "possess the principle of light and
you the principle of life." What is this *word
of life?* It means having the seed of life, that
is, the beginnings of life, possessing life itself. HOMILY ON PHILIPPIANS 9.2.12-16.[8]

2:17 Poured as a Libation

WHY AND TO WHOM DOES HE SAY THIS?
THEODORET: When he says *you* he means all
the faithful. . . . And he says this to work on
their souls and to teach them that his martyrdom is so great that it has the character
of a libation and a sacrifice. EPISTLE TO THE
PHILIPPIANS 2.17.[9]

2:18 Rejoicing with Paul

**READINESS TO DIE IN EQUAL CONCERN FOR
ONE ANOTHER.** MARIUS VICTORINUS: He
means, "Being prepared to die for you, so
long as I can serve you and strengthen your
faith, I rejoice and am glad for all of you. So
therefore you rejoice and be glad with me, so
that we may show equal concern for one another and rejoice in each other in turn." EPIS-
TLE TO THE PHILIPPIANS 2.17-18.[10]

REJOICE IN THE DEATH OF THE RIGHTEOUS.
CHRYSOSTOM: The death of the righteous,
therefore, deserves not tears but joy. If they
rejoice, one should rejoice with them. "But
we long for their company," you say. . . . If
you were going to remain here, you speak

---

[4]IOEP 5:94. [5]CCL 9A:286-87. [6]Jn 1:4. [7]BT 1972:93
[1213B]. [8]IOEP 5:94. [9]CPE 2:56. [10]BT 1972:93 [1213D].

reasonably; but in a little while you are going to recover the departed one. What sort of company is it that you desire? . . . "I suffer nothing terrible," he says, "but rather rejoice because I am departing to be with Christ.

And do you not rejoice? Rejoice with me." Homily on Philippians 9.2.17.[11]

[11]IOEP 5:95.

2:19-24 THE MISSION OF TIMOTHY

[19]I hope in the Lord Jesus to send Timothy to you soon, so that I may be cheered by news of you. [20]I have no one like him, who will be genuinely anxious for your welfare. [21]They all look after their own interests, not those of Jesus Christ. [22]But Timothy's worth you know, how as a son with a father he has served with me in the gospel. [23]I hope therefore to send him just as soon as I see how it will go with me; [24]and I trust in the Lord that shortly I myself shall come also.

Overview: The mission of Timothy reveals Paul's deep affection for the Philippians (Chrysostom) and his extraordinary praise of Timothy (Theodoret). Timothy's mission is an antidote to selfishness (Marius Victorinus), which Paul rebukes by his own humility (Marius Victorinus), repeating that all things depend on God (Theodoret). Our actions are completed in God (Marius Victorinus).

2:19 Sending Timothy to Them Soon

Our Actions Completed in God. Marius Victorinus: Because every act of ours must be referred to God so that it may be completed by God, he says, *I hope in our Lord Jesus Christ.* Epistle to the Philippians 2.19.[1]

His Solicitude. Chrysostom: He shows his love not only by telling them his news but also by asking for theirs. This is the mark of a soul that is constantly permeated with solicitude and consideration. . . . Why did he say not "so that you may know my affairs" but *so that I may know yours?* The reason is that Epaphroditus was going to bring news of him before Timothy. Homily on Philippians 10.2.19-21.[2]

2:20 One Anxious for Their Welfare

No One Like Him. Theodoret: The praises of the blessed Timothy are true, but the divine apostle has pronounced them at this

[1]BT 1972:94 [1214A]. [2]IOEP 5:96.

point both as a sign of his own affection for them (since he has sent to their assistance the only comforter of his soul) and as an exhortation to receive him with all hospitality as a mouthpiece of the truth. EPISTLE TO THE PHILIPPIANS 2.19-22.[3]

2:21 Christ's Interests

LOOKING AFTER CHRIST'S INTERESTS. MARIUS VICTORINUS: To the charge being given to Timothy as one *who is faithfully anxious on your behalf* he adds this explanation: The others *seek after their own interests;* that is, they are anxious to protect and keep what is theirs and in this are not Christians. For what is it to be a Christian? To seek rather in every companion and brother that which is Christ's. EPISTLE TO THE PHILIPPIANS 2.21.[4]

2:22 Timothy's Worth Known

SERVED WITH ME. MARIUS VICTORINUS: He says *he served with me,* not "he served me." EPISTLE TO THE PHILIPPIANS 2.22-24.[5]

2:23-24 Sending Timothy; Hoping to Join Them

I TRUST IN THE LORD. THEODORET: Even here he does not expressly announce that he will come but makes this depend on the providence of God. And clearly he has not yet wholly escaped his former peril. EPISTLE TO THE PHILIPPIANS 2.23-24.[6]

---

[3]CPE 2:56. [4]BT 1972:94 [1214C]. [5]BT 1972:95 [1215A]. [6]CPE 2:57.

2:25-30 THE MISSION OF EPAPHRODITUS

[25]*I have thought it necessary to send to you Epaphroditus my brother and fellow worker and fellow soldier, and your messenger and minister to my need,* [26]*for he has been longing for you all, and has been distressed because you heard that he was ill.* [27]*Indeed he was ill, near to death. But God had mercy on him, and not only on him but on me also, lest I should have sorrow upon sorrow.* [28]*I am the more eager to send him, therefore, that you may rejoice at seeing him again, and that I may be less anxious.* [29]*So receive him in the Lord with all joy; and honor such men,* [30]*for he nearly died for the work of Christ, risking his life to complete your service to me.*

OVERVIEW: A range of unusual qualities entitles Epaphroditus to be called *fellow soldier, minister, brother* and *apostle* (THEODORET, MARIUS VICTORINUS). God allowed his illness as a trial (AMBROSIASTER). His mission will bring a natural joy to the Philippians (CHRYSOSTOM) and so to Paul, despite his own loss (MARIUS VICTORINUS). He preempts any conflict by reminding them of Epaphroditus's services (AMBROSIASTER) and courage (CHRYSOSTOM) and bids them receive him with spiritual joy (CHRYSOSTOM). The desire for life is not to be demeaned (MARIUS VICTORINUS), especially when survival will conduce to the glory of God (MARIUS VICTORINUS, THEODORET).

2:25 Sending Epaphroditus to Them

EPAPHRODITUS IS BEING SENT SINCE TIMOTHY WAS DELAYED. MARIUS VICTORINUS: Although he has promised to send Timothy rapidly, nevertheless, because he still speaks of a certain delay, he now sends Epaphroditus. EPISTLE TO THE PHILIPPIANS 2.25.[1]

HOW THESE QUALITIES ARE DISTINGUISHED. MARIUS VICTORINUS: He commends the character of Epaphroditus by calling him *my brother and fellow soldier*. He is a *brother* in the law and a *fellow soldier* in the camp and in the work of the gospel. And he is called *your apostle*.[2] Note that he calls Epaphroditus an apostle. Everyone who is sent on account of the gospel can rightly be called an apostle. EPISTLE TO THE PHILIPPIANS 2.25.[3]

THE COMMENDATION OF EPAPHRODITUS. THEODORET: Paul attributes many accomplishments to Epaphroditus. He calls him not merely a *brother* but a *fellow worker* and a *fellow soldier*. And Paul has even called him *their apostle*, because he has been entrusted with their care. Thus it is apparent that those who were called *bishops* in the earlier part of the letter held their charge under Epaphroditus, being obviously presbyters. And he calls him a *minister to his need*,

because he had brought the necessities that they had sent, as was their duty, analogous to contributions for civic officers. EPISTLE TO THE PHILIPPIANS 2.25.[4]

2:26 Longing and Distress

THE SOLICITUDE OF PAUL. CHRYSOSTOM: See how earnestly Paul tries to forestall any tendencies toward lethargy or selfishness. He quickly removes the suspicion that it was through lack of concern for them that he did not come. For nothing is such a stimulus to progress in disciples as the conviction that their master truly cares about them. Paul shows that he feels sorrow on their behalf. This is a sign of his exceptional quality of love. HOMILY ON PHILIPPIANS 10.2.26-27.[5]

THEIR MUTUAL CONCERN. AMBROSIASTER: Both the congregation and Epaphroditus were sad because of his sickness. They hoped that they might, on seeing him, be reassured in his recovery of health and that he might be relieved of his present anxiety to see them. For he was their apostle, appointed by Paul when he sent him to them for their exhortation. EPISTLE TO THE PHILIPPIANS 2.27.1.[6]

2:27a Ill, Near to Death

HIS ILLNESS WAS INTENDED FOR HIS GROWTH. AMBROSIASTER: Is it possible that the apostle prayed for him and the prayer was not answered by his immediate recovery? Remember that signs are for unbeliev-

---

[1]BT 1972:95 [1215B]. [2]Or "minister." [3]BT 1972:95 [1215B]. [4]CPE 2:57. [5]IOEP 5:99-100. [6]CSEL 81.3:148-49.

ers. This man's illness was designed not for his hurt but for his growth. Many indeed are the trials of the faithful . . . and therefore the petition of the apostle was not spurned, but a better provision was made for him on whose behalf Paul prayed. EPISTLE TO THE PHILIPPIANS 2.27.2-3.[7]

2:27b God Had Mercy on Him and on Paul

GOD'S MERCY ON HIM. MARIUS VICTORINUS: Note what benefits we experience from the Lord even in this life. Hence we ought not hurry to death. For even if this world is a hotbed of sin and therefore to be shunned, yet the desire to live in the world comes from your nature and is not sin. Life ought to be desired. So it is right to say *God had mercy on him.* EPISTLE TO THE PHILIPPIANS 2.27.[8]

PRAYING FOR THOSE WHO ARE ILL. MARIUS VICTORINUS: Many are preserved and pitied by God because something is done through them which belongs to the ministry of salvation. At the same time we also should pray for those who are ill, lest we be saddened by the loss of those whose help we need in the performance, imparting and proclamation of divine grace. EPISTLE TO THE PHILIPPIANS 2.27.[9]

PAUL NOT DEPRIVED OF HIS FELLOW WORKER. THEODORET: The words *God had mercy on him* also reveal Epaphroditus's zeal for the contest. He did not wish to be rid of his wretched life, even knowing the gain that was to spring from it. "And God also pitied me," says Paul, "by not depriving me of my fellow worker." EPISTLE TO THE PHILIPPIANS 2.26-7.[10]

2:28a Eager to Send Epaphroditus

THE RELIEF OF SEEING THE SICK IMPROVE. CHRYSOSTOM: Hearing of those whom we desire to be well never makes us so glad as actually seeing them, especially when the event exceeds our expectations. HOMILY ON PHILIPPIANS 10.2.28.[11]

2:28b Lessening Anxiety

FULFILLING THEIR MUTUAL DESIRE. MARIUS VICTORINUS: Why does Paul add the phrase *and I may be less anxious?* Because he has already said that Epaphroditus had ministered to his needs. He did not want it to appear as though he was sad to be sending him. Since Epaphroditus desired to be with them and since they are going to be glad if they see him, Paul could then be *less anxious.* EPISTLE TO THE PHILIPPIANS 2.28.[12]

2:29 Receiving and Honoring Such Men

HIS WILLINGNESS TO DIE FOR THE GOSPEL. AMBROSIASTER: It is apparent that the people and Epaphroditus loved one another inseparably. He is commended by the apostle also, so as to make him all the more dear. . . . This is the reason for explicitly recalling the struggle of Epaphroditus: his unhesitating willingness to die for the sake of the gospel. EPISTLE TO THE PHILIPPIANS 2.30.[13]

RECEIVE HIM IN THE LORD. CHRYSOSTOM: *Receive him in the Lord*—this means spiritually, that is, with great eagerness. It means

---

[7]CSEL 81.3:149. [8]BT 1972:96 [1216A]. [9]BT 1972:97 [1216B]. [10]CPE 2:57. [11]IOEP 5:101. [12]BT 1972:97 [1216C]. [13]CSEL 81.3:150.

receive him in the Lord because it is God's will. "Give him, as saints ought to do, the reception due to a saint, *with all joy*." Paul says this for the sake of the congregation rather than Epaphroditus. The profit of doing good is greater than that of receiving reward. HOMILY ON PHILIPPIANS 10.2.29.[14]

2:30a *Risking His Life for Christ's Work*

HE NEARLY DIED. CHRYSOSTOM: He nearly died, says Paul, not "on my account" but *for the work of Christ*. This makes Epaphroditus all the more worthy of trust.... "He submitted himself as one who looked after me, whatever he had to suffer." But if he submitted himself to death for the sake of looking after Paul, how much more he would have suffered this for the sake of the proclamation of the gospel! HOMILY ON PHILIPPIANS 10.2.30.[15]

2:30b *Completing Service to Paul*

A SERVICE IN NEED OF COMPLETION. CHRYSOSTOM: The first obligation is to preserve those in danger. Do you see the wisdom of the apostle? This shows how much he cares for the faithful. He does this in order that they will not be elated over themselves but remain modest, and that they not think that they have done anything great but remain humble. He calls their deeds a service in need of completion. HOMILY ON PHILIPPIANS 10.2.30.[16]

HIS GREAT VALUE TO PAUL'S MINISTRY. CHRYSOSTOM: Epaphroditus had been sent by the community in Philippi to serve Paul. Perhaps he had brought something with him. He perhaps brought Paul supplies, as Paul shows near the end when he says *having received your gifts from Epaphroditus*.[17] It is likely then that when he arrived in the city of Rome Epaphroditus found Paul in grave and acute peril. Even those closest to Paul were not able to help him to safety. Epaphroditus, being a man of noble spirit, despised every danger. He visited Paul, ministered to him, did all that was needful. Paul gives two reasons for regarding him with such high respect: First, *he almost died* on Paul's account. Second, he did this as a representative of the whole city, so that in this danger the reward is reckoned to those who sent him, as though the whole city had sent him as an ambassador. So to receive him with kindness and to welcome him on account of what has happened is their way of sharing in his audacious enterprise. HOMILY ON PHILIPPIANS 10.2.28-30.[18]

---

[14]IOEP 5:101. [15]IOEP 5:101. [16]IOEP 5:101-2. [17]Phil 4:18. [18]IOEP 5:101-2.

3:1-3 TRUE AND FALSE CIRCUMCISION

¹*Finally, my brethren, rejoice in the Lord. To write the same things to you is not irksome to me, and is safe for you.* ²*Look out for the dogs, look out for the evil-workers, look out for those who mutilate the flesh.* ³*For we are the true circumcision, who worship God in spirit,*ᵉ *and glory in Christ Jesus, and put no confidence in the flesh.*

e *Other ancient authorities read* worship by the Spirit of God

OVERVIEW: Paul shows special concern for the Philippians in their despondency (CHRYSOSTOM). Those of the circumcision party are like dogs barking and attacking (AMBROSIASTER, CHRYSOSTOM). Paul urges them not to place any confidence in salvation by works (MARIUS VICTORINUS). He coins the ironic term *concision* (CHRYSOSTOM). Christians have the true circumcision of the heart (AMBROSIASTER). In such matters the Spirit illumines Scripture's deeper meaning (DIDYMUS THE BLIND).

3:1a *Rejoice in the Lord*

COMFORTING DESPONDENCY. CHRYSOSTOM: Despondency and worry deprive the soul of its vitality. They put an immoderate strain upon the soul. For this reason Paul comforts the Philippians, who were in great despondency because they did not know how things stood with Paul. They thought him already dead. . . . Note that he does not introduce his exhortation immediately, but after having heaped praises on them and expressed his wonder he praises them once again. HOMILY ON PHILIPPIANS 11.3.1-3.[1]

3:1b *Writing the Same Things*

READINESS TO REPEAT WHAT IS NECESSARY. AMBROSIASTER: He shows the concern that he feels for their faith walk. He repeats to them what is necessary for their benefit. EPISTLE TO THE PHILIPPIANS 3.1.[2]

3:2a *Wariness About Attackers*

BARKING AND ATTACKING DOGS. AMBROSIASTER: He uses this name for those who, in envy of the Gentiles, have overthrown them by their evil conversation and persuaded them to be circumcised. These he says should be absolutely avoided and rejected. They are like dogs that first bark and then mutilate the flesh with savage bites. EPISTLE TO THE PHILIPPIANS 3.2.[3]

GENTILES ONCE STRANGERS. CHRYSOSTOM: The Jews are no longer children. The Gentiles were once called *dogs* but now these [Judaizing Christians] are. Why so? Because, just as the Gentiles were once strangers to Christ and God, so these have now become.

---

[1]IOEP 5:111. [2]CSEL 81.3:151. [3]CSEL 81.3:151.

And he alludes to their stubborn shameless-ness and their great tenacity against the faith-ful. HOMILY ON PHILIPPIANS 11.3.1-3.[4]

3:2b *Looking Out for Evil Workers*

THE FALSE HOPE FOR SALVATION BY WORKS. MARIUS VICTORINUS: Divine Scrip-ture speaks of dogs which are of use and are defenders of the church, as David teaches in Psalm 68,[5] saying that these dogs are sated with the blood of enemies in the temple of God. And here he speaks of the opposite kind of dogs, who are obviously the Jews, be-cause they are *workers* and *evil workers*. For works are the sole exercise of their lives, without any knowledge of God, and from their works they hope for salvation. EPISTLE TO THE PHILIPPIANS 3.1-3.[6]

3:2c *Beware of Those Who Mutilate the Flesh*

WORDPLAY ON CIRCUMCISION. CHRYSOSTOM: The Jews attached great solemnity to circumci-sion. . . . Therefore Paul mutilates its name and says, *Beware of the concision*. He refrains from saying that circumcision is evil, that cir-cumcision is superfluous, so as not to alarm these people, but he conveys his point more wisely, turning them away from the act indeed but being gracious in his words, or rather more intent upon the issue. . . . He does not say that we try this circumcision and see whether it is

better. He does not even give it the name *cir-cumcision*. For what is he saying? "That cir-cumcision is mutilation." For when this happens unlawfully, it is nothing but a curtail-ment of the flesh, a "concision." Either this was the reason or else it was because they were trying to cut up the church in pieces. HOMILY ON PHILIPPIANS 11.3.1-3.[7]

3:3 *Worshiping God, Glorying in Christ Jesus*

THE TRUE CIRCUMCISION. AMBROSIASTER: It is evident that those who are faithful are circumcised in their own hearts. By cutting away the cloud of error, they see and recog-nize the Lord of creation. This is what it means to *serve in the Spirit* and *glory in the Lord Jesus Christ*. EPISTLE TO THE PHILIP-PIANS 3.4.[8]

THE SPIRIT ILLUMINES SCRIPTURE. DIDY-MUS THE BLIND: The word *spirit* signifies above all a deeper and mystic meaning in the holy Scriptures.[9] . . . This construction is supported by [the verse] *We are the circum-cision, who serve the Spirit of God and do not trust in the flesh*. ON THE HOLY SPIRIT 249.[10]

---

[4]IOEP 5:112. Cf. Theodoret *Epistle to the Philippians* 3.2.2 [CPE 2:58-59]. [5]Ps 68:23. [6]BT 1972:99 [1218A]. [7]IOEP 5:112. [8]CSEL 81.3:151. [9]Here Didymus cites 2 Corin-thians 3:6. [10]SC 386:366-69.

3:4-11 COUNTING ALL LOSS FOR CHRIST

[4]Though I myself have reason for confidence in the flesh also. If any other man thinks he has reason for confidence in the flesh, I have more: [5]circumcised on the eighth day, of the people of Israel, of the tribe of Benjamin, a Hebrew born of Hebrews; as to the law a Pharisee, [6]as to zeal a persecutor of the church, as to righteousness under the law blameless. [7]But whatever gain I had, I counted as loss for the sake of Christ. [8]Indeed I count everything as loss because of the surpassing worth of knowing Christ Jesus my Lord. For his sake I have suffered the loss of all things, and count them as refuse, in order that I may gain Christ [9]and be found in him, not having a righteousness of my own, based on law, but that which is through faith in Christ, the righteousness from God that depends on faith; [10]that I may know him and the power of his resurrection, and may share his sufferings, becoming like him in his death, [11]that if possible I may attain the resurrection from the dead.

OVERVIEW: Paul shows that he has not failed by the standards of the law (CHRYSOSTOM). Listing his credentials in the most impressive order (CHRYSOSTOM), he claims distinction by styling himself a Hebrew of the tribe of Benjamin (THEODORET, CHRYSOSTOM). Persecution of the church proves his zeal as a Jew (CHRYSOSTOM, THEODORET), but this was only a specious righteousness (AUGUSTINE). Using a metaphor from nature and Scripture (THEODORET, AMBROSE) he counts his former righteousness as refuse, but only by comparison with his new state (CHRYSOSTOM). His legal righteousness was external (AUGUSTINE) and worthless in comparison with that of God-given faith (THEODORET, CHRYSOSTOM). Paul alludes to those baptismal teachings that we must know (THEODORET) but stresses that these are profitable only when apprehended by a faith willing to suffer (CHRYSOSTOM, MARIUS VICTORINUS). This faith is from God (CHRYSOSTOM). Righteousness in this life awaits completion in the future life (MARIUS VICTORINUS).

3:4 Confidence in the Flesh

BORN A JEW. CHRYSOSTOM: Suppose Paul had been a Gentile and had condemned circumcision (not circumcision itself but those who underwent it inappropriately). It would then have seemed that he might be demeaning it because he did not have the good fortune to be born a Jew. He would have appeared to be ignorant of lofty things, having no experience of them. But Paul speaks as a Jew. He speaks as one who shares in Jewish culture. He does not despise as a nonparticipant but criticizes as one who has made a reasonable assessment, not in ignorance but with intimate knowledge. HOMILY ON PHILIPPIANS 11.3.4.[1]

3:5a Of the Tribe of Benjamin

WHY HE STATES HIS CREDENTIALS IN THIS ORDER. CHRYSOSTOM: Paul first mentions the very point that was their chief boast, the ritual of circumcision. He was, he says, *circumcised on the eighth day.* So he makes it clear that he comes *of the stock of Israel.* By this language he shows that he is not a proselyte (hence the eight day), nor was he born of a proselyte background (for he comes of the stock of Israel). And so that no one may suppose that *of the stock of Israel* means from one of the ten tribes, he further specifies that he is *of the tribe of Benjamin.* This is a highly respected Jewish identity, since the affairs of the priesthood fell to the lot of this tribe. HOMILY ON PHILIPPIANS 11.3.5.[2]

THE SIGNIFICANCE OF BENJAMIN. THEODORET: "My Jewish identity," he says, "is in no way ambiguous. I do not come from a family that was only partially Jewish. I am a plant of freedom, a son of Rachel the beloved, on whose behalf the patriarch[3] himself endured slavery." EPISTLE TO THE PHILIPPIANS 3.5.[4]

3:5b A Hebrew Born of Hebrews and a Pharisee

A HEBREW OF THE HEBREWS. CHRYSOSTOM: It was possible to be *of Israel* but not a *Hebrew of the Hebrews.* For there were many who had already misplaced their Hebrew heritage. Long residing among Gentiles, they had become ignorant of their Hebrew

tongue. Not so with Paul. HOMILY ON PHILIPPIANS 11.3.5.[5]

3:6a A Persecutor of the Church

THE IMPLICATION OF HIS FORMER ZEAL. CHRYSOSTOM: "If then it was because of my good breeding and my zeal and my way of life, and I had all the things that belong to life, why," he says, "did I let go those lofty things, unless I found that those of Christ were greater, and greater by far?" HOMILY ON PHILIPPIANS 11.3.6.[6]

BURNING WITH ZEAL FOR THE LAW. THEODORET: "When I was harrying the church," he says, "I was not driven by love of honor or vainglory or jealousy, like the rulers of the Jews. I was burning with zeal for the law." EPISTLE TO THE PHILIPPIANS 3.6.[7]

3:6b Under the Law Blameless

BLAMELESS UNDER THE LAW. AUGUSTINE: Before his conversion Paul fulfilled the law conspicuously, either through fear of the people or of God himself, even if he may have offended the law in his internal affections. But he was fulfilling the law through fear of punishment, not through love of righteousness. ON TWO LETTERS OF PELAGIUS 1.15.[8]

3:7 Gain Counted as Loss for the Sake of Christ

THE LADDER OF THE LAW NO LONGER NEEDED. CHRYSOSTOM: What do the false

---

[1]IOEP 5:114. [2]IOEP 5:114-15. [3]Jacob. [4]CPE 2:59. [5]IOEP 5:115. [6]IOEP 5:116. [7]CPE 2:59-60. [8]Migne PL 44:558. Cf. on Phil 3:15.

teachers[9] say about this passage? "See, the law is a *loss*; it is *refuse*. How then do you say it is of God?" In fact, all this is in favor of the law. How so? It is clear from this passage, if we attend closely to the words. He does not say "the law is privation" but *I count it loss*. And when he spoke of gain, he did not say "I count it" but *it was*. For the latter was true by nature, the former in his own estimation. So, whatever gain I had in the law, I count as loss *on account of Christ*. How then was the law ever *a gain*, and not in supposition but in fact? Consider what a great thing it was to restore the human form to people who had been turned to beasts. And without the law, there would be no grace. How so? Because the law served as a bridge. It was not possible to be raised from this extreme lowliness. So the law served as a ladder. Note that when a person has gone up a ladder, he no longer needs it. Yet he does not despise it but gives it thanks, because it is due to the ladder that he is in the state of no longer needing it. . . . It is not the law that is a privation but apostasy from Christ through adherence to the law. So when it leads us away from Christ it is a loss. When it leads us to him, no longer so. HOMILY ON PHILIPPIANS 12.3.7-9.[10]

3:8 The Surpassing Worth of Knowing Christ Jesus

THE HARD PART OF THE CHAFF IS REFUSE. THEODORET: It is not that I flee them[11] as base things but that I prefer what is superior. Having tasted the grain I throw away the refuse. For *refuse* means the denser and harder part of the chaff. It carries the grain but is discarded once the grain has been col-

lected. EPISTLE TO THE PHILIPPIANS 3.8.[12]

THE REFUSE METAPHOR IN ABRAHAM, JOB AND DAVID. AMBROSE: He had read that Abraham, when he confessed himself to be refuse and ashes, found God's grace in his extreme humility.[13] He had read that Job, sitting on his refuse heap, had recovered all his losses.[14] He had read in David's prophecy that *God raises the needy from the earth and the pauper from the refuse*.[15] ON PENITENCE 2.1.4.[16]

3:9a Righteousness Not His Own

NOT MY OWN RIGHTEOUSNESS. AUGUSTINE: Now what does he mean, *not having my own righteousness*, when that law was not his but God's? He can only have called it his own righteousness because, although it was from the law, he used to think that he could fulfill it without the aid of the grace that is through Christ. ON GRACE AND FREE WILL 26.[17]

3:9b Righteousness Through Faith in Christ

RIGHTEOUSNESS FROM GOD. CHRYSOSTOM: Righteousness comes from faith, which means that it too is a gift of God. For since this righteousness belongs to God, it is an unmerited gift. And the gifts of God greatly exceed any achievements of our own zeal. HOMILY ON PHILIPPIANS 12.3.7-9.[18]

---

[9]His reference is probably to the Antinomians and to followers of Marcion, who demeaned the Old Testament. [10]IOEP 5:123. [11]I.e., the commands of the law. [12]CPE 2:60; following Chrysostom *Homily on Philippians* 12.3.7-9 [IOEP 5:125]. [13]Gen 18:27. [14]Job 2:8; 42:10-17. [15]Ps 113:7. [16]CSEL 73:164. [17]Migne PL 44:896. [18]IOEP 5:125.

BY FAITH. THEODORET: If, as he tells the Colossians, *in Christ are hidden all the treasures of wisdom and knowledge*,[19] then everything, whatever it is, is to be reckoned of no account, so that we may attain to the height of this wisdom and knowledge. Not only sufficient but superabundant indeed is the righteousness that comes from faith. This salvation is freely given by the grace of God through the knowledge of Christ. It can hardly be said to be a gift of the law. For to know rightly the mystery of his incarnation and passion and resurrection is the perfection of life and the treasure of wisdom. EPISTLE TO THE PHILIPPIANS 3.9-10.[20]

3:10a *Knowing Christ and the Power of His Resurrection*

THE POWER OF HIS RESURRECTION KNOWN THROUGH FAITH. CHRYSOSTOM: Knowledge therefore comes through faith, and without faith there is no knowledge. How so? It is only through faith that we know the power of his resurrection. For what reasoning could demonstrate the resurrection to us? None, but it is through faith. And if the resurrection of Christ in the flesh is known through faith, how can the nativity of the Word be comprehended by reason? For the resurrection is far more plausible to reason than the virgin birth. HOMILY ON PHILIPPIANS 12.3.10-11.[21]

KNOWING THE BAPTISMAL CONFESSION THROUGH FAITH. THEODORET: To know *the power of his resurrection* means to know through faith that he is the God and Maker of all, he assumed our nature, he effected our salvation, and he was raised again in the

body that he had taken as he conceived the common salvation of all humanity. To know *the power of his resurrection* is to know the purpose of his resurrection. EPISTLE TO THE PHILIPPIANS 3.9-10.[22]

3:10b *Sharing in Christ's Sufferings*

SHARE IN HIS SUFFERINGS. CHRYSOSTOM: From faith comes our sharing in his sufferings. How? If we had not believed in him, we would not be suffering with him. If we had not believed that we will abide and reign with him, we would not have endured these sufferings. HOMILY ON PHILIPPIANS 12.3.10-11.[23]

3:11 *Attaining the Resurrection from the Dead*

THROUGH SUFFERING TO RESURRECTION. MARIUS VICTORINUS: We who believe in Christ endure sufferings with him and indeed all sufferings, even as far as the cross and death. From the knowledge of all these and from the sharing in suffering comes resurrection. And thus, as we are sharers in his death and his burden, we are enabled to share his resurrection. EPISTLE TO THE PHILIPPIANS 3.10-11.[24]

IF IN ANY WAY. MARIUS VICTORINUS: It is because Paul is still persevering in the fellowship of suffering, which is very similar to death itself, that he says *that if possible I may attain the resurrection from the dead*. There can be no doubt of his attaining to the resurrection. But what is this attaining to

---

[19]Col 2:3. [20]CPE 2:60-61. [21]IOEP 5:126. [22]CPE 2:60-61. [23]IOEP 5:126. [24]BT 1972:102 [1220B].

the resurrection of the dead? It is the perfect and full life of every individual which is elicited from the fellowship of Christ's sufferings by every means, which will appear clearly at that end time when the resurrec-

tion from the dead occurs, that is, when the dead come back to life. EPISTLE TO THE PHILIPPIANS 3.12.[25]

---

[25]BT 1972:102-3 [1220D-1221A].

3:12-16 PRESSING ON TO THE GOAL

[12]*Not that I have already obtained this or am already perfect; but I press on to make it my own, because Christ Jesus has made me his own.* [13]*Brethren, I do not consider that I have made it my own; but one thing I do, forgetting what lies behind and straining forward to what lies ahead,* [14]*I press on toward the goal for the prize of the upward call of God in Christ Jesus.* [15]*Let those of us who are mature be thus minded; and if in anything you are otherwise minded, God will reveal that also to you.* [16]*Only let us hold true to what we have attained.*

OVERVIEW: Paul's modesty is a lesson in humility for the Philippians (THEODORET), for he discounts even his labors as an evangelist (THEODORET), teaching us that all perfection lies in a gradual advance toward the future with God (JEROME). His entreaty combines both humility and aspiration (MARIUS VICTORINUS), hinting at prizes yet unseen (THEODORET). He claims maturity only in his aspirations and in the knowledge of his imperfection (AUGUSTINE). He banishes complacency (AMBROSIASTER), stressing the urgency of the tasks in which our actions are manifesting our reconciliation with Christ (CHRYSOSTOM, THEODORET, MARIUS VICTORINUS). He prays for the instruction of those who disagree (HILARY OF POITIERS) or offer new interpretations (MARIUS VIC-

TORINUS). He tells them to be content with the received doctrine (AMBROSIASTER) and to advance with the grace of God (AUGUSTINE).

3:12a Not Already Perfect

NOT THAT I HAVE ALREADY OBTAINED. AMBROSIASTER: Throughout the letter Paul bears witness to his joy in them and praises their obedience and faith. He is, however, concerned that they, like all who are subject to human conceits, might become elated as though they were already worthy. So he tells them openly, speaking of his own person, that something is still wanting for perfect righteousness. He urges them to good works. If he who is adorned with such dignity confesses that he is still wanting in perfection, they would understand how much more they must work to acquire the blessings of righteousness. EPISTLE TO THE PHILIPPIANS 3.12.1.[1]

3:12b *Pressing On*

STRAINING IN PURSUIT. CHRYSOSTOM: He says not "I run" but *I press on*. Consider how the pursuer strains in his pursuit. He sees nothing, he thrusts away all who impede him with great force, he cherishes his mind, his eye, his strength, his soul and his body, looking at nothing other than the crown. HOMILY ON PHILIPPIANS 12.3.12.[2]

NOW ACTIVELY PURSUING THE ONE WHO ONCE PURSUED ME. THEODORET: "It was he who first caught me in his net" Paul says in effect, "for I was fleeing him and was turned well away. He caught me as I fled. But now I in turn am the pursuer in my desire of catching him, that I may not be a disappointment to his saving work." EPISTLE TO THE PHILIPPIANS 3.12.[3]

MAKING MY OWN THE ONE WHO MADE ME HIS OWN. MARIUS VICTORINUS: Christ by his sufferings has set free all who follow him. He embraces everyone, but especially those who follow. The one who wants to follow and embrace Christ is bound to follow Christ in all his sufferings. Only in this way may he embrace Christ as Christ embraces him. For if Christ set everyone free by his sufferings, he embraces everyone in his sufferings. EPISTLE TO THE PHILIPPIANS 3.12.[4]

3:13a *Not Fully My Own*

NOT YET FULLY MADE IT MY OWN. MARIUS

VICTORINUS: If they compared themselves with Paul, the Philippians would understand how far they were from the blessings of freedom. How frequently had he shared in so many of Christ's sufferings: He had been beaten, imprisoned, thrown to wild beasts and burdened with other evils. Nonetheless even he did not think that he had already taken hold of Christ, as long as he was alive. EPISTLE TO THE PHILIPPIANS 3.13.[5]

3:13b *Straining Forward*

WHAT IS PERFECT TODAY MAY BE FALSE TO-MORROW. JEROME: Put the past out of mind. Set your mind to the future. What he has reckoned perfect today he ascertains to have been false tomorrow as he reaches for ever better and higher goals. By this gradual advance, never being static but always in progress, he is able to teach us that what we supposed in our human way to be perfect still remains in some ways imperfect. The only perfection is the true righteousness of God. DIALOGUE AGAINST THE PELAGIANS 1.15.[6]

FORGETTING WHAT LIES BEHIND. THEODORET: Some think that *paying no heed to the things behind* refers to life under the law. I think he says this of his labors as a preacher. For his custom was to be cursory and to mingle doctrinal statement with exhortation. What he says then is "I pay no heed to my previous labors, but I strive enthusiastically to press on to those ahead." EPISTLE TO THE PHILIPPIANS 3.13-14.[7]

---

[1]CSEL 81.3:154-55. [2]IOEP 5:128. [3]CPE 2:61. [4]BT 1972:103 [1221B]. [5]BT 1972:103-4 [1221C]. [6]CCL 80:18-19. [7]CPE 2:61.

3:14 *The Upward Call of God in Christ Jesus*

THE UPWARD CALL OF GOD. MARIUS VIC-TORINUS: Here then are two precepts for the one who is going to live the rest of life walking in the Christian way. First, the one who is still living under divine governance, however well and rightly he has acted in the past, should not think about all the actions he has already done as though he deserved to obtain something by them. Rather he should cast them into oblivion, always seeking the new tasks that remain. Second, he should nonetheless keep living under the divine rule, continually *pressing on* toward these things and observing the rule of Christ, even to death. EPISTLE TO THE PHILIPPIANS 3.13-14.[8]

THOUGH WE KNOW NOT THE FUTURE WE KNOW THE ONE WHO KNOWS IT. THEODORET: This is how we should think about the crowns laid up for us. For even if we do not perceive exactly what these are like, we ought at least to know that God, as Master of the contest, will reveal this to us. EPISTLE TO THE PHILIPPIANS 3.15.[9]

3:15a *The Mind of the Mature*

HOW THE MATURE IN FAITH ARE BOTH PERFECT AND IMPERFECT. AUGUSTINE: The apostle speaks of himself as both perfect and imperfect[10]: imperfect when he considers how much righteousness is still wanting in him but perfect in that he does not blush to confess his own imperfection and makes good progress in order to attain it. ON TWO LETTERS OF PELAGIUS 3.19.[11]

TO RUN PERFECTLY IS TO BE AWARE THAT WE ARE NOT YET PERFECT. AUGUSTINE:

All of us who are running the race perfectly should be aware that we are not yet perfect. The hope is that we may receive perfection in the place to which we are now running perfectly. ON THE PERFECTION OF HUMAN RIGHTEOUSNESS 19.[12]

3:15b *God Will Reveal Different Understandings*

DIFFERENT UNDERSTANDINGS OF MATURITY ALLOWED AMONG THE MATURE IN FAITH. MARIUS VICTORINUS: Assuming that this statement is complete and self-contained and need not be linked to his subsequent words, I think it must be understood as follows: "If there is anything in what I have said that you construe or understand in a different way, I allow your understanding to develop." Remember that he is speaking of the perfect, for so he says so: *we who are perfect....* "In due time *God will reveal this to you,* since both what you understand and what I have said are fitting." EPISTLE TO THE PHILIPPIANS 3.15.[13]

HOPING THEY WILL BE MADE PERFECT WHO IMAGINE THEMSELVES ALREADY PERFECT. HILARY OF POITIERS: If we, because of the tendency to err that lies within the human condition, take the meaning of anything for granted, we are not to refuse increase of understanding through grace.... For the apostle has already explained the thought of those whose thought is perfect.[14] As to those

---

[8]BT 1972:104 [1222A-B]. [9]CPE 2:62. [10]Phil 3:6. [11]Migne PL 44:602. [12]Migne PL 44:300. [13]BT 1972:105-6 [1223A]. [14]Those whose thought is perfect understand that they are still on the way to a maturity that is to be completed in the future with God. For those who think otherwise (i.e., that they have already attained), Paul hopes their imperfect thoughts will be brought to greater perfection.

who think otherwise concerning God's revelation, he hopes that their thoughts will be brought to perfection. ON THE TRINITY 11.24.[15]

3:16 Hold True to What Is Attained

HOLD TRUE TO THE CONSENT OF THE WHOLE CHURCH TO BAPTISMAL FAITH. AMBROSIASTER: Lest anyone should presume to think this was not from God and revealed by God he therefore adds the words *what we have attained*, that we should think in accord with the apostles. That means that we should not overstep the rule of doctrine[16] in understanding but accept what is commonly and humbly under-

stood in the truth of the gospel. EPISTLE TO THE PHILIPPIANS 3.16.[17]

THE PERFECT TRAVELER DOES NOT HOLD STILL BUT ADVANCES DAY BY DAY. AUGUSTINE: *Hold true* with the affections of the mind and habits of living, so that one is able to be perfectly in the possession of righteousness when, advancing day by day along the direct road of faith, one has already become a perfect traveler on the road. ON WHAT IS DUE TO SINNERS 2.20.[18]

---

[15]Migne PL 10:416A-B [390-91]. [16]The baptismal confession in the name of the Father, Son and Spirit. [17]CSEL 81.3:156. [18]Migne PL 44:164.

3:17-21 THE LOST AND THE SAVED

[17]Brethren, join in imitating me, and mark those who so live as you have an example in us. [18]For many, of whom I have often told you and now tell you even with tears, live as enemies of the cross of Christ. [19]Their end is destruction, their god is the belly, and they glory in their shame, with minds set on earthly things. [20]But our commonwealth is in heaven, and from it we await a Savior, the Lord Jesus Christ, [21]who will change our lowly body to be like his glorious body, by the power which enables him even to subject all things to himself.

OVERVIEW: The Philippians are instructed to imitate Paul even in his absence (CHRYSOSTOM). Those against whom he warns among the Philippians are already leading the Galatians into a new bondage (AMBROSIASTER). He predicts their destruc-

tion (MARIUS VICTORINUS). Christians have a future resurrection (HILARY OF POITIERS), which detaches them even now from the world (BASIL OF CAESAREA), in which they view themselves as pilgrims (CLEMENT OF ALEXANDRIA). The cross is the means of a transfiguration (MARIUS VICTORINUS), which does not destroy our bodies (TERTULLIAN) but frees them from corrupt desires (CASSIODORUS) and makes them spiritual (MARIUS VICTORINUS). God sets limits in the use of our bodies in the world (CHRYSOSTOM). The risen Lord subjects all things to himself, conferring upon our creation a new nature (AMBROSIASTER, HILARY OF POITIERS).

3:17 *Join in Imitating Me*

YOU KNOW MY MANNER OF LIFE. CHRYSOSTOM: Remember above when he said *beware of dogs*[1] and drew them away from those people? Now he directs them to what they ought to imitate. "If anyone," he says, "wishes to imitate me and tread the same path, let him hold fast to the faithful. And even if I am not present, yet you know my manner of walking— that is, my way of acting, speaking and living." For he taught them not through words only but also through deeds. In a chorus or a military camp you expect the others to imitate the director or the general. They should walk in the same good order. Otherwise the line can be broken by conflict. HOMILY ON PHILIPPIANS 13.3.17.[2]

3:18a *An Exhortation with Tears*

THEIR FEARFUL END. MARIUS VICTORINUS: An exhortation is stronger when it is accompanied by what is fearful in its alternative. . . . Paul expresses heartfelt affection when he describes the evils suffered by those who live otherwise, saying, *I say it with tears.* EPISTLE TO THE PHILIPPIANS 3.19.[3]

NOW WITH TEARS. AMBROSIASTER: Those who bring him to tears are the very ones who had already overthrown the Galatians. By treacherous proceedings they were destroying the churches in the name of Christ. . . . He speaks of these people with grief and tears. They were impeding the salvation of the faithful by raising questions about the eating of or abstinence from food. It is as though salvation were in food or as if *God were a belly,* one whom they believed to take delight in worldly foods according to the law while they gloried in the circumcision of their private parts. This is what it is to *think earthly thoughts.* One who *thinks spiritual thoughts* glories in faith, hope and charity. EPISTLE TO THE PHILIPPIANS 3.19.[4]

3:18b *Living as Enemies of the Cross*

ENEMIES OF THE CROSS SEE ONLY FLESH OR ONLY SPIRIT CRUCIFIED. MARIUS VICTORINUS: There are two types of misunderstanding of Christ, or rather one class of two descriptions, who are enemies of Christ. For some in their carnal thoughts deride the cross of Christ, thinking of Christ merely as a man raised onto a cross. . . . These pay attention to nothing but the flesh. To them *their god is a belly* and their *glory is in filthiness.* These are the ones who *think earthly thoughts* and whose end is death. On the other hand, there are those who think of Christ only as a spirit. They do not think of him as incarnate or crucified. They too are enemies to the cross of Christ, having death as their end. EPISTLE TO THE PHILIPPIANS 3.19.[5]

3:19 *Minds Set on Earthly Things*

---

[1]Phil 3:2. [2]IOEP 5:136. [3]BT 1972:107 [1224B-C]. [4]CSEL 81.3:157. [5]BT 1972:108-9 [1225A-C].

PUT BOUNDARIES ON THE BELLY. CHRYSOSTOM: Your belly is given to you so that you may nourish it, not so that it may burst. Your body is given you that you may rule it, not so that you may have it as a mistress. It is given that it may serve you for the nourishment of the other members, not so that you may serve it. Do not exceed these bounds. The sea in flood does not so much harm to the boundaries as our belly does to our bodies and our souls. The flood overwhelms only part of the land. The god of the belly overwhelms the whole body. Set self-constraint as a bound to it as God sets the sand to the sea. HOMILY ON PHILIPPIANS 14.3.18-21.[6]

THEY GLORY IN THEIR SHAME. CHRYSOSTOM: Those who *glory in their shame* some think is a reference to circumcision. I disagree. *To glory in their shame* means to take pride in what they ought to conceal. For it is bad enough to do shameful things. But if the doer is ashamed, it is only half so terrible. When, however, someone preens himself on his own shame, that is the extreme of shamelessness. HOMILY ON PHILIPPIANS 14.3.18-21.[7]

WHOSE GOD IS IN THEIR BELLY. CHRYSOSTOM: Let us build houses: where? On earth. Let us procure fields: on earth again. Let us get power: on earth again. Let us get glory: on earth again. Let us be rich: always on earth. These are the ones *whose god is their belly.* HOMILY ON PHILIPPIANS 14.3.18-21.[8]

3:20a *Our Commonwealth in Heaven*

WHETHER ANNIHILATION IS THE END. HILARY OF POITIERS: If it should be the case that both the blessed and the impious have an end and that end is understood as annihilation, the end makes religion and impiety equal. The common end of both would consist simply in not being. And where is our *hope in heaven* if our end simply makes us nonexistent? If hope is said to be owed to the saints and an end to the impious, even then the end cannot be simply annihilation. For how could it be a punishment of impiety to have no awareness whatever of the punishments that avenge it? Would not one who is annihilated not know the cause of his suffering? Better to distinguish a continuing place reserved for the blessed and another prepared for the wicked. ON THE TRINITY 11.28.[9]

CITIZENS OF HEAVEN. BASIL OF CAESAREA: We drag our body like a shadow along the ground, but we guard our soul as one that shares in the citizenship of heaven. ON BAPTISM 1.21.[10]

3:20b *Awaiting a Savior, the Lord Jesus Christ*

LIVING AS EXPATRIATES. CLEMENT OF ALEXANDRIA: We know that this is well said, for we ought to live as strangers and expatriates in the world . . . not using the creation to satisfy our passions but high-mindedly and with thanksgiving. STROMATA 3.95.[11]

3:21a *Our Body to Be Like Christ's Glorious Body*

---

[6]IOEP 5:144. [7]IOEP 5:143. [8]IOEP 5:143; commenting on Phil 3:20. [9]Migne PL 10:418B-C [392-93]. [10]SC 357:170-72. [11]CAO 2:303.

LIKE HIS GLORIOUS BODY. MARIUS VICTOR-INUS: When we rise and are changed and are made spiritual in soul, body and spirit (for all these three make up one man and are one spirit), the body in which we have been humbled will be raised. It will be of the same and an equal form to the body of Christ's own glory. So too we shall be spirits as he himself is a spirit. EPISTLE TO THE PHILIPPIANS 3.21.[12]

HOW CHRIST CHANGES OUR LOWLY BODY. MARIUS VICTORINUS: In this place of worship dwells the mystery of the resurrection. For what was fulfilled in Christ in the flesh was this: that he should save souls and also cause immortality to be given to the flesh through resurrection. This he accomplished by the power of his cross. EPISTLE TO THE PHILIPPIANS 3.21.[13]

THE SAME BODY WILL RISE. TERTULLIAN: If Christ coming from heaven will *transform the body of our humiliation into conformity with the body of his glory*, then this body of ours, which is humbled by sufferings and cast down into the earth by the very law of death, is the very body that will rise. For how will it be transformed if there is nothing? AGAINST MARCION 5.20.7.[14]

SIN NO LONGER DESIRED. CASSIODORUS: What he obviously means is that those who

no longer desire sins are immortal, since they enjoy divine delights. That is the rule ordained for the blessed, of whom it is said, *They shall be as angels.*[15] SUMMARY OF PHILIPPIANS 5.3.21.[16]

3:21b All Things Subject to the Lord

FROM NATURE TO NATURE. HILARY OF POITIERS: *The power that enables him to subject all things to himself* consists in the transition from one nature to another nature. Insofar as it ceases to be its previous nature, it becomes subject to its new nature. It does not stop existing but advances in existing. It ceases to be the old nature and becomes the new nature. It is subdued by transformation as it passes into the fashion of the new kind that it has assumed. ON THE TRINITY 11.35.[17]

THE POWER OF THE LORD MANIFEST. AMBROSIASTER: Through the resurrection of the dead and their transformation into glory the power of the Lord will be manifestly apparent, subduing all the principalities and powers so that he may be manifestly the God and Lord of all. EPISTLE TO THE PHILIPPIANS 3.21.[18]

---

[12]BT 1972:110. [13]BT 1972:109 [1226A]. [14]CCL 1:725. Cf. Irenaeus *Against Heresies* 5.13.3 [SC 153:170-75]. [15]Mt 22:30. [16]Migne PL 70:1350A. [17]Migne PL 10:422C-423A [397]. [18]CSEL 81.3:158.

4:1-7 COUNSELS OF PEACE

[1]*Therefore, my brethren, whom I love and long for, my joy and crown, stand firm thus in the Lord, my beloved.*

[2]*I entreat Euodia and I entreat Syntyche to agree in the Lord. [3]And I ask you also, true yokefellow, help these women, for they have labored side by side with me in the gospel together with Clement and the rest of my fellow workers, whose names are in the book of life.*

[4]*Rejoice in the Lord always; again I will say, Rejoice. [5]Let all men know your forbearance. The Lord is at hand. [6]Have no anxiety about anything, but in everything by prayer and supplication with thanksgiving let your requests be made known to God. [7]And the peace of God, which passes all understanding, will keep your hearts and your minds in Christ Jesus.*

OVERVIEW: Paul urges the Philippians toward constancy in the increase of virtue (AMBROSIASTER, MARIUS VICTORINUS). He pleads for peace between Euodia and Syntyche (MARIUS VICTORINUS). He asks help in this from someone he calls his *yokefellow,* who some (erroneously) speculated might be his wife (CLEMENT OF ALEXANDRIA). It is more probably a compassionate believer (THEODORET) and might possibly be Epaphroditus (MARIUS VICTORINUS). He commends the joy that arises from unity (MARIUS VICTORINUS) and increases with wholesome solemnity (CHRYSOSTOM). Forbearance and moderation draw us toward Christ (MARIUS VICTORINUS) and win others to him (AMBROSIASTER). We must wait vigilantly for the Lord (AMBROSIASTER), casting away worldly cares (MARIUS VICTORINUS) and giving thanks in every form of prayer (CHRYSOSTOM, MARIUS VICTORINUS). God's peace exceeds our hopes (CHRYSOSTOM) and brings perfect harmony (MARIUS VICTORINUS).

4:1a *Paul's Joy and Crown*

THE FUTURE CROWN. AMBROSIASTER: The constancy of the Philippians is Paul's joy, both for the present and for his future crown. For when his disciples are victorious in the contest, the master rightly receives the crown. EPISTLE TO THE PHILIPPIANS 4.1.[1]

4:1b *Stand Firm in the Lord*

THE BELOVED STAND TOGETHER AS ONE IN CHRIST. MARIUS VICTORINUS: Love, the sum of every virtue for the Christian, does not fittingly come to pass if the faithful do not stand united as one, thinking in harmony. This is what Paul means here by *Stand firm in the Lord, my beloved.* We may understand that he wants them to be united in understanding from the fact that he calls

[1]CSEL 81.3:158.

them [literally] *most beloved brethren*. Mutual love is the result of thinking in unison and standing together in Christ. When all have equal faith in Christ all of us stand together in him. EPISTLE TO THE PHILIPPIANS 4.1.[2]

4:2 Entreating Euodia and Syntyche

PAUL HANDLES A QUARREL BETWEEN TWO WOMEN. MARIUS VICTORINUS: He asks that these women should seek a common understanding in the Lord. Out of their belief in Christ, they should think and understand what the gospel says about Christ. But he says *I ask*, implying that this will be to their benefit. "I do not command or order; I ask." EPISTLE TO THE PHILIPPIANS 4.2.[3]

4:3a A True Yokefellow

WHETHER THIS YOKEFELLOW MIGHT BE PAUL'S WIFE. CLEMENT OF ALEXANDRIA: Paul at least is not afraid in one of his letters to give the name *yokefellow* to the one whom, for the convenience of his ministry, he did not lead about with him.[4] STROMATA 3.53.[5]

PAUL UNMARRIED. THEODORET: Now some have been foolish enough to suppose that the *yokefellow* was his wife, not considering that when he wrote to the Corinthians he reckoned himself among the unmarried.[6] . . . So the *yokefellow* is so called because he bore the same yoke of piety. EPISTLE TO THE PHILIPPIANS 4.3.[7]

WHETHER EPAPHRODITUS IS ASKED TO MEDIATE. MARIUS VICTORINUS: I have said above that he promised that Epaphroditus

would come to Philippi, and then I showed that Paul sent him when he said *and so I sent him in haste*. Therefore this is now, so to speak, added so that he may give him a command in the letter, praying and beseeching him to tell those women, Euodia and Syntyche, to have a common understanding in the Lord. . . . And that Epaphroditus is the one to whom he gives this command to help the aforesaid women to reach a common understanding can be perceived from the fact that he says, *I pray and beseech you, brother and yokefellow*, whereas above he said, *I thought Epaphroditus needful, my brother and fellow soldier*. EPISTLE TO THE PHILIPPIANS 4.3.[8]

4:3b Laboring Side by Side in the Gospel

THESE WOMEN TOILED WITH HIM SIDE BY SIDE IN THE GOSPEL. CHRYSOSTOM: Do you see how great is the virtue of these women, according to his testimony? As great as that which Christ told his apostles . . . *your names are written in the book of life*.[9] . . . Did they toil with him? Yes, he says. They contributed in no small part. Even though there were many fellow workers, yet in many affairs they also took a hand. Great therefore was the cohesion of the church at that time when the most respected, whether men or women, enjoyed such honor from the rest. There were many good consequences. HOMILY ON PHILIPPIANS 14.4.2-3.[10]

4:4 Rejoice in the Lord Always

---

[2]BT 1972:111 [1227B-C]. [3]BT 1972:112 [1228A]. [4]1 Cor 9:5. [5]CAO 2:276. [6]Here Theodoret cites 1 Corinthians 7:8. [7]CPE 2:64. [8]BT 1972:112 [1228A-C]. [9]Lk 10:20. [10]IOEP 5:146.

JOINED IN HEART. MARIUS VICTORINUS: This means that the consequence of having unity in understanding and faith is that they rejoice in the Lord and are always dear to one another. *Rejoice,* he says, *in the Lord*—this is too little: *again I say rejoice.* For when you are joined in heart you rejoice in the Lord, and when you rejoice in the Lord you are joined in heart and stand together in the Lord. EPISTLE TO THE PHILIPPIANS 4.4-5.[11]

AGAIN I SAY, REJOICE. CHRYSOSTOM: This rejoicing is not separable from grief,[12] for indeed it is rather deeply connected with grief. The one who grieves for his own wrongdoing and confesses it is joyful. Alternatively it is possible to grieve for one's own sins but rejoice in Christ.... On this account he says *Rejoice in the Lord.* For this is nothing if you have received a life worthy of rejoicing.... He is right to repeat himself. For since the events are naturally grievous, it is through the repetition that he shows that in all cases one should rejoice. HOMILY ON PHILIPPIANS 15.4.4-7.[13]

4:5a Let Everyone Know Your Forbearance

FORBEARANCE DEFINED. MARIUS VICTORINUS: Forbearance is individual patience that observes due measure without straining beyond its station. When we live among strangers and live in a way commensurate with our lowliness, God will lift us up. So it is here; we do well to recognize our lowliness. "Therefore let your moderation," he says, "be known to all." Why does he tell us this? So that we may make a pleasing show here? No, but so that when Christ comes he may raise up our lowliness

and exalt our moderation. EPISTLE TO THE PHILIPPIANS 4.4-5.[14]

LET OTHERS SEE, THAT THEY MAY PROFIT. AMBROSIASTER: Paul wants all to profit by good examples. When their forbearance becomes apparent as their regular way of life, their works will shine forth. There will be nothing lacking in those who imitate their virtue. They will be blessed not only from doing good deeds but also by inspiring good deeds in others. EPISTLE TO THE PHILIPPIANS 4.7.1.[15]

4:5b The Lord Is at Hand

BE WAKEFUL IN PRAYER. AMBROSIASTER: *The Lord,* he says, *is at hand.* They must be prepared and wakeful in prayer, giving thanks to God and putting away every worldly care, so as to hope and have before their eyes what the Lord promises. What he promises is, as he teaches, the reason for giving him thanks. EPISTLE TO THE PHILIPPIANS 4.7.2.[16]

4:6a No Anxiety About Anything

GOD PROVIDES ALL THAT IS NEEDFUL. MARIUS VICTORINUS: *Do not be anxious about anything.* This means: Do not be concerned for yourselves. Do not give unnecessary thought to or be anxious about the world or worldly things. For all that is needful for you in this life God provides. And it will be even better in that life which is eternal. EPISTLE TO THE PHILIPPIANS 4.6.[17]

---

[11]BT 1972:113 [1228C-D]. [12]Commended in Mt 5:4. [13]IOEP 5:150. [14]BT 1972:113 [1228D-1229A]. [15]CSEL 81.3:159. [16]CSEL 81.3:159. [17]BT 1972:113 [1229A].

4:6b *Prayer and Supplication with Thanksgiving*

THE COMFORT OF GIVING THANKS IN EVERYTHING. CHRYSOSTOM: It is comforting to know that the Lord is at hand. . . . Here is a medicine to relieve grief and every bad circumstance and every pain. What is it? To pray and to give thanks in everything. He does not wish that a prayer be merely a petition but a thanksgiving for what we have received. . . . How can one make petitions for the future without a thankful acknowledgment of past things? . . . So one ought to give thanks for everything, even what seems grievous. That is the mark of one who is truly thankful. Grief comes out of the circumstances with their demands. Thanksgiving comes from a soul that has true insight and a strong affection for God. HOMILY ON PHILIPPIANS 15.4.4-7.[18]

4:7 *The Peace of God*

THE PEACE OF GOD HELPS US UNDERSTAND GOD. MARIUS VICTORINUS: When the peace of God has come upon us we shall understand God. There will be no discord, no disagreement, no quarrelsome arguments, nothing subject to question. This is hardly the case in worldly life. But it shall be so when we have the peace of God, wherein all understanding shall be ours. For peace is the state of being already at rest, already secure. EPISTLE TO THE PHILIPPIANS 4.7.[19]

HOW THIS PEACE PASSES ALL UNDERSTANDING. CHRYSOSTOM: *The peace of God,* which he imparted to us, *passes all understanding.* For who could have expected and who could have hoped for such benefits? It transcends every human intellect and all speech. For his enemies, for those who hated him, for the apostates—for all these he did not refuse to give his only begotten Son, so as to make peace with them. . . . The peace which will preserve us is the one of which Christ says, *My peace I leave with you; my peace I give you.*[20] For this *peace passes all human understanding.* How? When he sees that we should be at peace with enemies, with the unrighteous, with those who display contentiousness and hostility toward us, how does this not pass human understanding? HOMILY ON PHILIPPIANS 15.4.4-7.[21]

---

[18]IOEP 5:152. [19]BT 1972:114 [1229D]. [20]Jn 14:27. [21]IOEP 5:152-53.

4:8-13 IMITATING PAUL

[8]*Finally, brethren, whatever is true, whatever is honorable, whatever is just, whatever is pure, whatever is lovely, whatever is gracious, if there is any excellence, if there is anything worthy of praise, think about these things.* [9]*What you have*

learned and received and heard and seen in me, do; and the God of peace will be with you.

[10]I rejoice in the Lord greatly that now at length you have revived your concern for me; you were indeed concerned for me, but you had no opportunity. [11]Not that I complain of want; for I have learned, in whatever state I am, to be content. [12]I know how to be abased, and I know how to abound; in any and all circumstances I have learned the secret of facing plenty and hunger, abundance and want. [13]I can do all things in him who strengthens me.

OVERVIEW: Paul concludes briskly (CHRYSOSTOM), indicating that one virtue follows from another (MARIUS VICTORINUS) so as to drive out the corresponding vices (CHRYSOSTOM). We must remember that all the virtues come from God (MARIUS VICTORINUS) and must be practiced sincerely (CHRYSOSTOM). Paul himself is the epitome of this (CHRYSOSTOM). The outcome is peace, both with one another (MARIUS VICTORINUS) and with God (AMBROSIASTER). He hints at slackness in the Philippians but praises their good will and service (CHRYSOSTOM). Abundance is as much a test as poverty (ORIGEN, AUGUSTINE), since neither is essential to the true good (CHRYSOSTOM).

4:8a A List of Six Virtues

HOW THE VIRTUES COMPLEMENT ONE ANOTHER. MARIUS VICTORINUS: *Whatever is true*—What are these *true* things? They are set out in the gospel: Jesus Christ is the Son of God and all that goes with that good news. When your thoughts are true, it follows that they will be *honorable*. What is true is not corrupted, which means that it is honorable. What is not corrupted is true. Then what is true and honorable will also be *just*, for it is made just or *justified*. And what is made just is pure since it receives *sanctification* from God. All that is *just, honorable, true* and *pure* is *lovable* and also *gracious*. For who does not love these saintly virtues? Who does not speak and think well of them? . . . Of this list some items pertain to true virtue in itself, while the later ones pertain to the fruit of virtue. To virtue it belongs to love *truth, honor, justice* and *purity*. To the fruit of virtue belongs that which is *lovely* and *gracious*. EPISTLE TO THE PHILIPPIANS 4.8-9.[1]

WHATEVER IS LOVABLE, TRUE, PURE AND HONORABLE. CHRYSOSTOM: *Whatever is lovable* refers to what is lovable to the faithful, lovable to God. *Whatever is true* refers to that which is virtuous. For what is really true is virtue. Vice is falsehood—its pleasure is false, its glory is false, and everything in it is false. Whatever is *pure* is the contrary of *thinking earthly thoughts. Whatever is honorable* is the contrary of those *whose god is their belly.*[2] HOMILY ON PHILIPPIANS 15.4.9.[3]

FINALLY, BRETHREN. CHRYSOSTOM: By now he has said everything he means to say. This is the letter of one who is pressing on and

---

[1]BT 1972:115-16 [1230C-D]. [2]Phil 3:19. [3]IOEP 5:153.

has no unworthy ties to the present. HOMILY ON PHILIPPIANS 15.4.8.[4]

4:8b Think About Excellent, Praiseworthy Things

WHY "IF"? MARIUS VICTORINUS: In saying *if there be any excellence, any praise*, he takes good note of the nature of things. For all things happen by the grace of God, who governs and rules through the Spirit that he sends into us. We count on nothing of our own, but on grace alone. This is why he speaks conditionally: *if any excellence*, for the virtues being nurtured in us are not from us but from God's grace. So not even the praise is ours. Therefore he also says *if there is anything worthy of praise*. EPISTLE TO THE PHILIPPIANS 4.8-9.[5]

THINK ON WHATEVER IS WORTHY OF PRAISE. CHRYSOSTOM: Paul did not say "look for praise" but "do what is praiseworthy"—but do not do it merely with an eye to praise. . . . When he says *whatever is of good report*, so that you will not suppose that he means simply from human reports, he adds, *If there be any virtue, any praise*. HOMILY ON PHILIPPIANS 15.4.9.[6]

4:9a Doing as Paul Has Taught Them

DO THESE THINGS. MARIUS VICTORINUS: *These things*, he says, *do*. And above he says *think about* these things. He adds *do* to show that these things are not only good to think about but to bring into action. EPISTLE TO THE PHILIPPIANS 4.8-9.[7]

DO WHAT YOU HAVE SEEN IN ME. CHRYSOSTOM: He sees that it is impossible to give pre-

cise instructions about everything—their going out, their coming in, their words, their inner condition and their company. All of these a Christian must think about in context. He says concisely and as it were in a nutshell, "Just do what you have heard and seen me do." HOMILY ON PHILIPPIANS 15.4.9.[8]

4:9b The God of Peace Will Be with You

THE NEED OF EVERY SOUL FOR PEACE. MARIUS VICTORINUS:Then he points to the blessing, as he has before: Do this and *the God of peace will be with you*. This is what the Philippians needed most, that there should be no discord, that all should think as one. Thus there will be peace in their church. The God of peace, who is the Father, with his Son Jesus Christ our Lord, will impart peace to every soul that is intimate with God. EPISTLE TO THE PHILIPPIANS 4.8-9.[9]

DISTINGUISHING GOD'S PEACE FROM THE PEACE THAT IS OF THE WORLD. AMBROSIASTER: Our God is truly *the God of peace*. We are constantly called to peace by God who himself is peace. His calling is not in timidity or weakness or in some show of strength. God is at peace with himself to such a degree that he even allows sins to be committed against him when he could certainly, by the terror of his manifested power and ineffable greatness, force even the unwilling into subjection. But peace of this kind is that of the world, not that of God, whose very na-

---

[4]IOEP 5:153. [5]BT 1972:116 [1230D-1231A]. [6]IOEP 5:154. [7]BT 1972:116 [1231A-B]. [8]IOEP 5:154. [9]BT 1972:116 [1231B].

ture is peace. EPISTLE TO THE PHILIPPIANS 4.9.[10]

4:10a Reviving Concern for Paul

WHAT WITHERED WAS REVIVED. CHRYSOS-TOM: *Revived* is a word for fruits that have once flourished, then dried up, then flourished again. By this word he shows that they were at first in bloom, then withered and then flourished again, so that *revived* conveys both reproach and praise. It is no small thing for what is withered to revive. HOMILY ON PHILIPPIANS 16.4.10-14.[11]

4:10b Concerned but Lacking Opportunity

CONCERNED OVER A LONG TIME. CHRYSOS-TOM: The Philippians had sent him things over a long period of time, conveying them through Epaphroditus. Now, as he prepares to send Epaphroditus back carrying this letter, see how he praises them. He shows that this is happening not only for the benefit of the one who receives but also for the one who gives. He wants those who do well not to fall into thoughtlessness. He urges them to become more zealous in well-doing, since they are thereby doing good to themselves. Those who are on the receiving end of gifts must not go on receiving thoughtlessly, lest they incur judgment. HOMILY ON PHILIPPIANS 16.4.10-14.[12]

4:11-12a Content in Any State

THE TEMPTATION OF ABUNDANCE. ORIGEN: Suffering poverty is often thought to be a tribulation, but abundance also may be an oc-casion for tribulation. The wise person restrains himself from being enervated by abundance. COMMENTARY ON ROMANS 4.9.[13]

KNOWING HOW TO ABOUND. AUGUSTINE: All sorts of people indeed can suffer poverty, but to *know how to suffer poverty* is a mark of greatness. Likewise, who is there who may not abound? But to *know how to abound* belongs to none but those who are not corrupted by abundance. ON THE GOOD OF MARRIAGE 25.[14]

4:12b In Any and in All Circumstances

THE AFFLUENT BECOME SLACK. CHRYSOS-TOM: Abundance does not yield either knowledge or virtue. How so? Because just as penury occasions much wrongdoing, so does plenty. Many who have become affluent have become derelict. They do not know how to bear their good fortune. But not so with Paul, for what he received he spent on others. He emptied himself for others. HOMILY ON PHILIPPIANS 16.4.10-14.[15]

4:13 Doing All Things in Christ

THE ONE WHO STRENGTHENS. CHRYSOS-TOM: Since this might seem like a great boast, see how quickly he adds: *I can do all things in Christ who strengthens me.* "Any achievement I have had belongs not to me but to the One who gave me strength." HOMILY ON PHILIPPIANS 16.4.10-14.[16]

---

[10]CSEL 81.3:160. [11]IOEP 5:158. [12]IOEP 5:158. [13]Migne PG 14:996 [539]; from Rufinus's Latin translation. [14]Migne PL 40:390. [15]IOEP 5:160. [16]IOEP 5:160.

4:14-23 PARTING WORDS

^{14}Yet it was kind of you to share my trouble. ^{15}And you Philippians yourselves know that in the beginning of the gospel, when I left Macedonia, no church entered into partnership with me in giving and receiving except you only; ^{16}for even in Thessalonica you sent me help^{f} once and again. ^{17}Not that I seek the gift; but I seek the fruit which increases to your credit. ^{18}I have received full payment, and more; I am filled, having received from Epaphroditus the gifts you sent, a fragrant offering, a sacrifice acceptable and pleasing to God. ^{19}And my God will supply every need of yours according to his riches in glory in Christ Jesus. ^{20}To our God and Father be glory for ever and ever. Amen.

^{21}Greet every saint in Christ Jesus. The brethren who are with me greet you. ^{22}All the saints greet you, especially those of Caesar's household.

^{23}The grace of the Lord Jesus Christ be with your spirit.

f Other ancient authorities read money for my needs

OVERVIEW: Paul praises the Philippians by recalling their past services, particularly their unique support at the outset of his ministry (AMBROSIASTER, CHRYSOSTOM). They have learned the secret of exchanging carnal for spiritual goods (CHRYSOSTOM). Paul spurs on their benevolence (MARIUS VICTORINUS) but with a hint of criticism (AMBROSIASTER). They have given him excellent support (CHRYSOSTOM). Their offerings, sweetened by poverty (THEODORET), are a sacrifice to God (CHRYSOSTOM). They will be blessed by God for their generosity (THEODORET, AMBROSIASTER). Everyone can benefit from God's bounty (CHRYSOSTOM), acknowledging him as common Source of all and Father of all (AMBROSIASTER), who never abandons his Son (THEODORET). There are numerous salutations to absent brethren, recalling their comfort (AMBROSIASTER). Many of them are distinguished (MARIUS

VICTORINUS). The conversion of the royal household is also a challenge to the Philippians (CHRYSOSTOM). Paul is already knowledgeable of their hopes (MARIUS VICTORINUS).

4:14 Sharing Paul's Trouble

SHARING OUR TROUBLES. CHRYSOSTOM: If Paul had disdained their relief, they would inevitably have become more lax. To prevent this, see how he treats the matter. What he has said may have distressed them, but what he is yet to say will give them a new zeal for life.... How had they shared his trouble? By ... suffering for Christ.... He does not refer simply to their giving but to their being partakers in Christ. This shows that the blessings are theirs insofar as they become partakers in Christ. He does not refer to his troubles being lightened but to his troubles

286

being shared. This is much more personal. Homily on Philippians 16.4.10-14.[1]

4:15a In the Beginning of the Gospel

Their Memory Goes Way Back. Ambrosiaster: He recalls these acts in order that, hearing that their good works are still held in mind and praised, they may have no doubt that they are counted acceptable in the Lord's sight, adding zeal in faith to their generosity. Epistle to the Philippians 4.17.[2]

No Previous Example. Chrysostom: What a great eulogy! What the Corinthians and Romans could have done had they been inspired by hearing of this! But no other church took the lead before the Philippians acted. Even in the beginning of the gospel they were already zealous on the saints' behalf. Even when they had no good examples before them they were the first to bear this fruit. Homily on Philippians 16.4.15.[3]

4:15b Entering into Partnership

How They Entered into Partnership. Chrysostom: The principle by which they entered this partnership was: Give useful gifts and receive back better spiritual gifts. You know how those who buy and sell hold conversation with one another in order to exchange their wares. This is what is happening here. There is nothing, nothing at all, more profitable than this sort of buying and selling. It begins on earth but ends in heaven. Homily on Philippians 16.4.15.[4]

4:16 Sending Help Again and Again

You Sent Me Help When I Was in Need.

Chrysostom: What great praise is this! When he was dwelling in the great capital city, he was being nourished by this little city of Philippi. He does not want to encourage them to be slack in generosity by telling them that he has no needs whatever. All he has to do is to indicate the bare outlines of his need. Homily on Philippians 16.4.16.[5]

4:17 Practicing Benevolence

The Fruit of Benevolence. Marius Victorinus: "I am not in want," Paul says, "nor do I ask for these things out of my own need. But you ought to practice benevolence simply in order that your abundance of benevolence may be for me the fruit of your good deeds. . . . When I either ask God on your behalf or give him thanks on your account, there is fruit for me in my prayer on your account, so long as I know that you are abounding in benevolence." Epistle to the Philippians 4.17.[6]

4:18a Receiving Full Payment and More

Full Payment. Ambrosiaster: It is not idle for him to tell them with exhortations that something needs to be done. He confesses that much has already been done. But some of that which was done was done more negligently and less freely than they might have wished it to be. His aim was that they should remember their previous works. Then they would realize that they are doing less now than at the beginning. Epistle to the Philippians 4.18.[7]

---

[1]IOEP 5:161. [2]CSEL 81.3:161. [3]IOEP 5:162. [4]IOEP 5:162. [5]IOEP 5:163. [6]BT 1972:119-20 [1233C]. [7]CSEL 81.3:162.

I Am Filled. Chrysostom: "You have made my life overflow through your giving," he says in effect. This was the distinctive mark of these people who were so very zealous. For the more philosophical the benefactors are, the more they are likely to seek thanks from their beneficiaries. On the contrary, Paul tells the Philippians that they have not only filled him up in what was lacking in the past but have exceeded all expectation. Homily on Philippians 16.4.18.[8]

4:18b *An Acceptable and Pleasing Sacrifice*

Why a Sacrifice? Chrysostom: "It is not I," he says, "who have received but God through me. So I personally have no need of your gifts. Let this not concern you. And God himself has no need either. Yet he accepts these gifts." . . . It is not the incense or the smoke that makes an acceptable offering but the will of the one who offers. Homily on Philippians 16.4.18.[9]

The Praise Enhanced by Their Poverty. Theodoret: "You gave to Epaphroditus," Paul says, "and Epaphroditus gave to me, and God himself received the sacrifice through me." Their praise is enhanced by their poverty. They were not prosperous when they sent their gifts but trapped in the utmost poverty. Epistle to the Philippians 4.18.[10]

4:19a *God Will Supply Their Needs*

God Will Supply Your Every Need. Theodoret: Their gifts are like an aroma of sacrifice, a sacrifice acceptable and well-pleasing to God. Paul prays that the givers will also be recipients of necessities for the present life. He prays that *God will supply every need of yours*. And there is nothing absurd in asking this blessing on them. For the Lord himself in the holy Gospels bids us say *give us our daily bread*.[11] Epistle to the Philippians 4.19.[12]

My God. Ambrosiaster: His promise is that *my God will supply every need of yours*, that God himself might stand ready to help them receive all that he has provided for them in the abundant greatness of his glory in Christ Jesus. It is indeed the glory of Jesus Christ when by the will of God the desires of Christians are fulfilled in accordance with the teaching of the gospel. Epistle to the Philippians 4.19.[13]

4:19b *The Riches of His Glory in Christ Jesus*

According to the Riches of God's Glory. Chrysostom: They were artisans and paupers. They had wives, reared children and owned houses. They had given these gifts freely from their small means. There was nothing absurd in praying that such people so situated should have sufficiency and plenty. He does not ask God to make them rich or affluent. He asks only that God may *supply their every need*—so they will not be in want but will have what they need. Homily on Philippians 16.4.19.[14]

4:20 *Glory to Our God and Father*

Why God and Father? Ambrosiaster:

---

[8]IOEP 5:164. [9]IOEP 5:164. [10]CPE 2:66. [11]Mt 6:11. [12]CPE 2:66-67. [13]CSEL 81.3:162. [14]IOEP 5:165.

Here he makes no distinction [as in 4:19] but prays to both our God and our Father. He calls upon God on account of awe. He calls upon the Father for the sake of honor and because every beginning is from him. EPISTLE TO THE PHILIPPIANS 4.20.[15]

HYMNS TO THE FATHER ARE HYMNS TO THE SON. THEODORET: Here he praises the Father alone, whereas elsewhere he praises the Son alone.[16] . . . He does not divide the Son from the Father or the Father from the Son. He offers the hymn to the divine nature as a whole. EPISTLE TO THE PHILIPPIANS 4.20.[17]

4:21 Greet Every Saint

EVERY SAINT MEANS ALL WHO BELIEVE. THEODORET: Not everyone who calls himself *a saint* is a saint but only the one who believes in the Lord Jesus and lives according to his teaching. EPISTLE TO THE PHILIPPIANS 4.21.[18]

MUTUAL CONSOLATION. AMBROSIASTER: The greeting of the brothers is an act of mutual consolation. It calls to mind those who have been split apart. EPISTLE TO THE PHILIPPIANS 4.22.[19]

4:22 All the Saints Greet You

FROM THE HUMBLEST TO THE GREATEST. MARIUS VICTORINUS: Many apparently have believed even from Caesar's household. These are people who would otherwise have walked proudly and thought of nothing but Caesar. The power of the gospel has been revealed to these people. Many others who have believed are humble people. He equally greets them all, humbly and affably, wherever they are. The word *especially* in relation to *those of Caesar's household* makes it apparent that they are taking pains to be pleasing in service. EPISTLE TO THE PHILIPPIANS 4.21-22.[20]

THE ROYAL HOUSEHOLD. CHRYSOSTOM: If those in the royal household have despised so much for the kingdom of heaven, how much more should the Philippians. It was a mark of Paul's love that he had spoken so much and so warmly of the Philippians as to inspire a desire for them to witness to those of the royal household. To these he sent greetings. HOMILY ON PHILIPPIANS 16.4.22-23.[21]

4:23 The Grace of the Lord Jesus Christ

GRACE BE WITH YOUR SPIRIT. MARIUS VICTORINUS: He knew that the Philippians, unlike those addressed in his other letters, held to correct teaching. They had not been seduced by false apostles. He is here writing only a short letter of exhortation. He prays that *the grace of our Lord Jesus Christ be with your spirit*. For if the Spirit dwells within them, they will respond rightly. EPISTLE TO THE PHILIPPIANS 4.23.[22]

THE LETTER SENT FROM ROME. THEODORET: The letter to the Philippians was sent from Rome by the hand of Epaphroditus. EPISTLE TO THE PHILIPPIANS 4.23.[23]

---

[15]CSEL 81.3:162-63. [16]Here Theodoret cites Romans 9:5. [17]CPE 2:67. [18]CPE 2:67. [19]CSEL 81.3:163. [20]BT 1972:121 [1234D-1235A]. [21]IOEP 5:167. [22]BT 1972:121-22 [1235A-1236A]. But cf. comments on Gal 6:18. [23]CPE 2:67.

Appendix

The following table lists where various early documents may be found in Cetedoc and TLG digital CD-Rom databases.

Ambrose

"On the Faith" (De Fide Libri V [ad Gratianum Augustum])	Cetedoc 0150
"On Paradise" (De Paradiso)	Cetedoc 0124
"On Penitence" (De Paenitentia)	Cetedoc 0156
"On the Sacraments" (De Mysteriis)	Cetedoc 0155

Athanasius

"Against the Arians" (Orationes Tres Contra Arianos)	TLG 2035.042

Augustine

"Against Faustus" (Contra Faustum)	Cetedoc 0321
"Epistle to the Galatians" (Expositio Epistulae ad Galatas)	Cetedoc 0282
"On Continence" (De Continentia)	Cetedoc 0298
"On Diverse Questions" (De Diversus Questionibus ad Simplicianum)	Cetedoc 0290
"On Faith and the Creed" (De Fide et Symbolo)	Cetedoc 0293
"On Grace and Free Will" (De Gratia et Libero Arbitrio)	Cetedoc 0352
"On Lying" (De Mendacio)	Cetedoc 0303
"On Marriage and Concupiscence" (De Nuptiis et Concupiscentia)	Cetedoc 0350
"On Nature and Grace" (De Natura et Gratia)	Cetedoc 0344
"On the Good of Marriage" (De Bono Coniugali)	Cetedoc 0299
"On the Grace of Christ and on Original Sin" (De Gratia Christi et de Peccato Originali)	Cetedoc 0349
"On the Perfection of Human Righteousness" (De Perfectione Iustitiae Hominis)	Cetedoc 0347
"On the Trinity" (De Trinitate)	Cetedoc 0329
"On Two Letters Of Pelagius" (Contra Duas Epistulas Pelagianorum)	Cetedoc 0346
"Question" (De Diversus Quaestioibus Octoginta Tribus)	Cetedoc 0289
"Questions of Genesis" (De Fenesi Contra Manichaeos)	Cetedoc 0265
"Tractate on the Gospel of John" (In Iohannis Euangelium Tractatus)	Cetedoc 0278

Basil of Caesarea

"On Baptism" (De Baptismo Libri Duo)	TLG 2040.052

Cassian, John

"Collation" (Conlationes XIIII)   Cetedoc 0512

Cassiodorus

"Summary of Ephesians" (Complexiones in Epistulas Apostolorum,
     Actus Apostolorum et Apocalypsim Iohannis)   Cetedoc 0903
"Summary of Galatians" (Complexiones in Epistulas Apostolorum,
     Actus Apostolorum et Apocalypsim Iohannis)   Cetedoc 0903
"Summary of Philippians" (Complexiones in Epistulas Apostolorum,
     Actus Apostolorum et Apocalypsim Iohannis)   Cetedoc 0903

Chromatius of Aquileia

"Tractate on Matthew" (Tractatus in Matthaeum)   Cetedoc 0218

Clement of Alexandria

"Excerpts From Theodotus" (Excerpta ex Theodoto)   TLG 0555.007
"Stromateis" (Stromata)   TLG 0555.004

Cyril of Alexandria

"Dialogues on the Trinity" (De Sancta Trinitate)   TLG 4090.123
"Letter to Acacius" (Epistula ad Acacium Beroeensem)   TLG 4090.X54-77
"On the Orthodox Faith to Emperor Theodosius"
     (Oratio ad Theodosium Imperatorem de Recta Fide)   TLG 4030.x06
"Scholium on the Incarnation of the Only-Begotten"
     (Scholia De Incarnatione Unigeniti)   TLG 4090.x62

Didymus the Blind

"On Genesis" (In Genesim)   TLG 2012.041
"On Zechariah" (Commentarii in Zacchariam)   TLG 2102.010

Epiphanius

"Ancoratus" (Ancoratus)   TLG 2021.001
"Panarion" (Panarion)   TLG 2021.002

Eusebius of Caesarea

"Commentary on Isaiah" (Commentarius in Isaiam)   TLG 2018.019
"Demonstration of the Gospel" (Demonstratio Evangelica)   TLG 2018.005
"On the Theology of the Church" (De Ecclesiastica Theologia)   TLG 2018.009

Eusebius of Vercelli

"On the Trinity" (De trinitate libelli septem)   Cetedoc 0105

Faustinus

"On the Trinity" (De Trinitate)   Cetedoc 0120

Filastrius

"Book of Heresies" (Diversarum Hereseon Liber)   Cetedoc 0121

Fulgentius

"On the Incarnation" (Sermo Dubius II: "Incarnationis diuinae mysterium")   Cetedoc 0841

"On the Remission of Sins" (Ad Euthymium de Remissione
   Peccatorum Libri II)   Cetedoc 0342

"On the Truth of Predestination" (De veritate praedestinationis et gratiae
   libri III ad Iohannem et Venerium)   Cetedoc 0823

Gregory of Elvira

"On the Ark of Noah" (De Arca Noe)   Cetedoc 0548

"On the Faith" (De Fide Orthodoxa Contra Arianos)   Cetedoc 0551

Gregory of Nazianzus

"Orations" (In Dictum evangelii: Cum consummasset Jesus hos sermones)   TLG 2022.045

Gregory of Nyssa

"Against Eunomius" (Contra Eunomium)   TLG 2017.030

"Antirrheticus Against Apollinarius" (Antirrheticus Adversus
   Apollinarium)   TLG 2017.008

"On the Three Days" (De Tridui Unter Mortem et Resurrectionem
   Domini Nostri Jesu Christi Spatio)   TLG 2017.031

"Oration on Song of Songs" (In Canticum Canticorum)   TLG 2017.032

"Refutation of Eunomius' 'Confession of Faith' "
   (Refutatio Confessionis Eunomii)   TLG 2017.031

Hilary of Poitiers

"On the Trinity" (De Trinitate)   Cetedoc 0433

Irenaeus

"Against Heresies" (Adversus Haereses)   TLG 1447.007

Jerome

"Dialogue Against the Pelagians" (Dialogi Contra Pelagianos Libri III)   Cetedoc 0615

"Epistle to the Ephesians" (Commentarii in Epistulas Paulinas)   Cetedoc 0591

"Epistle to the Galatians" (Commentarii in Epistulas Paulinas)   Cetedoc 0591

"Letters" (Epistulae)   Cetedoc 0620

John Chrysostom

"Commentary on Galatians" (In Epistulam ad Galatas Commentarius)   TLG 2062.158
"Homily on Ephesians" (In Epistulam ad Ephesios)   TLG 2062.159
"Homily on Philippians" (In Epistulam ad Philippenes)   TLG 2062.160

Lucifer of Cagliari

"On Dying for the Son of God" (Moriundum Esse Pro Dei Filio)   Cetedoc 0116

Marius Victorinus

"Against the Arians" (Adversus Arium)   Cetedoc 0095
"Epistle to the Ephesians" (Commentarii in Epistulas Pauli, ad Ephesios,
     ad Galatas, ad Philippenses)   Cetedoc 0098
"Epistle to the Galatians" (Commentarii in Epistulas Pauli, ad Ephesios,
     ad Galatas, ad Philippenses)   Cetedoc 0098
"Epistle to the Philippians" (Commentarii in Epistulas Pauli, ad Ephesios,
     ad Galatas, ad Philippenses)   Cetedoc 0098

Methodius

"Symposium" (Symposium)   TLG 2959.001

Novatian

"On the Trinity" (De Trinitate)   Cetedoc 0071

Origen

"Commentary on John" (Commentarii in Evangelium Iohannis)   TLG 2042.005
"Commentary on Romans" (Commentarii in Epistulam ad Romanos)   TLG 2042.037
"Epistle to the Ephesians" (Fragmenta ex Commentaries in
     Epistulam ad Ephesios)   TLG 2042.035
"On First Principles" (De Principiis)   TLG 2042.002

Quodvultdeus

"On the Creed" (Sermo I: De Symbolo I)   Cetedoc 0401
 (Sermo II: De Symbolo II)   Cetedoc 0402
 (Sermo III: De Symbolo III)   Cetedoc 0403

Tertullian

"Against Marcion" (Adversus Marcionem)   Cetedoc 0014
"On the Flesh of Christ" (De Carne Christi)   Cetedoc 0018
"On the Resurrection of the Dead" (De Resurrectione Mortuorum)   Cetedoc 0019
"On the Veiling of Virgins" (De Virginibus)   Cetedoc 0027

Theodoret

"Epistle to the Ephesians" (Interpretatio in XIV Epistulas Sancti Pauli)	TLG 4089.030
"Epistle to the Galatians" (Interpretatio in XIV Epistulas Sancti Pauli)	TLG 4089.030
"Epistle to the Philippians" (Interpretatio in XIV Epistulas Sancti Pauli)	TLG 4089.030
"Eranistes" (Eranistes)	TLG 4089.002

CHRONOLOGY

Clement of Rome, fl. c. 80 (92-101?)

Ignatius of Antioch, c. 110-112

Hermas, fl. 140/155

Marcion of Sinope, fl. 144; d. c. 154

Polycarp of Smyrna, c. 69-155

Justin Martyr (of Flavia Neapolis in Palestine), c. 100/110-165; fl. c. 148-161

Irenaeus of Lyon, b. c. 135; fl. 180-199; d. c. 202

Clement of Alexandria, b. c. 150; fl. 190-215

Tertullian of Carthage, c. 155/160-240/250; fl. c. 197-222

Montanist Oracle, mid-second century

Theophilus of Antioch, late second century

Origen, c. 185-c. 254

Novatian of Rome, fl. 235-258

Cyprian of Carthage, fl. 248-258

Euthalius the Deacon, fourth century?

Victorinus of Petovium (Pettau), d. c. 304

Methodius of Philippi, d. c. 311

Eusebius of Caesarea, b. c. 263; fl. c. 315-340

Cyril of Jerusalem, c. 315-386; fl. c. 348

Hilary of Poitiers, c. 315-367; fl. 350-367

Athanasius of Alexandria, c. 295-373; fl. 325-373

Liber Graduum, c. 303-c. 324

Arius, fl. c. 320

Basil of Caesarea b. c. 330; fl. 357-379

Eusebius of Emesa, d. c. 359

Acacius of Caesarea, d. 366

Ambrosiaster, fl. c. 366-384

Gregory Nazianzen, b. 330; fl. 372-389

Diodore of Tarsus, d. c. 390

Apollinaris of Laodicea, 310-c. 392

Gregory of Nyssa, c. 335-394

Ambrose of Milan, c. 333-397; fl. 374-397

Didymus the Blind of Alexandria, 313-398

Severian of Gabala, fl. c. 400

[Pseudo-]Constantius, fl. c. 405

Prudentius, c. 348-post 405

John Chrysostom, c. 344/354-407

Jerome of Stridon, c. 347-420

Pelagius, c. 354-c. 420

Theodore of Mopsuestia, 350-428

Augustine of Hippo, 354-430

Cyril of Alexandria, d. 444

Leo the Great of Rome (pope), regn. 440-461

Philoxenus of Mabbug, c. 440-523

Theodoret of Cyr, 393-466

Gennadius of Constantinople, d. 471

Pseudo-Dionysius the Aeropagite, post-482, pre-532; fl. c. 500

Symmachus of Rome, 498-514

Caesarius of Arles, 470-542

Gregory the Great (pope), 540-604; regn. 590-604

Oecumenius, sixth century

Luculentius, fifth-sixth centuries

Bede the Venerable, 673-735

John of Damascus, c. 645-c. 749

GLOSSARY

Ambrose of Milan (c. 333-397; fl. 374-397). Bishop of Milan and teacher of Augustine who defended the divinity of the Holy Spirit and the perpetual virginity of Mary.

Ambrosiaster (fl. c. 366-384). Name given by Erasmus to the author of a work once thought to have been composed by Ambrose.

Apollinaris of Laodicea (310-c. 392). Bishop of Laodicea who was attacked by Gregory Nazianzen, Gregory of Nyssa and Theodore for denying that Christ had a human mind.

Arius (fl. c. 320). Heretic condemned at the Council of Nicea (325) for refusing to accept that the Son was not a creature but was God by nature, like the Father.

Athanasius of Alexandria (c. 295-373; fl. 325-373). Bishop of Alexandria from 328, though often in exile. He wrote his classic polemics against the Arians while most of the Eastern bishops were against him.

Augustine of Hippo (354-430). Bishop of Hippo and a voluminous writer on philosophical, exegetical, theological and ecclesiological topics. He formulated the western doctrines of predestination and original sin in his writings against the Pelagians.

Basil of Caesarea (b. c. 330; fl. 357-379). Bishop of Caesarea and champion of the teaching on the Trinity propounded at Nicaea in 325. He was a great administrator and founded a monastic rule.

Basilides (fl. 2d century). Alexandrian heretic of the early second century who is said to have believed that souls migrate from body to body

and that we do not sin if we lie to protect the body from martyrdom.

Cassian, John (360-432). Author of a compilation of ascetic sayings highly influential in the development of Western monasticism.

Cassiodorus (c. 485-c. 540). Founder of Western monasticism whose writings include valuable histories and less valuable commentaries.

Chromatius (fl. 400). Friend of Rufinus and Jerome and author of tracts and sermons.

Chrysostom, John (344/354-407; fl. 386-407). Bishop of Antioch and of Constantinople who was famous for his orthodoxy, his eloquence and his attacks on Christian laxity in high places.

Cyprian of Carthage (fl. 248-258). Martyred bishop of Carthage who maintained that those baptized by schismatics and heretics had no share in the blessings of the church.

Cyril of Alexandria (375-55; fl. 412-444). Patriarch of Alexandria whose strong espousal of the unity of Christ led to the condemnation of Nestorius in 431.

Cyril of Jerusalem (c. 315-386; fl. c. 348). Bishop of Jerusalem after 350 and author of *Catechetical Homilies*.

Didymus the Blind (313-398). Alexandrian exegete who was much influenced by Origen and admired by Jerome.

Dionysius the Areopagite (post-482, pre-532; fl. c. 500). The name long given to the author of four mystical writings, probably from the late fifth century, which were the foundation of the apophatic school of mysticism in their denial that anything can be truly predicated of God.

Epiphanius of Salamis (c. 315-403). Bishop of Salamis in Cyprus, author of a refutation of eighty heresies (the *Panarion*) and instrumental in the condemnation of Origen.

Ephrem the Syrian (b. c. 306; fl. 363-373). Syrian writer of commentaries and devotional hymns which are sometimes regarded as the greatest specimens of Christian poetry prior to Dante.

Eunomius (d. 393). Bishop of Cyzicyus who was attacked by Basil and Gregory of Nyssa for maintaining that the Father and the Son were of different natures, one ingenerate, one generate.

Eusebius of Caesarea (c. 260-340). Bishop of Caesarea, partisan of the Emperor Constantine and first historian of the Christian church. He argued that the truth of the gospel had been foreshadowed in pagan writings, but he had to defend his own doctrine against suspicion of Arian sympathies.

Eusebius of Vercelli (fl. c. 360). Bishop of Vercelli who supported the trinitarian teaching of Nicaea (325) when it was being undermined by compromise in the West.

Faustinus (fl. 380). A priest in Rome and supporter of Lucifer and author of a treatise on the Trinity.

Filastrius (fl. 380). Bishop of Brescia and author of a compilation against all heresies.

Fulgentius of Ruspe (467-532). Bishop of Ruspe and author of many orthodox sermons and tracts under the influence of Augustine.

Gaudentius of Brescia (fl. 395). Successor of Filastrius as bishop of Brescia and author of numerous tracts.

Gnostics. Name now given generally to followers of Basilides, Marcion, Valentinus, Mani and others. The characteristic belief is that matter is a prison made for the spirit by an evil or ignorant creator and that redemption depends on fate, not on free will.

Gregory of Elvira (fl. 359-385). Bishop of Elvira who wrote allegorical treatises in the style of Origen and defended the Nicene faith against the Arians.

Gregory of Nazianzus (b. 330; fl. 372-389). Bishop of Nazianzus and friend of Basil and Gregory of Nyssa. He is famous for maintaining the humanity of Christ as well as the orthodox doctrine of the Trinity.

Gregory of Nyssa (c. 335-394). Bishop of Nyssa and brother of Basil, he is famous for maintaining the equality in unity of the Father, Son and Holy Spirit.

Hilary of Poitiers (c. 315-367). Bishop of Poitiers and called the "Athanasius of the West" because of his defense (against the Arians) of the common nature of Father and Son.

Irenaeus of Lyon (c. 135-c. 202). Bishop of Lyons who published the most famous and influential refutation of Gnostic thought.

Jerome (347-420). Gifted exegete and exponent of a classical Latin style, now best known as the translator of the Latin Vulgate. He defended the perpetual virginity of Mary, attacked Origen and Pelagius and supported extreme ascetic practices.

Leo the Great (regn. 440-461). Bishop of Rome whose *Tome to Flavian* helped to strike a balance between Nestorian and Cyrilline positions at the council of Chalcedon in 451.

Lucifer (fl. 370). Bishop of Cagliari and fanatical partisan of Athanasius. He and his followers entered into schism after refusing to acknowledge less orthodox bishops appointed by the Emperor Constantius.

Marcion (fl. 144). Heretic of the mid-second century who rejected the Old Testament and much of the New Testament, claiming that the

Father of Jesus Christ was other than the Creator God (*see* Gnostics).

Manichaeans. A religious movement that originated c. 241 in Persia under the leadership of Mani but apparently was of complex Christian origin. It is said to have denied free will and the universal sovereignty of God, teaching that kingdoms of light and darkness are coeternal and that the redeemed are particles of a spiritual man of light held captive in the darkness of matter (*see* Gnostics).

Marius Victorinus (b. c. 280; fl. c. 355). Grammarian who translated works of Platonists and, after his late conversion (c. 355), used them against the Arians.

Methodius of Olympus (fl. 290). Bishop of Olympus who celebrated virginity in a *Symposium* partly modeled on Plato's dialogue of that name.

Nestorius (b. 381; fl. 430). Patriarch of Constantinople 428-431 and credited with the foundation of the heresy that says the divine and human natures were associated, rather than truly united, in the incarnation of Christ.

Novatian of Rome (fl. 235-258). Roman theologian, otherwise orthodox, who formed a schismatic church after failing to become pope. His treatise on the Trinity states the classic Western doctrine.

Origen of Alexandria (b. 185; fl. c. 200-254). Influential exegete and systematic theologian. He was condemned (perhaps unfairly) for maintaining the preexistence of souls while denying the resurrection of the body, the literal truth of Scripture and the equality of the Father and the Son in the Trinity.

Pelagius (c. 354-c. 420). Christian teacher whose followers were condemned in 418 and 431 for maintaining that a Christian could be perfect and that salvation depended on free will.

Quodvultdeus (fl. 430). Carthaginian deacon and friend of Augustine who endeavored to show at length how the New Testament fulfilled the Old Testament.

Rufinus of Aquileia (c. 345-411). Orthodox Christian thinker and historian who nonetheless translated Origen and defended him against the strictures of Jerome and Epiphanius.

Sabellius (fl. 200). Allegedly the author of the heresy that maintains that the Father and Son are a single person. The Patripassian variant of this heresy states that the Father suffered on the cross.

Tertullian of Carthage (c. 160-c. 240). Brilliant Carthaginian apologist and polemicist who laid the foundations of Christology and trinitarian orthodoxy in the West, though he himself was estranged from the main church by its laxity.

Theodore of Mopsuestia (350-428). Bishop of Mopsuestia, founder of the Antiochene, or literalistic, school of exegesis. A great man in his day, he was later condemned as a precursor of Nestorius.

Theodoret of Cyr (c. 393-466). Bishop of Cyr (Cyrrhus), he was an opponent of Cyril, whose doctrine of Christ's person was finally vindicated in 451 at the Council of Chalcedon.

Valentinus (fl. c. 140). Alexandrian heretic of the mid-second century who taught that the material world was created by the transgression of God's Wisdom, or Sophia (*see* Gnostics).

BIBLIOGRAPHY

Ambrose. "De Abraham." In *Sancti Ambrosii Opera*. Edited by Carolus Schenkl. Corpus Scriptorum Ecclesiasticorum Latinorum, vol. 32, pt. 1. Vindobonae: F. Tempsky; Lipsiae: G. Freytag, 1896.

_____. "De Bono Mortis." In *Sancti Ambrosii Opera*. Edited by Carolus Schenkl. Corpus Scriptorum Ecclesiasticorum Latinorum, vol. 32, pt. 1. Vindobonae: F. Tempsky; Lipsiae: G. Freytag, 1896.

_____. "De Excessu Fratris." In *Sancti Ambrosii Opera*. Edited by Otto Faller. Corpus Scriptorum Ecclesiasticorum Latinorum, vol. 73. Vindobonae: Hoelder-Pichler-Tempsky, 1955.

_____. "De Fide ad Gratianum Augustum." In *Sancti Ambrosii Opera*. Edited by Otto Faller. Corpus Scriptorum Ecclesiasticorum Latinorum, vol. 78. Vindobonae: Hoelder-Pichler-Tempsky, 1962.

_____. "De Paenitentia." In *Sancti Ambrosii Opera*. Edited by Otto Faller. Corpus Scriptorum Ecclesiasticorum Latinorum, vol. 73. Vindobonae: Hoelder-Pichler-Tempsky, 1955.

_____. "De Paradiso." In *Sancti Ambrosii Opera*. Edited by Carolus Schenkl. Corpus Scriptorum Ecclesiasticorum Latinorum, vol. 32, pt. 1. Vindobonae: F. Tempsky; Lipsiae: G. Freytag, 1896.

_____. "De Sacramentis." In *Sancti Ambrosii Opera*. Edited by Otto Faller. Corpus Scriptorum Ecclesiasticorum Latinorum, vol. 73. Vindobonae: Hoelder-Pichler-Tempsky, 1955.

Ambrosiaster. "In Epistulam ad Efesios." In *Ambrosiastri Qui Dicitur Commentarius in Epistulas Paulinas*. Edited by Henricus Iosephus Vogels. Corpus Scriptorum Ecclesiasticorum Latinorum, vol. 81, pt. 3. Vindobonae: Hoelder-Pichler-Tempsky, 1966.

_____. "In Epistulam ad Filippenses." In *Ambrosiastri Qui Dicitur Commentarius in Epistulas Paulinas*. Edited by Henricus Iosephus Vogels. Corpus Scriptorum Ecclesiasticorum Latinorum, vol. 81, pt. 3. Vindobonae: Hoelder-Pichler-Tempsky, 1966.

_____. "In Epistulam ad Galatas." In *Ambrosiastri Qui Dicitur Commentarius in Epistulas Paulinas*. Edited by Henricus Iosephus Vogels. Corpus Scriptorum Ecclesiasticorum Latinorum, vol. 81, pt. 3. Vindobonae: Hoelder-Pichler-Tempsky, 1966.

Athanasius. "Orationes Contra Arianos." In *The Orations of St. Athanasius: Against the Arians According to the Benedictine Text*. Edited by W. Bright. Oxford: Clarendon Press, 1873.

Augustine of Hippo. "Contra duas Epistolas Pelagianorum, ad Bonifacium." In *Opera Omnia*. Patrologiae Cursus Completus, Series Latina, vol. 44. Edited by J.-P. Migne. Paris: Migne, 1865.

_____. "Contra Faustum Manichæum." In *Opera Omnia*. Patrologiae Cursus Completus, Series Latina, vol. 42. Edited by J.-P. Migne. Paris: Migne, 1865.

_____. "Contra Julianum Pelagianum." In *Opera Omnia*. Patrologiae Cursus Completus, Series Latina, vol. 44. Edited by J.-P. Migne. Paris: Migne, 1865.

_____. "Contra Mendacium." In *Opera Omnia*. Patrologiae Cursus Completus, Series Latina, vol. 40. Edited by J.-P. Migne. Paris: Migne, 1865.

_____. "De Bono Conjugali." In *Opera Omnia*. Patrologiae Cursus Completus, Series Latina, vol. 40. Edited by J.-P. Migne. Paris: Migne, 1865.

_____. "De Continentia." In *Opera Omnia*. Patrologiae Cursus Completus, Series Latina, vol. 40. Edited by J.-P. Migne. Paris: Migne, 1865.

_____. "De Diversis Quæstionibus." In *Opera Omnia*. Patrologiae Cursus Completus, Series Latina, vol. 40. Edited by J.-P. Migne. Paris: Migne, 1865.

_____. "De Fide et Symbolo." In *Opera Omnia*. Patrologiae Cursus Completus, Series Latina, vol. 40. Edited by J.-P. Migne. Paris: Migne, 1865.

_____. "De Gratia Christi et de Peccato Originali." In *Opera Omnia*. Patrologiae Cursus Completus, Series Latina, vol. 44. Edited by J.-P. Migne. Paris: Migne, 1865.

_____. "De Gratia et Libero Arbitrio." In *Opera Omnia*. Patrologiae Cursus Completus, Series Latina, vol. 44. Edited by J.-P. Migne. Paris: Migne, 1865.

_____. "De Libero Arbitrio." In *Opera Omnia*. Patrologiae Cursus Completus, Series Latina, vol. 32. Edited by J.-P. Migne. Paris: Migne, 1877.

_____. "De Mendaci." In *Opera Omnia*. Patrologiae Cursus Completus, Series Latina, vol. 40. Edited by J.-P. Migne. Paris: Migne, 1865.

_____. "De Natura et Gratia." In *Opera Omnia*. Patrologiae Cursus Completus, Series Latina, vol. 44. Edited by J.-P. Migne. Paris: Migne, 1865.

_____. "De Nuptiis et Concupiscentia." In *Opera Omnia*. Patrologiae Cursus Completus, Series Latina, vol. 44. Edited by J.-P. Migne. Paris: Migne, 1865.

_____. "De Peccatorum Meritis et Remissione." In *Opera Omnia*. Patrologiae Cursus Completus, Series Latina, vol. 44. Edited by J.-P. Migne. Paris: Migne, 1865.

_____. "De Perfectione Justitiæ Hominis." In *Opera Omnia*. Patrologiae Cursus Completus, Series Latina, vol. 44. Edited by J.-P. Migne. Paris: Migne, 1865.

_____. "De Trinitate." In *Opera Omnia*. Patrologiae Cursus Completus, Series Latina, vol. 42. Edited by J.-P. Migne. Paris: Migne, 1865.

Basil, Bishop of Caesarea. *The Letters*. 4 vols. Edited by R. Deferrari. The Loeb Classical Library. Cambridge, Mass.: Harvard University Press; London: W. Heinemann, 1926.

_____. *Sur le Baptême*. Edited by Jeanne Ducatillon. Sources Chrétiennes, vol. 357. Paris: Éditions du Cerf, 1989.

Cassian, John. *Iohannis Cassiani Conlationes XXIIII. Iohannis Cassiani Opera* Pars II. Edited by Michael Petschenig. Corpus Scriptorum Ecclesiasticorum Latinorum, vol. 13. Vindobonae: C. Geroldi Filium, 1886.

Cassiodorus, "Complexiones in Epistolas Apostolorum: Epistola ad Ephesios." In *Magni Aurelii Cassiodori Senatoris, Opera Omnia*. Patrologiae Cursus Completus; Series Latina, vol. 70. Edited by J.-P. Migne. Paris: Migne, 1865.

_____. "Complexiones in Epistolas Apostolorum: Epistola ad Galatas." In *Magni Aurelii Cassiodori Senatoris, Opera Omnia*. Patrologiae Cursus Completus; Series Latina, vol. 70. Edited by J.-P. Migne. Paris: Migne, 1865.

_____. "Complexiones in Epistolas apostolorum: Epistola ad Philippenses." In *Magni Aurelii Cassiodori Senatoris, Opera Omnia*. Patrologiae Cursus Completus; Series Latina, vol. 70. Edited by J.-P. Migne. Paris: Migne, 1865.

Chromatius, Bishop of Aquileia. "Tractatus." In *Chromatii Aquileiensis Opera*. Corpus Christianorum. Series Latina, vol. 9A. Edited by R. Étaix and J. Lemariè. Turnholti: Typographi Brepols Editores Pontificii, 1974.

Chrysostom, John. *Interpretatio Omnium Epistolarum Paulinarum Per Homilias Facta*. Oxford: T. Combe, 1849.

_____. *Sur l'Égalité Du Père et Du Fils: Contre les Anoméens Homélies VII-XII*. Edited by Anne-Marie Malingrey. Sources Chrétiennes, vol. 396. Paris: Éditions du Cerf, 1994.

Clement of Alexandria. *Clemens Alexandrinus*. Die Griechischen Christlichen Schriftsteller der Ersten Jahrhunderte, vols. 12, 15, 17, 39. Leipzig: J. C. Hinrichs; Berlin: Akademie-Verlag, 1936-1960.

_____. *Opera*. 4 vols. Edited by Wilhelm Dindorf. Oxford: Clarendon Press, 1869.

Cyprian, Bishop of Carthage. *Sancti Cypriani Episcopi Epistularium*. Corpus Christianorum. Series Latina, vol. 3C. Turnholti: Typographi Brepols Editores Pontificii, 1994.

_____. *Sancti Cypriani Episcopi Opera*. Corpus Christianorum. Series Latina, vols. 3A, 3B. Turnholti: Typographi Brepols Editores Pontificii, 1972.

Cyril, Bishop of Jerusalem. In *Opera Qua Supersunt Omnia*. Edited by W. K. Reischl and J. Rupp. Monaci: Sumtibus Librariae Lentnerianae, 1848-1860.

Cyril, Patriarch of Alexandria. "Doctrinal Questions and Answers." *Select Letters*. Edited and translated by Lionel R. Wickham. Oxford Early Christian Texts. Oxford: Clarendon Press, 1983.

_____. *Lettres Festales*. Edited by Pierre Évieux. Sources Chrétiennes, vol. 392. Paris: Éditions du Cerf, 1993.

_____. "Quod Unus Sit Christus." In *Opera quae Reperiri Potuerunt Omnia*, vol. 8. Edited by Joannis Auberti. Patrologiae Cursus Completus; Series Graeca Prior, vol. 75. Edited by J.-P. Migne. Paris: Petit-Montrouge: apud. J.-P. Migne,1863.

_____. "Scholia de Incarnatione Unigeniti." In *Opera quae Reperiri Potuerunt Omnia*, vol. 8. Edited by Joannis Auberti. Patrologiae Cursus Completus; Series Graeca Prior, vol. 75. Edited by J.-P. Migne. Paris: Petit-Montrouge: apud. J.-P. Migne, 1863.

_____. "To Acacius of Melitene." In *Select Letters*. Edited and translated by Lionel R. Wickham. Oxford Early Christian Texts. Oxford: Clarendon Press, 1983.

Didymus the Blind. *Sur la Genèse*. Edited by Pierre Nautin. Sources Chrétiennes, vol. 233. Edited by H. de Lubac and J. Daniélou. Paris: Éditions du Cerf, 1976.

_____. *Sur Zacharie*. Edited by Louis Doutreleau. Sources Chretiennes, vols. 83-85. Paris: Éditions du Cerf, 1962.

_____. *Traité Du Saint-Esprit*. Edited by Louis Doutreleau. Sources Chrétiennes, vol. 386. Paris: Éditions du Cerf, 1992.

Ephrem the Syrian. "Homily on Our Lord." In *Ephraim: Homilies*. Edited by John Gwynn. Library of the Nicene and Post-Nicene Fathers. Second Series, vol. 13. Edited by P. Schaff and Henry Wace. Edinburgh: T & T Clark, 1898. Reprint, Peabody, Mass.: Hendrickson, 1994.

Epiphanius, Bishop of Constantia in Cyprus. *Ancoratus*. Edited by Karl Holl. Die Griechischen Christlichen Schriftsteller der Ersten Drei Jahrhunderte, vol. 25. Leipzig: J. C. Hinrichs, 1915.

———. *Panarion*. Edited by Karl Holl. Die Griechischen Christlichen Schriftsteller der Ersten Drei Jahrhunderte, vols. 22, 31. Leipzig: J. C. Hinrichs, 1915-1922.

Eusebius, Bishop of Caesarea. "De Ecclesiastica Theologia." In *Eusebius Werke*. Edited by E. Klostermann. Die Griechischen Christlichen Schriftsteller der Ersten Drei Jahrhunderte, vol. 14. Leipzig: J. C. Hinrichs, 1906.

———. "Der Jesajakommentar." In *Eusebius Werke*. Edited by Joseph Ziegler. Die Griechischen Christlichen Schriftsteller der Ersten Drei Jahrhunderte, vol. 56. Leipzig: J. C. Hinrichs, 1975.

———. "Die Demonstratio Evangelica." In *Eusebius Werke*. Edited by I. A. Heikel. Die Griechischen Christlichen Schriftsteller der Ersten Drei Jahrhunderte, vol. 22. Leipzig: J. C. Hinrichs, 1913.

Eusebius, Bishop of Vercelli. "De Trinitate." In *Eusebii Vercellensis Episcopi Quae Supersunt*. Edited by Vincent Bulhart. Corpus Christianorum. Series Latina, vol. 9. Turnholti: Typographi Brepols Editores Pontificii, 1957.

Faustinus. "De Trinitate." In *Opera*. Edited by M. Simonetti. Corpus Christianorum. Series Latina, vol. 69. Turnholti: Typographi Brepols Editores Pontificii, 1967.

Filastrius. *Diversarum Haereseon Liber*. Edited by F. Marx. Corpus Scriptorum Ecclesiasticorum Latinorum, vol. 38. Vindobonae: Hoelder-Pichler-Tempsky, 1898.

Fulgentius, Bishop of Ruspa. "Ad Euthymium de Remissione Peccatorum Libri III." In *Opera*. Edited by J. Fraipont. Corpus Christianorum. Series Latina, vol. 91a. Turnholti: Typographi Brepols Editores Pontificii, 1968.

———. "Ad Iohannem et Venerium de Ueritate Praedestinationis et Gratiae Dei Libri III." In *Opera*. Edited by J. Fraipont. Corpus Christianorum. Series Latina, vol. 91a. Turnholti: Typographi Brepols Editores Pontificii, 1968.

———. "Liber ad Scarilam de Incarnatione Filii Dei et Uilium Animalium Auctore." In *Opera*. Edited by J. Fraipont. Corpus Christianorum. Series Latina, vol. 91. Turnholti: Typographi Brepols Editores Pontificii, 1968.

Gaudentius, Bishop of Brescia. "Tractatus XIX." In *S. Gavdentii Episcopi Brixiensis Tractatvs ad Fidem Codicum*. Edited by Ambrosius Glueck. Corpus Scriptorum Ecclesiasticorum Latinorum, vol. 68. Vindobonae: Hoelder-Pichler-Tempsky, 1936.

Gregory of Elvira. "De Fide Orthodoxa Contra Arianos." Edited by Vincent Bulhart. In *Gregorii Iliberritani Episcopi Quae Supersunt*. Corpus Christianorum. Series Latina, vol. 69. Turnholti: Typographi Brepols Editores Pontificii, 1967.

———. "Tractatus de Arca Noe." Edited by Vincent Bulhart. In *Gregorii Iliberritani Episcopi Quae Supersunt*. Corpus Christianorum. Series Latina, vol. 69. Turnholti: Typographi Brepols Editores Pontificii, 1967.

Gregory of Nazianzus. "Discours 37: Sur la Parole de l'Évangile: 'Lorsque Jésus Eut Achevé ces Discours.' " In *Discours 32-37*. Edited by Paul Gallay. Sources Chrétiennes, vol. 318. Edited by H. de Lubac and J. Daniélou. Paris: Éditions du Cerf, 1985.

_____. "Lettre 101." In *Lettres Theologiques*. Edited by Paul Gallay. Sources Chrétiennes, vol. 208. Edited by H. de Lubac and J. Daniélou. Paris: Éditions du Cerf, 1974.

Gregory of Nyssa. "Antirrheticus Adversus Apolinarium." Edited by Fridericus Mueller. *Gregorii Nysseni Opera*, vol. 3, pt. 1. Edited by Wernerus Jaeger. Leiden: Brill, 1958.

_____. "Commentarius in Canticum Canticorum, Oratio XIV." Edited by Hermann Langerbeck. In *Gregorii Nysseni Opera*, vol. 6. Edited by Wernerus Jaeger. Leiden: Brill, 1960.

_____. "Contra Eunomium Libri." In *Gregorii Nysseni Opera*, vol. 2. Edited by Wernerus Jaeger. Leiden: Brill, 1960.

_____. "De Tridui Spatio." Edited by Ernest Gebhardt. In *Sermone: Pars I. Gregorii Nysseni Opera*, vol. 9. Edited by Wernerus Jaeger. Leiden: Brill, 1967.

_____. "Refutatio Confessionis Eunomii." In *Gregorii Nysseni Opera*, vol. 2. Edited by Wernerus Jaeger. Leiden: Brill, 1960.

Hilary of Poitiers. "Commentarius in Psalmus 127." In *Opera Omnia*. Patrologiae Cursus Completus; Series Latina, vol. 9. Edited by J.-P. Migne. Paris: Migne, 1844.

_____. "De Trinitate." In *Opera Omnia*. Patrologiae Cursus Completus; Series Latina, vol. 10. Edited by J.-P. Migne. Paris: Migne, 1845.

Irenaeus, Bishop of Lyon. *Contre les Heresies*. Sources Chrétiennes, vols. 100, 152-53, 210-11. Paris: Éditions du Cerf, 1965.

Jerome. "Commentarius in Epistolam S. Pauli ad Ephesios." *Sancti Evsebii Hieronymi Opera Omnia*. Patrologiae Cursus Completus; Series Latina, vol. 26. Edited by J.-P. Migne. Paris: Migne, 1845.

_____. "Commentarius in Epistolam S. Pauli ad Galatas." *Sancti Evsebii Hieronymi Opera Omnia*. Patrologiae Cursus Completus; Series Latina, vol. 26. Edited by J.-P. Migne. Paris: Migne, 1845.

_____. "Dialogus Adversus Pelagianos." In *S. Hieronymi presbyteri opera 79, pars III and 1: Opera Polemica*. Edited by C. Moreschini. Corpus Christianorum. Series Latina, vol. 80 Turnholti: Typographi Brepols Editores Pontificii, 1982.

_____. "Sancti Evsebii Hieronymi Epistvlae." *Eusebii Hieronymi Opera* (Sect. I, Parts I-III). Edited by Isidorus Hilberg. Corpus Scriptorum Ecclesiasticorum Latinorum, vols. 54-56. S. Vindobonae, F. Tempsky, 1910.

Leo the Great. "Ad Flavianum Epistola." In *De Fide et Symbolo: Documenta Quaedam Nec Non Aliquorum Ss. Patrum Tractatus*. Edited by C. Heurtley. Oxford: Parker, 1909.

Lucifer, Bishop of Cagliari. "Moriundum Esse Pro Dei Filio." In *Luciferi Calaritani Opera Quae Supersunt*. Corpus Christianorum. Series Latina, vol. 8. Turnholti: Typographi Brepols Editores Pontificii, 1978.

Methodius of Olympus. "Symposium." In *Methodius*. Edited by G. Nathanael Bonwetsch. Die Griechischen Christlichen Schriftsteller der Ersten Drei Jahrhunderte, vol. 27. Leipzig: J. C. Hinrichs, 1917.

Nestorius, Patriarch of Constantinople. *The Bazaar of Heracleides*. Translated and edited by G. R. Driver and Leonard Hodgson. Oxford: Clarendon Press, 1925.

Novatian. "De Trinitate." In *Opera, Quae Supersunt Nunc Primum in Unum Collecta ad Fidem*

Codicum, Qui Adhuc Extant, Necnon Adhibitis Editionibus Veteribus. Edited by G. F. Diercks. Corpus Christianorum. Series Latina, vol. 4. Turnholti: Typographi Brepols Editores Pontificii, 1972.

Origen. "Apologia pro Origene" In *Opera Omnia,* vol. 7. Patrologiae Cursus Completus; Series Graeca Prior, vol. 17. Edited by J.-P. Migne. Paris: Migne, 1857.

_____. "Commentaria in Epistolam B. Pauli ad Romanos." In *Opera Omnia,* vol. 4. Patrologiae Cursus Completus; Series Graeca Prior, vol. 14. Edited by J.-P. Migne. Paris: Migne, 1862.

_____. "The Commentary of Origen upon the Epistle to the Ephesians." J. A. F. Gregg. *Journal of Theological Studies* 3. London: Macmillan and Co., 1902: 233-44; 398-420; 554-76.

_____. "De Principiis." *Origenes Werke.* Edited by Paul Koetschau. Die Griechischen Christlichen Schriftsteller der Ersten Drei Jahrhunderte, vol. 22. Leipzig: J. C. Hinrichs, 1913.

_____. "Expositio Origenis de Psalmo Nonagesimo Primo." *Gregorii Iliberritani Episcopi Quae Supersunt.* Edited by Vincent Bulhart. Corpus Christianorum. Series Latina, vol. 69. Turnholti: Typographi Brepols Editores Pontificii, 1967.

_____. *Origenes Werke.* Die Griechischen Christlichen Schriftsteller der Ersten Drei Jahrhunderte, vols. 2-3, 10. Leipzig: J. C. Hinrichs, 1899-1955.

_____. *Origenous Ton Eis to Kata Ioannen Euangelion Exegethokon* [The Commentary of Origen on S. John's Gospel]. 2 vols. Edited by A. E. Brooke. Cambridge: University Press, 1896.

_____. *The Philocalia of Origen.* Edited by J. Armitage Robinson. Cambridge: University Press, 1893.

_____. "Sur le Psaume 118." *La Châine Palestinienne sur le Psaume 118 (Origène, Eusèbe, Didyme, Apollinaire, Athanase, Théodoret).* Edited by Marguerite Har with Gilles Dorival. Sources Chrétiennes, vols. 189-90. Edited by H. de Lubac and J. Daniélou. Paris: Éditions du Cerf, 1972.

Pamphilus. "Apologia pro Origene." *Opera Omnia,* vol. 7. Patrologiae Cursus Completus; Series Graeca Prior, vol. 17. Edited by J.-P. Migne. Paris: Migne, 1857.

Pseudo-Athanasius. "Orationes Contra Arianos." In *The Orations of St. Athanasius: Against the Arians According to the Benedictine Text.* Edited by W. Bright. Oxford: Clarendon Press, 1873.

Pseudo-Augustine. *Pseudo-Avgustini Quaestiones Veteris et Novi Testamenti CXXVII. Accedit Appendix Continens Alterius Editionis Quaestiones Selectas.* Edited by Alexander Souter. Corpus Scriptorum Ecclesiasticorum Latinorum, vol. 50. Vindobonae, F. Tempsky, 1908.

Pseudo-Dionysius the Areopagite. "De Divinus Nominibus." Edited by Regina Suchla. *Corpus Dionysiacum.* Patristische Texte und Studien, vol. 33. Edited by K. Aland and E. Mühlenberg. New York: De Gruyter, 1990.

Pseudo-Vigilius of Thapsus. "Contra Varimadus the Arian." *Florilegia Biblica Africana.* Edited by B. Schwank. Corpus Christianorum. Series Latina, vol. 90, pt. 1. Turnholti: Typographi Brepols Editores Pontificii, 1961.

Quodvultdeus, Bishop of Carthage. "De Symbolo." *Opera Quodvultdeo Carthaginiensi Episcopo Tributa.* Corpus Christianorum. Series Latina, vol. 60. Turnholti: Typographi Brepols Editores Pontificii, 1976.

Schaff, Philip, et al., eds. A Select Library of the Nicene and Post-Nicene Fathers of the Christian Church. 2 Series (14 vols. each). Buffalo, N.Y.: Christian Literature, 1887-1894. Reprint, Grand Rapids, Mich.: Eerdmans, 1952-1956. Reprint, Peabody, Mass.: Hendrickson Publishers, 1994.

Tertullian. "Adversus Marcionem." *Opera*. Corpus Christianorum. Series Latina, vol. 1. Turnholti: Typographi Brepols Editores Pontificii, 1953.

_____. "De Resurrectione Mortuorum." *Opera*. Corpus Christianorum. Series Latina, vol. 2. Turnholti: Typographi Brepols Editores Pontificii, 1953.

_____. "De Virginibus Velandis." *Opera*. Corpus Christianorum. Series Latina, vol. 2. Turnholti: Typographi Brepols Editores Pontificii, 1954.

Theodore, Bishop of Mopsuestia. "Commentarii." In *Epistolas Beati Pauli Commentarii: The Latin Version with the Greek Fragments*. Edited by H. B. Swete. Cambridge: Cambridge University Press, 1880-1882.

_____. Fragments in *Catenae Graecorum Patrum in Epistulas Pauli*. Edited by J. A. Cramer. Oxford: Clarendon Press, 1854.

Theodoret, Bishop of Cyrrhus. *Commentarius in Omnes B. Pauli Epistolas*. 2 vols. Edited by Charles Marriott. Bibliotheca Patrum Ecclesiae Catholicae. Oxford: J. H. Parker, 1852-1870.

_____. *Eranistes*. Edited by Gerard H. Ettlinger. Oxford: Clarendon Press, 1975.

Victorinus, Marius. "Adversus Arium." *Opera Theologica*. Edited by Albrecht Locher. Bibliotheca Scriptorum Graecorum et Romanorum Teubneriana. Leipzig: Teubner, 1976. "In Epistulam Pauli ad Ephesios."

_____. "In Epistulam Pauli ad Ephesios." *Commentarii in Epistulas Pauli ad Galatas, ad Philippenses, ad Ephesios*. Edited by Albrecht Locher. Bibliotheca Scriptorum Graecorum et Romanorum Teubneriana. Leipzig: Teubner, 1972.

_____. "In Epistulam Pauli ad Galatas." *Commentarii in Epistulas Pauli ad Galatas, ad Philippenses, ad Ephesios*. Edited by Albrecht Locher. Bibliotheca Scriptorum Graecorum et Romanorum Teubneriana. Leipzig: Teubner, 1972.

_____. "Liber ad Philippenses." *Commentarii in Epistulas Pauli ad Galatas, ad Philippenses, ad Ephesios*. Edited by Albrecht Locher. Bibliotheca Scriptorum Graecorum et Romanorum Teubneriana. Leipzig: Teubner, 1972.